CHURCHILL
in Parliament

DENNIS BARDENS

South Brunswick and New York:
A. S. Barnes and Company

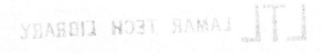

For
Marie *and* Peter

Contents

	Note on Sources	11
	Preface	13
1	The Beginner	15
2	First Steps to Westminster	23
3	The Cockyollybird	30
4	His Father's Son	37
5	Maturing Years	49
6	Reformist Zeal	56
7	The Maelstrom	64
8	Peace—and War	75
9	The War Unfolds	83
10	The Dardanelles	92
11	In the Wilderness	99
12	Peace	122
13	Defeat of the Liberals	128
14	Post-war Problems	143
15	Sans Everything . . .	151
16	The General Strike	163
17	The Twenties	168
18	In Opposition	172
19	The Years of Drift	176
20	Appeasement	186
21	The Phoney War	199
22	A Fighting Leader	216
23	A New Phase of War	240
24	Still Under Fire	263
25	The Turn of the Tide	277
26	In God's Good Time	289
27	Victory	302

Contents

28 His Majesty's Opposition   310
29 Prime Minister Again   336
30 Journey's End   360
    Bibliography   369
    Index   371

1940

This be for epitaph: in that fell hour
Dour and all-dominant he calmly stood;
Recked well the odds; then, with resistless power
Unleashed the angered lions in the blood.
                                James Edward Holroyd
(*From the* Evening News *of 30th January 1965*)

Note on Sources

Not only was Sir Winston Churchill's life a crowded one, but the events in which he was involved, and the historical background over so long a period, cannot but include too many sources of information to be given in complete detail.

Nevertheless, future generations will assess and re-assess the career of this remarkable man. Those who attempt it will find an immensity of documentation. Further, they will have to weigh the facts adduced against the source—for temperament, integrity, bonds of family, party, national or group loyalty affect not only the presentation of facts but the selection of them. The more important books concerned are listed in the Bibliography.

All who investigate Sir Winston's life, however, must have resource to *Hansard*, the official record of Parliamentary debates, and a treasure-house of objective reporting on the most detailed matters, admirably indexed. The Parliamentary reports of *The Times* are a useful supplement to this, while the vivid and contemporary accounts of such brilliant journalists as C. F. G. Masterman of the *Daily News* are living history. The files of *Punch*, the *New Statesman and Nation* and *The Spectator* are valuable for their commentaries on past and long-forgotten sensations and controversies, while local newspapers such as the *Dundee Advertiser*, *Oldham Standard* and *Leicester Mercury* throw interesting and often surprising light on past election campaigns.

My thanks are due to Odhams Books Limited, for permission to quote from Winston S. Churchill's *The World Crisis* and *The Aftermath*; to Mrs. Bambridge and Methuen and Company Limited for the Rudyard Kipling poem from *The Seven Seas*; to Mr. Frank Owen and Hutchinson and Company Limited for the quotes from *Tempestuous Journey*; and to Cassell and Company Limited for the quotes from Churchill's *Second World War* (The Gathering Storm) and *A King's Story* by H.R.H. The Duke of Windsor, K.G.

It goes without saying that Sir Winston Churchill's own works, especially *The World Crisis* and *The Second World War*, will forever remain an indispensable source of study for those who would attempt to study his life and works. As with all factual works, they reflect his temperament and preferences and criteria of selection; but they are not less valuable because of that.

D.B.

Preface

In the year in which Britain celebrated the 700th Anniversary of the granting of Magna Carta and the birth of parliamentary freedom Sir Winston Churchill, the greatest parliamentarian this country has ever known, passed from our midst.

He was part of Parliament and it was part of him. The sense of being at the very centre of authority, of watching history in the making and helping it to be made; of championing what he believed to be right and good and attacking without quarter what he conceived to be wrong; the showmanship, the colour, the tradition, the challenge, the moments of high drama, the cut-and-thrust of fierce debate—all these things made a deep and abiding appeal to him.

Churchill was not only The Great Commoner; he was the greatest commoner.

That is my theme. For over sixty years he was a central figure in the Mother of Parliaments. Often, during that time, Britain was in violent metamorphosis and twice was convulsed by two disastrous and protracted wars. The pattern of politics, social organization, industry and economics, religious thought and attitudes to philosophy and science changed in those decades almost beyond recognition. Yet, amazingly, Churchill was never left behind by events; he refused to live in the past, to the last moment of his life exulting in the present, with all its transient sweetness, trial or challenge.

Therefore, I do not attempt to describe or assess his life as such —his interest in art, his soldiering, his social life, domestic circle, manifold hobbies. I pass lightly over his literary career which, had Churchill been stripped of every other distinction and achievement, would, in itself, have earned him a lasting and honoured place in history. There were too many Churchills for one canvas to do justice to them all. It is as a man of Parliament and as a politician (the two, of course, cannot be separated) that he will, primarily, be remembered by posterity.

This book is not nor ever was intended to be, a panegyric, tribute or memorial. It was not conceived because of his last illness and subsequent death, but was planned some time before both. In any case, a man of such stature needs no praise of mine and I doubt if any Englishman has ever been showered with so many superlatives both during his lifetime and afterwards—Man of Action; Man of the Century; The Greatest Englishman . . . the sonorous eulogies have been exhausted.

They were deserved. Churchill had many lives and they were all remarkable. Nevertheless, it is his political career which provides the main thread of continuity and the main outlet for his brilliance, restlessness, aggressiveness, humour and love of action; it was the political path, towards the end of which it fell upon his broad shoulders to bear the heaviest burden of all, which led him to the apotheosis of achievement. But for his courage, Europe would have gone down into the abyss of medieval cruelty and darkness, for an indefinite period.

I have, of course, in the interests of objectivity, recorded some of the criticisms to which he was exposed and which, in his early days, he seemed to encourage as well as sometimes to deserve. In his early years he was distrusted, hated and even ostracized by influential sections of the Conservative and Liberal Parties, and during the inter-war years he was for most of the time in the political wilderness. He could be tough with opponents but never intentionally vindictive. He was inordinately ambitious. Of his showmanship and vanity—his love of dressing up, of being the centre of interest—there is no question. But other great Englishmen have been like that, such as Wellington or Nelson.

The number of informants is too great for all to be acknowledged individually, and I ask them to accept this general token of thanks. I am indebted to Dr. George Morey for much helpful advice, to Miss Dawn Tindall, Librarian of the Reform Club, to Mrs. Vivienne Semmence for assistance with research, and to Mr. David Curnock for suggesting the theme.

After the long, poignant tribute of a State Funeral had been paid and the mortal remains of Sir Winston Churchill borne to their last place of rest, one of Her Majesty's Heralds said to me, 'It is the end of an era.' This everyone felt. I hope that this account, with all its limitations, will recall something of that era and of The Great Commoner who has left the impress of his personality indelibly upon Parliament and upon the world.

Reform Club,
Pall Mall, S.W.1

DENNIS BARDENS

I

The Beginner

The year was 1899. It was still what Sir Winston Churchill described
—on the death of King George VI—as 'the august serenity of the
Victorian era'. Britain was the greatest power in the world, at the
height of its prestige and pride and economic strength.

Nevertheless, the country was in transition, although it did not
know it. An era was drawing to a close. Gladstone, who had four
times been the Queen's Prime Minister, had died at Hawarden the
previous May 1898. Only two years ago Queen Victoria had celebrated her sixty years upon the throne; but now, although she made
a few public appearances, she was getting tired. Her sight was
failing, although with unflagging determination she continued to
sign documents and attend to all necessary matters of State.

Mr. Winston Churchill, aged 25, was probably the best known
young man in the country. Most people had heard of him, many
admired him and not a few disliked, if not actually hated him.

Already he had crammed more adventure and personal initiative
into his few years of manhood than many were to experience in a
whole lifetime. And it may be that his driving restlessness and
hunger for action and adventure reflected a desperate need for self-
assertion after a childhood which had been happy only in patches
and more often miserable. Born at Blenheim Palace—prematurely—
as the elder son of Lord Randolph Churchill, famous Tory leader
and former Chancellor of the Exchequer and Lady Churchill (*née*
Jennie Jerome)—he had suffered from disadvantages in belonging to
so distinguished a family. Lord Randolph had been too busy with
his political career to give Winston the companionship he might
otherwise have done. Lord Randolph Churchill was sensitive,
imaginative, highly-strung, ambitious, complex and, in certain
moods, unapproachable and often for months on end inaccessible;
Winston in the nature of things saw little of him, although regarding
him with awe mixed with an affection that never waned.

And as a very young boy, Winston had not seen as much as he

wished of his beautiful, witty and talented mother, one of three daughters of a wealthy American who had lost and won fortunes and had become a powerful figure in the world of finance and publishing. Hearing that the Duke of Marlborough regarded the prospect of his son's marriage to Jennie Jerome with some misgivings, Leonard Jerome was almost beside himself with anger and disposed to prohibit the marriage. But the couple were married in Paris on 31st January 1874, irrespective of the tension between their respective parents.

For his mother, too, Winston felt the deepest affection. There is no doubt that she loved her son, but on the level of society in which she had been accustomed to move she had become used to a busy social life, and continued with it after marriage; indeed only six weeks before Winston was due to be born, she went to a ball at Blenheim Palace, and, feeling the pangs of childbirth, tried to reach her bedroom and hurried through the vast ornate rooms. Instead of reaching her bedroom, she gave birth to the baby in a smallish room serving for that night as a ladies' cloakroom.

It is clear from all that Sir Winston has written and said during his long life that his childhood years were not happy, despite the aristocratic lineage and sumptuous homes. The loneliness was mitigated by the devoted companionship of his nanny, Mrs. Everest, whose memory he treasured all his life; but at the age of seven he was sent as a pupil to St. James's School, near Ascot, a boarding school which could scarcely have been a less suitable environment for a boy of seven. Stark, dull, and fear-ridden because of the sadistic headmaster who loved to terrorize and beat the boys until they screamed, it was surely here that Winston Churchill's stubborn pride was put to the test. A hopeless scholar, he was beaten so unmercifully that years afterwards at the age of nineteen he made his way back to the school with the express intention of giving the cruel master a thrashing before all the scholars. But it was not to be; the school had gone and the headmaster too.

After two years of misery, at last noticed by his parents, Winston was sent to a preparatory school in Brighton run by two kindly ladies. He learned little but at least was not so actively unhappy. In 1888 he entered Harrow School in the lowest form—in fact his scholastic level was so poor that it is doubtful if he would have been accepted at all but for his illustrious name. Here again, he was a poor scholar. He enjoyed fencing and swimming but cared little for football and cricket. Possibly by over-compensation for the loneliness he had felt during the frequent absences of his parents and his unhappy experiences at the hands of the brutal headmaster in Ascot, his temper was hot and his pride so excessive as to be thought arrogance. He had some firm friends, but many more critics and not a few enemies, amongst his companions.

One factor, of considerable importance in understanding the zest and pushfulness with which Winston Churchill was to tackle his political career, is his admiration for his father and realization as a small boy that he was a national—as well as a controversial figure. He would not be the first boy to attempt to model himself, knowingly or unknowingly, on his father. He knew that his father before a huge audience at Dartford, in Kent, had in 1886 outlined a programme of Tory reform which had incensed diehard Tories and angered Radicals who felt he was trying to steal their thunder.

He could not fail to have known of the surprise occasioned by his father's resignation from office as Chancellor of the Exchequer in December 1886, for the papers were full of it. Lord Randolph Churchill wanted to make economies on defence expenditure. The War Office and the Admiralty did not. After an audience with the Queen at Windsor, Lord Randolph sent a letter of resignation to Lord Salisbury, the Prime Minister, using the royal writing-paper at Windsor Castle. The Prime Minister took his irate Chancellor at his word and accepted his resignation made in a fit of nervous exhaustion and self-dramatization. Lord Randolph Churchill had over-played his hand and thrown to the winds a brilliant career.

There seemed very little indication that his son would do as well. Winston once described his years at Harrow as 'the only barren and unhappy period of my life'. He found it almost impossible to assimilate anything, was cheeky to friend and foe alike, and even to the masters. Once, when the headmaster admonished him sternly, 'I have very grave reason to be displeased with you,' he replied in a flash, 'And I, Sir, have every grave reason to be displeased with you!'

What to do with him? It was clear that he would not qualify for a university. With a poor educational standard, a capacity for antagonizing not only companions of his own age but others of any age, with little to show for years of schooling but a fencing prize, an excellent memory and an inordinate passion for playing with toy soldiers, it is hardly surprising to find his grandmother, Mrs. Jerome describing him as 'a naughty little sandy-haired bulldog' who seemed backward.

His passion for toy soldiers offered a potential cure for Lord Randolph's increasing desperation about his son's future prospects. At Harrow Winston was prepared for the entrance examination which would enable him to go to the Royal Military College at Sandhurst. After two failures he was sent to a crammer's school for six months in London in order to fit him for the entrance examination. At the third attempt he succeeded and was accepted for the cavalry, passing out of Sandhurst eighth in order of merit out of one hundred and fifty.

The following year—in 1895—his father died. From this period Winston Churchill's life became a constant round of adventure, controversy and variety. It is not the function of this book to describe these years of early youth and early manhood, for he has described them himself in the words of a master, and with all the humour and self-revelation of which he was capable. Increasingly, he came into the public eye. Like his father, he showed himself no respecter of persons and, also like his father, he enjoyed and exploited the privilege of his upper-class background whilst retaining a lively and perhaps unreasonable scepticism about the aristocracy.

In March 1895, two months after the death of his father, Winston Churchill was gazetted to the 4th Hussars. The period between his nursery days and entry to Sandhurst had been in his own words 'a sombre grey patch upon the chart of my journey . . . an unending spell of worries'. Longing for adventure, he obtained permission to visit the Spanish Army, then in action against the rebels in Cuba, and secured from the *Daily Graphic* a commission to write for them at the not very princely rate of five pounds per article (his father had been paid two thousand guineas for a series of articles on South Africa). Winston Churchill could not fail to have known that in view of his father's association with that newspaper, its editor would be predisposed to give the new, unlikely contributor a chance to show his mettle as a journalist. In those days it was permissible for a soldier to write as well as serve, a state of affairs which no longer exists.

On his twenty-first birthday Churchill was under fire in the jungle near Arroyo Blanco. As the bullets whizzed past him, he kept his saddle calmly, and on his return to England for six months' leave he felt the elation every man knows who has walked (or ridden) with death and finds himself the victor. His confidence now was in full flower; many people, then and later, found him over-confident.

Thence with his regiment to Bangalore in India, to lead a life which was a mixture of privilege, glamour and adventure as a gentleman officer; but when fighting broke out on the North-west Frontier nobody was in a greater hurry to forsake the delights of sports and mess companionship for active fighting.

In between all these adventures he had cultivated the habit of voracious reading and here his prodigious memory ensured that what he read his mind retained. His passion for the English language had been noted at Harrow. Despite polo and campaigns, every normal day in India included hours set aside for reading. Gibbon's *Decline and Fall of the Roman Empire* was a masterpiece that enthralled his youthful imagination, recapturing for him the sweeping panorama of the past, with all its grandeur and tragedy. So, too, did Lecky's *History of European Morals* and Winwood Reade's *Martyrdom of Man.*

Winston had come home on leave in 1897 in time to enjoy the tremendous celebrations of Queen Victoria's Jubilee, the sixtieth anniversary of her reign. England and especially London were in festive mood, and there was a glittering round of dinners and parties and balls.

In the midst of these jollifications came the news—for him, good news—that revolt had broken out among the Pathan tribesmen near the Malakand Pass on the North-west Frontier. Sir Bindon Blood, the general in charge of operations, knew Churchill and had once said that if opportunity arose he would give him a chance of active service. Churchill wired him that he was leaving at once for Brindisi *en route*. However, learning that there was little chance for him unless he came as a war correspondent, he obtained accreditations from *The Pioneer* newspaper of Allahabad and from the *Daily Telegraph* (the latter on his mother's intervention).

His war despatches were brilliant, and he embodied them in a book, *The Story of the Malakand Field Force*, which appeared in March 1898. Its clarity, continuity, confident and expressive phrasing, graphic description and sheer exposition are still a model to all authors, and its success was not only inevitable but made his name increasingly a household word.

The *Malakand Field Force* contained many strictures upon the organization of the British Army and the limitations of officers in high command, and such widely-published castigations from a mere subaltern earned him dislike in high quarters. The Prince of Wales had written to him enthusing about the book, and the Prime Minister had sent for him and complimented him highly. Yet even the Prime Minister could not persuade Sir Herbert Kitchener—then Sirdah of the Egyptian Army, who was moving south with six brigades to avenge the murder of General Gordon in Khartoum and crush the Mahdist rising—to accept Churchill for service with the 21st Lancers, then under Kitchener's command as part of the Army in Egypt.

Churchill, twice rebuffed (a previous application had been curtly refused) enlisted the goodwill of the Adjutant-General, Sir Evelyn Wood, who by good fortune was a friend of the Churchill family and no friend at all of the imperious Kitchener. The revelation that the Sirdah had refused a request from the Prime Minister spurred Sir Evelyn to action, and Churchill for the third time of trying secured his wish—an attachment to the 21st Lancers. And in the course of that campaign he experienced the most exciting adventure of his life so far, the cavalry charge at Omdurman. Three hundred horsemen, lances at the level, thundered towards three thousand waiting Dervishes and in the mêlée Churchill, who killed several with his Mauser pistol, narrowly escaped death himself, at one point becoming detached from his men.

But in later years he was to write of it: 'Talk of fun. Where will you beat this! On horseback, at daybreak, within shot of an advancing enemy, seeing everything and corresponding directly with Headquarters.'

Triumphantly, Churchill rode into defeated Omdurman at sunset with Kitchener.

Winston Churchill's reporting of the Sudan campaign had added even further to his mounting reputation as a writer. The general principle of a serving officer acting as a serving writer was a different matter; the two roles are not easily compatible and from a disciplinary point of view it is military nonsense to have subordinates serving under you who can without hindrance or restriction or censorship expose you to criticism and obloquy to a huge section of the population. The War Office decided that the two roles would in future be separate; war correspondents could not be soldiers nor soldiers war correspondents.

This decision was, in the fulness of time, to be of immense benefit to the British people. For Churchill's heart was in the Army, and he had intended to make it his career. But the Churchills were not wealthy, and he could not indefinitely accept an allowance from his family. His articles in the *Morning Post* had been well paid, whereas the Army could not offer him a satisfactory living.

How to start in politics? In the broadest sense, Mr. Churchill was already involved; genetically or intuitively he was copying the father whom he had loved and admired from a distance, and whose meteoric rise and sudden fall had given him a sense of mission, a feeling that he should carry on the torch. His father, an aristocrat, enjoyed and used the privileges of his class whilst initiating or advocating reforms which put him at loggerheads with them. Mr. Winston Churchill had begun to do this, too. He had pulled all manner of strings, or his mother had pulled them for him, and then would not hesitate to criticize the hierarchy, as he had castigated those he considered inept in the military world. The fact is that, just as he sought action in battle 'for the hell of it' he loved a verbal fight too, a battle of ideas for which, with his turn of phrase, ready wit and natural belligerence, he was well fitted.

And so, in 1899, elegantly and impressively dressed as ever, he made his way to the labyrinthine offices of the Conservative Central Office in St. Stephen's Chambers, opposite the Houses of Parliament where his father was remembered with awe as a dynamic and controversial Tory leader who might one day have been Premier but for his mercurial temperament. A distant relative, Mr. FitzRoy Stewart, worked there as a volunteer, and Winston sought his advice on the prospect of finding him a constituency which he could contest.

In the course of their talk Winston noticed a book of speakers. Did this mean, he inquired, that they needed speakers? Indeed yes, said Mr. Stewart. After some discussion it was agreed that Winston should go to Bath in ten days' time to speak at a Primrose League gathering in a park owned by Mr. H. D. Skrine and overlooking the city.

Churchill followed a technique which served him well in later life. He wrote out a speech which he could deliver with effort in twenty minutes and comfort in twenty-five. This he knew by timing himself with his stop-watch. A first political speech was no matter for slipshod planning. He well knew that he was over-shooting the fifteen minutes of time promised to him. He rehearsed the speech to himself again and again until he was word perfect, so that instead of fumbling with words he could deliver them with appropriate expression of voice and with gestures which seemed natural though contrived. He was in truth an actor playing a part, which is not to say that he did not personally believe what his lines said. Such care, he considered, was due to his hosts, his party and his public.

Thoughtfully, he had told the *Morning Post* of the forthcoming engagement, and when he caught the train from Paddington to Bath the reporter was there too, clad as was the fashion in an elegant grey frock-coat. The reporter served as a guinea-pig, and to the rhythm of the train's wheels Churchill declaimed loud and long in defence of the Government.

Amidst the paraphernalia of a fairground and funfair, and speaking from a dais formed of planks placed over upturned beer barrels, he was introduced in glowing terms by Mr. Skrine and delivered his speech to an audience whose applause must have warmed his heart. His appetite for rhetoric could be seen in some of his phraseology, such as 'England would gain more from the rising tide of Tory Democracy than from the dried-up drain-pipe of Radicalism'. Everyone was satisfied. The *Morning Post* reported his speech at length and added the compliment of a leader welcoming a new and bright recruit to the Tory ranks. He went back to India, briefly, resigned his commission, and returned to Britain to enter politics as a career.

2

First Steps to Westminster

The seed which Churchill had sown during his visit to the Central Office had fallen on good soil. There was the fact of his father's long and—if one excepts his closing years—successful service to his Party; there was the fact that Winston Churchill was already, as a young man, a name well known to most people; there was his ambition, his energy and his gift of expression. Not every young man of twenty-five could lay claim to all those advantages at once.

He was offered the chance to stand as Conservative candidate in a by-election to be held in the important constituency of Oldham. It was not likely to be a walkover, nor could new and untested candidates expect to be offered one. A predominantly working-class neighbourhood, it was marked by a strong radical tradition. It had many powerful trade unions. It was regaining its prosperity as a textile town, but there were still thousands who could remember how operatives were thrown out of work by the cotton famine in 1865—and Alexandra Park was a constant reminder of it, for it was laid out by unemployed operatives at the time. For eleven years it had been a county borough, and it had returned two members to Parliament since 1832.

The Labour Party as we know it did not exist then. There were two Conservative candidates—Mr. Churchill and Mr. J. Mawdsley —and two Liberals, Mr. A. Emmott and Mr. Walter Runciman, later Lord Runciman.

Whether it was any advantage to be fighting side-by-side with a Conservative candidate who was also a prominent local trade unionist (Secretary of the Amalgamated Society of Operative Spinners) and who surprised and antagonized some of the working class by lining up with the Tories, then largely identified with the landowning and commercial classes, may be doubted.

Churchill had enjoyed the advantage of a wonderful panegyric in the *Daily Mail* by G. W. Steevens, the famous war correspondent who had travelled back with him to England. In an article entitled

'The Youngest Man in Europe' he showered the young man with compliments, some of which were strangely prophetic:

> He has qualities which make him, almost at will, a great popular leader, a great journalist or the founder of a great advertising business . . . at the rate he goes, there will hardly be room for him in Parliament at thirty or in England at forty. . . .

Furthermore, the *Oldham Standard* found it effective to reprint *in toto* Winston Churchill's reference in *Who's Who*:

> CHURCHILL, W. L. S. Lt. The Queen's Own Hussars; eldest son of the late Rt. Hon. Lord R. Churchill, 3rd son of the 7th Duke of Marlborough, born 30th November 1874. Educated Harrow, Sandhurst. Entered Army, 1895. Served with the Spanish forces in Cuba, 1895 (1st Class (Spanish) Order of Merit); served, attached 31st Punjab Infantry, with Malakand Field Force, 1897; present at operations at Bajaur, including actions of 16th and 30th September (despatches, medal with clasp); served as Orderly Officer to Sir W. Lockhart with Tirah Expeditionary Force 1898 (clasp); served, attached 21st Lancers, with the Nile Expeditionary Force. Present at the Battle of Khartoum (medal with clasp).

The *Oldham Standard* in its assessment of the contestants left no doubt where its preference lay. Of Mr. Churchill, 'the soldier son of the great statesman,' it asked:

> What is the object of his getting into Parliament? He is imbued largely with the noble ideals, sought after by his illustrious father, and his ambition to enter Parliament is that he may make this great Empire grander and more glorious, richer and more powerful, and that he may make his fellow men happier and more prosperous. Broadly, those are Mr. Churchill's reasons for seeking to enter the British House of Commons.

Mr. Mawdsley, too, was 'just the man for Oldham'. For years he had tried to better the lot of cotton operatives in Oldham. But Mr. Emmott, described by the paper, with an initial show of impartiality as having achieved 'considerable local distinction'—what were his motives? '. . . to have M.P. tacked on to his name, and if he were to get into Parliament we might possibly, once a year, receive a report of a dull statistical speech delivered in a half-empty and sleepy House. . . .'

As for 'Mr. Runciman, the wealthy shipowner, we may dismiss him in a sentence' (but the paper didn't). 'He is a professional politician who wants to get into Parliament for commercial and partly social reasons. As regards the latter, his aspirations are well known in Newcastle. He is desirous of moving in a higher groove of society and an M.P. would be very useful to this end. Oldham is asked to be the instrument. To what base ends. . . .'

The laws of libel were not so strict in those days and the good faith of a candidate could be impugned as much as his policies.

It was a lively and interesting campaign, waged for several weeks and with Mr. Churchill attending crowded meetings, often several a day, in which he propounded the glories of Empire and the prosperity and contentment attendant upon them. In ringing tones he told his audience in Oldham's Theatre Royal that 'the conscious-ness of dominion over subjects alone increases the self-respect of every Englishman. The Radicals, it appears, would have no Empire at all, whilst the Imperialist desires to have one, that all may share the glory.'

There is a distinct Churchillian sonority about the picture he drew of England's future:

> . . . marching steadily forward on the path of progress, combining all the pomp and glitter of an ancient throne, armed with Imperial Power, comforted with the spoils of commerce and enriched with the rewards of industry, beating all rivals, beating down all opponents. . . .

Such passages, commented the *Manchester Guardian* dryly, were worth quoting as they represented the kind of thing that drew a Tory Democratic cheer. It added an invitation to Mr. Churchill to explore some of the back streets of Oldham, where a less roseate picture could be seen.

Churchill's exploits abroad had indeed fired him with a fierce pride of Empire and a sure sense of England's destiny. It was a natural enough feeling in a young aristocrat to whom authority came naturally as an hereditary privilege, who although never having had enough money, had nevertheless never been without it, and whose environment was that of an upper class firmly entrenched and separated by an unbridgeable economic gap from the mass of working people. At that time he knew little or nothing of their circumstances or problems or reactions.

But Churchill, with his pungent phrases, ebullient confidence and natural aggressiveness was not to be put off by such tactics. His meetings were attended by tremendous enthusiasm. He knew too well how to turn a political opponent's attack. Mr. Runciman, in one speech had said indiscreetly that he, for his part, had not been 'swashbucklering' his way around the world. That, said Churchill, was just the sort of attitude the Radicals took to the two fighting services, but a county like Lancashire, fond of manly games, would not take up that attitude. Why, a Lancashire regiment was up the Nile! 'Is that swashbucklering?' the young Churchill cried, lifting his jaw defiantly and glaring at his audience. 'Mr. Runciman, of course, has not had the same experience as the Queen's Own Lancashire Fusiliers. They fought at Omdurman, he at Gravesend; he fought for himself, they for their Queen and country, and while he was beaten they fought and won.' This broadside brought deafening applause.

He invented some remarkable turns of phrase in the course of his election speeches. Perhaps the strangest, taking advantage of Mr. Mawdsley's participation on the Conservative side, was the description of his party (to an audience in the Co-operative Hall, Greenacres) as the Conservative Labour Party. Mr. Mawdsley's selection, he said, was proof of the sympathetic connection existing between the Conservative Party and the working class of Britain. He instanced the Government's measures for improving the lot of the working class, such as the Truck Act, which compelled employers to pay their men in coin of the realm; the Conciliation Act, intended to pour oil on troubled industrial waters and, especially, the Workmen's Compensation Act which would spare workers injured on the job the privations of want and destitution.

This particular speech, characteristic of scores which he delivered during the election campaign, underlines his extraordinary energy. It was a speech of over 8,000 words which had not only to be prepared but memorized. Its references to the economics of the cotton industry are detailed and extensive.

A good deal of lobbying of candidates went on. The Temperance Party worried everyone, asking them to commit themselves on regarding alcohol as an evil. They had little luck with Mr. Churchill.

There were deputations of dissatisfied sub-postmasters, of the Shop Assistants Association which was pressing for a bill reforming shop hours (at that time as much as sixteen hours a day); the Early Closing Association League and the Suffragettes, agitating for votes for women.

The Suffragettes got short shrift from Mr. Churchill. He was, he told them 'very much against' women having Parliamentary votes. 'I am afraid,' he told them, 'that the entry of women into the political arena would tend to lessen that great respect and admiration which all men very rightly have.' Lest this refusal should appear too curt, he qualified it with a rider that 'the entry of women into political life if it benefited either party, would tend to the advantage of Conservatism, because woman, with her superior instinct, would naturally make the wiser choice. . . .' From Mr. Mawdsley, Mr. Churchill's Conservative companion-in-battle, the Suffragettes received a favourable reply.

On the eve of the election, Mr. Churchill had one final, mighty verbal smack at his opponents. Mr. Runciman, he said, had come to Oldham and said he was not a believer in the eight-hour day for miners, but had changed his mind and now believed that labour should be restricted. They could see his address placarded on every wall in town, a long bill 'almost as tall as a factory chimney and very nearly as hollow'. Of Mr. Emmott's speeches he quoted this rhyme:

> Peter was dull, he was at first
> Dull, oh, so dull, so very dull;
> Whether he wrote, spoke or rehearsed
> Still with this failing he was accursed.
> Dull, beyond all conception, dull.

And at one of the eight meetings he addressed that day—speaking in the process something like 100,000 words or the equivalent of a lengthy novel—Churchill worked up to a climax of glowing patriotism tempered judiciously with a note of reformist zeal:

. . . all the world is looking to Oldham. Not only in England, but those beyond the seas. All over the world the great machinery of Empire is grinding out prosperity and happiness of the people of this island. We must send a worthy reply. Our flag will be high upon the seas and our voice heard in the nations of Europe under a Sovereign supported by the love of her subjects; and with a country guarded by the gallantry of its sons, we shall pursue our path. Not only will we pursue our dominion in many lands, but will also gratify those instincts and desires for practical social reform which are planted so deeply in the heart of the Tory democracy, and were planted by one whose name I have the honour to bear. . . .

Election day found Oldham in a fever-pitch of excitement, but the Conservatives were hampered by a lack of carriages; a large number of Radicals were well-to-do manufacturers who gave up their landaus, Victorias and dog-carts—130 of them—to bring voters to the poll. Churchill and Mawdsley could only muster ninety vehicles. Lady Randolph Churchill added a touch of colour and drama by accompanying her son in a landau and pair, with gaily-ribboned and rosetted postillions, while she was dressed entirely in blue. The new horseless carriage which Mr. Churchill had expected from Coventry broke down at Stafford.

In the event the Radicals carried the day. Mr. Emmott, despite his dullness, polled 12,976 votes, the allegedly social-minded Mr. Runciman 12,770. Mr. Churchill polled 11,477—no mean start for a beginner—and Mawdsley 11,449.

At the Conservative Club, as the night wore on, the rooms filled and towards midnight the result was announced. Churchill was unable to speak for several minutes because of the storm of cheering. In a tactful but forceful way he alluded to the weak organization of the Conservatives, adding a topical touch by an analogy with the Dervishes who fell to Kitchener's army—'they had the valour and enthusiasm, but had not the discipline their enemies had. That fact had its lessons. . . .' He added, with an ebullience that went down well, that 'I am a young man, and perhaps no young man can expect to go far in the world without getting one or two smacks in the eye. . . .'

To prove his point, *The Times of India* said that

Mr. Churchill makes no secret of his convictions and aspirations. Like his father, he aims at becoming the champion of the new Tory democracy . . . as he is not fettered by any lurking doubts of his own capacity—with very good reason, as those who know him can testify—he will probably become one of the lions of modern Conservatism before many years are over. He seems to have inherited his father's gift for saying smart things. His friends, in fact, would feel more confident about his future if he showed a little more reticence and restraint. His readiness as a writer and speaker, too, perilously approaches that fatal fluency which is the bane of the serious politician, and in England the politician who is not taken seriously cannot hope to attain real eminence. The average Tory voter likes to think that the quality he values most in a politician is solidity; we suspect that it might better be described as stolidity. Mr. Churchill, whatever he will develop into, will never become stolid. . . .

However, Churchill was not cast down by his defeat. Two days after war broke out with South Africa he was on his way to the scene of battle as war correspondent of the *Morning Post* at two hundred and fifty pounds a month, in those days a prodigious sum and the highest ever paid for such services. Time was to prove that he was not overpaid.

3

The Cockyollybird

For his role as war correspondent Winston Churchill was ideally suited. He had the physical energy, the mental curiosity, a cocksure independence of outlook and a sense of occasion—of throwing himself into the thick of complicated or chaotic situations and making sense of them in explicit and often exquisite prose. He was unique in his field, and Oliver Borthwick, editor of the *Morning Post* had been quick to see it.

This driving appetite for adventure which the young Churchill had was to prove the ideal conditioning and toughening-up required for a future political career, which is no ambition for the thin-skinned. To size up situations, to express himself clearly upon subjects without opportunity to swat them up beforehand, to be philosophic about unpopularity in some quarters and to court rebuff cheerfully after numerous reverses—we may all be thankful that he could do these things, at the age of only twenty-five.

Somehow, before leaving, he had seen to press his two-volume *The River War*, a graphic and masterly account of the reconquest of the Sudan. Joseph Chamberlain, Colonial Secretary, had received him before he left and, like many others, under-estimated the magnitude of the war ahead, causing Churchill to write in later life: 'Always remember, however sure you are that you can easily win, that there would not be a war if the other man did not think he also had a chance.'

The declaration of war was on 11th October 1899. Soon the Boers invaded British territory at several points, so that in the early stages British action consisted of several different campaigns—in the west the Boers moved to surround Mafeking, the siege of which began on 16th October and was not lifted until the following 17th May. To the south, Kimberley, the centre of the diamond mines, was besieged. Two Boer invasions crossed into Cape Colony, necessitating two British actions, while in the east nearly thirty thousand Boers entered Natal and after various engagements surrounded and contained Sir George White and his twelve thousand men. By the time Churchill arrived in South Africa everything was happening at once. But knowing that Ladysmith was besieged his inevitable instinct was to get there for an eye-witness's report. But in November, an armoured train moving towards Ladysmith, with Churchill standing on a box in the rear truck, was derailed by Boers at Estcourt.

Churchill had been asked to tell two other correspondents, Amery and Atkins, of the forthcoming foray into enemy lines, but forgot about it until the last moment, when, leaving the tent to discover on behalf of all of them whether and when the expedition was leaving, he caught the train only in the nick of time, and could not return to warn them to get moving—they were still in their sleeping bags. As the armoured train was derailed it came under withering Boer fire, to see which Churchill jumped off the train. After an hour's skirmishing he helped to load the wounded on to the locomotive and, as it moved slowly away for home, he jumped off and went to look for the beleaguered infantry. He had left his Mauser pistol on the train and, to his intense mortification, found himself a prisoner of the Boers.

His amazing adventures have been told often enough, and most expressively of all by himself, in *My Early Life*. He was not badly treated by the enemy—a fact which he emphasized later, to the disgust of many bloody-minded non-combatants at home. He would read, chat with the guards and play chess, but he could not leave. Having planned a mass breakout, he found himself going it alone because the others had lost their nerve, and by jumping trains, starving and hiding in a coal mine—by a strange coincidence he had met a stranger who turned out to be manager of a local colliery, and was from Oldham—he was able to rejoin the fighting forces and get to Durban. There he had a hero's reception (for the Boers had put a price on his head) and was able to see more action, this time as a lieutenant with the South African Light Horse, whose members, because of their 'cowboy' hats and waving plumes were known as the 'cockyollybirds'.

The news of his exploits, conveyed by other war correspondents and supplemented byhis own vivid despatches to the *Morning Post* had rocketed Churchill to popularity at home and abroad. At home, he typified the patriotic Englishman, risking life and limb for his Queen. He was flooded with telegrams and letters, many of them from people in Oldham who had voted against him at his last election, and wanted him to know that on a future occasion they would vote for him. It was heartening news, because such publicity was precisely what he needed as a budding politician; in politics you may be liked or disliked, but in either event people must have heard of you. People in 1899 did not have the benefit of wireless or the intrusive television lens to transport them vicariously to the scene of action; only the skilled and courageous war correspondent stood between them and ignorance. It was a misfortune to have been taken prisoner, but as Churchill said of this later, '. . . if I had not been caught, I could not have escaped, and my imprisonment and escape provided me with materials for lectures and a book which brought me in enough money to get into Parliament in 1900. . . .'

This time, getting into Parliament was comparatively easy; I say 'comparatively' because election campaigns were as strenuous then as now—once again it entailed a round of meetings, often several in a day, with long speeches (one of nearly ten thousand words) to be written and memorized before delivery.

Lord Salisbury's Conservative government had decided to have an election in October 1900 because the war fever was propitious for them; the tide had turned in South Africa and in the resultant glow of fervent patriotism at home, credit for this must, it was realized, redound to the government's favour.

Not only was Churchill on the crest of this emotional wave, but he enjoyed the added and incomparable advantage of having been 'on the spot' and being accepted by many as the hero of the hour. Oldham was bedecked with flags and bunting, Union Jacks predominating. From the station to the Conservative Club the streets were packed with people. The six carriages carrying Conservative notabilities, Churchill being one and the other Conservative candidate, the war correspondent C. B. Crisp, being another, were given an escort of mounted police. There was a municipal delegation to greet them. As he took his seat in the landau with Mr. Crisp, Alderman Whittacker and Alderman Waddington, he waved his panama hat again and again and grinned appreciatively as the Glodwick Brass Band struck up 'See The Conquering Hero Comes' followed—for good measure—by 'Soldiers of The Queen'. At several points, as the huge procession made its way through Wellington, King, Manchester, Yorkshire and Union Streets, his carriage had to be pulled to a halt while he stood up in it to receive the plaudits of the crowd. 'Everywhere eyes were strained to catch a glimpse of the manly face and figure of Mr. Churchill,' wrote a local journalist.

All this was in the hey-day of British imperialism. But supporters of the Liberal candidates, Emmott and Runciman, were often more grudging about Churchill's exploits and indignant at what was blatantly a 'khaki election'—an election in which emotion would play a greater part than political argument. Certainly Churchill put inordinate emphasis on the South African campaign, but it was, after all, the burning issue of the moment and permitted the inference that anybody not voting for the Conservative government would in some strange way be letting down the British fighting men in South Africa. Pictures of war scenes were everywhere displayed. A Mafeking touch was added by what the *Daily Telegraph* proudly described as 'electrical and gas devices'.

After the orgy of successful writing, which included two highly profitable best-selling books, *From London to Ladysmith via Pretoria* and *Ian Hamilton's March*, Mr. Churchill could be sustained by the thought that he was now of independent means. He had several thousand pounds saved, a fundamental preliminary to a parliamentary career, since Members of Parliament were not paid in those days, the political dice being heavily loaded thereby in favour of the Conservatives.

In those days neither radio nor television could achieve 'blanket' coverage of a nation, and although the newspapers, solid or popular, had given copious space to his despatches and reports about himself, it was possible for Churchill to make a speech in several different places and for the speech to have interest and novelty in each place.

As a climax of two days' celebrations to welcome his homecoming and his participation in Oldham's election, a huge meeting was held at the Empire Theatre, Oldham, in which Mr. Churchill's lengthy speech, interrupted frequently by wild bursts of cheering and clapping, was devoted entirely to the South African war. The greatest storm of applause, of course, came when he revealed that it had been an Oldham man who had hidden him in a mine and helped him to reach Delagoa Bay. Mr. Churchill, in the course of his long and descriptive narrative of the war and his adventures in it, said, 'You know that I had the misfortune to be taken prisoner' (a

voice: 'But you got out of it') and to the good-humoured interruption Churchill, quick as a flash, quipped, 'I found it necessary
to leave without the usual farewell addresses.'

'And whilst I was wandering about in the great tract of country
stretching between Pretoria and the Portuguese Territory, a distance
about three hundred miles as the crow flies—but I could not walk so
fast as the crow flies—(laughter)—one of the men who . . . at the
risk of his life gave me succour and assistance, was an Oldham
lad. . . .' The peroration was drowned in cheers.

Mr. Churchill left his listeners in no doubt as to his feelings about
South Africa. 'We will not have (if it lies within our power, as it most
assuredly does lie) a Republican form of government in South
Africa' although he was all for giving the Boers 'the widest measure
of self-government, the greatest extension of civil liberty'. Yet to
read that speech of his is to relive the excitement and drama and
tragedy of that now-forgotten war.

Realizing that Churchill was an election asset in other parts, he
was used as a star turn in numerous other towns such as Newcastle
and Manchester, for the Colonial Secretary, Joseph Chamberlain,
knew that the South African war was a national and not a local issue.
But Churchill's continual lambasting of Radicals evoked some acid
comments, especially from the *Oldham Chronicle*:

W. Churchill did not apparently exhaust his bad manners in his
speech at Newcastle. It might have been thought that the jet of
abusive epithets . . . would have completely drained the vials of his
spleen. But there were a few dregs left which were utilised in be-
spattering the political reputation of our borough members. He
insinuated that they were 'slippery customers' and that they had
assumed 'the cloak of imperialism'. By what right does Mr.
Churchill speak in this way? The vulgar parody about Emmott
changing its spots was an exhibition of bad taste. Mr. Churchill
can behave better than this and in Oldham he will be expected to
do so. The Liberal Party are quite prepared to deal with him as a
politician, but they will not sit quietly down whilst men whom
they regard with the highest respect are abused by a roaming
person fresh from the camp.

'The roaming person' was described in the *Newcastle Daily Leader* as
'. . . clean shaven, rather below the average height; if anything he is
facially very like his father. He is a pert youth, extremely "cocky"

—"gobley" as one of the audience termed him. Full of animation of delivery, he has an aptitude for phrase-making . . . he is somewhat nervous and apt to lose his way in a long sentence. . . .' Certainly Churchill knew how to combine alliteration with vehemence; he described the Liberal Party as 'a squabbling disorganized rabble, without purpose, plan, policy or power.' The *Newcastle Daily Chronicle* noted that he seemed 'anxious and nervous' and even when he had gained his audience and was in full swing 'there was a constant impediment or lisp to spoil the velvety flow of the well-arranged sentences.' But there was earnestness. 'In clerical garb' the writer concluded, 'Mr. Churchill would have looked an engaging sample of curate who could play cricket, and who could reasonably look forward to prospects, matrimonial or otherwise.'

Another writer made play with Churchill's adventures with the 'Cockyollybirds' or South African Light Horse. 'The cock's feather in his hat is not the only sign by which his connection with the cockyollybirds is signalled. He has a distinct tendency to crow, which much practice is making perfect. There is also a stretching of the neck, a strutting in the walk, a proud glancing of the eye. . . .'

It was not simply vanity. Churchill's instinct regarding elections was sound. To pursue too many contentious issues at once is politically complicated and confusing to the voter. The South African War gave him a clear-cut issue and canalized into political channels his well-deserved popularity as a writer.

Despite his violent criticism of Liberal policies, many Liberals switched their votes to Mr. Churchill, enabling him to scrape through with a margin of two hundred and thirty votes. His companion Mr. Crisp was defeated, as was the Liberal Mr. Runciman. Emmott, whose party Churchill had been telling Oldham was 'without purpose, plan, policy or power', polled the highest vote of all. So young Churchill, although elected for Oldham, was reminded that the town had not forsaken its radical tradition.

After speaking at a few more election meetings in other towns, he went on a lecture tour in the United States, where he was boosted as 'the future Prime Minister of Great Britain'; Churchill must surely have appreciated the compliment implied, but insisted on the description being withdrawn.

Mr. Churchill was in Minneapolis on 22nd January 1901 when Queen Victoria passed away at Osborne after a reign of sixty-three years. His exhausting tour of America finished, he returned to

England to challenge his tremendous physique further by yet another lecture tour. He was a complete realist where money was concerned; its possession alone gave freedom of choice, action and the opportunity of a Parliamentary career. How many young men of twenty-five could earn ten thousand pounds within a few months (and the pound then was worth five or six times as much as it is today)?

He returned to find the country plunged in sorrow at the Queen's death. King Edward VII, after a long wait, was now monarch. The South African war still dragged on. China was in a ferment after the Boxer rising and the savage reprisals of the western nations. Ireland was seething with discontent. The Empire might be far-flung but Britain, despite the wealth of her industrial revolution, had plenty of social problems at home. Abroad, friends were few. As Lord Salisbury put it: 'We can have no security; we cannot have any confidence in the feelings and sympathy of other nations . . . we can have no security except in the efficiency of our own defences. . . .'

A new century had begun and a new era. And the cocky young man in his middle twenties entered Parliament to play his part in their making.

4

His Father's Son

That Winston Churchill should have entered Parliament at this particular time was in keeping with his life. He thought and he acted big. His ambitions were clear-cut. The care he expended on the preparation of his speeches, with their hours of memorization and practice in front of mirrors, the judicious money-making as a necessary preliminary to independence, and the tremendous sense of showmanship which enabled him to make political capital out of any situation—these were to serve him well.

Churchill had arrived at the first stage of his career just when King Edward VII was to attend a State opening of Parliament for the first time in his reign. There had not been such a colourful and elaborate opening for forty years; its customary glitter and pomp and ceremony had been whittled down to almost Cromwellian simplicity by Queen Victoria. Now the old colour and glamour were restored by the worldly but warm-hearted King Edward. The famous stage coach, built for George III at the then prodigious cost of £7,000, was redecorated and re-upholstered. The Royal Procession appeared in all its historic splendour, by the King's command; the Yeomen of the Guard, Gentlemen in Waiting, Pursuivants, Heralds all appeared again.

And so, on 14th February 1901, Winston Churchill—immaculate in his grey topper and impeccable morning suit—took a back bencher's seat in the House of Commons Chamber and with the rest waited for the minatory knocks of Black Rod on the door of the Chamber, to announce that the King awaited them in the House of Lords, to read his first address.

'I address you for the first time,' the King said, 'at a moment of national sorrow . . . my beloved mother, during her long and glorious reign, has set an example before the world of what a monarch should be. It is my earnest desire to follow in her footsteps.'

The King spoke of trouble in South Africa, China and Ashanti,

37

of the proclamation of the establishment of the Australian Commonwealth at Sydney on 1st January and of his intention to visit that
country as his mother had intended, and to visit also Canada and
New Zealand. He then bowed to his Lords and Commoners, and,
taking the Queen by the hand, led the procession back to the
robing room.

It was a doubly historic occasion; the first State opening for
forty years, and the first Parliament of a new century.

It was more. The back-bencher had no intention of staying a
back-bencher, nor was any one likely to underestimate his ambition.
But only a few, such as Steevens of the *Daily Mail* could foresee that
he would reach political eminence. I think it true to say that having
a famous father makes others predisposed to think that his son is
unlikely to equal him in achievement. Such people forget that
Winston Churchill was totally indifferent to physical danger and
rebuffs, had an insatiable appetite for adventure and asserted
authority quite naturally and enjoyed responsibility. These are
valuable qualities of leadership. To him a difficulty was a challenge
to be taken up with zest; many men would shrink from making
speeches when they remembered they had a speech impediment
which some might ridicule. The impediment simply made Churchill
speak all the more, especially in public, in order that it might be
overcome.

The *Daily Mail* described the impression which the new Member
made upon the House:

> Ten minutes after he had been sworn, he was leaning back
> comfortably on the bench, silk hat well down over his forehead,
> figure crouched in the doubled-up attitude assumed by the
> Ministers, both hands deep in his pockets, eyeing the place and
> its inmates critically as if they were all Parliamentary novices.

For all this superficial show of confidence, Churchill's armoury
of confidence was incomplete. He lacked one quality which he
would have dearly loved to possess, the gift of improvisation, as a
result of which he was in a state of nerves. He had prepared a speech
with his usual care but now found that he would have a job to make
it sound spontaneous. Most parliamentarians spoke from the
briefest of notes, which contained facts impossible to memorize or
mere points on which the speaker could elaborate. But Churchill

needed a cue, some phrase of a previous speaker upon which he could seize, making a convenient link with the proceedings, showing his listeners that he was an attentive listener with a capacity for analysis and criticism.

But Churchill was fated to follow David Lloyd George, a 'damned Radical' whose young eyes flashed with Celtic fire and whose impassioned speeches endorsed their message. Lloyd George had embarrassed the methodical Churchill by not moving the amendment which he had put upon the order paper. Certainly the subject of debate was on the South African War, upon which no Member of the House, whether young or old, was more fitted to speak than Churchill, and he had waited for a subject which would give him the greatest chance of making a favourable impression.

The subject, of course, was highly contentious. Lord Roberts, when he handed over his command to Kitchener in November 1900, told the government at home that the war was over except for small isolated pockets of trouble-makers. There were, in fact, still over twenty thousand Boer fighters about, using guerilla tactics. Kitchener, a hard man himself, thought Lord Milner's 'squeeze them till the pips squeak' policy too harsh, with its pitiless system of concentration camps for women and children, the wholesale arson and needless slaughter. There should, he thought, have been an amnesty.

Lloyd George, then, echoed the misgivings of a good many British people at home who, while loyal to King and Empire, felt that our soldiers in the field were being compelled to be too cruel and ruthless.

As he waited for the Welshman's glowing oratory to end, Churchill fidgeted nervously. Where was his cue? By changing his tactics Lloyd George had deprived Churchill of a convenient lead-in. Churchill's speech was already prepared, but one couldn't just recite it, like a school recitation, with no reference to what had gone before. Sensing his embarrassment, George Bowles gave him a friendly tip—why not say that Lloyd George would have been better to have moved his moderate amendment instead of making a violent speech? As Lloyd George sat down amidst cheers, Churchill rose and the eyes of the House were upon him; his voice was loud and clear and rang with conviction:

I understood the Honourable Member, to whose speech the

House has just listened, had intended to move an Amendment to the address. The text of the Amendment, which had appeared in the papers, was singularly mild and moderate in tone; but mild and moderate as it was, neither the hon. Member nor his political friends had cared to expose it to criticism or challenge a division upon it, and indeed, when we compare the moderation of the amendment with the very bitter speech which the hon. Member has just delivered, it is difficult to avoid the conclusion that the moderation of the amendment was the moderation of the hon. Member's political friends and leaders and that the bitterness of his speech was all his own. It has been suggested to me that it might perhaps have been better, upon the whole, if the hon. Member, instead of making his speech without moving his amendment, had moved his amendment without making his speech.

Then came (after this rather dull introduction) a speech which, although not brilliant by his later standards, was competent, well delivered and had the necessary ingredients of controversy and independence. For example, he was too magnanimous to denigrate the enemy, whose integrity and fighting qualities he had learned, by personal contact, to admire. Quite a few Members gasped as he continued:

. . . I do not believe that the Boers would attach particular importance to the utterances of the hon. Member. No people in the world received so much verbal sympathy and so little practical support as the Boers. If I were a Boer fighting in the field—and if I were a Boer I hope I should be fighting in the field—I would not allow myself to be taken in by a message of sympathy, not even if it were signed by a hundred hon. Members. . . .

He reminded the House of the objects, as originally stated, of the war. The original negotiations with the Boers had been 'to extend the franchise to the people of the Transvaal'. At that time there were two and a half times as many British and non-Dutch as there were Boers, and 'before the outbreak of the war every train was crowded with British subjects who were endeavouring to escape from the approaching conflict, and so it was the Uitlanders were scattered all over the world'. The population balance, he thought, should be restored, and as for which form of government was best, he was against 'irksome' military government.

Although I regard British officers in the field of war, and in dealing with native races, as the best officers in the world, I do not believe that either their training or their habits of thought qualify them to exercise arbitrary authority over civil populations of European race. I have often myself been very much ashamed to see respectable old Boer farmers—the Boer is a curious combination of squire and peasant, and under the rough coat of the farmer there are often to be found the instincts of the squire—I have been ashamed to see such men ordered about peremptorily by young subaltern officers, as if they were private soldiers.

The rest of his speech was a reasoned appeal for a settlement combining commonsense with honour, and he finished with an oblique reference to his father, whose memory was, of course, still very fresh with many of the Members he was addressing: 'I cannot sit down without saying how grateful I am for the kindness and patience with which the House has heard me, and which have been extended to me, I well know, not on my own account, but because of a certain splendid memory which many hon. Members still preserve.'

Joseph Chamberlain, Colonial Secretary, shifted uncomfortably. The pointed reference to the dignity and integrity of the enemy was, he thought, 'a way to throw away seats'. This was not support for the Government at all, and if a new member could behave that way on his very first entry to the House, what on earth would he do later? Was the writer in *Vanity Fair* right, then, when he had predicted, 'He can write and he can fight . . . he is ambitious . . . he means to get on, and he loves his country. But he can hardly be the slave of any party.'? Some Tories noted, not entirely with pleasure, that as much applause came, at the end of his speech, from the Liberal side of the House as from their own. But Churchill was not abashed; he had learned early that one can move amongst those having authority without submitting to them. A man not overawed by Lord Kitchener, who himself managed to intimidate most of the War Office except perhaps the Adjutant-General, was hardly likely to be bothered by a few M.P.s or even the stern, appraising gaze of the elderly Premier, Lord Salisbury, who adjusted his pince-nez to get a better view of the new arrival.

Afterwards Churchill exchanged guarded pleasantries with Lloyd George, thereby beginning, in his own words 'an association which has persisted through many vicissitudes'.

Joseph Chamberlain's misgivings about the new Tory recruit were soon to be confirmed. Churchill had no idea whatsoever about political party discipline. He did what he wanted and said what he wished, almost as though he were a party in his own right. He had criticized government policy in South Africa within weeks of first entering Parliament; and before long he was to be sniping at his own ranks again, to the mortification of his Tory colleagues and the jubilation of the Liberals on the other side of the House.

It is commonly assumed that in early life Churchill was calculating in pursuing his ambition, which was to get into Parliament and get into office. One wonders whether his natural zest, courage, energy and fluency of expression were not canalized by intuition. I feel that he was following in his father's footsteps in far more senses than one. He bitterly resented what he considered the rejection of his father by Lord Salisbury (actually Lord Randolph Churchill resigned, and his resignation had been accepted by the Prime Minister). Winston Churchill's sniping at Chamberlain makes sense, too, when one remembers that Chamberlain was an old opponent of Lord Randolph Churchill.

But a third Tory was to draw Churchill's fire. He was Mr. William St. John Brodrick, Secretary of State for War. Fifteen years ago he had been Under-Secretary to William Henry Smith, the War Minister whose army estimates were considered by Winston Churchill's father, then Chancellor of the Exchequer, to be excessive. Lord Salisbury had stuck by his War Minister's judgement, causing—as Winston Churchill saw it—the sacrifice of Lord Randolph's career.

Winston Churchill did and said everything he could to vindicate his father's memory. In many ways he considered himself as carrying on his father's policies.

Mr. Brodrick, now seized in the glare of Mr. Churchill's angry gaze, had submitted a scheme to the House for the reorganization of the British Army and the remedying of its more glaring weaknesses, some of which Mr. Churchill had himself pin-pointed in his books. To be fair to Churchill, one must remember that he was not the only opponent of Brodrick's scheme, which demanded an army budget of £30 million and recommended the re-grouping of regular and irregulars into six army corps (of which half would be held in readiness for immediate embarkation to anywhere). Kitchener, certainly no friend of Churchill's, thought Brodrick's scheme 'futile' and resisted all efforts to bring him back to England to do the job instead.

Churchill has been quite frank about how he began and sustained his running battle against his father's old enemy and would-be re-organizer of the British Army: 'I resolved to oppose this scheme,' he wrote in *My Early Life*, 'whenever the Army Estimates should be introduced. I took six weeks to prepare this speech, and learnt it so thoroughly off by heart that it hardly mattered where I began it or how I turned it.'

As a beginning in a campaign which he sustained for two years, Churchill tabled an amendment acknowledging the necessity for Army Reform but insisting on economies. In so doing he further antagonized the Tory hierarchy and was castigated by *The Times* for his 'disastrous mistake'.

It was a battle of wits and arguments which Churchill relished. He reminded them of how his father had found thirty-one millions too much for both the Army and Navy, and here was a man called Brodrick who asked for twice as much. What, he asked, was the point of such vast expenditure? In effect, it looked as though it was to allow generals to play at being soldiers even when there was no soldiering to be done. 'When they come home from South Africa with no more worlds to conquer they must keep their hands in, and they must be provided with an army, even if it costs thirty millions a year to save them getting out of practice. . . .'

Once again he brought his father's name into the debate, a frequent habit which some thought overdone. He made it clear that he was speaking 'in a cause I have inherited, and a cause for which the late Lord Randolph made the greatest sacrifice of any Minister in modern times'.

For a new M.P. he was doing well; he had managed to offend the Prime Minister, the Colonial Minister, the War Minister and the Financial Secretary to the Treasury all within a few weeks. He had bitter things to say about Ministers and spoke with the candour of one who knew what fighting entails:

'I have frequently been astonished since I have been in this House to hear with what composure and how glibly Members, and even Ministers, talk of a European war.' Once wars could be limited 'but now, when mighty populations are impelled against each other . . . when the resources of science and civilization sweep away everything that might mitigate their fury, a European war can only end in the ruin of the vanquished and the scarcely less fatal commercial dislocation and exhaustion of the conquerors.'

He made a pointed hint that arms races lead to war. 'The possession of a very sharp sword offers a temptation which becomes irresistible to demonstrate the efficiency of the weapon in a practical way.' He thought the Navy our primary defence—'The only weapon with which we can expect to cope with great nations is the Navy. . . .'

Churchill's party insubordination at least served to focus public attention on to the Conservatives at a time when their prestige was quite certainly on the wane. He became the nucleus of a 'ginger group' of Conservatives who were dissatisfied with their Party's ineffectual grip on the public imagination. It became known as the 'Hughligans', supposedly after Lord Hugh Cecil, the Prime Minister's younger son, who was one of the group's leading lights. Others, aristocrats all, included Arthur Stanley, son of Lord Derby and Ivor Guest, son of Lady Wimborne and cousin of Winston.

Lord Salisbury resigned his office of Prime Minister in July 1902 and was succeeded by a nephew, Arthur Balfour, more notable for his intelligence than strength, and whose role was to be scarcely more than that of caretaker in a house soon to be vacated.

After living with his mother for a time at Great Cumberland Place, near Marble Arch, Churchill shared a flat in Mount Street, Mayfair, with his brother Jack. His day started with work in bed, and when he was not in the House of Commons he would, most of the time, be sitting at his father's desk, drafting speeches and memoranda, answering a heavy correspondence and writing for the press.

In his own memoirs, Churchill prefers the actual word 'Hooligans' to describe the group. But they were, apart from their political dissidence, a gentlemanly crowd, given to dining well—'We shall dine first and consider our position afterwards,' Mr. Churchill liked to say. Once Lord Salisbury entertained them in his home, and even Austen Chamberlain was their guest. Chamberlain was getting more than a little tired of Churchill's sniping. He had been under fire in April 1902 because of the Government's refusal to admit to this country a Mr. Cartwright, who had been imprisoned in South Africa during the war there for writing an article attacking Britain. The decision seemed to Churchill petty and stupid, and he told Chamberlain so. 'What is the use of supporting your own government only when it is right?' Chamberlain demanded. 'It is just when it is in this sort of pickle that you ought to have come to our aid.'

When he was leaving he gave them a hint of his next political enthusiasm, and one which Mr. Churchill certainly did not share. 'You young gentlemen have entertained me royally and in return I will give you a priceless secret. Tariffs! Study them closely and make yourself masters of them, and you will not regret your hospitality to me.'

Probably some did not. Perhaps Mr. Chamberlain did. He had warned Mr. Churchill that he proposed to advocate a policy which Mr. Churchill found anathema. Churchill believed in free trade. A country which could feed only half its population and needed to earn enough by its exports to buy the rest of the food abroad could not afford, Mr. Churchill believed, to penalize importers wanting to bring goods into Britain. If he raised tariff walls, surely so would they. It was a form of warfare in which everyone would find themselves poorer.

While the prestige and power of the Conservatives were in decline, the Liberals, previously divided, were becoming united and confident under Sir Henry Campbell-Bannerman. Mr. Churchill's continual forays were a delight and a help to the Liberals. How true, I wonder, are the Countess of Warwick's references to a shooting party held in 1901, in which Mr. Churchill is said to have told Cecil Rhodes that 'he had just been on a visit to Lord Rosebery and he said he was inclined to leave the leadership to Mr. Balfour and proclaim himself a Liberal. He wanted power, and the Tory road to power for a young man was blocked by the Cecils and other brilliant young Conservatives, whereas the Liberal path was open. Cecil Rhodes was all in favour of Winston turning Liberal. . . .'

Was this the course of Winston Churchill's reasoning so early in his career? Whether the Countess of Warwick reported correctly or not, Winston Churchill's words and actions were leading him, inexorably, into the Liberal camp.

From the outset, it is clear, he did not regard his loyalty as being due primarily to a party, but to the people. He did not see himself as a mere delegate, sent like a messenger to convey the intentions and inhibitions of the majority of his constituents. However resentful his own party might be, and however restive the Oldham voters, who in a fit of war fever, had voted him into Westminster, his independence was impressive. And if one accepted the premise of loyalty to a party, how could one expect unlimited allegiance to a party divided within itself, proclaiming wholly opposed and inconsistent policies?

On 15th May 1903 the Tory Party's inherent confusion and indiscipline were manifested in a striking way. In a speech at Birmingham Mr. Joseph Chamberlain declared in favour of protective tariffs. On precisely the same day the Prime Minister, Mr. Balfour, made a speech espousing Free Trade. Thus two principals of the Tory Government could be seen to be at loggerheads on fundamentals of policy, to the dismay of the Tories and the jubilation of Liberals.

Prominent—indeed, foremost—amongst those who attacked the proposed tariff policy was Mr. Churchill. In December 1903 he sent the Liberal candidate at Ludlow by-election a letter of support. 'Thank God we have a Liberal Party!' he told Free Traders at Halifax.

His alienation from Tory policies deepened all the time. To some extent he was influenced by an increased interest in social questions and the economic conditions of the working man, whose problems, in his rather exalted social position, had hitherto been a closed book to him. His interest in social reform was stimulated by meetings with those trade union pioneers, Beatrice and Sidney Webb. Beatrice found him 'egotistical, bumptious, shallow-minded and reactionary, but with a certain personal magnetism, great pluck and some originality.'

Churchill sustained his attacks upon Chamberlain and Balfour. He attacked what he considered Tory smugness and insularity during a debate on the Trade Disputes Bill in April 1904 when he told the House that 'the influence of Labour on the course of legislation is ludicrously small'. The *Daily Mail* condemned this next day as 'Radicalism of the reddest type'. One feels that Winston Churchill must have enjoyed being called a Red. It was during that speech that he lost the thread of his argument, which was rare for him. But he could be excused a certain tension. Thick-skinned though he was, he was surrounded by tension and hostility, and had decided to cut away from the Tories and join the Liberals.

That it was to prove practicable for him to do this was due, at least indirectly, to his championship of an unpopular cause, that of Jewish refugees who came to this country to escape the terror of Tsarist pogroms. In Russia thousands were killed in massacres and many thousands injured in sponsored or condoned anti-Semitic riots. To limit their arrival, the Aliens Bill of 1904 was mooted, giving the Home Office, Mr. Churchill maintained, far too much authority. There was a distinct anti-Semitic tone about the proposed legislation and Mr. Churchill attacked the Bill with all his might.

During the Easter Recess Mr. Nathan Laski, a leading Liberal in Manchester and a pillar of the Jewish community there, approached Mr. Churchill on behalf of the Liberal Association of North-west Manchester, and asked if he would be willing to stand as Liberal candidate for their constituency in the next General Election. This he agreed to do.

After the Easter Recess Mr. Churchill crossed to the Opposition benches and sat next to Mr. Lloyd George. Churchill's old colleagues looked across with contempt and anger. He, cherubic and seemingly relaxed, engaged in animated conversation with his Liberal colleagues. There was uproar when he attempted to speak, and so rowdy were the catcalls and comments from the Conservative benches that Mr. David Shackleton, a Labour M.P., interceded with the Speaker on Mr. Churchill's behalf, asking for a fair deal. Mr. Churchill roundly accused Mr. Chamberlain of conniving at a conspiracy to gag him, which drew the Minister white and taut to his feet. Was it in order, he demanded, 'for the junior Member for Oldham to say that there is a conspiracy against him in which I am an accomplice, which is absolutely untrue.' The Speaker rebuked Churchill for his accusation, which he withdrew.

Chamberlain took a surprisingly charitable view of young Churchill's defection. 'I think you are quite right, feeling as you do, to join the Liberals. You must expect to have the same sort of abuse flung at you as I have endured. . . .' This prophecy was more than fulfilled. 'Blenheim Rat' was perhaps the least offensive of the epithets levelled at him.

But Churchill did not simply spend his time travelling from Mount Street to Westminster, making speeches and listening to debates. Sensitive to the course of events, he could see that the Tory Party was breaking up. He spent much time discussing and planning future policy with Liberal leaders, and in working on his biography of his father, which was published in 1906 and widely acclaimed by friend and foe alike as a masterpiece.

On 4th December 1905 Mr. Balfour resigned. The following day the leader of the Liberals, Sir Henry Campbell-Bannerman, was invited by King Edward to form a government, and accepted. A week later Mr. Winston Churchill was His Majesty's Under-Secretary of State for Colonies in the first Liberal government for ten years.

He was to learn, too, not to weaken his case by abuse or crude attack, but to rely upon the skilful marshalling of facts, forceful expression, timeliness of reference and sheer oratory. His youthful 'cockiness' was to mature somewhat (it had been a popular music-hall joke, always guaranteed to bring the house down with laughter 'Oo d'yer think you are, Winston Churchill?'). But hardly had he joined the Liberals than he was criticizing them too, causing Sir Charles Dilke to warn him: 'Look out, Winston. You can "rat" once, but no one can "rat" twice. That finishes any man.'

In the General Election of 1906 Mr. Churchill stood as Liberal candidate for North-west Manchester in opposition to the un-imaginative and pedantic Sir William Joynson-Hicks, a solicitor known as 'Jix'. The constituency included a fair number of sober tradesmen and Campbell-Bannerman doubted whether Churchill's ebullience and cheek were the qualities to attract their votes. However, Churchill threw himself into the election campaign with his accustomed zest, profiting by the dullness of his opponent and Joynson-Hicks' foolishness in relying too much upon abuse of Mr. Churchill in the hopes of winning votes for himself. Polling 5,639 votes against Joynson-Hicks' 4,398, he came back to Parliament. The election had been one of the greatest political landslides in British history, the Liberals returning in triumph with 401 seats against 157.

This Liberal administration was destined to last nearly ten years before becoming part of a Coalition during the First World War. Mr. Churchill, now a Minister at the age of thirty-one, was to remain within the maelstrom of activity, to be free to assert the authority, shoulder responsibility and enjoy all the controversy which his restless and adventurous nature demanded. Many who had called him 'Blenheim Rat', 'Turncoat' and 'a political Vicar of Bray' had themselves been swept out of office and in many cases even out of politics. Their careers were, in many cases, ended. Churchill's, in the true sense, had begun in earnest.

5

Maturing Years

The ousting of the Conservatives after twenty years of ascendancy in Parliament and the Liberal revival were events of unprecedented importance in British social history. It was the beginning of a more democratic era. Being able to reckon, on most measures, on the support of 83 Irish Nationalists and 51 Labour members, the Liberals had an overwhelming majority of 300.

It is true that the British Empire exercised a strong appeal to many; but Imperialism as such had been rejected. Chamberlain's advocacy of tariffs had to some extent encompassed the defeat of his party; but the conduct of the war in South Africa and the flogging of Chinese coolies there had made many ordinary people ask what else was done in their name but without their knowledge.

Churchill's heart was full as he took his seat in the new Parliament, which met on 20th February 1906. There were so many new faces—but never had the old House met with such an air of expectancy and zest. The Campbell-Bannerman administration included a brilliant and varied array of talent. On the Liberal side there was Lloyd George, the fire-eating Welshman who was to be a great wartime Prime Minister but for the moment was President of the Board of Trade. Mr. Asquith, the lawyer with a mind like a rapier, yet solid Yorkshire stuff refined in the best universities, was Chancellor of the Exchequer and formidable in debate. There was John Burns, the first manual worker ever to become a Cabinet Minister, as President of the Local Government Board—who may be said to have established the tradition of h-dropping in Parliament when he said, at the time of his appointment, to the Prime Minister, 'Sir 'Enery, this is the most popular thing you 'ave done.'

There were others in that House, too, of brilliance if wholly different in temperament and aspiration. Mr. F. E. Smith (later Lord Birkenhead) with smooth, unruffled legal mind and dry, drawling humour; he was at his most dangerous in debate when he appeared most casual. There was the ascetic, tense-faced Philip

Snowden of the Independent Labour Party, forever leaning on his two sticks and bending forward as though flinging himself into battle, sticks and all; Keir Hardy, the poor baker's boy who had been fired summarily for being late at work after staying up all night with his dying brother and cheated of his week's pittance by his well-fed and sanctimonious boss—now Hardy was Chairman of the Parliamentary Labour Party. There was Ramsay MacDonald, with dark curly hair and flashing black eyes, a strategist distrusted by many within his own Labour Party, but a future Prime Minister nevertheless.

Least colourful of all his associates was Winston Churchill's boss, Colonial Secretary the Earl of Elgin. He had been Viceroy of India but was without governmental experience; he was an impatient listener, taciturn and gave the impression that he did not expect much good of anybody. Churchill he seemed even to resent, often ignoring him when his advice might reasonably have been sought, by-passing him on innumerable occasions and on others even snubbing him. Perhaps he felt that Churchill was a man who wanted to go too far too soon.

In 1906 the Colonial Office was a ministry of far-flung importance. For one thing, it administered South Africa. The task of piloting through the House a Bill for a new Transvaal Constitution was one much to Churchill's liking. He had conceived a great respect for the Boers and urged the House to agree to the creation of 'a tranquil, prosperous, consolidated Afrikander nation under the protecting aegis of the British Crown.' He tried to keep the whole issue away from party politics. South Africa should start its life anew after the schisms and miseries of protracted war. 'There must be no difference in this grant of responsible government between Boer and Britain in South Africa,' he told the House. 'With all our majority we can only make it the gift of a party. You can make it a gift of England.'

During his holiday in France during the summer recess of 1906 Mr. Churchill wrote long letters to King Edward about the problem of South Africa. He also found time to attend German Army manoeuvres, where the Kaiser treated him with imperial hospitality. The debate on the Transvaal continued until 17th December 1906 and in the course of it Mr. Churchill learned that a clever *riposte* can sometimes prove too clever. During the General Election the Liberals had made much capital out of Chinese 'slave' labour in South Africa and the infliction of corporal punishment upon them.

The Liberals had used the word 'slavery' as a stick with which to beat their Conservative opponents.

Now the boot was on the other foot. The Liberals were now in power and the Chinese, beaten or unbeaten, were still in South Africa. They were there on labour contracts, and it was no easy matter for a Minister sitting in London to whisk them back to their original countries. Churchill was pressed about this. Could indentured labour really be called 'slavery' (which was what the Liberals had called it)? No, said Mr. Churchill in effect, it was not. '. . . it cannot, in the view of His Majesty's Government, be classified as slavery in the extreme acceptance of the word without some risk of terminological inexactitude.' Conservatives were not slow to seize the phrase 'terminological inexactitude' and to say that it was a mere euphemism for a lie, and an admission that the Liberals had lied about alleged Chinese slavery in order to get into Parliament.

Mr. Churchill ran into further trouble when William Byles, a Liberal back-bencher, moved a vote of censure on Lord Milner (now back from South Africa and in the House of Lords) for having authorized the flogging of Chinese coolies. But as Lord Milner had already admitted his mistake in making such an authorization, and apologized for it, the government did not want to re-open old wounds.

To Mr. Churchill fell the unenviable job of condemning Lord Milner on one hand and persuading the House to leave him alone on the other. His speech, unexceptional in its textual form, sounded harsh, patronizing and ungenerous in its delivery. Milner, he said, having dealt with men 'rich beyond the dreams of avarice' was now 'poor, and honourably poor. After twenty years of exhausting service under the Crown he is today a retired Civil Servant, without pension or gratuity of any kind whatever. . . .' *Honourably poor?* What did the phrase mean? That Milner's poverty was some kind of providential judgement? King Edward was shocked at Mr. Churchill's speech and told the Prime Minister so.

The 1906 sessions of Parliament were arduous. There were many bills to be worked out and debated, some highly controversial, such as the Trade Union Bill and the Education Bill. In this year alone Mr. Churchill spoke in Parliament no less than ninety times, and some of his speeches, consisting of as many as ten thousand words or more, involved detailed research on specialized and diverse subjects. All these had to be written, amended and memorized before delivery. The Parliamentary work in any case was additional to the ordinarily heavy routine of his daily life—the long hours at the Ministry, the endless procession of callers, the meetings, conferences, correspondence and travels. Not only his brilliance but his vitality were the envy of all. He was, certainly, as one rival put it 'the most hated man in Parliament' but he was acknowledged ungrudgingly to be the most energetic.

It was fortunate for Mr. Churchill that a disgraceful incident in Egypt—then under British administration—did not involve him as Junior Minister. Egypt came under the jurisdiction of the Foreign Office, which had therefore to deal with a gross abuse of imperial power. Five British officers tried to shoot some pigeons belonging to the inhabitants of the village of Densharwai on the Nile Delta. They were tame pigeons—valued pets—and the incensed villagers sprang to the defence of the helpless and harmless birds. In the resulting skirmish a British officer was beaten with clubs and subsequently died.

The skirmish had arisen through the tactless arrogance of the British officers; theirs was the provocation and theirs the responsibility for the attack upon themselves. But Lord Cromer's administration responded to the incident with much brutality. A special court was convened with no right of appeal. Four villagers were condemned to be hanged, twelve received prison sentences ranging from one year to life, and others were flogged, some receiving as many as fifty lashes. The men were hanged or flogged on the site of their offence and in the presence of their relatives and friends.

Sir Edward Grey, the Foreign Secretary, and Lord Cromer supported the action taken on the argument that a challenge to authority, if not met decisively, encourages even greater insurrection —a line of reasoning used once to attempt to justify the massacre at Amritsar. Liberals were disturbed at the affair. Cromer issued an order that in future pigeons were not to be shot, which must have been a belated consolation for the inhabitants of Denshawai, and his successor released the prisoners two years later.

Those who care to study Mr. Churchill's Parliamentary pronouncements of those early days will get a surprise. Not for nothing was he dubbed 'a damned Radical'. How many know that he was one of the earliest advocates of nationalization? 'I am very sorry that we have not got the railways of this country in our hands,' he declared, and it took nearly forty years before a Labour Government did precisely that. 'We are all agreed,' he also said, 'that the State must increasingly and earnestly concern itself with the care of the sick and the aged and, above all, of the children. I look forward to the universal establishment of minimum standards of life and labour, and their progressive elevation as the increasing energies of production permit. . . . I would recommend you not to be scared in discussing any of these proposals, just because an old woman comes along and tells you they are Socialistic.'

It would be surprising if any one as pugnacious and outspoken as Mr. Churchill had not committed a few indiscretions. The Imperial Conference of 1907 was an occasion for one. For the Premiers of Australia, Canada, New Zealand and The Cape pressed for Imperial Preference. Mr. Asquith, the Prime Minister, had to tell them that his government was voted into office on its promise to uphold the principle of Free Trade, and could not be committed by the 'Tariff Reformers' or Protectionists of the previous government. Churchill, with far less tact, told the Prime Ministers that the door to Imperial Preference had been 'banged, barred and bolted' and, as Earl Winterton has said, enabled Conservatives to say 'what we sincerely believed at the time, that Sir Winston was an enemy of the Empire.'

Towards the end of 1907 Campbell-Bannerman began to crack up from the excessive strain of overwork, anxiety and emotional strain through the death of his much-loved wife. Colleagues had found him, his head buried in his hands, sobbing his heart out. He did not realize how ill he really was, and to sustain his morale, his colleagues did not tell him, and suffered the painful ordeal of watching a friend and leader literally dying on his feet. At the commencement of the 1908 session he made a brief appearance and resigned in April, dying three weeks later on 22nd April. Mr. Asquith became Prime Minister and, after discussions with King Edward, who had formed a favourable opinion of Winston Churchill despite criticisms on detail, promoted him to the office of President of the Board of Trade, which gave him cabinet rank.

So far, so good, but for Mr. Churchill this entailed an initial embarrassment and complication. It was at that time obligatory for any M.P. admitted to the Cabinet to submit himself for re-election. This was easier said than done. At his previous election, Mr. Churchill had declared himself against Votes for Women and in the meantime the Suffragettes had become more and more militant. Their tactics were surprise, obstruction, shock and mere emotion. Impervious to argument, they stormed into his meetings and heckled him unmercifully. He devised no way of dealing with these female guerillas except to look glumly on while they were ejected forcibly. The dull but pro-Suffragette Joynson-Hicks took full advantage of Churchill's discomfiture and when the results were announced it was seen that he had lost by 491 votes. 'Winston Churchill is OUT, OUT, OUT, OUT!' screamed the *Daily Telegraph* but the young Parliamentarian was not discouraged. Relaxing over a brandy and cigar in the portentous Manchester Reform Club, he heard that he had been nominated as Liberal candidate in Dundee.

Even Dundee, however, was not to be a walkover. The city of jam, jute and journalism had many Labour supporters who saw Churchill as an aristocrat and an Imperialist. The Conservatives hated him as a political turncoat and a Radical whose radicalism appeared to have no definable bounds. The Suffragettes in Manchester had forewarned their militant colleagues in Scotland to converge upon Mr. Churchill and give him a taste of feminine hell. This they did, one tall and terrifying female drowning his speeches by the loud clanging of a handbell.

But Mr. Churchill enjoyed the campaign and showed his shrewd understanding of the political scene. There was no more talk of armies, Imperialism, South Africa—these were no rallying cries to over-worked shop assistants and ill-paid factory hands. But while accepting—indeed, advocating—collective State action for the common good, he attacked Socialism with its assumption ('a monstrous and imbecile conception') of State monopoly on a large scale.

Mr. (now the 'Rt. Hon.') Winston Churchill was elected by 7,079 votes against the Unionist poll of 4,370 votes. Not surprisingly the unlucky Mr. Scrymgeour, the Prohibition candidate, polled only 655 votes.

So now The Rt. Hon. Winston Churchill, M.P., was a member of the Cabinet at the age of 33. Of course, the Board of Trade could only be a stepping-stone to higher office; Churchill, to use his own graphic expression, had no real appetite for 'those damn dots'. But it was a better choice than the alternative proffered him by Asquith, of going to the Local Government Board. 'I refuse to be shut up in a soup-kitchen with Mrs. Sidney Webb' Churchill told his faithful secretary, Edward Marsh.

The comment sounds like a sneer; but it was not. Churchill had conceived a healthy respect for Sidney Webb and his able wife. From them he had learned much about the impact of unemployment and the hardships of poor wages and sweated labour. The whole business of finding work or finding somebody to do work was too hit-or-miss. A man would trudge around all day, seeing many employers yet missing the very one who could have used his services. Why not Labour Exchanges? Why should the Government not have skilled staff, and local premises which would be a clearing house for labour? Where a man might go who needed work, and where there would be information about the jobs vacant locally, so that he could be sent after one suited to his skills? We take this particular social service for granted now, but in those days the idea was revolutionary and a great step forward socially. And it was Mr. Churchill, keeping a wary eye on other openings, and labouring among 'those damn dots' who brought it about.

6

Reformist Zeal

The parliamentary session which began in autumn, 1908, was a memorable one—for the country and for Mr. Churchill. For one thing, so far as his personal life was concerned, he had taken the most important step of all. In September 1908 he had married Clementine Hozier, daughter of Lady Blanche Hozier, daughter of the seventh Earl of Airlie. He had met her at the house of a friend during the Dundee campaign. Despite aristocratic connections and descent, Clementine Hozier was not wealthy and had been giving French lessons to help maintain the home she shared with her mother in Kensington. Churchill fell in love with her and, as he so charmingly put it in his memoirs 'lived happily ever after'. All who saw them together, then and in the intervening half a century, could not fail to be touched by their mutual devotion. 'My ability to persuade my wife to marry me was quite my most brilliant achievement,' Churchill once proudly remarked, adding that he could never have gone through all he did in peace and war without his 'better half'.

His marriage at St. Margaret's, Westminster, was the social event of the season attended by the notabilities of the country. Presents flooded in on the couple and a mere list of them filled a column in *The Times*. King Edward sent a gold-mounted stick bearing the Marlborough coat-of-arms; Haldane, the founder of the modern Army, sent a silver bowl, Lloyd George a silver fruit bowl. Members of all political parties attended the wedding. He had married for love and for no other reason, but as it happened, his choice spiked the guns of his less generous political enemies, who would liked to have been able to say that the aristocrat-turned-working-man's-champion had married for money.

Churchill had found a large and comfortable house at 33 Eccleston Square in the City of Westminster, only a short walk from the Houses of Parliament which, in another sense, were also to be his home for the better part of his lifetime. His great book-lined study on the first floor was the workroom in which he drafted countless speeches, memoranda, notes and letters, his output of written work being far in excess of that of most professional full-time writers with no other things to do. In this house his children were born. Here he would entertain friend and foe, discoursing volubly on anything and everything. His home and his household had the stability of rock; it was a refuge and a fortress, a source of strength which he always happily acknowledged.

Mr. Churchill soon found that there was more to the Board of Trade than he had imagined. Its ramifications were wide indeed, covering trade and transport, working conditions and trade disputes, development plans and production problems, as well as trade both domestic and international.

Asquith's choice of Churchill was a wise one. Despite the tremendous majority gained by the Liberals in 1906, their political prestige was on the wane. Only a bold programme which could capture the country's imagination could sustain the Liberals in power. Churchill, like the other firebrand Lloyd George (with whom he had struck up a lasting friendship), did much to reinvigorate Parliament.

With Mr. Churchill in the Cabinet were Grey of the Foreign Office, Haldane at the War Office and Lloyd George, Chancellor of the Exchequer, whose budget of 1909 was to create a storm. It was Lloyd George who had sparked off the Radical streak in Churchill. He, and the Webbs—Beatrice and Sidney—had made him realize that for all Britain's vast wealth there were millions living below subsistence level. A whole programme of reform was embarked upon, laying the foundations of the welfare state—old age pensions, sickness insurance, labour exchanges and trade boards for fixing wages and hours of work.

Was Churchill a Liberal from conviction or for reasons of expediency? Did he cross the floor of the House because the Conservatives were—at that time—a dying cause and the Liberal party, therefore, a better path to political promotion and success? Those who knew him intimately at the time were convinced that, despite being born in a palace, of moving by right amongst the country's élite, his Radicalism was sincere. Lord Simon has said:

His tolerance, his sympathy with the oppressed and the underdog, his courage in withstanding clamour all derive from a heart and a head which made him in his early days of Ministerial office, a Liberal statesman. This liberal outlook was sincerely adopted and his liberal views were embodied in well-argued speeches and were not a mere pose. . . .

A word on the origin of Labour Exchanges, for so long a feature of our welfare services. The idea originated with the late Lord Beveridge—then William Beveridge, a barrister who had studied at Oxford and was especially interested in social work. He was a friend of the Webbs and through them met Churchill at their house for dinner. The Webbs, who had researched deeply into social problems, did not attempt to implement any of their ideas or ideals through the Labour Party, which lacked the strength and substance necessary for the launching of a bold and effective programme of reform. As the Webbs expounded the idea to Churchill, he was quick to see its usefulness (it is true that at most stages of his parliamentary career he would pursue an idea if he thought it good, even though it might not be in line with party policy; but in this case the Asquith government was in general committed to improving the lot of the middle and labouring classes at the expense of the well-to-do). Beveridge, too, spoke with all the earnestness of the young idealist with facts at his fingertips. Within a few days Churchill had set the wheels in motion by having Beveridge taken on to the Board of Trade Staff, cutting ruthlessly through Civil Service red tape to avail himself of his services immediately.

Together, Churchill and Beveridge established a country-wide network of labour exchanges, under Board of Trade Control. Churchill argued the case for such exchanges with great eloquence in Parliament, and within two years they were functioning. He insisted that they should not be staffed entirely by former civil servants, as recruitment demanded quite different qualities.

In the Cabinet, Churchill was irrepressible. There was no such thing, so far as he was concerned, as being a *junior* member of the Cabinet. You were either in it or you were not, and if you were deemed good enough to be in it you did not have to be diffident about expressing your views. And he certainly was not. He expounded at length on anything that concerned him and quite a few things that did not—including the business of other Ministers. Once, when the young Minister had almost monopolized the

Cabinet's time, Sir Edward Grey the Foreign Minister, remarked in despair, 'Winston, very soon, will become incapable from sheer activity of mind of being anything in the Cabinet but Prime Minister.'

Apart from this, Churchill bombarded members of the Cabinet and almost everybody else with notes and lengthy memoranda embodying his views on many matters remote from the province of the Board of Trade. After all, his lengthy missives to King Edward were often paternalistic in tone; he was not likely to be overawed by a mere Prime Minister.

In April 1909 Lloyd George presented what became known as the 'People's Budget'. One feature of it was that Lloyd George wanted to save on naval estimates in order to spend money on social services. But Germany's expansionist ambitions were becoming increasingly recognized. Lloyd George, with Winston Churchill's support, recommended four Dreadnoughts. McKenna, First Lord of the Admiralty, and Admiral Fisher, First Sea Lord, wanted six. The Cabinet was split over this issue and Liberal prestige lowered by this public quarrel. Eventually those who clamoured, 'We want eight, and we won't wait!' got what they wanted—four Dreadnoughts approved and four to come.

But the real controversy of the Budget itself was the introduction of supertax of twopence in the pound for incomes of over £5,000 a year, the increase of death duties by one third, and the valuation of land—a possible prelude to further taxation based on such valuation. The House of Lords was predominantly Conservative and, being an hereditary body which included some of the country's greatest landowners, could be expected to remain so. The Finance Bill which would provide the means with which to implement the Budget proposals was debated by the Commons for seventy days and caused 554 divisions. Churchill, despite his aristocratic background, supported Lloyd George in his stand that land monopoly was a bad thing; it was, he declared, '. . . a perpetual monopoly . . . the mother of all other forms of monopoly . . . land which is a necessity of human existence which is the original source of all wealth . . . land, I say, differs from all other forms of property. . . .'

Such was the contention aroused by the Finance Bill that the Liberals formed a Budget League with Churchill as President, the Tories forming an Anti-Budget League. By summer it seemed obvious that the House of Lords would reject the Bill, and Joseph

Chamberlain was urging them to do it. Lloyd George, sensing this, sought to arouse public support by making a violent speech in Limehouse which became known as the 'Slimehouse' speech. It was an attack on landowners, whose vast incomes, he declared, were gained not by their own effort but that of those who had worked and developed the land:

Who created that increment? Who made that golden swamp? Was it the *landlord*? Was it *his* energy? was it *his* brains, *his* forethought? It was not! It was the combined efforts of all the people engaged in the trade and commerce of that part of London—the trader, the merchant, the shipowner, the dock labourer, the workmen—of everybody *except* the landlord!

Some of the landowners, notably the Duke of Westminster, he attacked by name. Afterwards he and Winston Churchill went off to have a luxurious dinner at the Carlton Hotel, which happened to be on the Duke of Westminster's estate. King Edward was gravely offended by the speech, which at one point contained a reference to him. He accused Lloyd George of fostering class warfare.

On 4th November 1909 the Commons passed the Finance Bill and on 28th November the Lords threw out the Bill. Now no government can carry out its programme without the finance necessary. Not for 250 years had the Lords attempted to veto a Finance Bill from the Commons. Their precedent meant that a Conservative Upper House, and an hereditary one, could negate the legislation of the Commons whenever they chose. This would make elections to the Commons meaningless.

However, the challenge having been made, Asquith determined to press for the reform of the House of Lords, and to get a mandate from the people of Britain. Parliament was dissolved on 3rd December 1909, a General Election was held and the Liberals returned to power—but only just. The Government lost 104 seats, giving them a majority of a mere two seats over the Conservatives, and making them dependent on the 81 Irish Nationalist and 40 Labour M.P.s.

On 29th April the People's Budget was passed by the Commons and later by the Lords. Their grudging compliance was due to the introduction of three resolutions for reforming the legislative procedure of the House of Lords—that the Lords could veto a Bill only three times, after which the Commons could pass it into law; that the Lords could not veto a Finance Bill; that the life of any Parliament should be restricted to five years instead of the previous seven. Asquith made it clear to the Lords that if they opposed *this* Bill, he would advise the Sovereign on how this might be made law. There were many things which might have been done, such as the creation of enough new Liberal peers to swamp the House of Lords.

King Edward tried hard for compromise and was much distressed at the manner and matter of the Liberal attack on the Lords. He became depressed and ill, and although both parties must share some measure of blame, there is no doubt that, in his debilitated condition, the controversy did something to hasten his end. He died on 6th May 1910.

All parties were sobered by his death, and anxious that the new King should not start his reign amidst the turmoil of a constitutional crisis. So the Bill was eventually passed by both Houses, rendering impossible any future rejection of a budget by the House of Lords.

Mr. Asquith being on holiday in the Mediterranean when King Edward died, it fell to Winston Churchill to make arrangements for the King's Accession Council.

In the January election of 1910 Mr. Churchill had been returned as Member for Dundee with only 282 votes more than his Labour opponent. He was given the job of Home Secretary. He was full of enthusiasm and ideas but he was gaining for himself, in some quarters, the reputation of being an impulsive show-off. During the miners' strike of 1910 a dangerous atmosphere of violence had set in. Churchill followed it all with distaste and misgivings. He had laboured long and hard, at the Board of Trade, devising legislation to improve their lot—to limit their working hours to eight hours a day, to compensate them for injury or illness, to introduce better first-aid training and facilities. He was to follow up with the Coal Mines Act, which introduced better and regular inspection of mines, pit-head baths and improved and stricter safety precautions.

But for the moment, there was the threat of riots and there had been incidents of violence. Churchill's Eight Hours Act had had the opposite effect to that he had intended; in D. A. Thomas's collieries in Rhondda it had limited earnings and caused resentment.

The men having stopped the ventilating machinery and formed a cordon around the mine, the Chief Constable on the spot appealed for troops. Two squadrons of Hussars and two companies of infantry were despatched, but Churchill ordered them to be held up in Swindon and despatched instead two hundred Metropolitan Policemen to keep order. His disinclination, in this instance, to use soldiers for the control of civilians could not, however, rule the day. For riots broke out, and the soldiers had to be sent in to restore order. Churchill was blamed by some miners for the very military intervention he had tried to prevent, and for years afterwards the miners of South Wales and trade unionists in general, held this affair against him.

Early in 1911 came an incident which produced one of the best-known press photographs in the world, a masterpiece of suspended animation. A cobbled street in the East End, damp and muddy with the night rain. The mahogany and glass bay of Walker's public house, a recessed entry on either side, each with soldiers carrying rifles and peering warily round the corner. Next door, and half concealed, a crowd of police, some armed, led by an eager Home Secretary in top hat and long, fur-collared overcoat.

One December night the police in the East End had interrupted some burglars in Houndsditch and were met by withering fire in which three policemen were shot dead. Mr. Churchill was in his bath when he learned at ten o'clock that the gang believed responsible for the murders had been traced to a room at 100 Sidney Street and were holding out with arms and ammunition. Winston agreed to the use of troops and hurried to the scene, recapturing some of the thrill of his youthful adventure in South Africa, India and the Sudan. Within minutes of arrival he was telling the Royal Engineers, the Royal Artillery and anyone else within earshot what to do. The criminals were anarchists from the Baltic, led by a notorious character known as Peter the Painter. The house was bombarded until it caught fire. Two charred bodies were found in the ruins but Peter the Painter was not found.

There were aspects of this melodramatic affair which caused some criticism. One was that the Home Secretary ought to confine himself to policy and administration and not embarrass men on the spot; the next was that, when the house was seen to be alight he had specifically ordered the fire brigade to let the house burn itself out. Balfour, leader of the Opposition, said later in the House of Commons:

'We are concerned to observe photographs in the illustrated

papers of the Home Secretary in the danger zone. I understand what the photographer was doing, but not the Home Secretary.' But Winston Churchill *did* know why he was there. He could not resist action. When he returned to the Home Office a senior civil servant, irked at the Minister's unconventional approach to his duties, demanded, 'What in hell have you been doing now, Winston.' Churchill grinned broadly. 'Now Charlie,' he said, 'don't be cross. It was such fun!'

7

The Maelstrom

Many verbal battles have raged in the House of Commons ('The object of Parliament,' Churchill said, in later life, 'is to substitute argument for fisticuffs.'); but the struggle to pass the Parliament Bill, which was intended to deprive the House of Lords of any right of veto on legislation passed by the House of Commons, became an acute constitutional crisis.

It was a strange position for Winston Churchill, descendant of the noble Marlboroughs, an aristocrat himself and a descendant of aristocrats, to appear in the forefront of this attack upon the House of Lords. Yet the Lords had only themselves to blame. In rejecting the 1909 Budget they made it imperative to ensure that such a contingency should not occur again.

However, the Bill drafted after much discussion and committee work in the House of Commons was returned by the House of Lords so altered that it was, as Asquith put it indignantly, 'as if no General Election had taken place.' In July 1911 the Cabinet informed King George V that, if the Lords proved obdurate the Monarch would be asked to exercise his prerogative. In less devious language, this meant that the King would be asked to flood the House of Lords by the creation of 400 Liberal-minded peers, rendering the existing opposition completely ineffective. Asquith informed Mr. Balfour, Leader of the Unionists in the Commons, and Lord Lansdowne, Leader of the Opposition in the House of Lords, that this course would be pursued if necessary.

Churchill was in the House on 24th July to witness what he afterwards described to the King as a disgraceful scene. When Mr. Asquith rose to move 'That the Lords Amendments be now considered' he was howled down with cries of 'Traitor!' In vain the Speaker appealed to Members to see that 'the ordinary decencies and decorum of debate should be observed.' Continual abuse and interruptions made it impossible for the Prime Minister to get a hearing and the Speaker was obliged to adjourn the House for reasons of 'grave disorder'.

The Lords were split into two camps—the 'Ditchers' (those who would concede nothing, resisting to the last ditch) and the 'Hedgers' (those who despite fulmination were uncommitted as to the stand they would take in the last resort). It was for both camps an impossible quandary. A policy of no compromise would find the Lords overrun by newly-created peers, including, some thought, not a few *parvenus* who in status and privilege would be equated with the scions of families dating back for a thousand years or more. Submission to the Commons would relegate the Lords to the role of consultants, whose advice and judgement could be ignored. But Asquith, Lloyd George and Churchill—together with Liberal supporters generally—would not flinch from their task; they knew the temper of the ordinary people of Britain, who would not tolerate what would have amounted to government by an hereditary Upper Chamber whose members by their upbringing, background and financial isolation were semi-feudal in outlook. Shop assistants were getting restless at their ruthless exploitation; industrial workers were organizing themselves to fight inadequate wages, unhealthy and dangerous working conditions and the prospect of an eventide of poverty and indignity after a lifetime of hard work. This was no time for the Lords to veto Liberal reforms in the field of social welfare, reforms long overdue.

But Churchill's position in all this was a curious one. Only latterly had he begun to appreciate the problems of the working class. He was an aristocrat, born of a noble line, accustomed to privilege, moving with ease with the greatest in the land. His support of the Liberals in their battle with the Lords brought coals of fire upon his head. He told the House: 'The time has come for the Crown and the Commons, acting together, to override the Lords'— a statement which his friend F. E. Smith described as 'a shameful speech'. It was common knowledge in society, too, that Churchill had helped to draw up a list of the invading peers whose sudden preferment was to weight the scales; such an act seemed nothing less than treason to his class.

But it must not be supposed that unpopular ideas or decisions worried Churchill overmuch. From the outset of his career he took it for granted that one cannot please everyone, and that it was as stupid as it was cowardly to try such a thing, apart from the fact that it would have been alien to his robust temperament. Indeed, he rather relished controversy, and the piquancy of his wit made him respected by all who joined issue with him. Once Sir William Joynson-Hicks, in the middle of a speech, noted that Winston was shaking his head in dissent, and emitting those very audible, disapproving grunts which could be so admirably timed.

'I see my right honourable friend shakes his head,' said Hicks, directing towards the cherubic Churchill a chill, minatory look, 'but I am only expressing my opinion.'

'And I,' said Churchill, 'am only shaking my own head.'

On another occasion Churchill had so angered a Member that the man sprang to his feet, red in the face and so bursting with indignation that he could not express himself effectively. Churchill listened calmly and then said, gently, 'My right honourable friend should not develop more indignation than he can contain.'

What would the Lords do? The atmosphere in the Lords' Chamber was almost suffocating in the course of the two days' debate there on 9th and 10th August 1911 for it was the hottest two days for seventy years. The pitiless sun streamed through the mullioned windows, heating the red leather benches. But the Ditchers still fought. 'Nothing in the world will induce me to vote for a bill which I believe to be wrong and immoral and a scandalous example of legislation,' declared Lord Halsbury. But amidst tension and excitement the Bill was passed and the House of Lords curtailed its powers. The Liberals had won the day—and Winston Churchill had added many more influential enemies to his already considerable legacy.

But much else was happening in 1911. The world was changing shape and so was Britain. Churchill knew that the old, comfortable days of squirearchy were on the way out. The frightening facts about poverty and social conditions in Britain could no longer be ignored. Industrialism had outpaced trade unionism in growth, but the working class was growing more vocal and better organized. Quick and vast fortunes had been made and were still being made by industrialists and shopkeepers, who had grown richer while many sections of the working class had grown poorer. The dangerous rift between the two classes was largely responsible for the epidemic of strikes in the shipyards, textile industries, coal mines and railways.

Churchill spoke eloquently in the House in favour of Mr. Lloyd George's National Insurance Bill, introduced in May 1911 and passed into law early the following year. Churchill had been fore-most in insisting that sickness and unemployment benefit should be firmly based on insurance and it was because of this sound basis that it became possible, in the ensuing decades, to expand its scope by a series of simple amendments to embrace all industrial workers. He fiercely resisted Cabinet attempts to cut unemployment benefit from seven to five shillings a week (money was worth five times as much then as it is now, and the difference of two shillings was by no means a trivial matter).

Churchill also backed his protégé Beveridge by supporting legislation to improve the Poor Laws. He rejected the underlying, and for so long unchallenged, assumption that poverty was a crime and its victims legitimate objects of disdain and patronage; the old workhouse maintained its inmates at a bare subsistence level.

Prison reform absorbed much of his time at the Home Office. He had himself once been a prisoner and well understood that ill-treatment apart, it was no small hardship to lose one's freedom. With characteristic energy and curiosity he visited prisons, questioned judges and looked into every aspect of the judicial and penal system.

Hearing of Churchill's constructive attitude, the venerable General Booth, founder of the Salvation Army, called upon him at the Home Office, asking that his men could visit prisoners and help in their rehabilitation. Churchill listened sympathetically, and betrayed no sign of impatience as Booth switched from the salvation of prisoners in general to the salvation of Mr. Churchill in particu-lar. The old man, with his flowing beard and gleaming patriarchal eyes, went down on his knees and prayed aloud to the Almighty to guide, sustain and enlighten the Home Secretary who, when the unorthodox interview was over, escorted him to the door with every civility and a promise to consider all he had said.

To the Suffragettes, who had lobbied and picketed him un-mercifully and even sabotaged his election meetings (a Miss Maloney pursued him with a muffin bell at all his meetings, clanging it with ferocious feline energy every time he opened his mouth) Churchill showed a certain clemency. Break the law they might, but though their ideas might be good or bad, their primary motive was to improve the law. Many feminists went on hunger strike in prison, and submitting them to the brutal indignity of forcible feeding had become in some prisons as much an act of official malice as of necessity. It was said that Churchill insisted on being forcibly fed to discover just what it entailed. One Suffragette attempted to horsewhip him on a train journey. She missed, and he pocketed the whip as a souvenir. Churchill decided that Suffragettes must be denied martyrdom, and not be treated as harshly as ordinary prisoners. Certainly Mrs. Pankhurst incited her followers to hysterical violence, but most Suffragettes were more peaceable. Churchill mitigated their lot, although he did not believe in votes for women.

Mr. Churchill often talked to prisoners as well as Governors, and it was made plain to all that little would escape his questing mind. He did not hesitate to show clemency when he considered it justified. One reform on which he insisted was an improvement in prison clothes. 'It is an infamy,' he said, 'to clothe a man in a boy's jacket and knickerbockers and deny him enough shirt to cover his loins.' He hated particularly his task, as Home Secretary, of confirming death sentences, tossing and turning on his bed in sleepless anguish on the night before an execution. But some of his proposals were eccentric and bizarre. He confided in his friend Wilfred Blunt that he regretted the abolition of public executions. 'To the man himself, shut in for weeks by the four walls of his prison, with nerves unstrung by solitude and that perpetual longing for a sight of trees and fields, and contact once more with the busy life he formerly enjoyed, it must surely have lessened by a great deal the pang of death to be set for one last half hour in the light of day outside those walls, and thus get a breath of the ópen air of heaven, and with it the courage to endure his pain.' He even thought that it might mitigate the condemned man's sufferings if relatives and friends could attend his execution, forgetting that although it might comfort the man's last moments it could prove an appalling and permanent shock to those who survived him.

The 'slum shop' conditions as exposed by H. G. Wells in such novels as *Kipps* and *Mr. Polly* (based on experience, for Mr. Wells once worked in a drapery store) were also a matter for legislative reform.

But such domestic matters were overshadowed by the Agadir crisis of July 1911. In 1906 Britain, by the Anglo-French Algeciras Convention, had acknowledged France's rights in Morocco. But the Kaiser, seeing that France had a weak Premier, decided to chance his arm and sent, as Mr. Churchill put it 'suddenly and unexpectedly, on the morning of 1st July . . . his gunboat *Panther* to Agadir to maintain and protect German interests . . . all the alarm bells throughout Europe began immediately to quiver. France found herself in the presence of an act which could not be explained, the purpose behind which could not be measured. Great Britain, having consulted the Atlas, began to wonder what bearing a German naval base on the Atlantic coast of Africa would have upon her maritime security.'

Britain had not been consulted by Germany, and an inquiry from Sir Edward Grey, our Foreign Minister, had been ignored for seventeen days. Was this a straw in the wind? Was this the rumbling of a distant drum? Churchill was certain that it was. The Foreign Minister, the War Minister and the First Lord of the Admiralty had long been accustomed to receive from the indefatigable Mr. Churchill long, detailed and usually unsolicited memoranda saying what the Government in general and the Minister in particular should do. Solicited or not, the missives, first considered an intrusion, earned increasing respect by their mastery of fact and clear and cogent exposition. And as the Agadir crisis unfolded, Churchill heeded Lloyd George's warning that 'the thunderclouds are gathering'. Churchill wrote to Sir Edward Grey pressing for a Triple Alliance of Britain, France and Russia to save the Low Countries and Scandinavia. Lloyd George, for his part, had made a speech in the City of London which was a plain warning to Germany:

. . . if a situation were forced upon us under which peace could only be preserved by the surrender of the great and beneficent position Britain has won by centuries of heroism and achievement, by allowing Britain to be treated, where her interests were vitally affected, as if she were of no account in the Cabinet of Nations, then I say emphatically that peace at that price would be a humiliation intolerable for a great country like ours to endure. . . .

Churchill had a clear mandate from Lloyd George to think continually on defence. 'I am inclined to think that the chances of war are multiplying,' Lloyd George wrote in a letter dated 27th August 1911, '*Be ye therefore Ready*.'

Churchill was alarmed at the unpreparedness of Britain for a war which looked like being sprung upon the country at any moment. He believed in action, not in worrying, brooding or idly speculating about inevitable doom. At a garden party given by the Premier at 10 Downing Street he learned that his Ministry was for some odd administrative reason responsible for the protection of the Navy's cordite dumps and that the handful of constables entrusted with the protection of this crucially important material could easily be overcome by 'a handful of Germans'. Without a second's hesitation Churchill left the party and telephoned the Admiralty to insist on better protection for the dumps. His well-meant intervention was resented and he was told, in effect, to look after his Home Office and mind his own business. The rebuke only served to goad him into renewed activity, and by bringing pressure on Haldane, the War Minister, he achieved his object. The incident shows how alert Churchill was when he felt the security of his country was threatened.

This sparked off further Churchillian investigations. What other vulnerable points might there be? In what further respects were our defences lacking or badly organized? What effective checks were there against espionage and the careless handling of important papers?

In August the recrudescence of strikes was so acute that the King telegraphed Churchill asking him if he were confident of his ability to maintain law and order. 'The difficulty is not to maintain order, but to maintain order without loss of life,' Churchill replied. This was true, though it was doubted if Churchill was the best man to handle strikes. Lucy Masterman, the astute and witty wife of the famous journalist, says that Churchill 'enjoyed immensely mapping the country and directing the movements of troops. Charlie (her husband) thinks that in the main he did right, but that he did it in an amazingly wrong way, issuing wild bulletins and longing for "blood".' During the railway strike his bulletins infuriated the strikers and made a bad job worse. There were many violent demonstrations up and down the country, and he despatched troops to no less than thirty-one places. At Llanelly soldiers opened fire and some people were killed.

Churchill was openly discouraged at the ineffectiveness of his methods. 'The men have beaten us,' he said, gloomily. 'We cannot keep the trains running. There is nothing we can do. We are done!' Lloyd George, with the support of Ramsay MacDonald, leader of the Labour Party, and Arthur Henderson, felt that the use of troops was a provocation which should cease. Lloyd George won the day. And he managed to settle the strike. The move which earned Churchill most unpopularity amongst the working class and his own Cabinet colleagues was a telegraphed order from the Home Office to General Officers Commanding the various military areas 'to use their own discretion as to whether troops are, or are not, to be sent to any particular point.' The Army Regulation which required a requisition for troops from a Civil Authority was suspended—thereby transferring responsibility for local action from the civil authority to the military.

One glaring omission in Britain's defence arrangements shocked Churchill profoundly. The War Office had worked out plans for a British Expeditionary Force which could, in the event of war with Germany, protect France and Belgium—but the Admiralty had made no plans for its transport. Indeed, Sir Arthur Wilson, who had succeeded the gruff and dictatorial Admiral Fisher as First Sea Lord, saw no necessity for an expeditionary force at all. Lord Haldane, the War Minister, had written repeatedly to the Prime Minister urging action by the Admiralty and asking to be transferred to it so that he could put the necessary plans into effect and achieve the necessary co-ordination between the planning of the Army and the Navy.

Asquith did not favour this. While appreciating the arguments of Haldane and Churchill, he felt that Haldane's arrival at the Admiralty would create resentment. For his part, Haldane was opposed to Asquith's idea that Churchill should shift to the Admiralty, going so far as to comment: 'I feel that, full of energy as he is, he does not know his problem or the vast field of thought that had to be covered . . . it is only a year since he has been doing his best to cut down mechanized armies and the Admiralty would receive the news of his advent with dismay.' He added another cogent reason: 'He is apt to act first and think afterwards, though of his energy and courage one cannot speak too highly.'

Hardly two weeks after his 'protect the cordite stores' move, Churchill had presented the Prime Minister with a masterly summary of the facts to be considered in the event of war. Entitled 'Military Aspects of the Continental Problem', it combined detailed analysis with prophecy. For example, he forecast that, in any future European war, the twentieth and fortieth days could be crucial—and so, three years later, they proved to be.

This was only of meagre satisfaction to Churchill. As he puts it
in Volume i of *The World Crisis*, 'I could not think of anything else
but the peril of war. I did my other work as it came along, but
there was only one field of interest fiercely illuminated in my mind.'

This field of interest was not 'fiercely illuminated' in many
British minds at the time. It was a weakness of the long Liberal
administration that it was almost wholly preoccupied with domestic
matters and social reform, and that foreign affairs received surprisingly little debating time in the House of Commons; in the
event this neglect of foreign affairs was a contributory factor in a
war which was to cost thirty million lives, hopelessly outweigh
any benefits that might have accrued from the social reforms, and
leave Europe a disillusioned and impoverished ruin.

But Churchill did see the peril. Partly as a result of his agitation,
an urgent and secret meeting of the Committee of Imperial Defence
was convened on 23rd August 1911 while Parliament was in recess,
with the Prime Minister in the chair. General Wilson outlined the
Army's plans for landing a British Expeditionary Force in France,
whilst later Admiral Sir Arthur Wilson expounded his plan, so far
as a plan could be said to exist. War Office and Admiralty were now
plainly seen to be at loggerheads. The Navy, Britain's traditional
defence, regarded the Army's role as secondary; the war would
need to be won at sea first, then the Army would be permitted to
support raids upon the enemy coast. But the Army insisted that
an Expeditionary Force must land in France at the same time as
the French Army was mobilized. It is interesting to note that
Edward (later Viscount) Grey clears Churchill of any aggressive
ambitions. 'Let me not be supposed to imply,' he wrote, 'that
Churchill was working for war, or desired it: he followed all the
diplomacy closely, but never either in Council or in conversation
with me did he urge an aggressive line. It was only that his high-
mettled spirit was exhilarated by the air of crisis and high events.'

For weeks Churchill was in constant contact with the War Office
and Admiralty. He wanted a Triple Alliance between Britain,
France and Russia to safeguard the independence of Belgium,
Holland and Denmark.

Asquith, meanwhile, was pondering gravely on how to achieve
close-knit co-operation between Army and Navy. Clearly, McKenna,
the First Lord, must go. Who had the patriotism, the foresight, the
interest, intelligence and driving force to bring it about?

There was only one answer—Winston Spencer Churchill. Nor is there the least doubt of the great joy it gave him to be entrusted with this new and heavy responsibility. Writing to King George V, Mr. Churchill said:

In delivering my seals to Your Majesty this morning I should be sensible of many regrets at ceasing to be Your Majesty's Principal Secretary of State, were it not for the fact that the great service of the sea, upon which the life and honour of the realm depends, is one with which Your Majesty is so intimately associated by a lifetime of practical experience, and that I know I may recur to Your Majesty for aid and support in the duties entrusted to me by Your Majesty's gracious favour.

In many ways the appointment was a strange one. Churchill knew little of naval affairs, and memories were young enough to recall his vehement and persistent appeals for economy in the Army estimates. And there were two schools of thought in the Liberal Party; those who were, broadly, pacifist, those who hoped that if we minded our own business and spent the minimum on arms, we should be left alone in peace to enjoy our social welfare schemes; and the more realistic Liberals who suspected German ambitions and dreaded the thought of Britain being found defenceless in a crisis.

Churchill's letter to the King shows his pride and sense of destiny in receiving his appointment. But he had once, according to Sir Austen Chamberlain 'pooh-poohed' the office of First Lord of the Admiralty. When he met Sir Austen at Dunrobin in 1902, he asked Chamberlain, who was then Postmaster-General, what he wanted to become. Sir Austen replied that he had always thought the Admiralty 'one of the pleasantest offices and the post of First Lord one of the proudest positions that any Englishman could occupy.' This Churchill thought 'a poor ambition'.

But times had changed. England was in peril. Here was a job promising drama and excitement and high responsibility. Sir Winston has said that when, in October 1911, Prime Minister Asquith invited him to stay with him in Scotland and, the day after he arrived, asked him quite abruptly if he would like to go to the Admiralty, he had replied, 'Indeed I would.' In *The World Crisis* he describes an incident which (having thrown off his youthful anticlericalism) seemed to him prophetic:

3*

That night when I went to bed, I saw a Bible lying on a table in my bedroom . . . I opened the Book at random and in the 9th Chapter of Deuteronomy read:

> Understand therefore this day, that
> the Lord thy God is He which goeth
> over before thee; as a consuming fire
> He shall destroy them . . . Not for thy
> righteousness, or for the uprightness
> of thine heart dost thou go to possess
> their land: but for the wickedness of
> these nations the Lord thy God doth
> drive them out from before thee.

It seemed a message full of reassurance.

'The life and honour of the realm' did, indeed, depend in those days upon 'the great service of the sea' and it was with a sense of destiny that Churchill relinquished his office of Home Secretary and moved into the Admiralty as First Lord. Perhaps it was not so tactful to take with him, and display so prominently on his desk, his favourite bust of Napoleon, for there were many traditionalists and diehards at the Admiralty who awaited his coming with grim misgivings. What, so now they were going to let this bumptious fellow, this soldier, play at being a sailor?

8

Peace—and War

Part of Mr. Churchill's mandate at the Admiralty was to develop a War Staff, a nucleus of experienced men who would draw up a war plan in close harmony with the War Office plans. He was to see that the Navy 'is in a state of instant and constant readiness for war in case we are attacked by Germany.'

In this matter, many influential Liberals had undergone a change of heart. Had not Lloyd George once slightingly referred to the War Minister as 'Minister for Civil Slaughter?' Churchill realized that to gain the confidence of his subordinates he must study hard. For eight months of the year he was afloat in the Admiralty yacht. Every ship, dockyard and installation received a visit from him. He would arrive, beaming and alert, his pockets bulging with notes and questions—probing, pertinent and detailed queries on almost every aspect of organization, function and operation. His object, to quote his own words, was 'to know what everything looked like and where everything was and how one thing fitted into another.'

A year ago the energetic, autocratic and brilliant Admiral Fisher had retired from his post as First Sea Lord. Fisher had been behind Mr. Churchill's predecessor in insisting that Britain's primary defence demanded the building of Dreadnoughts, heavily armed battleships worth several smaller craft. His brilliance was to some extent offset by a hot temper and an unshakable belief in the infallibility of his judgement; but Churchill valued his advice highly. He did not invite him back to the Admiralty, but asked him to act as adviser. This the touchy admiral did with a vengeance, plying Churchill with memoranda and notes running to half a million words. Such prodigious outpouring did not dismay Churchill, always a tremendous reader and an enthusiastic writer of memoranda of equal length. The pungency of Fisher's language amused Churchill; Fisher's missives would finish 'Yours till Hell freezes' or 'Yours till charcoal sprouts'.

One of Churchill's first steps was to appoint Rear-Admiral Beatty as his Private Secretary. The decision astonished and dismayed many, including Fisher. Beatty was considered to have gone too far too soon, to have too many shore interests for a sailor, and had—almost unforgivably, according to Admiralty precedent—declined an appointment with the Atlantic Fleet. He had been left clicking his heels for eighteen months and his superiors intended that he would be quietly retired within three years. But two things weighed with Churchill. Beatty was the youngest Flag Officer in the Fleet and he had commanded a gunboat which had come up the Nile at close quarters to support the 21st Lancers, to which he was attached in 1890, when they made the charge at Omdurman. That settled it! He 'disregarded this unfortunate advice' (to pass Beatty over).

Churchill's appointment of Sir John Jellicoe as Commander-in-Chief of the Home Fleet was highly pleasing to Fisher, who regarded it as his personal triumph: 'My two visits to Winston were fruitful. I'll tell you the whole secret of the changes—to get Jellicoe Commander-in-Chief of the Home Fleet prior to October, 1914, which is the date of the Battle of Armageddon. . . .' Indeed, the First World War did start late in 1914; Fisher's prescience was only out by two months. But before long Fisher was taking the arrogant line that for Churchill not to follow his advice was something like insubordination. He was speechless with fury when the First Lord made three appointments of which he did not approve. ('I fear,' he wrote, 'that this must be my last communication with you on any matter at all . . . I consider that you have betrayed the navy in these three appointments and what the pressure could have been to induce you to betray your trust is beyond my comprehension.'

Churchill's reaction to such presumption would, one would have expected, been explosive. Instead, he followed Fisher to Naples in the Admiralty yacht *Enchantress* in company with the Prime Minister. Fisher, despite personal appeals from Churchill and Asquith, was obdurate, but when the three attended church that Sunday the preacher, by a happy coincidence which has never been explained, referred in his sermon to the fact that 'No man possessing all his powers and full of vitality has any right to say "I am now going to rest as I have had a hard life. . . .", for he owes a duty to his country and fellow men.' It was said that prior to the service, Winston Churchill had a useful, as well as an interesting, conversation with the preacher, whose arrow hit the target. Fisher relented.

The naval manoeuvres of spring 1912, with the trim and majestic vessels in proud array, pennants fluttering in the breeze, the King in his royal yacht, and all the disciplined bustle of a great fleet, were a heart-warming experience for Churchill. But the Kaiser, who had hoped Churchill's appointment presaged a soft-pedalling on naval expansion (he remembered Churchill's agitation for economy on the Army estimates) noted grimly that he had doubled the rate of battleship construction in his estimates for 1912. By so doing Churchill angered Liberals preoccupied with home affairs and the Tories who had never forgiven his defection from their Party.

It was partly to placate those Liberals who were restive about his militant approach to naval rearmament that Churchill figured prominently in support of the government's Home Rule Bill. It is difficult for us now to imagine with what vehemence, even hatred, politicians aligned themselves for or against Home Rule for Ireland. Protestant Ulster did not want to be incorporated into a self-governing Ireland which would be largely Roman Catholic. And Britain's role in Ireland was a constant source of local violence and a possible cause of civil war. Half a million Ulstermen had signed a covenant pledging themselves to use 'all means . . . to defeat the present conspiracy to set up a Home Rule Parliament in Ireland.' As Asquith introduced his Bill into the House of Commons, the Ulstermen were fully determined and prepared to fight.

Churchill's father had once said, on this subject, 'Ulster will fight and Ulster will be right', but in this instance Winston Churchill did not try to perpetuate or implement his father's policy, but to oppose it. He would not, he told the Commons, acknowledge a policy which would give encouragement to 'every street bully with a brickbat and every crazy fanatic fumbling with a pistol.' So casual an assessment of the deep divisions between the two parts of Ireland, not unconnected with vicious and futile religious conflicts in the past, incensed loyal Ulstermen.

The Parliament Act entitled the House of Lords to delay, though not to veto, House of Commons legislation. So far as the Home Rule Bill was concerned, this enabled the Irish question to become more vexed and complicated by delay, even though the respective policies of Tories and Liberals came nearer and nearer to unanimity towards 1914. But some of the debates in the Chamber read like a street brawl.

The 13th November 1912 was the scene of unprecedented tumult in the Commons. Two days previously Sir F. Banbury had moved an amendment on the report stage of the financial resolution for the Home Rule Bill. The Government had been unable to defeat the Opposition's amendment, 228 votes being cast in favour of it and only 206 in support of the Government. The House had been at once adjourned and on 12th November Mr. Asquith announced that on the following day he would move to rescind the decision.

This was an extraordinary and arbitrary thing to do; the Tory sense of outrage was justified, although their methods of expressing it were not. Pandemonium ensued. In vain the Speaker, J. W. Lowther, appealed for order. Again and again Members were shouted down. An hour's adjournment, during which the Speaker hoped tempers would cool, achieved nothing and the House was again adjourned.

Winston Churchill, one of the Government's principal advocates of the Bill, moved with Colonel Seely, Secretary for War, from the front bench, smiling acknowledgements to his enemies as they hissed 'Rats!' at the pair. Churchill's smile vanished, however, when an Ulster Member, Ronald McNeil, seized a copy of Standing Orders and threw it across the table at Churchill, hitting him full in the face and grazing his forehead. Horrified at the assault, and seeing that Winston Churchill was tensed and poised for swift retaliation, bystanders of all parties put themselves between the contestants. Churchill left the Chamber and McNeil, appalled at his want of self-control, hurried after the First Lord intending to offer an apology, but could not find him.

The following day McNeil apologized in the House and Churchill accepted it with unqualified good grace. 'I can assure the hon. Member that I have not, nor have I had at any time, any personal feeling in the matter, and if I had any personal feelings the observations he has thought proper to address to the House would have effectually removed them.'

The act of violence was trivial compared with those which might erupt in Ireland at any moment. Arms smuggling into Ulster proceeded on a heavy scale, and volunteers drilled openly in the parks.

It would be wrong to conclude that Mr. Churchill was pursuing a policy of 'my Party, right or wrong.' There was a strategic reason for his open if unpopular advocacy of Home Rule at the expense of Ulster. Time was to prove him wrong on that issue, and in due course Ulster was treated as a separate problem. He wanted to get on with his reorganization of the Navy. But by 1913 he was receiving opposition from surprising quarters. His old friend (and rival for higher office) Lloyd George was, as Chancellor of the Exchequer, irritated by Churchill's expensive naval programme. Acrid notes were exchanged over the Cabinet table:

> Churchill: I consider you are going back on your word; trying to drive me out after we have settled, and you promised to support the estimates.
> Lloyd George: I agreed to the figure for this year and I have stood by it and *carried* it, much to the disappointment of my economical friends. But I told you distinctly that I would press for a reduction of new programme . . . and I think quite respectfully that you are unnecessarily stubborn. It is only a question of six months' postponement of laying down. This cannot endanger our safety.
> Churchill: No. You said you would *support* the estimates. The estimates included the new programme.

And not only notes, but letters. Lloyd George wanted economy; Churchill would brook no delay in the building of ships. 'There is no act of Admiralty administration for which I am responsible which cannot be vindicated to the House of Commons. I cannot buy a year of office by a bargain under duress . . . I recognize your friendship but I ask no favours and I shall enter into no irregular obligation. I am now approaching the end of my resources and I can only await the decision of my colleagues and the Prime Minister.'

To this Lloyd George replied bitterly: '. . . your letter has driven me to despair. . . . I now thoroughly appreciate your idea of a bargain; it is an arrangement which binds the Treasury not even to attempt any further economies in the interest of the taxpayer, whilst it does not in the least impose any obligation on the Admiralty not to incur fresh liabilities . . . I have been repeatedly told that I was being made a fool of; I declined to believe it. Your candour forces me to acknowledge the justice of the taunt.'

Lloyd George's line had the support of the radical Press. In pursuing his policy of strengthening the Navy, Churchill was forfeiting such popularity as remained to him. Meanwhile, behind the scenes, Churchill fostered and sustained many friendships with politicians in the Tory camp, particularly with F. E. Smith and Sir Austen Chamberlain. Churchill thought interests vital to the country above party politics. Sir Austen Chamberlain records in his diary, '. . . I was engaged with others to find a compromise on the Irish question which both parties could accept. Mr. Churchill was the prime mover in this overture and again suggested a coalition to make a national settlement of some of the great problems of the day. . . .'

The scrupulous courtesy with which Churchill treated political opponents has received too little attention. They might oppose, even abuse him, in the House, but he would not consider it beneath his dignity to keep them informed of his intentions and the reasons for them. On the country's important matters he sought understanding, whatever the political line-up might be. 'My dear Austen,' he wrote from the Admiralty on 13th December 1913, 'I send you herewith a couple of papers I circulated to the Cabinet two years ago. They are purely speculative; but for what they are worth, would you care to turn them over in your mind. Will you send them back?' What Churchill was thinking of was the possibility of having an English Parliament and Executive side by side with an Imperial Parliament and Executive, a kind of far-flung federalism, a sort of Commonwealth League of Nations. It was an ambitious and highly original project.

One great achievement of Churchill as First Lord of the Admiralty was the conversion of the fleet from coal to oil and the guarantee of adequate supplies of oil. The first project was resolutely opposed and obstructed by certain elements in the Navy, but Fisher had been all for it and that was enough for Churchill. In any case, coal was dirtier, heavier and more awkward. Churchill set up a Royal Commission to investigate the oil position, with Lord Fisher presiding. Its findings were secret, but in effect gave the go-ahead for the total conversion of naval vessels from coal to oil. One result was the conclusion of a long-term contract between the British Government and the Persian Oil Company, which secured for the Navy a high proportion of its peacetime output of oil, and in the event of war a right to its entire output. The contract was highly favourable to British security, matching in importance Disraeli's deal over the Suez Canal. It was, says Sir Reginald Bacon in his life of Fisher, 'a great feat of statesmanship, for which the country should be grateful.' But Churchill was bitterly assailed in the Commons over the deal and proved, as usual, impervious to hostile criticism.

Lloyd George had wanted a six months' delay in the shipbuilding programme and Churchill would not give it. Six months? What difference could six months make? As things turned out, quite a lot. For 28th June 1914 saw the first beginnings of the nightmare which had haunted Churchill and spurred him to unrelenting action. The Archduke Franz Ferdinand was assassinated at Sarajevo in Bosnia, and by a process of chain reaction Europe was soon to be at war. When Miss Frances Stevenson, Lloyd George's secretary, came round with a red despatch case from the Foreign Office and Lloyd George extracted the telegram and read it he spoke three words: 'This means war.'

That summer Churchill had cancelled naval manoeuvres and, whether by prescience or planning ordered instead a test mobilization of the second and third fleets, followed by a naval review by King George V on 17th–18th July of the greatest assembly of naval might ever seen in history.

This was ten days before the assassination that set Europe aflame. Nevertheless, instead of dispersing the fleets, allowing the reservists to go home and giving shore leave to the crews, he gave orders on 20th July that the First Fleet, concentrated at Portland, should not disperse, and that all vessels of the second fleet should remain at their home ports in proximity to their balance crews.

On 28th July Austria declared war on Serbia. Three days later Germany sent an ultimatum to Russia, whose troops had begun to mobilize on the Austrian border.

That evening—31st July—Churchill dined alone at the Admiralty, reading the ceaseless flow of telegrams and despatches, one of which read 'Germany had declared war on Russia'. He set off post-haste for 10 Downing Street, to tell the Prime Minister, who was there with Sir Edward Grey, Lord Haldane and Lord Crewe, that he intended to mobilize the fleet without Cabinet authority and take full responsibility for his action. On the way out Sir Edward Grey told Churchill, 'You should know that I have done a very important thing. I have told Cambon (the French Ambassador in Berlin) that we shall not allow the German fleet to come into the Channel.'

On Sunday, 2nd August 1914, while the British Cabinet was still debating the issue of peace or war, Churchill, on his own responsibility, ordered the completion of naval mobilization.

On 4th August Britain delivered Germany an ultimatum demanding that she withdraw her troops from Belgium. By 11 p.m.

of 4th August Britain was at war with Germany—and, thanks to
Churchill's initiative the British fleet was ready.

In *The World Crisis* Churchill describes the last moments of
peace:

> Now, after all the stress and convulsion, there came to us at the
> Admiralty a strange interlude of calm. All the decisions had been
> taken. The ultimatum to Germany had gone: it must certainly be
> rejected. War would be declared at midnight. As far as we had
> been able to foresee the event, all our preparations were made.
> Mobilization was complete. Every ship was at its station: every
> man at his post. All over the world, every British captain and
> admiral was on guard . . . In the War Room of the Admiralty,
> where I sat waiting, one could hear the clock tick. From Parlia-
> ment Street came the murmurs of the crowd: but they sounded
> distant, and the world seemed very still. The tumult of the
> struggle for life was over: it was succeeded by the silence of ruin
> and death. We were to awake to pandemonium. . . .
> The minutes passed slowly. Once more now in the march of
> centuries Old England was to stand forth in battle against the
> mightiest thrones and dominations. . . .
> It was eleven o'clock at night—twelve by German time—when
> the ultimatum expired. The windows of the Admiralty were
> thrown wide open in the warm night air. Under the roof from
> which Nelson had received his orders were gathered a small group
> of Admirals and Captains and a cluster of clerks, pencil in hand,
> waiting. Along the Mall from the direction of the Palace the sound
> of an immense concourse singing 'God Save the King' floated
> in. On this deep wave there broke the chimes of Big Ben; and, as
> the first stroke of the hour boomed out, a rustle of movement
> swept across the room. The war telegram, which meant 'Com-
> mence hostilities against Germany' was flashed to the ships and
> establishments under the White Ensign all over the world.
> I walked across the Horse Guards Parade to the Cabinet Room
> and reported to the Prime Minister and the Ministers assembled
> there that the deed was done.

9

The War Unfolds

Upon the broad shoulders of Winston Churchill, then still under forty years old, rested the fate of Britain. The Royal Navy was the basis of all defence and offence. It must guard the straggling shores of Britain, make practical British-French co-operation, and by blockading Germany could prevent the full and immediate exploitation of Germany's superiority in man-power and supplies against the French. Our 65 per cent of naval superiority was more impressive on paper than in practice, since in the nature of naval warfare our range of activities was widely scattered, but it was nevertheless a fact. The protracted agony of a war which many confidently asserted would be 'over by Christmas' was disastrous enough, but without the braking power and fighting power of a powerful Navy, France would have been overrun within months and Britain certainly could not have escaped invasion. One man could have been thanked for this; Winston Churchill. With what bitterness, and sometimes even malice, had he been assailed as he set to re-organizing the old-fashioned Admiralty! How vehemently had Lloyd George criticized his heavy naval expenditure, even to the point of threatening to resign. If Churchill had not constantly to justify and defend his estimation of future needs, would an economy of a million pounds have been forced upon him—as it was—and would Scapa Flow in the Orkney Islands, the most suitable base for the Grand Fleet, have been left without repairing facilities or really effective defences?

Britain did command the seas. Not only did food supplies reach Britain, but the British Expeditionary Force and its later reinforcements were safely landed. Escorts were provided for the troops leaving Commonwealth countries such as India, Canada and South Africa, and for those leaving Britain for India, Egypt and other distant places.

From his large, homely office at the Admiralty, with its mahogany furniture and grandfather clock, Churchill directed and watched the unfolding drama. He was a member of the War Cabinet, and

Lord Kitchener, now War Minister, who had once treated Churchill
with ill-disguised contempt and hostility, now accepted him as an
equal, a gentleman and an able fighting man. Sir John French,
Commander of the British Forces in France, was a close friend of
Churchill's, so that these close top-level contacts, combined with
Churchill's own experience as a soldier and absorbing study of the
inter-related problems involved in the war he saw was coming,
served to keep him well in the picture.

At the end of August came an action dear to Churchill's heart—a
daring attack on German naval bases in Heligoland, known as the
Battle of Heligoland Bight of 28th August, when British light
cruisers and destroyers, supported by battle-cruisers under the
command of the same Beatty whom Churchill had rescued from
obscurity and premature retirement, sunk three German cruisers
—the *Mainz*, *Köln* and *Ariadne*. Public elation at this daring
enterprise was offset shortly afterwards by the German bombardment of Hartlepool, Whitby and Scarborough on 16th December,
when the German vessels escaped unscathed. The grave menace of
the German submarine fleet was underlined by the loss of the
British cruisers *Cressy*, *Hogue* and *Aboukir*, all sunk by one German
submarine in the North Sea (the first two had closed in to rescue
survivors) with the loss of fourteen hundred men. The *Audacious*
was sunk by a mine, the *Bulwark* blown up in the Medway, and the
Amphion and *Speedy* lost by mines also.

The Germans, realizing that Britain—thanks largely to Churchill
—possessed superior naval strength and fire power, relied mostly
on mines and submarines. This irked Churchill, who always considered attack the best form of defence and knew that morale flags
under too much passivity and delay. He was, and remained until the
end of his days, something of a schoolboy, delighting in action. He
also liked directing the actions of others on a grand scale, and his
critics and enemies often forgot that, underlying his seemingly
impulsive enthusiasms was a tremendous capacity for hard work,
statesmanlike foresight and adamantine courage. There were some,
with memories of the Sidney Street siege, who felt he treated matters
of life and death with too much levity, that the fate of nations and
the threat of doom that hung over millions of people was to him a
great big game in which he saw himself as the principal player.
Some of the jests of prominent men carried this inference. Of
Winston Churchill's fervent hope that he might succeed in tempting

the German Grand Fleet to emerge from their secure hiding places and fight it out, Lloyd George remarked: 'Winston is like a dog sitting on the Dogger Bank, looking at a rat who has just poked his nose out of the hole at the other side of the water.'

The description was hardly apt, because Winston Churchill liked to be the first to move. Before Britain's ultimatum to Germany expired, Churchill was having the German ship *Goeben*, which was then cruising in the Mediterranean, shadowed by the British ships *Indomitable* and *Indefatigable*. The *Goeben* was the gravest possible menace to troop transport, being able to outstrip in speed any French vessel; thousands of soldiers might be drowned if the *Goeben* were not neutralized. Churchill had ordered that if she attacked, battle was to be joined at once; but he was restrained by the Cabinet. No act of war, it decreed, could be permitted until the ultimatum expired. As it happened, she did not attack French transports, but even if she had Churchill's hands would have been tied. At about five o'clock on 4th August Prince Louis of Battenberg, First Sea Lord whose whole heart was in the Navy, but who was later to be sacrificed because of his German antecedents, said that the *Goeben* could be sunk before dark, if authority could be given. Churchill waited restively, chafing at this observance of formal niceties when we were clearly on the brink of war. 'Little did we imagine,' he comments in *The World Crisis*, 'how much this spirit of honourable restraint was to cost us and all the world.' Despite the restraints, Churchill hoped that the *Goeben* might be neutralized on 5th August, for the ultimatum expired at midnight on the 4th. But by then it would be dark. Could she gather speed and give the two British battle-cruisers the slip? Their speed was 22 knots. In the event, 'she shook off her unwelcome companions and vanished gradually in the gathering gloom, her speed reaching at times the peak of 26 or 27 knots.'

If only Churchill's instinct had been given rein over the matter of the *Goeben*! As it was, she slipped away to the Dardanelles, trained her powerful guns on Constantinople, bringing in Turkey on the side of Germany. Greece and Rumania were favourably inclined to Britain and France. Bulgaria was still vacillating between her traditional friendship with Russia and her quarrels with Greece and Serbia. With Turkey on Britain's side, the Dardanelles would have been opened to us, giving us access to Russia. Serbia was fighting Austria valiantly at that time and, together with Britain, Russia and a pro-Allied Balkan bloc, would have split and conquered the Austro-Hungarian empire. How Churchill groaned inwardly at this disaster! It was not of his making, although he realized that the blame woud be laid at his door. He was under Cabinet pressure to respect the neutrality of Italy, and by telegraph had forbidden the British Commander-in-Chief, Sir Berkeley Milne, to enter the Straits of Messina and attack the *Goeben* and the *Breslau*. Milne was still following the *Goeben* eastwards on 8th August when he received an Admiralty message, 'We are at war with Austria.' This Milne took to mean 'break off the engagement with the *Goeben* and concentrate your forces at Malta.' The fault was Milne's entirely. Not only did he abandon the hunt for the *Goeben* but had already miscalculated that the *Goeben* would come out at the northern end —his ships were in the wrong place. Critics maintained that the Admiralty left too little initiative to the man on the spot; historians may decide that sometimes the Admiralty allowed too much.

Then there was the disastrous Battle of Coronel on 4th November, off the coast of Chile. The obsolete but re-fitted British cruisers *Good Hope* and *Monmouth*, the light cruiser *Glasgow* and the armed merchantman *Otranto*, under the command of Sir Christopher Craddock, were attacked by Vice-Admiral von Spee by two armoured and three light cruisers. The *Good Hope* and *Monmouth*, hopelessly outclassed, were sunk and the *Glasgow* badly disabled though able to limp away to the Falkland Islands and join the *Canopus*, which Craddock had left at a distance because of her slow speed.

The Admiralty had instructed Craddock to 'be prepared to meet the enemy' and 'to search' and a later telegram telling him not to attempt a fight with Von Spee without *Canopus* was not received. Even if it had been, the British guns would have been like pea-shooters against those of the *Scharnhorst* and the *Gneisenau*, which could steam around out of harm's way and still bombard the British ships with their heavier guns.

The factors actuating Churchill's decisions are too numerous to list and the imponderables too complex to assess, least of all in retrospect. Mistakes are bound to be made in war. Certainly, when the sombre news reached the Admiralty, Churchill acted with energy and decision. The battle-cruisers *Invincible* and *Inflexible*, the light-cruisers *Carnarvon*, *Cornwall*, *Kent*, *Glasgow* and *Bristol*, together with the armed merchant ship *Macedonia*, joined by the *Canopus* and *Glasgow* cornered Spee's fleet at the Battle of the

Falkland Islands on 8th December, sinking the *Scharnhorst*, *Gneisenau* and *Nürnberg* with the loss to Germany of 1,800 men, including Spee, who fought to the last and drowned with his two sons. The *Dresden* escaped to perish a few weeks later. Not until the two fleets met at the Battle of Jutland on 31st May 1916 was there to be another great naval battle, the result of which was that the German fleet escaped but never again chanced a show-down, and that by being able to escape, could blockade the Baltic, prevent relief reaching Russia and help to create the conditions of suffering and unrest which made possible the Russian Revolution.

This, however, is to anticipate events. To return to 1914. By the end of the year, despite the reverses, the seas were freed of enemy warships. The complexity of naval warfare makes any type of public explanation impossible—you cannot inform the public without informing the enemy as well. Your resources, the reasons for your dispositions, your future plans, cannot be disclosed. Not even to Parliament. The only way to keep anything secret is not to disclose it. If the secret must be shared for the sake of co-ordination, the fewer people who know, the less the danger of leakage and the greater the chance of discovering who was responsible for it.

How could Churchill tell the House of Commons that the victory at the Battle of the Falkland Islands was a triumph not only for the brave sailors who fought it, but for the department of Naval Intelligence, which came under his control? That the Admiralty were intercepting German wireless messages, and that Admiral Sir Reginald Hall had caused a British intelligence agent to broadcast to German ships a bogus instruction to attack the Falkland Islands? That British warships had been diverted from their task because of France's inability to safeguard her troop shipments?

In Parliament and out of it the rumour-mongers were busy: Churchill thought war was one great, glorious game. He was a dictator, flashing out irresponsible messages to commanders on the spot, who knew better than he possibly could, in his Admiralty fastness, what was the best course to take. He was basically a soldier playing at being a sailor. Meanwhile the seas had been cleared of surface raiders, though not of submarines or mines. Mighty battles raged on land, involving casualties never dreamed of by any who committed their thoughts to paper in the planning stage, culminating in the tremendous Battle of the Marne, which Churchill had predicted two years earlier almost to the day.

But Churchill was caught up in another drama which again, because of the speed with which war unfolds and the innumerable factors—technical, political and human—which cannot be easily explained or understood, was to damage his reputation still further and prepare the way for a serious crisis in his political life. This became known as 'The Dunkirk Circus'.

Churchill's day at the Admiralty stretched into the night. Even on the morning of 24th August, at 7 a.m. he was sitting up in bed reading memoranda, despatches and telegrams on the progress of the war on land and at sea. His bedroom door opened and there stood Lord Kitchener, the embodiment of strength, imperturbability and dour judgement. But now even his demeanour showed distress. 'Bad news,' he said, handing Churchill a telegram.

It was disastrous news. The Allies were already on the brink of catastrophe. Sir John French reported that his troops were holding a line east and west through Mons, but had received news from the G.O.C. Fifth French Army that Namur had fallen. Namur, one of the most powerful of the Belgian fortresses! And French was talking of retreating, and urging fortifying Havre, the Channel port.

Churchill's 'Dunkirk Circus' at the end of August, had started with the sending, on his orders, of a squadron of R.N.A.S. planes to Dunkirk to safeguard the Channel from that side. Commander Kette protected his base by improvising rudimentary tanks—commandeering cars, putting armour on them, and scouring the countryside attacking Germans and putting new heart into French and Belgians dismayed by the speed and immensity of the German onslaught. Reinforcements of marines and Yeomanry made the whole outfit a sort of commando force, constantly attacking the oncoming German forces and upsetting their lines of communication. Churchill flew over frequently to witness these operations and dispense advice and directives far and wide, strengthening the criticism at home that for him the war was a grand backcloth against which he, as principal actor, could disport himself. The usefulness of that highly unorthodox force is now generally acknowledged, but it was not obvious at the time.

Churchill was paying another of his fleeting visits to Dunkirk when his train to Dover was stopped near London and put in reverse. He was told to see Kitchener, who imparted the terrible news that the Belgians were on the point of surrender. Reinforcements were to be sent to enable Antwerp to hold out a little longer, but one could scarcely tender them this advice without being on the spot and taking in the situation.

The Belgian Army had retreated to Antwerp after their defeat at Namur. If France and Britain could move quickly enough, linking up to push the Germans back into eastern Belgium, some time could be saved, otherwise the Germans would swing round to the north, most of France would fall and the Channel ports be lost. Antwerp was the gateway through which, if it fell, the Germans would race to the coast and face Britain across the Channel.

It was Kitchener's wish that Churchill should go to Antwerp and rally the Belgians to further effort, if possible. His mission was not easily understood by others. An American journalist commented upon his dramatic arrival, resplendent in the uniform of an Elder Brother of Trinity House, reminding him of a hero in melodrama 'dashing up bare-headed on a foam-flecked horse' to save the heroine or the old homestead.

In the tragic circumstances of Antwerp at that time, a diffident man in drab civilian garb could scarcely have saved the day. Theatricality was not only permissible but essential. Morale was at its lowest ebb, and the beaming, bulky Englishman with his out-stretched hands and traditional uniform, exuding courage and confidence from every pore, was precisely what was needed.

He put new heart into the Belgian Premier, De Broqueville. He took charge happily of everyone from the King to the humblest Belgian private. The desperate situation stimulated him, as im-possible challenges always did. The outer forts were being shattered and stormed and subjected to merciless bombardment from German howitzers. There were no obvious means of saving any of them against superior gunfire and manpower, and in due course the assault must reach the inner forts. The soldiers were exhausted by ceaseless fighting, bombardment and want of sleep. Everything—food, munitions, equipment—was running short and there was no water supply.

Churchill was in his element. He visited the front while shells whistled over his indifferent head, saw the trenches which afforded no protection to the tired and hungry troops. He walked and drove through shrapnel, heartening everyone by his utter indifference to physical danger and impervious to exhaustion or despair. The Belgians had taken a cruel beating without adequate support for too long: 'Despondency in the face of an apparently irresistible artillery, and the sense of isolation, struck a deadly chill.'

He visited General Paris's Headquarters after sending urgent messages to Lord Kitchener for reinforcements and to discuss the arrival of two Naval Brigades. Shrapnel filled the air, killing a man at his side. Resistance was prolonged, but the German attack intensified. Churchill, having tasted action, begged Asquith to release him from his job as First Lord of the Admiralty and let him assume command of the forces at Antwerp. His old enemy, Lord Kitchener, was all for it but Asquith would not consider it and so, making his way through the streams of wounded and refugees, and having at least prolonged Antwerp's resistance by five days, Churchill returned to England. At home, more was expected of his mission than was reasonable and his motives were completely misunderstood. Lord Mottistone, sent by Sir John French to see Churchill at work there, reported that given 20,000 troops in time he could have saved Antwerp, but the 8,000 men of the Naval Division were mostly untrained youngsters and it was, indeed, from an almost fatherly feeling towards them that Churchill wanted to take charge, rather than to expose them to hazards for which they were not truly prepared.

Churchill had weakened his status with Asquith, who had followed his exploits with increasing impatience. He was particularly annoyed that he should even contemplate leaving the Admiralty when so much hinged on Britain's naval supremacy. It was freely, and quite inaccurately, alleged that Churchill had gone to Antwerp against Kitchener's advice, whereas he had gone at his request. In fact his swift and fearless action did prevent the incalculable tragedy of the loss of the Channel ports; the defence of Ypres succeeded by so narrow a margin that Antwerp may fairly be said to have decided the issue.

But back in London, Churchill was fully aware of his own waning prestige, and powerless in Parliament to give all the facts which would permit a proper understanding of his own actions. As he admits in his own words:

My own position was already to some extent impaired. The loss of three cruisers had been freely attributed to my personal interference. I was accused of having overridden the advice of the Sea Lords and of having wantonly sent the squadron to its doom.

Antwerp became a cause of fierce reproach. One might almost
have thought I had brought about the fall of the city (Antwerp)
by my meddling. The employment of such untrained men as the
Naval Brigades was generally censured. The internment in
Holland of three of their battalions was spoken of as a great
disaster entirely due to my inexcusable folly. One unhappy phrase
—about 'Digging rats out of holes' which had slipped from my
tongue in a weary speech at Liverpool, was fastened upon and
pilloried. These were the only subjects with which my name was
connected in the newspapers. My work at the Admiralty—such
as it was—was hidden from the public. No Parliamentary attack
gave me the opportunity of defending myself. In spite of being
accustomed to years of abuse, I could not but feel the adverse and
hostile currents that flowed about me. One began to perceive that
they might easily lead to a practical result. Luckily there was not
much time for such reflections. . . .'

He had, indeed, achieved so much, but as he so nicely put it,
'eaten bread is soon forgotten.'

If Parliament had been functioning normally, Churchill, with his
gifts of brilliant exposition, could have given an account of his own
actions step by step, with all the necessary background against which
to form rational judgements. In default of this, 'the adverse and
hostile currents' were in their due course to 'lead to a practical
result' and one which he knew in his bones must come about unless
there were some dramatic turn in his fortunes. One thing was to
decide that issue, fulfilling his worst misgivings and nearly bringing
him to the end of his Parliamentary career: the Dardanelles Campaign.

10

The Dardanelles

Winston Churchill knew how pressure of circumstances, or an adverse turn of fortune, or the clash of personalities, or emotion —even mere intrigue—could cause the end of a man's career and set at nought his devoted and able services to his country. He had seen the First Sea Lord, Prince Louis of Battenberg, thrown aside after a lifetime of service inspired by love of the Royal Navy and a selfless patriotism. Lord Haldane, whose long and arduous labours at the War Office had reformed the Army and made the perfect planning of the British Expeditionary Force (his idea) possible had been thrown to the wolves, with the ignoble insult of 'Traitor!' ringing in his ears. Both were victims of base ingratitude and un-thinking emotion. Their fate can have left Churchill with few illusions as to the hazards, as well as the alleged rewards, of public life.

It was partly from a sense of public injustice that Churchill had brought Lord Fisher back from retirement into the office of First Sea Lord. Fisher was a fierce though brilliant individualist, dog-matic in his views, inclined to treat an opinion contrary to his own as an act of personal hostility and of manifest stupidity. He alter-nated between tremendous enthusiasm and womanly touchiness. Churchill had enlisted his aid in the war because he felt the country needed his drive and vast experience at so grave an hour. He was considerate and understanding in his dealings with the dour old man, even adjusting his own hours of work to suit Lord Fisher, whose fits of pique, rage, huffiness and frequent threats to resign Churchill accepted as one of the burdens of office. Nobody who looks closely at the workings of politics and Government at that period can but marvel at Churchill's patience and tolerance of Fisher. It was, of course, a tolerance based on human considera-tions; Churchill would not compromise on principles, or consent to the shame of inaction in face of duty. But to Churchill the battle of ideas was a manly game permitting of no rancour or malice; he could disagree violently with people, resisting or opposing them with every weapon in his impressive armoury, but remain their friend and respect their individuality. As events were to prove—with Fisher as with others—such magnanimity is not always reciprocated. King George V, a shrewd judge of men, had strongly counselled Churchill against Fisher's recall to the Admiralty, pointing out that the Navy did not trust him. He thought the appointment a mistake and agreed to it with reluctance.

The Dardanelles Campaign of 1915, which has ever since been a subject of controversy, analysis and re-analysis, was an epic drama destined to involve the death of thousands of brave men and a tremendous number of wounded and missing. So of course were the other battles then raging, but the Dardanelles has always raised doubts as to whether it was soundly conceived and competently executed. Frank Owen, in his biography of Lloyd George, says that 'The Dardanelles was Operation Disaster, because it was Doubt and Delay from the word Go.' The strategic conception was sound enough, and if promptly and energetically pursued might have justified the risks. If it had succeeded, it could have shortened the war by years.

It will be remembered how Churchill had always been desperately anxious to intercept the *Goeben* before it eluded the Royal Navy, and how he had been restrained by the Cabinet. In the event, partly because of the threatening presence of the German battleship in her home waters, Turkey aligned herself with Germany and her Allies. Russia had asked Britain to help her against Turkey, which was attacking in the Caucasus. Turkey was preparing to attack the Suez Canal with men based in Palestine. A combined naval and military assault, forcing the heavily fortified sea gateway and moving on to capture Constantinople would have knocked out the Turks, demoralized and eventually disabled the Central Powers, and linked the West with Russia.

Lloyd George had not been in favour of the scheme. Lord Kitchener was, although the limited military support which he afforded it was a guarantee of its failure. The Tory leaders Bonar Law and Lord Lansdowne, invited to join the War Council of the Cabinet, largely at the insistence of Churchill—who hoped thereby to achieve a unity of purpose and of effort at a time when the war was going badly for Britain—were unenthused.

The scheme was proceeded with, but under disadvantages which were to prove fatal to its success. Because of the tremendous casualties being sustained in the battles on land, Sir John French had appealed to Kitchener for reinforcements. In vain did Churchill plead that Russia was asking for help, which she should be given promptly if her soldiers and civilians were not to become demoralized and Russia were not to drop out of the conflict—or even throw in her lot with the Germans. Kitchener decided that he could not spare troops. That was the first snag; the initial phases of the assault would be largely a naval operation. Next, Lord Fisher, as First Sea Lord, would not spare the most powerful battleships. A squadron of more ancient vessels was grudgingly assigned by him, reinforced by the mighty battleship *Queen Elizabeth*, whose tremendous guns would support them at long range. Churchill, whether he knew it or not, had antagonized Fisher, who resented being subordinate to a much younger man. He had originally been in favour of the Dardanelles scheme and at no stage during Cabinet discussions had he raised his voice against it. But he had since nurtured a scheme of his own which, in his own heart, he thought superior.

The dice, therefore, was heavily loaded against Churchill, as it was against the men whose lives and courage were treated so lightly. The requirements of the campaign were secrecy, speed and drive. All were lacking. The intentions of the Allies were advertised by a successful preliminary bombardment on 19th February 1915 which smashed the outer defences of the seaway.

The secrecy of the operation being thus lost, the full-scale naval attack was begun a month later, on 18th March, in the course of which three British battleships were lost and three damaged. But the warships had penetrated six miles up the straits. The Turks, as was discovered afterwards, were nearly out of ammunition, utterly tired and demoralized and the Sultan was making ready to evacuate to the highlands of Anatolia. But Admiral de Robeck stopped the engagement, much to the amazement (and gratification) of the Turks. Had the Navy pressed forward on the day afterwards, with sufficient military support, they would have encountered virtually no opposition, and that easily crushed. Constantinople would almost certainly have fallen.

But not only did the Navy not follow up its initial success (the sinking of the battleships, which struck a minefield, was horrifying enough, but the casualties were small compared with the tremendous losses in the land battles then raging) but after conferring with

General Sir Ian Hamilton it was decided to hold up further operations until there was adequate Army support.

At home, an appalling policy of Governmental drift and inefficiency was endangering England's very existence. From 6th April to 14th May the War Council was not even convened. Lloyd George, sick with anxiety at the lack of liaison between Britain and Russia, kept urging Asquith to send some high emissary there to ascertain the position and give Russia effective support; pro-German elements in Russia were gaining ground. They were short of rifles to arm the men who were needed to replace the 40,000 Russians lost as prisoners each month. Lord Kitchener, whom Lloyd George disliked almost to the point of hatred, did little to keep his Cabinet colleagues in the picture, treating the Army side of the war as though it were his own private affair. Lord Fisher demanded the return of the *Queen Elizabeth*, the mainstay of naval offence in the Dardanelles operation. And from Field Marshal Sir John French, whose men were dying like flies in the battle of Neuve Chapelle (where a mere square mile of land had claimed 12,892 British dead) came an agonized appeal for ammunition. 'What we stint in material, we squander in life' Lloyd George commented, wearily. In a speech on 20th April, the Prime Minister denied that there was a shell shortage despite the desperate telegram from French to Kitchener 'compelled to abandon further offensive operations until sufficient reserves are accumulated.' Kitchener had kept this grave news to himself, and actually obstructed Lloyd George in his efforts to get order and discipline into munitions output. The highly-paid workers in the munitions industry and shipyards were slacking, contracts were being fulfilled late or not at all, and excessive drinking among the workers was a growing menace to morale and production.

Winston Churchill struggled still against this weight of muddle and obstruction (Kitchener even obstructed efforts to secure a firmer control of the munitions industry). But the temporary cessation of activity in the Dardanelles had sinister undertones. Certainly troops were to be sent; Kitchener had agreed to the 29th Division going out there. But the troops had to be assembled, and transported with all their vast equipment to the theatre of war. In the meantime, the Turks and Germans availed themselves of the welcome lull to re-fortify the Dardanelles and prepare a deadly welcome for the tardy invaders. Furthermore, there was more

muddle in the sending of stores equipment to Egypt for this cruci-
ally-important operation. To avoid delays in unloading and using
it, the things needed most urgently should have been packed on
top, and so on downwards in order of planned priority. But nothing
of the kind was done.

And so it was not until 25th April, nearly three months after the
opening bombardment, that the 29th Division, together with the
Australian and New Zealand Army Corps (the 'Anzacs') landed on
the Gallipoli Peninsula at Bulair. Fisher, meanwhile, recalled the
battleships, too important for what he dismissed ill-humouredly as
'subsidiary operations'.

Such a force might have been adequate at the beginning, in
February or March. But the extra fortifications now made it inadequate.

Back at the Admiralty, Churchill saw the writing on the wall. He
told his friend Lord Riddell that the new fortifications would mean
the loss of many lives, but 'it is better to risk lives in this way than
to allow the war to drag on indefinitely.' But if the operation proved
unsuccessful, his career could be ended. 'They may get rid of me,'
he told Riddell. 'If they do, I cannot help it. I shall have done my
best. My regiment is awaiting me.'

In fact, more men were not sent until July, and despite the utmost
heroism the day was lost; they secured an initial victory but failed
to follow through. The expedition was abandoned.

Churchill did not remain in office long enough to have any say
in what followed. And to all these misfortunes was added the final,
fatal ingredient of intrigue. Fisher's long-pent-up resentment
exploded into open revolt and on 18th May he resigned. 'I can stand
it no longer,' he told Lloyd George, referring to Churchill. In vain
Lloyd George reminded Fisher that as a member of the War
Cabinet it had been open to him—indeed, had been his duty—to
speak his mind openly, and that he had offered no dissent on policy
or planning of the Dardanelles Campaign. Fisher claimed that he
had protested privately to the Prime Minister before the War
Council meeting of 28th January—a protest which, if made, the
Prime Minister never passed on to the Council. In any case, no
sailor could have deserted his post without swift and condign
punishment; why should the First Sea Lord have been allowed to
throw in his hand on a personal whim, without prior discussion
with those involved, and—worse still—while important naval

operations were under way? King George V was scandalized at such behaviour, which confirmed his original misgivings about Fisher.

Fisher, having resigned, retired to his room at the Admiralty, locked the door and booked himself a seat on the train to Scotland despite a command from the Prime Minister 'in the King's name' to stay at his job, and a conciliatory letter from Churchill. Not only did Fisher behave like a fractious child, but a deliberately mischievous one; he sent an anonymous letter to Bonar Law, Leader of the Opposition, informing him of the resignation, thereby ensuring the break-up of the Government, for Bonar Law refused to co-operate further with the existing Government. Within two days a Coalition Government was formed, with Asquith still as Premier, but including the Unionist leaders Balfour, Lansdowne, Bonar Law, Curzon, Austen Chamberlain, Walter Long and Selbourne. Churchill was excluded from the Cabinet. 'What are we to do for you?' Asquith asked him. Lloyd George suggested that Churchill should go to the Colonial Office but Churchill flouted this suggestion—his Tory enemies, he knew, would never tolerate such a proposal. Instead, he was offered and accepted the meaningless though comfortable sinecure of Chancellor of the Duchy of Lancaster.

The Coalition was inevitable. The deplorable publicity given to the Governmental disunity, born of feuds and follies, would, if subject to the usual Parliamentary tactics of open opposition, cause further scandal abroad and demoralization at home. The Unionists insisted that if they were not to fulfil their role of Opposition in the House, they must participate in the Government. And so it was.

Who can gauge Churchill's feelings at that hour? When Lord Riddell called on him at the Admiralty on 20th May, he found him worn out and unhappy. 'I am the victim of political intrigue. I am finished!' he said.

Riddell could hardly believe his ears. 'Not finished at forty, with your remarkable powers!'

'Yes,' said Churchill, deliberately, 'finished in respect of all I care for—the waging of war; the defeat of the Germans. I have had a high place offered to me—a position which has been occupied by many distinguished men . . . but all that goes for nothing. This is what I live for. I have prepared a statement of my case, but cannot use it. The foreign situation prevents me from doing so.'

Riddell: 'Do you think the Prime Minister has been weak in the conduct of the war?'

Churchill: 'Terribly weak—supinely weak. His weakness will be the death of him.' A week later, as they strolled together to the Bath Club, Churchill told him: 'I leave the nation a Navy in a state of perfect efficiency . . . I shall give the Government my support. I shall make a few speeches, and then I shall go to the Front. I could not continue to hold a sinecure office at such a time.' Churchill, incidentally, thought that Lloyd George had devised and carried through the Coalition. In fact Lloyd George had gone to see the Premier only after Bonar Law and Lord Lansdowne had made it plain that without a share in Government they would bring the Government down. Of Asquith's action in dismissing Churchill, Lloyd George says in his memoirs:

Mr. Asquith honoured me with his particular confidence in these discussions. The appointments took up valuable time, but at last they were concluded. The most notable change was the taking of Mr. Winston Churchill out of the Admiralty and placing him in charge of the Duchy of Lancaster, a post generally reserved either for beginners in the Cabinet or for distinguished politicians who had reached the first stages of unmistakable decrepitude. It was a cruel and unjust degradation. The Dardanelles failure was due not so much to Mr. Churchill's precipitancy as to Lord Kitchener's and Mr. Asquith's procrastination. Mr. Churchill's part in that unfortunate enterprise had been worked out by him with the most meticulous care to the last particular and nothing had been overlooked or neglected as far as the naval operations were concerned.

It was, said Lloyd George, unnecessary, in order to propitiate his enemies the Unionists, to fling him from the masthead, whence he had been directing the fire, down to the lower deck to polish the brass. 'The brutality of the fall stunned Mr. Churchill, and for a year or two his fine brain was of no avail in helping in its prosecution.'

11

In the Wilderness

Before Winston Churchill the prospect was bleak. He took it manfully but he was deeply hurt. Asquith had not given him the support he deserved; Fisher, whose brilliance he had been the first to acknowledge and whom he had brought out of retirement at the age of 73, had bit the hand that fed him. Churchill had hoped to shorten the war by decisive action, and so save lives, and was condemned as one who by irresponsibility born of personal vanity, had wasted tens of thousands of men.

He still had a seat on the Dardanelles Committee, but nobody as he well knew, was disposed to listen to him. In early summer he retired to Hoe Farm in Surrey to collect his troubled thoughts. He saw a box of paints belonging to John Spencer Churchill and found solace—and a new hobby—in painting. He also tried planting potatoes, with rather less success. Lord Fisher, who with much bluster and imposing many a condition, had tried to reinstate himself in the Admiralty with complete control of everything and everybody, was told in a letter from Asquith, 'I am commanded by the King to accept your tendered resignation of the office of First Sea Lord of the Admiralty.' And that was that. He had harmed Churchill and done himself no good in the process.

Churchill found himself bored and frustrated. When Asquith was reconstituting the Dardanelles Committee into a smaller War Council from which Churchill was to be excluded, he found this the last straw. Writing to the Prime Minister on 11th November 1915, Churchill said: 'Nor do I feel able in times like these to remain in well-paid inactivity. I therefore ask you to submit my resignation to the King. I am an officer, and I place myself unreservedly at the disposal of the military authorities, observing that my regiment is in France.'

The Times commented, 'Mr. Churchill's resignation . . . was not unexpected. He was an eager, active member of the old War Committee; it was obvious that his exclusion from the new War

Committee . . . vitally affected his position. Mr. Asquith wished to find a place for him in the new committee. Critics proved too strong for him. No man of spirit would consent to kick his heels in the office of the Duchy of Lancaster in times like these. The House of Commons will undoubtedly approve Mr. Churchill's decision to join his regiment in France, much as it will regret the passing of his brilliant personality. Nobody imagines that his disappearance from the political arena will be more than temporary. Mr. Churchill's great gifts and vivid imagination have been amply demonstrated in his ten years of office, and there are few who would venture to predict his permanent withdrawal from public life. Only time can show whether a parallel can be drawn between his resignation and that which closed his father's career. Lord Randolph Churchill "forgot Goschen" when he resigned the office of Chancellor of the Exchequer in Lord Salisbury's government in 1886. The circumstances of his son's resignation are equally dramatic, but those who know the man best think that he will come again. No man of his calibre can be content for long with a minor part.'

Churchill had told Asquith in his letter that 'I have a clear conscience, which enables me to bear my responsibility for past events with composure. Time will vindicate my administration of the Admiralty and assign me my due share in the vast series of preparations and operations which have secured us the command of the seas.'

Asquith hoped that was that; at last he would be free of the restless, troublesome man whose endless energy betokened so much complication. But Churchill was never one to retire timidly. He was not going to slink away like a guilty man. He would tell the House of Commons the reasons for his action and why he felt justified in following the policy and taking the decisions which he had done.

On 15th November the House of Commons was crowded and excitement was at fever pitch. Churchill was always a good speaker but now, so to speak, he had been dismissed from high office and was to stand up for himself. There was so much about the war that was never explained to Members of Parliament.

His personal statement to the House was restrained in delivery, though not without sting in its content interspersed with flashes of mordant humour. It may be said that in the House were only two real friends who really cared about his future and felt sorry for him

—Lloyd George, whom he had once helped to save from public disgrace by standing up for him at the time of the Marconi Scandal in 1913, and his old friend and member of the Opposition, F. E. Smith.

But the atmosphere of the House was friendly. Members do not like to feel that one of their number, of whatever party, has been treated injustly, and earnest attention was paid to him. As usual, Churchill had memorized his extremely long speech of over 10,000 words and went through it faultlessly despite the mass of detail it contained. He rose from the corner seat immediately behind the Treasury Bench and was received with cheers.

He said:

Mr. Speaker—My letter to the Prime Minister gives fully and truthfully the reasons which have led me to ask for release from His Majesty's Government . . . but I think it important to point out these reasons do not apply to any other member of the Cabinet. No other Minister who does not hold a laborious office and is not on the War Council has been so closely connected as I have with the conduct of the war for the first ten months. In the second place, I alone have open to me an alternative form of service to which no exception can be taken, and with which I am perfectly content (cheers). Neither does the fact that I do not take my place on the Front Opposition Bench imply any criticism of those who do (laughter). In truth I earnestly hope that the right hon. Member for Dublin University (Sir Edward Carson) will find it possible to be constantly in attendance in the House . . . that bench (the front opposition bench) is the right hon. gentleman's war station, and I hope he will continue to occupy it for the good of the House, for the good of the country and for the good of the Government (laughter).

I have had great doubts as to whether I should trouble the House at all this afternoon, but I felt that I ought not to leave this country without dealing to some extent, and as far as the public interest will permit, with certain episodes and incidents in Admiralty war direction which occurred during my tenure of office. These have been the subject of much comment in the country, and I have lain under serious reproach in regard to them (hear, hear). The incidents are, first, the destruction of Admiral von Spee's squadron in the series of operations which included the actions at Coronel and the Falkland Islands; secondly, the loss of the three 'Bacchante' cruisers; third, the attempt to relieve

Antwerp; and fourth, the initiation of the naval attack on the Dardanelles.

He then proceeded to give chapter and verse of all these operations. Of the first he maintained that an objective examination of relevant papers (and Churchill always committed all his observations and directives in writing) would show

that the Admiralty's dispositions were sound, probably the best that could be made in all the circumstances . . . all my directions and comments had been made in writing. All my business at the Admiralty was conducted in writing, and my right hon. Friend has my full authority to quote or publish any minute of mine which may be considered relevant or of interest. More than that I cannot say.

With regard to the three 'Bacchante' cruisers I must be more definite. The definite charge has been made, and publicly repeated, that I overruled the naval authorities in keeping these cruisers out against their advice, and that the disaster was due personally to me. That charge is not true. I take general responsibility for what was done or not done, but it is not that invidious responsibility which falls upon a Minister who incompetently overrules his professional advisers. . . .

I now come to Antwerp. The project of sending a relieving army to Antwerp did not originate with me. It originated with Lord Kitchener and the French Government. I was not concerned or consulted in the arrangements until they had advanced a long way, and until large bodies of troops were actually moving, or under orders to move.

He then retraced the situation at Antwerp and the desperate necessity of persuading the city to hold out a little longer.

His exposition of the Dardanelles campaign was brilliant and well-ordered. Every word of it was followed with rapt attention.

I now come to the Dardanelles. What am I going to prove or try to prove about the Dardanelles? I am not going to prove that we forced the Dardanelles. No amount of argument, however excellent, will do that. Nor am I going to try to prove that the plan we adopted was the best plan that could have been adopted. No amount of argument will do that. Nor, least of all, am I going to try to prove that my responsibility in the matter is not a great one.

I am concerned to make it clear to the House, and not only to the House but to the Navy, that this enterprise was profoundly, maturely, and elaborately considered, that there was a great volume of expert opinion behind it, that it was framed entirely by expert and technical minds, and that in no circumstances could it be regarded as having been undertaken with carelessness or levity. That, I am concerned to prove. It is important to me to do so and it is also important in the general interest.

... In the month of December last the political situation in the South-East of Europe was stagnant and torpid, and the immense currents of opinion which were then favourable to the Allied cause flowed sluggishly or even ebbed. In Italy our negotiations made little progress. The Russian Government asked the Foreign Office whether some action against Turkey was not possible to relieve the pressure in the Caucasus? In consequence of those communications from the Foreign Office and the War Office I began to draw the attention of the First Sea Lord and other naval advisers to the possibility of action in Turkish waters. The Dardanelles stood out as incomparably the most decisive operation that was open.

Of course, from the beginning we all recognised at the Admiralty that a joint naval and military operation by surprise was the best way of attacking the Dardanelles. As early as 3rd November, over a year ago, we obtained from the War Office their appreciation of the number of troops necessary to seize the Gallipoli Peninsula by a joint amphibious *coup de main*. On 30th November I sent a minute to my Noble Friend Lord Kitchener offering to congregate transports for 40,000 men . . . sufficient for the first echelon of an Army for the purpose in Egypt, on the chance of their being wanted, as I could see that the situation was developing in the direction of an attack in the Eastern Mediterranean on the Turkish Empire. *We were informed that no arms were available*; and further, in the early discussions which took place among us, and also at the War Council, it was clearly the opinion that even if they were available, they should not be used for attacking the Gallipoli Peninsula.

As a result of these representations and discussions, I telegraphed on 3rd January to Admiral Carden, who was our Admiral blockading the Dardanelles, and who had been there since the Turkish declaration of war, and I put to him this specific question 'Do you consider the forcing of the Dardanelles by ships alone a practical operation?' The admiral replied to the effect that the Dardanelles could not be rushed, but could be reduced by a regular and sustained naval bombardment. I put the same question simultaneously to Sir Henry Jackson, and I received from him an almost similar answer. The coincidence of opinion . . . made a profound impression upon me.

Admiral Carden was asked to formulate plans, which came before the War Council on 13th January.

This meeting was attended by the principal Members of the Cabinet, by various high military officers, by the First Sea Lord and by Sir Arthur Wilson. The War Council was immensely impressed with the political advantages of the plan if it could be carried out, and they pressed the Admiralty to find a way to carry it out. No one spoke against the methods proposed. No expert adviser indicated any dissent.

The whole plan was searchingly examined by the Admiralty War Staff, who pronounced in its favour. Lord Fisher gave Churchill, on 25th January, a memorandum of naval policy and

this memorandum did not question the feasibility of the particular operation which was being studied, but it deprecated reducing our margins in home waters or using fighting ships for bombarding purposes except in conjunction with military operations. It was a memorandum not against the Dardanelles operation, but against others which were being very strongly pressed forward at the time. . . . I attach importance to the fact that at no time did I receive from Lord Fisher any criticism of the definite method of attack proposed. On the principle he had doubts and objections, but on the special technical and professional points involved I received from him at no time any expressions of adverse criticism . . .

He then retraced the unhappy chronology of a campaign.

I have gone through this story in detail in order to show and to convince the House that the naval attack on the Dardanelles was a naval plan, made by naval authorities on the spot, approved by naval experts at the Admiralty, assented to by the First Sea Lord and executed on the spot by admirals who at every stage believed in the operations. . . . I am bound to make that clear. I will not have it said that this was a civilian plan, foisted by a political amateur upon reluctant officers and experts. I am not going to

embark upon any reproaches this afternoon, but I must say that
I did not receive from the First Sea Lord (Lord Fisher) either the
clear guidance before the event or the firm support afterwards I
was entitled to expect. If he did not approve the operation, he
should have spoken out in the War Council. . . . If the First Sea
Lord had not approved the operations, if he believed that they
were unlikely to take the course which was expected of them, if
he thought that they might lead to undue losses, it was his duty to
refuse consent. No one could have prevailed against such a refusal. The operations would never have been begun. That was the
time for resignation.

On the other hand . . . I do not at all regret having insisted on
Lord Fisher's return, in face of great opposition, to the Admiralty
in November 1914.

Churchill then paid a tribute, and a handsome tribute, to Lord
Fisher's contribution to Britain's naval greatness. He finished his long
explanation on a note of hope and courage which we have long
associated with his name, and which could, had Government and
people believed in him more, have cheered them at one of the
most terrible periods in British history, when the flower of Britain's
youth were being mown down by a monster scythe in battles that
achieved nothing:

There is no reason to be discouraged about the progress of the
war. We are passing through a bad time now, and it will probably
be worse before it is better, but that it will be better, if we only
endure and persevere, I have no doubt whatever. . . . It is no doubt
disconcerting for us to observe the government of a state like
Bulgaria convinced, on an impartial survey of the chances, that
victory will rest with the Central Powers. Some of these small
States are hypnotised by German military pomp and precision.
They see the glitter, they see the episode; but what they do not see
or realise is the capacity of the ancient and mighty nations against
whom Germany is warring to endure adversity, to put up with
disappointment and mismanagement, to recreate and renew their
strength, to toil on with boundless obstinacy through boundless
suffering to the achievement of the greatest cause for which mankind has ever fought.

The Prime Minister in his reply to the House said the safe
minimum. It was not a very generous response since he could,

however briefly, have acknowledged his own share of responsibility for misfortunes for which Churchill was being made the scapegoat.

The House is always accustomed, and properly accustomed, to give great latitude . . . to explanations from a Minister of the Crown who has resigned his office, and my right honourable friend has taken advantage of the privilege in a manner which, I think, will be generally appreciated and admired. I only wish to say two things. I think my right hon. friend has dealt with a very delicate situation not only with ability and eloquence, but also with loyalty and discretion. He has said one or two things which I tell him frankly I had rather he had not said, but on the other hand he has necessarily and naturally left unsaid some things which, when the complete estimate of all these transactions has to be taken, will have to be said. But that does not affect his personal position at all, and I desire to say to him and of him, having been associated with him now for ten years in close and daily intimacy, in positions of great responsibility and in situations varied and of extreme difficulty and delicacy, I have always found him a wise counsellor, a brilliant colleague and a faithful friend. I am certain, Sir, he takes with him to the new duties he is going to assume . . . the universal good will, hopes, and confident expectations of this House and of all his colleagues.

A lunch with his friend Lord Northcliffe, and the following day Churchill arrived at Boulogne and made his way to the headquarters of his friend Sir John French. French, of course, was delighted to see Churchill and, having the soldier's inborn distrust and dislike of professional politicians, and remembering that Churchill was originally a soldier, warmed to him in his situation.

He offered Churchill a brigade, which would have given him the command of 4,000 men and, as a brigade commander, the rank of brigadier-general. Winston accepted gladly, making it a condition that he should before assuming command undergo a month's training in trench warfare. So Major Churchill of the Oxford Yeomanry, having chosen the Guards Division, found himself with the 2nd Grenadier Guards, riding with the Colonel and his adjutant and followed by weary guardsmen struggling to keep their bearing in the mud and drizzle. The farmhouses of Artois tilted crazily or lay in ruins from shell-fire. It was raining. The ex-Minister who had held one of the highest offices in the land heard the Colonel say to him in a voice as cold as the rain, 'I think I ought to tell you that we were not at all consulted in the matter of your coming to us.'

They reached a ruined farmhouse and while having some hot tea the body of a dead guardsman was brought in. Major Churchill's kit had not been brought, except for his shaving kit and a pair of socks. As a sleeping place he had the choice of a crowded signals office, used by four signallers and echoing to the Morse tapper, and a flooded dugout. He preferred the former, and was quite unperturbed by his cool welcome. He had not come to France for a holiday.

But Churchill's craving for action found complete satisfaction in this environment of war and death. His complete fearlessness and continual cheerfulness earned the respect of his superiors. In due course he presented himself once more at French's headquarters, but here bitter disappointment awaited him. He had worked hard to prepare himself for the responsibility of a brigade, but French had been recalled. He spent a sad last day with him, accompanying him in the car as he went his rounds paying farewell to his troops, and learned that French's successor, Haig, would allow him only a battalion. He was bitterly disappointed. In fact, it was not Haig's decision originally. When French told Asquith, while on leave, that he proposed giving Churchill a brigade, Asquith was horrified. 'For God's sake don't give him a brigade—don't give him anything more than a battalion!' He feared Churchill's impetuosity.

Lord Beaverbrook summed up the Prime Minister's intervention in a few words:

This really was rough. A Premier may have to throw a colleague overboard sometimes to save the ship, but surely he should not jerk from under him the hen-coop on which the victim is trying to sustain himself on the stormy ocean.

As Lieutenant-Colonel Churchill, he took over command of the 6th Royal Scots Fusiliers and by his energy and enthusiasm immediately won the support of his officers and men. As one might expect, his methods were often unorthodox. He would rouse his battalion at odd hours during the night to blast the enemy—'Fire ten rounds—wake those fellows up!' he would bellow and hear with satisfaction the roar and whistle of shells. The enemy, left with no choice, would lob over a few shells in retaliation, no doubt cursing Churchill's nocturnal enthusiasms. His new tactics scarcely endeared him to the villagers of Ploegsteert who within days decided to move out, Churchill lending them wagons to carry their goods and waving them on with a smiling '*C'est la guerre!*'

In between action, Churchill worked hard on a treatise on the use of tanks in war, an idea which he had put forward in a memorandum to Asquith late in 1914. An armoured car which would resist heavy fire and crush trenches and fortifications much occupied his mind, and after some trial and error and revision of his ideas, a test of a caterpillar truck was arranged for him on Horse Guards Parade. Indeed, acting on his own authority—ignoring both the Board of Admiralty and the Army Council who deserved to be ignored for their utter lack of encouragement—he placed an order for eighteen 'landships' or tanks at a cost of £70,000. 'Winston's folly' they were called, but from the carnage and chaos of the Western Front Churchill was determined that this decisive new weapon should be developed and used. The dreadful stalemate of trench warfare, which he was now witnessing and participating in, could only be broken by such a weapon.

If Parliament hoped it had seen the back of Churchill, the reverse was certainly not true. He was an Army officer, but still an M.P., and occasionally he would fly over to lecture the Commons on why they should do what they were doing in some different way or not at all, and what they were omitting to do. The marshalling of his arguments and the factual research on which they were based made such statements difficult to refute, as during his speech on the Navy Estimates in March 1916.

At this time there was increasing apprehension amongst Churchill's numerous and influential enemies that he might be taken back into the Government. The violent reactions which the mere mention of his name evoked at this time are reflected in a particularly cruel attack upon his good name in the columns of *The Spectator* in May 1916. The anonymous writer said:

> The return of Colonel Churchill to the House of Commons, which we are told is going to be permanent, has set a number of rumours going as to the future of the most audacious and brilliant figure of public life. . . .
> We must state the reasons which should prevent any sane Government from availing themselves of the brain power, vigour

and action that Colonel Churchill undoubtedly possesses. With Colonel Churchill we have no personal quarrel. It is on his public acts alone that we judge him . . . he has a restlessness of mind and an instability of purpose, joined with the restless egotism of the political gambler, which would make him a most dangerous element. . . .

In another issue the denunciation was such as would send most men rushing to their lawyers:

In private life Col. Churchill may very likely have all the virtues, or even the graces, of personal conduct. We should not be surprised that he was scrupulously loyal to his friends, and willing always to think of others first and himself last; that he scorned the marauder's motto 'Thou shalt want ere I want', that he was unselfish in thought, word and deed; and that he could be trusted implicitly under temptation; that he was a man who would never take advantage of any man's friendly indulgence and willingness to share burdens he need not share; in fact that he was chivalrous, straightforward, open and sincere, a man who would scout anything in the nature of an intrigue and who would no more engage in tortuous action than stab a friend in the back or strike a secret and felon blow in the dark. But if these are the qualities which Col. Churchill shows in private life, as for aught we know they are, they are not his qualities in public life. That there may be disparity between a man's public and private record is unfortunately no new experience. Too often political ambition sweeps away the safeguards of domestic honour and somehow makes a man justify to himself action in public life from which he would shrink back in horror in any other sphere of activity . . . it is impossible to say that he has conformed to the standard which we are willing . . . to allow him as a private individual.

No man can review his public career . . . without having to admit that Col. Churchill has lowered instead of having raised the moral standard. He has played the part of a political adventurer, and played it with a skill and audacity, but also with a want of scruple and want of consideration of public interests, and with a reckless selfishness to which our history affords no parallel, or affords it alone in the life of Charles James Fox. Here are Pope's lines on the restless party demagogue who keeps his callous, unscrupulous course, who knows no doubts and has no fears as long as he thinks the action will pay him, will lead him to self-advancement and the satisfaction of his own ambitions:

> See the same man, in vigour, in the gout
> Alone, in company, in place, or out
> Early at business and at hazard late,
> Mad at a fox chase, wise at a debate,
> Drunk at a borough, civil at a ball
> Friendly at Hackney, faithless at Whitehall.

This broadside created a sensation in political circles and the clubs buzzed with talk of it. But by going too far, it rallied Churchill's friends to the same extent that it heartened his enemies.

Furthermore, many Members had written to him in France urging him to make his own highly individual contribution to Parliamentary debates and to shake the complacency of Asquith's administration. F. E. Smith, now Attorney-General, had visited him in France (managing to get himself arrested, ironically enough, for not having a permit!) and given Churchill similar encouragement. He knew that a Commission of Enquiry was examining in detail the whole Dardanelles fiasco, and that the documents and archives were bound to vindicate his honour and integrity. What was extraordinary was a passage in that speech advising the recall of Lord Fisher, whose tantrums had so grievously affected the course of his own career. But he cannot seriously, one feels, have expected them to do so.

Later in 1916 he was active in the Commons in pressing for the creation of an Air Ministry. He himself had learned to fly, although even his closest friends were relieved if he did not offer them a lift. Cigar in mouth, grinning broadly, he would grab the joystick with as much indifference as he might the reins of a mount, and roar into the air as though riding an air filly. Once his plane burst into flames. On another occasion it somersaulted. People used to say he had a charmed life; perhaps he had, for no man risked physical danger more cheerfully or even invited it.

No, they were certainly *not* rid of him. There was the Irish rebellion, the terrible slaughter of the Somme, the intrigues and disunity still rampant in Mr. Asquith's Cabinet, the gathering storm in Russia. Surely there would be a change of government; he must assert himself, be on the scene, show that he had much to give and was anxious for service in those fields where his abilities could best be utilized. He sent to the Cabinet a long and lucid condemnation of Haig's handling of the offensive in France, gave evidence before the Dardanelles Commission and awaited with patience the inevitable crash of Asquith's government.

Winston Churchill's political orientation at this time is curious. He was a Tory turned Liberal, possibly because the Tories were a hierarchy of old men disinclined to give a young and pushful man an opening, and now a Liberal disenchanted with their almost fatal preoccupation with social reform and their appalling neglect of foreign affairs. Their obsession with domestic matters was dispelled by war and its endless holocaust, through which they muddled their way while they bickered among themselves.

At this time Churchill had more enemies and critics than he had friends. The latter were equally divided between Tories and Liberals. Most of the Cabinet and a considerable body of M.P.s disliked and distrusted him; he was well aware of his isolation and determined to clear his name. Significantly, it was mostly Tories who pressed him to return to Parliamentary life—people like Edward Carson, Arthur Markham and F. E. Smith. Churchill was like 'the gadfly, spurring the cow to action' and Parliament badly needed his invigorating if irritating presence. Its somnolence could have proved fatal to Britain's existence, and was proving so; somebody was needed with the audacity to harass autocrats like Haig (Kitchener, a legendary figure, had been drowned in the *Hampshire* on his way to Russia).

F. E. Smith summarized the essential quandary of Churchill at the outset of his political career in *Contemporary Personalities*:

'He can wait' has always been the Tory formula which has chilled the hopes of young and able men ... and so chance after chance of modest promotion went by ... Winston characteristically jumped the whole fence. That he should have done so is one of the tragedies of modern politics, simply because fundamentally he has always been, of our generation, the most sincere and vivid believer in the stately continuity of English life.

But he was like a restive young thoroughbred. He had an extraordinarily thick-witted and clumsy rider, and he jibbed tragically. I suspect, without knowing, that he has always regretted it. If he has true perspective he ought to regret it, because he took a sudden, and it may be an irretrievable, step which placed him out of alignment with his natural allies. ...

In other words, he was a natural-born Tory forced by circumstances to throw in his lot with the Liberals as the only immediate pathway to political advancement. Smith thought that

his able, restless, ambitious temperament was hardly content with its own legitimate ambit. He saw too much, and he tried to do too much. No one department, hardly one war, was enough for him . . . his fundamental conceptions were sound and even brilliant, but they marched too far in front of the material resources which even he could command. He was right about Antwerp; he took great personal risks to make the Antwerp policy successful; but it was doomed to failure before the attempt was made. His conception about the Dardanelles was daring, brilliant and masterly. If successful the attack, as he conceived it, would probably have shortened the war by two years; there would possibly have been no Revolution in Russia and no Bolshevism, with all that this would have meant to the civilisation of Europe and to the security of the world. And had he only been supreme with the uncontrolled power of appropriating from the Western Front what was necessary—and it was so little—to make the Dardanelles Campaign a certain success, he would have been acclaimed today by the whole world as the statesman whose brilliant and intuitive genius won the war.

As 1916 drew to a close a long-developing political crisis at home came to a head. It was a crisis destined to affect the course of the war, and encompass the eventual disintegration and doom of the Liberal Party. The prime instigator of this decline of Liberalism was the Liberal Lloyd George himself.

A Coalition such as Asquith led, as Prime Minister, can only function effectively so long as its different political sections can agree on broad principles. This is particularly true on a ministerial level, for in wartime even more than in times of peace, the activities of different Government departments are intricately interlocked, and internecine warfare between Ministries completely clogs the machine.

Things were going badly at the Front. Lloyd George, as Minister of State for War, felt that the structure of administration was ineffective. He wanted to see the creation of a small, compact War Committee whose directives would be mandatory in connection with every aspect of the war effort. The Cabinet would only be involved if it wished to reverse a decision. Asquith would have none of it. If such a committee were formed, he told Lloyd George, the Prime Minister would have to be Chairman, and the Cabinet must be the ultimate source of authority. For all practical purposes this was a flat rejection of Lloyd George's idea.

Asquith found himself caught up in an intrigue which was too much for him. He had long been under a barrage of attack from Lord Northcliffe's newspapers, in implementation of Northcliffe's persistent and pitiless feud with Asquith, and his public prestige had been proportionately weakened. Lloyd George wanted Asquith to go because Sir William Robertson, Chief of the Imperial General Staff, was obstructing Lloyd George's urgent appeals for action by the Salonika force in concert with Roumania—and Robertson enjoyed the support of Asquith and would continue to be an obstacle until Asquith himself was deposed.

Bonar Law, the Conservative Leader and member of the Coalition, had his own reasons for wanting Asquith out. The Conservative Party had been split ever since one of its most colourful and dynamic members, Sir Edward Carson, had flounced out of the Coalition and joined the Opposition. The Party's further disintegration seemed certain unless Carson could be brought back into the fold —and this could never be while Asquith was Prime Minister. Sir Edward himself was bitterly opposed to Asquith though not averse to office under other direction. Max Aitken—afterwards Lord Beaverbrook—brought them together in what was, for practical purposes, an intrigue, although one which all of them felt sincerely to be in the interests of a more vigorous prosecution of the war effort.

His plan for a War Committee rejected (at least in the form in which he believed it could be effective), Lloyd George resigned. Asquith had announced on 4th December that he had 'decided to advise His Majesty the King to consent to a reconstruction of the Government'. It was plain that Lloyd George's plan was not to be implemented.

As anticipated, Asquith himself then resigned; he had heard that Bonar Law and the Conservatives would refuse to serve under him and had no other choice. On the evening of 5th December Bonar Law went to Buckingham Palace and was charged with forming a Government. He asked Asquith to serve under him but the elderly statesman, feeling it impossible to accept a subordinate office after being the leading Minister, refused. An all-Party conference at

Buckingham Palace failing to find a solution, Bonar Law advised the King to send for Lloyd George. On 6th December Lloyd George received the King's commission to form a Government.

That Bonar Law would not be able to form a Government even if asked to do so, and that he would as the only seeming alternative, suggest Lloyd George, was all pre-arranged.

All these machinations Churchill watched with lively interest and growing hope. With the 'Welsh Wizard' in supreme power, surely Churchill, his friend, would find himself back in harness again?

Unpopular he knew himself to be, but his conscience was clear and Lloyd George knew that; they dined together on the eve of the crisis, but Sir Max Aitken hinted to Churchill that he could not expect an appointment. Bonar Law would not have Churchill in the government at any price, and when somebody told him that Churchill was 'more dangerous as a critic than as a colleague', Law replied, 'I would rather have him against me every time.'

Lloyd George sent a friend to explain to Churchill why he could not be included in the new Government. His response was dignified and patriotic: 'I don't reproach him. His conscience will tell him what he should do. Give him that message and tell him that I cannot allow what you have said to fetter my freedom of action. I will take any position which will enable me to serve my country. My only purpose is to defeat the Hun, and I will subordinate my own feelings so that I may be able to render some assistance.'

The publication of the report of the Dardanelles Commission in March 1917 vindicated Churchill and showed Mr. Asquith in a less favourable light. Lloyd George promised Churchill that he would bring him back to office at the first opportunity and his enemies noted with grim displeasure that the former First Lord was in increasing favour with the Prime Minister.

In 1917 it dawned belatedly upon the Allies that despite the prodigious expenditure of their countries' lives and treasure, no coordinated strategic plan existed between them. Unity of plan and purpose were essential, the Russian Revolution freeing German troops for attacks in the west, as Russia abandoned her obligations to her Allies. The disaster at Caporetto led to the formation of a Supreme War Council. Meanwhile, the unrestricted use of submarines and mines added to the burden thrown upon the British Navy. Admiral Jellicoe, in *The Crisis of the Naval War* said: 'Who

would have had even the temerity to predict that the Navy, con-
fronted by the second greatest naval power in the world, would be
called upon to maintain free communications across the Channel
for many months until the months became years in face of the
naval forces of the enemy established on the Belgian coast, passing
millions of men across in safety as well as vast quantities of stores
and munitions? Who would have prophesied that the Navy would
have to safeguard the passage of hundreds of thousands of troops
from the Dominions to Europe, as well as the movement of tens of
thousands of labourers from China and elsewhere? Or who would
have believed had he stated that the Navy would be required to keep
open the sea communications of huge armies in Macedonia, Egypt,
Palestine, Mesopotamia and East Africa against attacks by surface
vessels, submarines and mines, whilst at the same time protecting
the merchant shipping of ourselves, our Allies and the neutral
powers against similar perils, and assisting to secure the safety of
the troops of the United States when they, in due course, were
brought across the Atlantic?'

The stepping-up of submarine and mine warfare meant that as
much merchant shipping was sunk by the Germans in six weeks of
1917 as during the whole of 1915.

A new factor was the declaration of war by the United States on
6th April and the arrival of Admiral Sims, U.S.N. three days later;
the arrival of a destroyer flotilla at Queenstown on 2nd May and,
later, the arrival at Scapa Flow of a division of U.S. battleships to
join the Grand Fleet. Churchill, knowing of America's intentions
urged the Commons, in a speech given in secret session as early as
March, that Britain should abstain from large-scale military offensives on the Continent until the added support of the United States
could give such offensives a chance of success.

Lloyd George wanted and needed Churchill, but could he afford
him in face of the hostility of so many members of the House of
Commons? Nobody doubted his brilliance. All had seen his love of
action. Most had heard him speak. He was not simply disliked for
his alleged mistakes, but for his enigmatic character. When Lloyd
George did some kite-flying as to Churchill's possible reinstatement,
a colleague wrote to him:

May I again and for the last time urge you to think well before
you make the appointment (W. Ch.) which we have more than

once discussed? It will be an appointment intensely unpopular with many of your chief colleagues—in the opinion of some of whom it will lead to the disruption of the Government at an early date, even if it does not lead, as it may well do, to resignations now.

X tells me that it will be intensely unpopular in the Army. I have every reason to believe the same of the Navy. He is a potential danger in opposition. In the opinion of all of us he will as a member of the Government be an active danger in our midst.

An active danger! Another Minister spoke of Churchill as 'a dangerously ambitious man'. Yet another predicted that Churchill in the Government would 'bring about a very grave situation. . . .' Northcliffe was against any appointment, and the power which he wielded with his newspapers was immense.

The campaign against Churchill gathered in bitterness and invective as, belligerent and uncontrite, he took his usual place in the House, intervening with unpredictable and explosive effect. Admiral Sir Charles Beresford informed Bonar Law that, having heard of a move to bring Churchill back, he had organized a committee of protest and arranged for protest meetings to be held up and down the country. At a huge meeting at Queen's Hall in London Beresford accused Churchill of 'gambling with the lives of men in the most reckless way'. *The Sunday Times* said that if 'the intrigue by a powerful clique' succeeded and Churchill returned it would 'constitute a grave danger to the Administration and the Empire as a whole . . . his public record has proved beyond all argument or doubt that he does not possess those qualities of balanced judgement and shrewd far-sightedness which are essential to the sound administration. Gambles today mean not only the jeopardizing of the Empire; they mean the sacrifice of men's lives. . . . We say with all deliberation and with the utmost emphasis that nothing would tend more effectively to damn Mr. Lloyd George's Government in the eyes of the whole country than the co-option of Mr. Churchill. . . .'

Lloyd George owed a debt of gratitude to Churchill, who had stood by him during the Marconi Scandal of 1913, when it was alleged that certain Ministers, including Lloyd George, had profited by corrupt means. Apart from that, he was a genuine admirer of his gifts, though shrewd enough to see his shortcomings. What, Lloyd George asked himself, was the reason for Churchill's tremendous unpopularity? It could not be his defection from party; many public men had done that before. Then he decided:

Here was their explanation. His mind was a powerful machine but there lay hidden in its material or its make-up some obscure defect which prevented it from always running true. They could not tell what it was. When the mechanism went wrong, its very power made the action disastrous, not only to himself but to the causes in which he was engaged and the men with whom he was co-operating. That was why the latter were nervous in his partnership.

But when Lord Northcliffe was away in America Lloyd George made Churchill Minister of Munitions. There was a tremendous job to do there, in particular in the manufacture and delivery of the tanks needed for the last, tremendous effort for victory.

There was an immediate outcry from all quarters. The news was passed on in the lobbies of the House of Commons and some of the comments were insensate in their fury. 'Down with Lloyd George and Churchill!' the cry went and sometimes, as Churchill overheard the comments, he gave his critics a friendly smile. That was the worst part. A man unafraid of shells could not easily be dismayed by words.

Newspapers on the morning of 18th July 1917 gave the news; Carson would leave the Admiralty for the War Cabinet; Vice-Admiral Geddes to be First Lord; Montagu to become Secretary of State for India, Addison to be Minister of Reconstruction and Churchill to be Minister of Munitions. *The Times* accepted his appointment with fair grace, adding a warning to him not to meddle with experts with his 'amateur strategy'. The *Daily Express* was friendly, but then so was its owner, Sir Max Aitken. The true-blue *Morning Post* was beside itself with rage. So were the Liberal and Labour newspapers.

For days the House of Commons business was delayed by questions and resolutions. Over a hundred Tory M.P.s supported a resolution of protest against his appointment. Mr. Evelyn Cecil 'asked the Prime Minister whether, in view of the feeling which exists in many quarters in this House that the inclusion of the right Hon. Member for Dundee in His Majesty's Government, and particularly at this time, as Minister of Munitions, is a national danger, he will give a day for the discussion of the appointment?'

Mr. Bonar Law: The subject can, I understand, be raised on the Vote of Credit if my right hon. friend desires.

Mr. Cecil: Arising out of that answer, may I ask the Right Honourable Gentleman to convey to the Prime Minister that in the opinion of many of the usual followers of the Government such an appointment must gravely compromise the policy of successfully getting on with the war?

Mr. Speaker: Order! Order! The Right Hon. Gentleman is making a statement.

Lloyd George had made a brave and statesmanlike gesture in bringing Churchill back. It was a happy moment when the Prime Minister, after a good dinner at 10 Downing Street, linked arms with Churchill and led him into a small room. There, framed and on the wall, was a *Daily Express* placard of 1913 issued at the time of the Marconi scandal: CHURCHILL DEFENDS LLOYD GEORGE. Now, at long last, the boot was on the other foot.

It was a good thing for Churchill that he was not thin-skinned. When his intentions ran counter to those of his colleagues, he was accused of being dictatorial—which beyond question he often could be. When he tried to please, his motives were impugned.

In making Churchill Minister of Munitions, thereby jeopardizing his own status and popularity besides exposing Churchill himself to attack from all sides, Lloyd George was not simply paying a debt of gratitude for past support. He needed somebody to put ginger behind the munitions output programme. There must be no more shell shortage. There must be tanks a-plenty; nobody knew how long the war might last, and the mechanical equivalent of Hannibal's army of elephants might yet be needed.

His first task was to organize the 12,000 civil servants into a manageable unit. There had been over fifty groups concerned with various aspects of stores and equipment. These he reduced in number, and set up a committee on which were represented some of the finest industrial brains in the country. When one considers the value of the pound then compared with its vastly depreciated purchasing power today, the sums of public money entrusted to his care were staggering. But as he had always thought big (even as a journalist he had received £1,000 for two articles, an enormous sum then) he was not unduly excited in placing a £100,000,000 order for medium guns, or planning the production of 10,000 tanks which would have necessitated a corps of 100,000 men. Before this last scheme could be realized the Armistice had made it unnecessary.

One almost intractable problem which Lloyd George left him as a legacy was industrial unrest. For a while, he tried appeasement and the donkey-and-carrot technique. The carnage of the great war, which had got entirely out of hand leaving the world's leaders bewildered and totally without clear objectives, would surely get worse if, once again, the British Army was denied the arms it needed to fight with. He knew how depressed his friend Lloyd George was, how sorely tempted to wash his hands of the whole terrible business. 'I warn you,' Lloyd George told C. P. Scott, Editor of the *Manchester Guardian* in December 1917, 'I am in a very pacifist temper. . . . If people really knew, the war would stop tomorrow, but of course they don't know, and can't know. The correspondents don't write, and the censorship wouldn't pass the truth. The thing is horrible and beyond human nature to bear, and I feel I can't go any longer with the bloody business; I would rather resign.'

To the world, the Prime Minister presented an exterior of stern confidence. But we know his real thoughts. By contrast, Churchill never lost his confidence. Even when badly hurt over his rejection by Asquith he continued to press for those things he thought important and to bombard all concerned with long and detailed memoranda. Just as Lord Chesterfield's son must have blanched at the sight of the postman 'Oh no! not another letter from my father!' so they quailed at the sight of the bulky missives on the direction of the war which he continued to send even when in 'exile' in France and everyone hoped they had effectually got rid of him.

Knowing his unpopularity, he once addressed a meeting of munition workers with the preface: 'We have heard that no Minister can expect to be popular. In that respect, at least, I start from scratch.' The disarming admission brought cheers and laughter —and a relaxed atmosphere.

One of Churchill's problems was that skilled workers could, at a time of labour scarcity due to the decimation of healthy men on the battlefields, command almost any terms they pleased. Often they threw in their work to do better paid but unskilled work. This trend would disorganize production and place the country in jeopardy. So he raised the wages for skilled time-workers by $12\frac{1}{2}$ per cent.

The timing of this move was not felicitous. Churchill was a member of a committee which was already dealing with this problem. It was embarrassed at the immediate effect of Churchill's unilateral action. Semi-skilled workers in the engineering, building, textiles and railways demanded the same increase while piece-workers followed up by a demand for a 7 per cent increase. In effect, what Churchill said would cost £14,000,000 would cost instead £40,000,000. George Barnes, a Socialist minister, roundly accused Churchill of 'butting in' with his much-advertised concession to the workers, and following a storm of critical questions in the Commons (his critics had been waiting for an opening such as this) the *Morning Post* fired its guns:

> Mr. Churchill has a genius for exploiting his opportunities. Mr. Churchill's idea in entering upon his office was simple; he desired to make himself popular with what is called Labour. He argued thus: the working man has a vote; he will vote for those who please him; he is pleased with a rise in wages; therefore let me give him 12½ per cent. That there was any other side to the wages dispute probably did not occur to Mr. Churchill. . . .

In the House of Commons every type of sensational rumour flew around. Lloyd George had told Churchill to go! Churchill wanted to resign! The Cabinet was up in arms against him again!

But Lloyd George badly needed stalwart support. The supply position was serious, and he was quite glad to have a tough man to deal with the situation—the output of the shipbuilding industry, for example, had fallen by fifty per cent. When an epidemic of strikes broke out and production of desperately-needed equipment was still further endangered, Churchill found a swift and salutary answer. In effect it was: 'get on with the job or go to the Front.' Soldiers were falling like flies in the mud; a quarter of a million of them, at Passchendaele. Under fire from field-batteries, mortars and machine-guns, strafed by diving planes, they pushed and plodded through the viscous yellow mud, trapped up to the knees, holding their rifles aloft. The gun carriages sank up to the axles, and in vain did General Gough appeal to Haig to call off the advance. Sometimes they were neck deep in the mud. Sometimes they drowned in it. Nobody had the wit to stop the senseless carnage, or to dismiss Haig. The home government and the public were kept in ignorance. Casualties were stated to be 148,470 for August and September 1917, when in fact they were nearly double that.

Churchill, who paid frequent flying visits to France and flew over almost every area of battle, visiting the front in many places, was in no mood to argue about strikes with munition workers who had a roof and warmth, food and physical security. His threat to withdraw their immunity from military service if they did not pull their weight in the war effort worked like a charm.

There was, of course, another side to the coin. The trade unions had watched with dismay their hard-won liberties whittled away. Decades of struggle had brought them to the point, just before war broke out, when at last their members were organized against exploitation, poor wages and inferior working conditions. But after all soldiers were in an even worse plight.

12

Peace

Churchill's position in the House at this time was of great delicacy. Where were his friends? He was not a man to lean, and he needed lessons from no man on how to manœuvre. With the Tories against him, an influential section of the Liberals hostile and the Labour members watching with baleful eyes for any encroachment on proletarian rights, he had to compromise more than he would have chosen. In August 1918 he had to modify considerably measures for permitting 'dilution' of labour. He was to discover that measures which may suit a government can be, from a human point of view, intolerable.

Sir Croydon Marks, having heard a summary of Churchill's intentions said, 'I rejoice tonight that we have a Minister of Munitions who is about to endeavour to get by goodwill that which he could never have got by regulation,' while Major Hills quoted the case of a skilled worker who had spent his life at his trade as a skilled fitter. His wife went to munitions work when war broke out, and at the end of the second week on Saturday night. 'She brought back £4, threw it on the table and said: "There is my little lot; you can stay at home and mind the baby." That shows the point I want to bring out, that it is not only the injury to a man's pocket but the injury to his self-respect. He sees boys and girls whom he himself has taught earning more than he does.'

Early in 1918 the Germans mustered a million men in a determined effort to drive a wedge through the Front of the British Third and Fifth Armies. There seemed a good chance that they might succeed, for they outnumbered the Allies by 62 divisions to 24. They hoped to reach Paris and the Channel ports before the much-advertised American contingents could join forces with the British and French. For no known reason, General Haig had not made provision for sufficient reserves with which to repel a concentrated attack, and as for 'the plans drawn up in combination with the French Military Authorities' and alleged to have been worked out in detail, mentioned in one of his dispatches, they never materialized. Lord Milner, in a letter to Lloyd George on 14th March 1918 said, almost in despair, that 'Haig is quite obdurate about the reserve. He will have none of it. Desperately stupid and very awkward for all of us.' Although Allied strength on the Western Front more than equalled the Germans', the enemy were concentrated on certain sectors with a superiority of three to one, joined in what Lloyd George described as 'the most stupendous battle fought on earth'.

Within three days it was apparent that the plans for mutual support said to exist between Haig and Pétain were not being put into operation. On Sunday, 24th March 1918, Haig learned from Pétain that orders had been given for the French to retire towards Paris, thereby splitting the Allied Front. As the battle raged, it seemed as though all the sacrifice of four years might be lost. The C.I.G.S. went to France and suggested that Foch should co-ordinate the two armies, and so it was agreed at Doullens by Clemenceau, Poincaré, Milner, Foch, Pétain and Haig—nobody thought of inviting General Bliss, the American Chief-of-Staff, to the meeting. But Foch had not been made Allied Commander-in-Chief, nor did his 'co-ordinating' powers extend to the Americans.

In a desperate and hurried attempt to achieve unity of effort, Lloyd George appealed to Churchill to go to the spot. Churchill flew to France, and reported that reserves were badly needed—'Our armies require strengthening by every conceivable means.' He got along well with the French Prime Minister, Clemenceau, finding him 'a tower of strength and courage'.

The Battle of Amiens drew towards its climax and the future of Europe hung in the balance. But at last, at Beauvais, it was agreed to give Foch powers of action besides vague 'co-ordination' and a mandate to manage the strategic deployment of military operations, but the respective Commanders-in-Chief had the right of tactical control, and of appeal if they felt the safety of their armies to be in jeopardy. Eventually, after much argument, Foch was made General-in-Chief of the Allied Armies.

On 12th April Haig had issued his famous appeal, 'With our backs to the wall, and believing in the justice of our cause, each one of us must fight to the end.'

Churchill, meanwhile, could see the end of the war coming. The Germans, with the greatest army they could muster, had failed to make the breakthrough. When hostilities ceased, there would certainly be a General Election—the Liberal Government, solely because of the war, had extended its normal period of influence as the predominating sector of the Coalition, and must submit themselves again to the electorate. What would Churchill's future be? Was he a Liberal still?

Churchill at this point gave grave offence to Lloyd George, saying in effect that before committing himself as to his own political allegiance, he would like to know what was to be the composition of Lloyd George's next Government. He was anxious that it should not contain 'any unrepresentative or reactionary elements'. It is hardly surprising that the Prime Minister, who in face of opposition and to the jeopardy of his own standing, had rescued Churchill from obscurity, was angered by such presumption. 'Surely,' he wrote sharply, 'this is an unprecedented demand. The choice of the Members of the Government must be left to the Prime Minister, and anyone who does not trust his leadership has but one course, and that is to seek leaders whom he *can* trust.' Lloyd George added that he valued their fourteen years' friendship and political co-operation, but that if Churchill had any doubts, he need not wait until a General Election before doing something about it. But early in 1918 Churchill had admitted to his friend Riddell that he was not really happy as a Liberal. 'I wish I was in Opposition. When the war is over I shall resign. I could not stop with this Government; I would prefer Opposition. Whilst the war is on I must help to the best of my ability, and I was miserable while I was unemployed. . . .' But the relationship of these two intensely ambitious men was often strained.

At last the long and bloody struggle drew to its close. As the German Army suffered its crushing defeat, new fears gripped the British Cabinet. The social and economic chaos of war might produce anarchy and Communism, with implications of violence spreading like a prairie fire which acknowledges no frontiers. There was the sinister precedent of the Russian revolution—a nightmare which obsessed Churchill and would later on, but for restraining hands, have driven him to extravagant follies. Men everywhere, tired and bitter, were asking what sort of leaders the world possessed, that these enormities had persisted so long? The German Navy mutinied. Was this a matter for Allied rejoicing? No! The German officers were murdered by their ratings. But there was plenty of bad blood in the British Army too.

Churchill has described in *The World Crisis* how the war ended:

It was a few minutes before the eleventh hour of the eleventh day of the eleventh month. I stood at the window of my room looking up Northumberland Avenue towards Trafalgar Square, waiting for Big Ben to tell that the war was over . . . the minutes passed . . . and then suddenly the first stroke of the chime. From the portals of one of the large hotels absorbed by Government Departments darted the slight figure of a girl clerk, distractedly gesticulating while another stroke resounded. Then from all sides men and women came scurrying into the street. Streams of people poured out from all the buildings. Northumberland Avenue was now crowded by people in their hundreds, nay, thousands, rushing hither and thither in a frantic manner, shouting and screaming with joy. I could see that Trafalgar Square was already swarming.

Around me in our very headquarters, in the Hotel Metropole, disorder had broken out. Doors banged. Feet clattered down corridors. Everyone rose from the desk and cast aside pen and paper. All bounds were broken. The tumult grew. It grew like a gale, from all sides simultaneously. The street was now a seething mass of humanity. Flags appeared as if by magic. Streams of men and women flowed from the Embankment. They mingled with torrents pouring down the Strand on their way to acclaim the King. Almost before the last stroke of the clock had died away, the strict, war-straitened, regulated streets of London had become a triumphant pandemonium. . . .

My wife arrived, and we decided to go and offer our congratulations to the Prime Minister, on whom the central impact of the whole struggle had fallen, in his hour of recompense. But no sooner had we entered our car than twenty people mounted upon it, and in the midst of a wildly cheering multitude we were impelled slowly forward through Whitehall. . . .

Churchill was in the House of Commons—in common with everyone else who could get there—as the Speaker, W. J. Lowther, took the chair at 2.45 in the afternoon. The protagonists of Parliament were hushed. The Prime Minister was solemn. Andrew Bonar Law, whose neat aspect and sombre clothing, trim moustache and sober, almost sad, shrewd eyes made him look like the epitome of an English business gentleman, sat quietly; Mr. Asquith, with his flowing grey hair and patriarchal geniality; Mr. Philip Snowden, the crippled Socialist who had remained truculently pacifist throughout the war, waited in dour silence. But generally the atmosphere was one of humble thankfulness. The war had lasted so long that nobody could foresee an end. Parliament had still remained in action as a legislative body, but executive decisions involving the life and death of hundreds of thousands of people were taken without consultation with the mass of M.P.s and often wholly without their knowledge. In normal times a probing account is given by the Government or demanded by the Opposition. In times of war security considerations limit the information which can be given. This takes much of the cut-and-thrust out of debates.

Lloyd George rose and said:

'I beg to move that this House do now adjourn.

'The Armistice . . . was signed this morning at five o'clock, after a discussion which was prolonged all night. I will read to the͵ House the conditions of the Armistice in so far as they have reached us up to the present. . . .' (He then read the conditions of the Armistice.)

'Thus at 11 o'clock this morning came to an end the cruellest and most terrible war that has ever scourged mankind. I hope we may say that thus, this fateful morning, came to an end all wars.

'This is no time for words. Our hearts are too full of a gratitude to which no tongue can give adequate expression. I will, therefore, move "That this House do immediately adjourn, until this time tomorrow, and that we proceed, as a House of Commons, to Saint Margaret's, to give humble and reverent thanks for the deliverance of the world from its great peril".'

Mr. Asquith: 'I join with a full heart in his aspiration, not only that this war may not be resumed, but that now we have entered upon a new chapter in international history, in which war will be recognized as an obsolete anachronism, never to be revived. As the Prime Minister has said, there is nothing we can do in conditions so unexampled as these than as a House and on behalf of the nation, to acknowledge our gratitude to Almighty God.'

The question was put and agreed to. The Speaker then said: 'I propose to proceed at once to Saint Margaret's, and I will invite the House to follow.'

That night Churchill dined with the Prime Minister at 10 Downing Street, in a huge room adorned by portraits of Pitt and Fox, Nelson and Washington. Lloyd George was cheerful, but not ebullient. He was, Churchill records, fully aware that although one war was finished, a different kind of battle had begun—the immense task of rehabilitation and reconstruction. Churchill was in no mood for the popular clamour of squeezing Germany 'until the pips squeak'. Germany must remain part of Europe, and must not go down in Communism, which would constitute as grave a menace to her neighbours and to Europe in general as Prussian Chauvinism.

Neither statesman had an appetite for the Mafeking-style celebrations raging throughout London and the rest of the country, although the upsurge of emotion was understandable. Furthermore, there was now the need for a General Election. What Government would get in, whose side should he support, and what line would he take in the election?

Churchill, despite the verbal maulings he had suffered both inside the House and out of it, was determined to continue as a Member of Parliament and indeed as a Minister if he could.

And in his mind too was the broader vision, so beautifully expressed in *The World Crisis*, by which one can see how cruel and unjust the accusation of 'warmonger', so commonly levelled against him, really was:

'Is this the end? Is it to be merely a chapter in a cruel and senseless story? Will a new generation in their turn be immolated to square the black accounts of Teuton and Gaul? Will our children bleed and gasp again in devastated lands? Or will there spring from the very fires of conflict that reconciliation of the three giant combatants, which would unite their genius and secure to each in safety and freedom a share in rebuilding the glory of Europe?'

13

Defeat of the Liberals

On 2nd November 1918, with victory in sight, Lloyd George decided that there should be an early General Election, and discussed the prospect with Mr. Bonar Law. A memorandum of 5th November by Lord Stamfordham shows that King George V was against the idea. So early an election would virtually disenfranchise the Service men—their votes just would not arrive in time. The King pointed out that the Government already had the support of the House of Commons and that Mr. Asquith, who was now Leader of the Opposition, had recently stated that his Party would continue their support.

Lloyd George told the King that he was not overmuch worried about the difficulties which an early election would pose for serving men (in fact only a quarter of them had a chance to vote in time) and emphasized that Parliament had overrun its normal term of office by a considerable period.

The King granted his permission for an early dissolution of Parliament. The moment this was announced, the Labour Party decided not to stand as Government supporters, but independently. There was strong pressure on Lloyd George to unite the Liberal Party by coming to terms with Asquith. This Lloyd George firmly refused to do. The background to this strange refusal, which weakened the Liberal Party irreparably and marked the emergence of the Labour Party as the main political opposition, may seem remote now, but was important then.

On 21st March the British Army on the Western Front was attacked by nearly half the German Army. Sir Douglas Haig had been compelled, against his wishes, to agree to the extension of the British part of the front by fourteen miles. He was refused reinforcements from home, where 300,000 troops were available, and so his force of 300,000 men came under overwhelming attack from 800,000 Germans.

Reinforcements were sent—too late to prevent grievous loss of life—and scapegoats were found in General Gough, commander of that part of the front which was weakened by the British and French Governments' insistence on the extension, who was relieved of his command, and Sir Frederick Maurice, Director of Military Operations. Sir William Robertson, Chief of the Imperial General Staff and a thorn in the side of Lloyd George, had already been dismissed and replaced by Sir Henry Wilson.

On 7th May 1918 Sir Frederick Maurice wrote a letter to *The Times* claiming that the Prime Minister had misled the House of Commons about the state of the British Expeditionary Force and the extension of the line. Asquith demanded a Select Committee to investigate the matter; Lloyd George, naturally enough, could not agree to an airing of military information at a time when the country was still fighting a desperate enemy, but would agree to a tribunal of two judges. Asquith pressed the attack and his motion was put to the vote. The Vote of Censure was defeated by 293 to 106—but the 106 Liberals who voted with Asquith were marked down by Lloyd George for political ostracism.

Hence Lloyd George's refusal to make peace with Asquith. Instead, he arranged with Bonar Law that all candidates loyal to the Coalition would receive a letter of recommendation signed jointly by Bonar Law and himself. This device Asquith denounced as 'a coupon' and from then on the General Election of December 1918 became known as the 'Coupon Election'.

In the atmosphere of emotional hysteria generated by victory, these coupons were almost a guarantee of the candidate's success at the polls. The Coalition had pulled the country through; Lloyd George was seen as the greatest wartime Prime Minister the country had ever known.

Sir George Younger, Chairman of the Unionist (Tory) Party Organization, having virtual control of the election machinery, naturally saw to it that the larger proportion of 'coupons' went to Tory candidates.

Lloyd George's strategy was, clearly, to see returned to power a Coalition which would accept him as Prime Minister, and to exploit to the utmost the Mafeking atmosphere. Many candidates, including Lloyd George himself, appealed directly to crude emotion. He himself undertook to see that the Kaiser would be prosecuted, that Germans in Britain would be sent packing, and that Germany herself would be squeezed of the last penny by way of reparations.

Otherwise, the issues of the election were few: (1) The character of the peace treaty; (2) the nature of reconstruction; and (3) the type of government which the electors desired. As to the Peace Treaty, the main public issues were whether to try or hang the Kaiser (or both) and to what extent and in what way Germany should be forced to pay the cost of the war.

The law of elections had been revolutionized by the Representation of the People Act of 1918 and this was the first general election to be held under its influence. The changes in procedure, briefly, were that all polls were to be taken in one day instead of being spread over three weeks, as in the past; there were to be three different methods of voting—personally, at the polling booths; by post, in the case of soldiers and sailors; and by proxy for those living at too great a distance from a booth. Plural voting was largely abolished. It was the first time that women over the age of thirty were granted a vote, providing that they or their husbands owned or occupied land or premises worth at least £5 a year. Thus another two million names of men and eight and a half million women were added to the voting list, almost doubling the electorate. It is hardly surprising that Lloyd George made friends with the Suffragettes, even to the extent of trying to find for the irrepressible Mrs. Pankhurst a place in Parliament, and that Mr. Churchill was less vocal than last time about his aversion to women having the franchise.

Once again Mr. Churchill contested Dundee, other candidates being A. Wilkie (Labour), J. S. Lloyd (Unionist), J. Glass (Unionist) and the Prohibitionist candidate Mr. E. Scrymgeour. In a statement of policy to Dundee Liberal General Committee, Mr. Churchill declared:

... not only have we got to make the transition back to peace ... but on top of this immense transformation full of difficulty and inconvenience and disturbance, and no doubt of much disappointment, there will soon be coming back three million men looking for a fair chance and a square deal and the means of earning a livelihood and keeping a home together. Who is to say they have not deserved it? Unless we pull together with the same loyalty and manliness and British pluck which has carried us through the late fearsome perils, all the splendour of our victory and all its immense possibilities will disappear into thin air, short commons and bad temper.

The times are hard and rough, and every man and every

woman must choose their part and play it with all their might. Personal interests, party interests, class interests, sectional interests—all these will have to take second place to National interests if we are to get round the corner without disaster. Whatever government is in power, whoever are the Ministers employed, they will want all the help their countrymen can give them and there is no help more needed than the help of a good and vigorous House of Commons, freshly returned by a million votes.

Lastly, there is stability and order, without which no revival is possible. To rally the people round the throne on the unshakable foundation of freedom and prosperity, so that our island life will long remain the wonder of the world and an example to all—that is our hope and our firm resolve.

At his election meetings Churchill avoided the sort of jingoism so freely indulged in by other candidates. He actually resisted the more hysterical over-simplifications. He was not for hanging the Kaiser, though not against his being brought to trial. Through the fog of revenge he could glimpse greater problems. For example, the revolution in Russia was a precedent of which the world had not heard the last; there was considerable social unrest in Britain and widespread sympathy amongst trade unionists with the Bolsheviks in Russia. The Tsarist Government which had been overthrown was reactionary, despotic, cruel and corrupt, supported by an insidious secret police; the Bolshevik Government which had seized power was also reactionary, despotic, cruel and corrupt and supported by the dreaded Cheka, but to the British working class it seemed a straightforward act of the Russian working class sacking their unworthy masters and deciding the course of their own destinies.

Mr. Churchill was returned with a good majority. He polled 25,788 votes as a Coalition-Liberal; Mr. Wilkie polled 24,822 votes while the abstemious Mr. Scrymgeour polled the astonishing number of 10,423 votes, standing this time as Independent and not specifically as a Temperance candidate, although he had in no wise forsaken his hatred of drink. Many of his votes came from serving men who had heard about the excessive drinking of munition workers who earned good money while they fought abroad. Mr. J. S. Brown (Labour) polled 7,769.

The General Election Poll was held on 14th December 1918, but the postal votes took a long time to come in, and only a fortnight later was the result declared. *The Times* could announce HUGE COALITION VICTORY. With a majority of 262 the Coalition Government had an easy mandate, but the significant fact was that of its 478 seats 335 were held by Conservatives. Asquith's Liberals gained only 33 seats, thus becoming an insignificant minority and constituting the virtual end of the Liberals as an effective or important political force. Equally significant was the fact that the Labour Party, for the first time, returned 59 Members, becoming the official Opposition and the only alternative government should a crisis arise. The Irish Nationalist Party dwindled to seven members, while 73 Sinn Feiner Members were returned but did not appear, refusing to sit in the House of Commons. As everyone expected, the Pacifists were routed. What it really meant, although few could see it, was that except for Labour Governments in 1924 and from 1929–31, Britain was in for two decades of Conservative government.

In a message to the electors of Dundee Mr. Churchill said:

The result of the election constitutes a grand affirmation by the city of faith in the destinies of Britain and a condemnation of tyranny, whether it takes the form of Kaiserism or Bolshevism. Our path lies between these perils which, from one side in the shape of autocracy and from the other in the shape of anarchy, threaten and impede the onward march of peoples. The political experience and sober virtues of the British Nation have hitherto enabled us to beat down foes abroad and restrain folly at home. Here in this land we have found a way to preserve the continuity of our history without preventing progress. . . . One glorious page in the story of the British people is closed. Let us so act that another may now be written in which the fruits of victory will be enjoyed by the masses who have fought and won.

The new Government was to be both the climax and the end of the 'Welsh Wizard's' meteoric career. Lloyd George was back as Prime Minister. Bonar Law, melancholy, unstimulating but of unshakable integrity and keen perception, was made Lord Privy Seal. His sense of public service, abstemious habits (which included an indifference to honours and decorations) and good health made him a sobering and steadying influence amongst the careerists. His own sacrifice in the war had not been a small one; his two elder sons were killed on active service. Arthur Balfour, now seventy, was Lord President of the Council. As with all brilliant men, he was the subject of quite opposite assessments of his character; Lord Beaverbrook thought him a 'crafty man' of few friends, an indifferent speaker and one who 'didn't believe in anything or anybody'; Lord Birkenhead found Balfour 'luminous in judgement, unrivalled in knowledge, unquestioned in integrity, whose charm dissolves all personal enmity, an ex-Premier, an ex-Foreign Secretary, an ex-leader of the Conservative Party. . . .'

There was Lord Milner, like Mr. Balfour a bachelor, as Colonial Secretary. It was not an appointment he relished. And his appointment of Secretary of State for War in April 1918 had not been wholly popular with the public, either; he was born in Germany of a father who was a German national despite English ancestry. Lord Birkenhead was Lord Chancellor. Sir A. Geddes, former First Lord of the Admiralty and member of the War Cabinet, 'a strong, silent man' who had a coin-operated phone box in his home near Brighton to avoid incurring phone bills, was President of the Board of Trade.

And Churchill? What was to be done with Churchill? At first he was offered a choice between the Admiralty and War Office, with the Air Ministry tagged on as a sort of extra. The ink was scarcely dry on his delighted acceptance of the Admiralty when the offer was withdrawn and he was appointed Secretary for War instead. The complexity of and controversy inherent in this job required a strong man with an inexhaustible capacity for hard work.

A tremendous task awaited him there. The Army was in a state of near-mutiny, seething with discontent. It was partly due to the boring interim between the demands of active service and the uncertain prospects of civilian life. Many were just sick of the war and even more sick of the civilians who snapped up the best jobs, and of the remote, seemingly smug and manifestly affluent hierarchy whose bunglings, they thought, had prolonged or even caused the awful conflict. 'The land fit for heroes to live in' as promised by Lloyd George was a far from comfortable place. There was a general strike in Belfast. There were bloody riots in Glasgow, an actual mutiny at Folkestone. In Luton an outraged mob burned down the Town Hall.

It is as well that Churchill, sizing up the situation, took prompt action both to ascertain and redress the worst grievances. To serving men 'first in, first out' seemed only commonsense and justice; they were not concerned with economic theories about

Britain's future, however logical. They were human beings whose exertions and nerves had been stretched to breaking-point and now wanted their freedom, whatever its problems.

The most ominous point was when hundreds of soldiers on leave, shouting curses and execrations on the Government, marched on Whitehall, becoming in the process a demonstration of over 3,000 people. Churchill, an ex-soldier, understood what passions were being unleashed:

> Certainly there were factors which nobody could measure and which no one had ever before seen at work. Armies of nearly four million men had been suddenly and consciously released from the iron discipline of war. . . . All these vast numbers had been taught for years how to kill; how to punch a bayonet into the vital organs; how to smash the brains out with a mace; how to make and throw bombs as if they were no more than snowballs. All of them had been through a mill. . . . To all, sudden and violent death, the woeful spectacle of shattered men and dwellings was . . . the commonest incident of everyday life. If these armies formed a united resolve, if they were seduced from the standards of duty and patriotism, there was no power which could ever have attempted to withstand them.

In one week no less than thirty cases of revolt were reported, the Army Service Corps in Grove Park and the Mechanical Transport Depots at Kempton Park being among the worst offenders. In many towns there were actual threats to march on the town and seize it.

Then there was the 'Horse Guards Revolution'—an ugly straw in the wind. At Victoria Station over three thousand soldiers from various units were incensed over the muddle created for their return to France after their leave. Tired, hungry—nobody had given them anything to eat or drink—and resentful at having to return anyway, they formed the angry legions who marched on Whitehall, and cornered the staff of London Command in the Horse Guards building.

Churchill, who had observed the Guards drawn up along the Mall and discovered the reason for it when he reached his office, took prompt action. A reserve battalion of the Grenadiers and two troops of the Household Cavalry closed in on the armed men—the Grenadiers with fixed bayonets. All the 3,000 men were arrested and taken to Wellington Barracks where they were fed. There were no casualties and very few were punished, as Churchill was satisfied that the authorities were to blame for their muddling.

Nevertheless, Britain was nearer to revolution than she had been for a long time. The dissentients were not organized; authority was. If the pockets of discontent had ever come together with a common aim there was indeed, as Churchill has said, 'no power which could ever have attempted to withstand them.' One had seen what had happened in Calais, where the British Army went into open revolt, three or four thousand armed men seizing the town and order being restored only when two divisions were sent against them.

But the British Tommy, as Churchill knew too well, had much to be angry about. What prodigious patience and valour had four million men shown through the long years of carnage and suffering! In the dangerous post-war situation, a weaker man could have made a bad job worse; as usual, Churchill refused to shrink from responsibility.

Military commitments in Russia were a more tricky matter. Prior to the Revolution, Russia had been Britain's ally against Germany. When Churchill took over the War Office, Russia was convulsed by revolution and counter-revolution. Although the Bolsheviks had seized the central government, a number of anti-Bolshevik movements led by Admiral Denikin, General Koltchak and General Wrangel continued operations. Britain, of course, encouraged this continued resistance because in 1917 we did not want Russia to drop out of the war and so release more German troops for an attack on the West.

During the Tsarist regime tremendous quantities of munitions from Britain had poured into Murmansk, Archangel and Vladivostock. When the Russians signed the Treaty of Brest-Litovsk with the Germans in March 1918, there was a danger of these vast reserves falling into German hands and British troops were despatched to protect them or effect their delivery. Thus there were about 12,000 British and 11,000 Allied troops in North Russia and in the icy wastes of Siberia two British battalions. Thus Denikin in the south and Koltchak in the east fought both Germans and Bolsheviks but by the time Churchill assumed office, there was little case for further involvement in Russia's agonizing metamorphosis.

What should be done? Lloyd George was deeply preoccupied with the peace discussions at Versailles. Churchill asked for guidance, and Lloyd George countered by asking for some idea of costs.

He remembered that after so long and terrible a war, the British people were in no mood for new military adventures or sacrifices; the industrial classes and trade unionists were also deeply suspicious of Governmental intentions in Russia. Labour leaders cherished the illusion that Bolshevik Russia was a promised land where the worker was triumphant at last, where arrogant hereditary privilege was ended, worldly religion snuffed out and be-medalled aristocrats silenced.

There was substance in the Prime Minister's suspicions. Churchill dearly loved adventure. Lucy Masterman, an acute observer, had noted his 'whiff of grapeshot' attitude towards crises of different kinds. Churchill's telegrams alarmed Lloyd George to such an extent that he told him:

> I am very alarmed at your second telegram about planning war against the Bolsheviks. The Cabinet have never authorised such a proposal. They have never contemplated anything beyond supplying Armies on anti-Bolshevik areas in Russia with necessary equipment to enable them to hold their own . . . and I also want you to bear in mind that the War Office reported to the Cabinet that according to their information intervention was driving the anti-Bolshevik parties into the ranks of the Bolsheviks. . . .

He warned Churchill 'not to commit this country to what would be a purely mad enterprise, out of hatred of Bolshevik principles.'

Churchill sharply reminded the Prime Minister that he, Lloyd George, had told the Cabinet that Britain was making war on the Bolsheviks and pointed out that he, as War Minister, was simply preparing a brief on resources and possibilities which the Supreme War Council could consider.

In November 1918 Allied ships had sailed up the Dardanelles and Constantinople had been occupied. Through the Black Sea, now opened, French troops disembarked at Odessa. They fraternized with Russian revolutionaries, and before long the French Black Sea Fleet mutinied. Truly, thought Churchill, Bolshevism is an infectious thing. Introducing his Army Estimates in the House of Commons in March 1919, Churchill said that the British Expeditionary Force in Russia could not leave 'that ice-bound shore' until summer and in the meantime must be kept supplied. On 20th May he gave the House an optimistic estimate of Admiral Koltchak's progress ' . . . the prospect of a far better solution of our own problems than we could ever see before. Whereas a few months ago our only plan was to withdraw our troops and carry with them as refugees 30,000 or 40,000 inhabitants upon whom the Bolsheviks would have wreaked vengeance—people, that is to say, who have been friendly to us and who had worked for us at the time of the German war—there is now a good prospect of the whole of North Russia becoming self-supporting within a reasonable time, and of purely Russian forces maintaining themselves against the Bolsheviks in that theatre.'

Six days later the Supreme War Council expressed themselves willing to help Admiral Koltchak and his forces 'with munitions, supplies and food, to establish themselves as the Government of all Russia.' Admiral Koltchak, of course, accepted the offer and Churchill threw himself—with undisguised enthusiasm—into its implementation.

'Churchill,' said Lloyd George irritably, 'has Bolshevism on the brain.' Within weeks Koltchak was in full retreat, and when Churchill rose in the House of Commons on 29th July 1919 to ask for a supplementary vote of £107,000,000 he was under fire from all sides. J. R. Clynes warned Churchill that the combined forces of the miners, railwaymen and transport workers, 'a formidable organization' had just passed a resolution calling for a general strike to bring intervention in Russia to an end.

Churchill stood by his guns. The states bordering on Russia, he said, would certainly have to bear the brunt of Bolshevist fury but for the fact that they were preoccupied in fighting the White Russians; but for this, the Allied powers would have to send reinforcements to protect them, since they were wards now of the League of Nations. Denikin, on the Southern Front, had taken 'an enormous area of country, where he has been welcomed by great masses of people.' On 10th August General Ironside, by an offensive at the River Dwina, created a diversion which made possible the successful evacuation of the British Expeditionary Force. But it was not the end. Denikin was advancing and a General Yudenitch with a combined force of White Russians and Esthonians was advancing on Petrograd.

There is little doubt that, but for the restraining hand of the Prime Minister, Churchill would have encouraged continually increased intervention in Russia. In September 1919 Lloyd George begged him 'to throw off this obsession which, if you will forgive me saying so, is upsetting your balance.'

Churchill suggested using the Baltic States as springboards for attack. Lloyd George was horrified. 'You want us to recognize their independence in return for their attacking the Bolsheviks? They would ask us to (1) *guarantee* it, (2) supply them with equipment and cash to fight with. And in the end whoever won in Russia, the Government there would promptly recover the old Russian Baltic ports. Are you, Mr. Churchill, prepared to have a war with perhaps an anti-Bolshevik Government of Russia to prevent that?'

In the event, all these questions were answered by the Russians themselves. The White Russians lost the day, the vast continent was overrun by the Bolshevists and a vast bloodbath began. Churchill's estimation of what Communist revolution would mean to Russia and to the world was near the mark, but unchecked, his enthusiasm for intervention would have been disastrous. Britain had neither the men nor the money for such an adventure, and even if she had, the temper of the workers would never have allowed it. Uppermost in the minds of those who watched Churchill at this juncture were memories of Antwerp and the Dardanelles. Who were we to decide what sort of government the Russians should have? If we abrogated to ourselves such a right, where would the precedent take us? Churchill's reputation for instability and impulsiveness was not helped by this situation. The Russians never forgave him, while at home the Labour Party stigmatized him as the enemy of the 'proletariat'.

The romantic emotionalism of the Labour Party towards the Bolshevik Revolution became the roots of Mr. Churchill's strong anti-Socialist bias, which was to grow stronger with the years. The Bolsheviks seized power by terrorism and in subsequent years maintained and extended that dominion by the same methods, precisely as Mr. Churchill forecast in a historic speech to the House of Commons during a stormy debate on Army Estimates:

We are bound to take sides . . . neither can we remain indifferent to the general aspects of Bolshevism. Bolshevism is not a policy; it is a disease. It is not a creed; it is a pestilence. It presents all the characteristics of a pestilence. It breaks out with great sudden-ness; it is violently contagious; it throws people into a frenzy of excitement; it spreads with extraordinary rapidity; the mortality is terrible. . . .

So far as that prophecy goes, it may be said to be accurate. It did spread. It engulfed vast continents. It engaged in endless 'purges' to eliminate opposition present and potential. But Mr. Churchill, like many others, hoped that his own vehement opposition was the measure of Communism's inevitable decline:

> Like other pestilences, the disease tends to wear itself out. The populations of the regions devastated by its first fury are left in a sort of stupor. Then gradually and painfully they begin to recover their sanity; they are feeble, they are shattered; and the light of human reason once again comes back to their eyes. Those regions which have been most afflicted by the fury of this storm are the first to recover, and having once recovered—let my honourable and gallant Friend mark this—they are specially immune from all subsequent attacks.
> Col. Wedgwood: Would it cure my right honourable and gallant Friend from reverting to Liberalism?
> Mr. Churchill: Thus Bolshevism is dying out in all the original centres of its power, and is keeping itself alive only by finding new areas to ravage and new populations to devour . . . thus great and terrible suffering attends the closing stages of the disease, but this suffering is the prelude to recovery. It is this recovery which we are endeavouring to aid in Russia. We are, for that purpose, supporting all the anti-Bolshevist forces now in the field. . . .

Mr. Churchill went on to tell the House that following the victory of the anti-Bolshevist forces in Russia, the 'five great victorious powers' would insist on the summoning there of a Constituent Assembly on a democratic franchise.

The assumption that the new fanaticism would spend itself was entertained by many other great statesmen; the fatal combination of an ideology which captured men's minds and a one-party bureaucracy sustained by a secret police, which could enslave people's bodies, had not been seen fully in operation. Nor had the cumulative disgust of ordinary people at the corruption of churches and the flaunting arrogance of rulers been correctly assessed. After all, Mr. Lloyd George, the Prime Minister, told the House on 16th April 1919:

> Bolshevism itself is rapidly on the wane. It is breaking down before the relentless pressure of economic facts. This process must inevitably continue. . . .

The weight of responsibility which Mr. Churchill had to carry at this time was so great that, even allowing for his confidence and superb physical and mental stamina, one wonders how it was possible to carry it. Within a single fortnight, for example, between 19th May and 6th June 1919, he had to speak in the House on no less than two hundred occasions. Admittedly some of those speeches were replies to questions, but equally some perorations ran to thousands of words, involving much research and thought. And on top of all this he had the day-to-day work at the War Office itself.

Churchill came heavily under fire from M.P.s in respect of a circular which he caused to be sent to Army commanders:

Secret and Urgent

I am directed to request that until further notice you will furnish information on the headings hereunder as regards the troops in your area and that you will arrange for a report to reach this office without fail not later than first post each Thursday morning.

Some of the points on which information was requested were:

(a) Will troops in various areas respond to orders for assistance to preserve the public peace?
(b) Will they assist in strike breaking?
(c) Will they parade for draft to overseas, especially to Russia ?

This directive was to be forwarded to all officers commanding Stations, Formations and Units in command areas. And the following was also issued to Station Commanders:

Will you please let me have the following information . . . with regard to the Units on the Station under your command:
(a) Whether there is any growth of trade unionism among them.
(b) The effect outside trade unions have on them.
(c) Whether any agitation from internal or external sources is affecting them.
(d) Whether any soldiers' councils have been formed.
(e) Whether any demobilisation troubles are occurring and if so (1) what troops are demonstrating; (2) the numbers involved; (3) what their grievances are; (4) what has been done.

Mr. Adamson, raising the matter, asked, 'Did the Secretary of State for War expect that because they had gone into the Army they

14

Post-war Problems

'I have always made myself the spokesman for the greatest possible freedom of debate even if it should lead to sharp encounters and hard words,' Churchill once said. He spoke in the House directly and with force. Once Woodrow Wyatt, M.P., who had criticized him severely in the debating chamber, came up to him in the lobby and said that he hoped he had not been too hard. 'I ask for no quarter and I bear no malice,' Churchill growled.

In the period immediately following the First World War, Churchill was not always at his witty best. The weight of responsibility was too great, and the tragic post-war problems which fell to him to solve hardly lent themselves to light-hearted treatment.

As a War Minister he was one of the best, perhaps the best, Britain had ever had. The mistakes he made as a comparative amateur were trifling compared with those made by brasshats who had spent their lives in the Army. Some of the worst features of Army life were cleaned up by his reforming hand.

In presenting the immense estimates in 1919 he had a difficult time. Almost vainly, he tried to assure Members of Parliament that there was still a need for an Army although the war was over. 'There have been several difficulties in framing the Army Estimates for this year. We are halfway between peace and war. Almost every factor with which we have to deal is uncertain and fluctuating . . . the greater part of Europe and the greater part of Asia are plunged in varying degrees of disorder and anarchy. Vast areas in both these Continents... are convulsed by hunger, bankruptcy and revolution.' He quoted two adages:

Do not be carried away by success into demanding or taking more than is right or prudent.
Do not disband your army until you have got your terms.

And he coined two adages of his own: 'The finest combination in the world is power and mercy. The worst combination in the world is weakness and strife.'

His analysis of the state of the world and the uncertainties of 'peace' attracted much sceptical scrutiny. Sir Donald Maclean pointed out that the Army's cost would be ten times more than it was in the last pre-war Army statement. Allowing for the cost of pensions and separation allowances, it amounted to £400,000,000 —'a staggering sum'. Mr. Hogge congratulated Mr. Churchill 'on having put into an hour a great scheme of this kind. It is not every Minister who can spend £500,000,000 inside an hour, as my hon. Friend did this afternoon.' To this Mr. Churchill replied that his 'honourable Friend' would have been more accurate to have said that Mr. Churchill had *saved* £500,000,000 in an hour, as 'vast as the expenditure is, it is practically half of the expenditure of the year that has just closed,' an argument which took no account of the fact that the war was supposed to be over.

Mr. Churchill, as a result of pressure from some Members, appointed a Committee of Enquiry into the Army's method of running courts-martial.

Mr. Bottomley told of a young man, scarcely sixteen when he joined up in 1914, invalided out after some tough fighting and being wounded, and after surgical treatment re-enlisted. He was charged with disobeying an order. The first hearing—comparable with a civilian's preliminary appearance in a magistrate's court— was before superior officers when he was not allowed to speak on his own behalf, or to be represented. At the court-martial he was given as defence a junior officer who could spare only half an hour. In rank, therefore, defending 'counsel' was subordinate to the President of the Court, who interrupted his eloquent speech of defence by the peremptory order, 'I wish you would take your hands out of your pockets, Sir'—a trivial point to raise when a man's life was at stake, for the original charge of disobedience had been changed (without the soldier being informed of it until the actual court-martial took place) to one of cowardice in the face of the enemy, an offence punishable by death. He was found guilty and sentenced to death. Fortunately Field-Marshal Haig, on examining the documents of the trial when it came to confirming the sentence, felt the trial had not been a fair one and commuted the sentence to one of ten years' imprisonment. This was subsequently reduced to two years, and later scrapped altogether.

'But for the action of the Field-Marshal that gallant young officer, whose record is a magnificent one, would have suffered the death penalty without being allowed by the rules and regulations to write to his relatives on the night before his execution. He has no right to tell his friends that he is lying under sentence of death and he is not allowed to do anything to obtain assistance outside the theatre of war.'

Major Hayward, only recently back from the Front, questioned Mr. Churchill about the infamous and degrading Field Punishment No. 1 under which a soldier had to carry on fighting, but would be pulled out of the ranks for two hours a day on three successive days and his hands and feet tied. Apart from the discomfort, which could be extreme according to the zeal or vindictiveness of those entrusted with the task of inflicting the punishment, there was the humiliation. 'I have seen men tied up in the public streets in France, and to gateways facing the street and French civilians and French children passing during the time,' Major Hayward told Churchill. 'I have seen men tied up to sign-posts in the middle of a French village. . . .' And of one victim he declared, 'I saw him undergoing the punishment and he saw I saw him, and ever afterwards when I met him a look came into his eyes like the look of a wounded, stricken dog.'

Mr. Bottomley, incidentally, quoted the case of a young officer who was sentenced to death and executed, when had he been given an adequate defence he would certainly, in the light of facts which were disclosed later, have been acquitted.

Mr. Churchill pressed energetically forward with reforms which guaranteed an end to such abuses.

In 1921 Churchill became Colonial Secretary on the resignation of Lord Milner. One of his first jobs was to go to Cairo to sort out the muddle created by contradictory pledges given to the Arabs in return for their support for the Allied cause. The Conference over which Churchill presided appointed the Arab King Feisal to rule over the new state of Iraq, Churchill working hand-in-glove with the romantic eccentric, Lawrence of Arabia. He came away with a presentation copy of *The Seven Pillars of Wisdom* and the knowledge that, by devising a scheme for the protecting of Iraq by the Royal Air Force, he had cut Britain's bill in Iraq from £40,000,000 to £5,000,000.

But Britain owes another long-forgotten debt to Churchill. Although an avowed Imperialist (he had soft-pedalled somewhat on this because of his alliance with the Liberals, the only party which at the early stages of his political career appeared to offer scope) he was tired of the long-drawn-out agony of Ireland. Irish efforts at self-rule had been harshly put down by Sir Hamar Greenwood, whose 'Black and Tans'—so called because they wore khaki uniforms and black belts—attempted to crush the Irish Republic Army (IRA) with terror, torture and wanton destruction. Arthur Griffith, Michael Collins and Eamon de Valera were leaders of the party aiming at political unity. The IRA also resorted to much ruthlessness in pursuit of its programme; members of the Royal Irish Constabulary were ambushed, assassinated, kidnapped or their families terrorized.

Repression sparked off revenge, and revenge brought fresh terror by way of reprisal. There seemed no end to it, and few people of conscience in England could avoid feelings of shame at stories of the things done in their name. By winter 1920 martial law was declared and in December the hated Black and Tans burned the city of Cork. During 1921 the situation deteriorated and there was a widespread desire in England to see an end to the whole miserable business, subject to Ulster, predominately Protestant, not being left to the mercies of their Roman Catholic kindred over the border.

With Lloyd George's support, Churchill conducted delicate negotiations with the IRA leaders, culminating in 'Articles for Agreement of a Treaty' by which Ireland became the 'Irish Free State' with the status of a Dominion comparable with that enjoyed by Canada, Northern Ireland being given the option of retaining its status outside of the Republic if it so wished.

When Collins, Griffifth and de Valera came to London to see Churchill they did so with hearts full of bitterness and suspicion. One night Collins and Griffifth came to Churchill's London house to meet Lloyd George. Lord Birkenhead and Churchill were left with Collins, who was seething with pent-up fury. 'You hunted me day and night; you put a price on my head!' he hissed at Churchill.

'Wait a minute,' said Churchill, 'you were not the only one.' He produced a framed copy of the reward notice issued by the Boers when Churchill was on the run, offering £25 for his capture dead or alive. At least, said Churchill, with a disarming grin, the British had thought Collins worth £5,000—two hundred times as much as

Churchill! The ice was broken and they talked as honourable protagonists.

The Treaty was not the end of all troubles, for Ireland was to know the full horrors of civil war and Irishman fought Irishman until 1922 when at last things settled down. But Churchill, despite his reputation in some quarters as a reactionary and dyed-in-the-wool last-ditcher, did not waver from his aspiration of freedom for the Irish. He understood their fierce pride and respected their ancient history. In moving the Irish Free State Bill he reminded Members how insuperable the problem had seemed to be before the war. 'Then came the Great War. . . . Every institution, almost, in the world was strained. Great Empires have been overturned. The whole map of Europe has been changed. The position of countries has been violently altered . . . but as the deluge subsides we see the dreary steeples of Fermanagh and Tyrone emerging once again. The integrity of their quarrel is one of the few institutions that have been unaltered in the cataclysm which has swept the world. . . .'

But trouble continued in Ireland, in the form of war between the provisional government of the newly-formed Irish Free State and the rebels against its authority. Churchill's hard and patient effort to bring peace seemed destroyed by a single shot when, in June 1922, Field-Marshal Sir Henry Wilson, who had recently finished his term as Chief of the Imperial General Staff, was shot dead outside his home in Eaton Square by two assassins who were caught red-handed and found to be Irishmen.

Churchill faced a grim House of Commons. Where were his fine words now? Once more a picture of rosy hopes, said his critics, had culminated in disaster; he seemed to have a special genius for underestimating risks. Were these the sort of Irishmen who were to be given equality in the Commonwealth?

But he did not lose his head. The gravity of the murder he fully acknowledged. His problem was to bring home to the newly-formed Government their obligation to keep order without resorting to the sort of language which would be taken as a threat and provide ammunition to that Government's own enemies at home.

I should not be dealing honestly and fully with this subject if I left in the minds of the House the impression that all that is needed is patience and composure. No, Sir. Firmness is needed in the interests of peace as much as patience. The constitution which has been published, satisfactorily conforms to the Treaty. It has now to be passed through the new Irish Parliament. There is no room for the slightest diminution of the Imperial and Constitutional safeguards which it contains. . . . The resources at the disposal of His Majesty's Government are various and powerful. They are military, economic and financial sanctions . . . hitherto we have been dealing with a Government weak because it had no contact with the people . . . but now the Provisional Government is greatly strengthened.

It is armed with the declared will of the Irish Electorate. It is supported by an effective Parliamentary majority. It is its duty to give effect to the Treaty in the letter and in the spirit. . . . A much stricter reckoning must rule henceforward. The ambiguous position of the so-called Irish Republican Army, intermingled as it is with Free State Troops, is an affront to the Treaty. The presence in Dublin in violent occupation of the Four Courts, of a band of men styling themselves the Headquarters of the Republican Executive, is a gross breach and defiance of the Treaty. From this nest of anarchy and treason, not only to the British Crown but to the Irish people, murderous outrages are stimulated and encouraged, not only in the twenty-six counties, not only in the territory of the Northern Government, but even, it seems most probable, here across the Channel in Great Britain. . . .

If either from weakness, from want of courage or for some other even less creditable reason, it is not brought to an end, and a very speedy end, then it is my duty to say, on behalf of His Majesty's Government, that we shall regard the Treaty as having been formally violated, that we shall take no steps to carry out or legalise its further stages, and that we shall resume full liberty of action in any direction that may seem proper and to any extent that may be necessary to safeguard the interests and rights that are entrusted to our care. . . .

The House listened with growing respect. What else could they, in his position, have done or said? In effect he was saying to Ireland: 'You have your freedom. You have no excuse—if ever there was excuse—for terrorism now. Stop the terror, or we shall both be back where we started. And we shall play it tough.'

Churchill continued to encourage Collins. 'This has been a terrible ordeal for you,' he wrote. 'But I believe that the action you have taken with so much resolution and coolness was indispensable if Ireland was to be saved from anarchy and the Treaty from destruction. We had reached the end of our tether over here at the same time as you had in Ireland. I could not have sustained another debate in the House of Commons on the old lines without fatal consequences to the existing governing instrument in Britain, and the Treaty would have fallen too. Now all is changed. Ireland will be mistress in her own house. . .'

In August Collins was shot by an Irish terrorist, a fate he had foreseen, since he had been accused of treachery in negotiating with the British. Only a day or so before this happened he had sent a message to Churchill: 'Tell Winston we could never have done anything without him.'

A crisis called then the Chanak crisis, now long forgotten, brought Churchill's Parliamentary career to an unexpected and temporary end. Turkey, who had fought against Britain in the war, had under the Treaty of Sevres been forced to agree to the break-up of the Ottoman Empire. A garrison of British, French and Italians was stationed in Constantinople and in part of the Dardanelles known as Chanak. The Turkish revolutionary, Mustapha Kemal—later President of the Turkish Republic—refused to acknowledge the Treaty as a result of which a Greek Army, encouraged by Lloyd George and the Allies, joined issue with the Turks.

The Greeks were routed and Kemal's forces bid to move outwards into Europe. The legend of 'the terrible Turk' and memories of their wholesale massacre of the wretched Armenians were still fresh in European memories. Churchill, like Lloyd George, was convinced that the Turks must be contained within their own territories and that if they were not they might start a Balkan war. He wanted reinforcements to be sent straightway to Constantinople and for the British Fleet to proceed to the sea of Marmora and open fire if need be.

Churchill was a realist, but the British people were not. They were sick and tired of war. When a communiqué setting out British intentions was drafted by Churchill and issued at the request of the Prime Minister to the Press, there was a nation-wide uproar.

What! *Another* Dardanelles? Would nothing stop this fat, noisy, cherubic sabre-rattler from playing at sailors? Here he was breathing fire again and wanting to send the Navy to its doom in Turkish waters again! The closing words of the communiqué read almost like a declaration of war:

. . . It is the intention of His Majesty's Government to reinforce immediately, and if necessary to a considerable extent, the troops at the disposal of Sir Charles Harington, the Allied Commander-in-Chief at Constantinople, and orders have also been given to the British Fleet in the Mediterranean to oppose by every means any infraction of the neutral zones by the Turks or any attempt by them to cross the European shore.

The communiqué was a political bombshell. Bonar Law's Conservatives protested that they would not police the world. Poincaré withdrew his French troops from the Dardanelles.

The Coalition had long been dependent for its existence on Tory support, being already unpopular with the Labour Party and Independent Liberals. Curzon, the Foreign Minister, resigned in protest. Stanley Baldwin, a junior Tory Minister, persuaded Bonar Law to emerge from retirement. A meeting of Conservative M.P.s was held at the Carlton Club on 19th October 1922 at which it was decided to withdraw from the Coalition, which virtually ceased to exist. Lloyd George resigned, and King George V invited Bonar Law to form a Government. Within a month there was a General Election. Mr. Churchill, hardened to election campaigns, was to find it the most remarkable of his mixed and turbulent career.

15

Sans Everything . . .

In the General Election of November 1922 Bonar Law had appealed for 'tranquillity and freedom from adventures and commitments both at home and abroad'. The inference was that Churchill in particular and his associates in general would achieve the opposite. Churchill, as a realist, liked to state a danger plainly. There *was* a danger of the Turks spilling into Europe. The bellicose communiqué which outraged the war-weary British public did inhibit Kemal Attaturk sufficiently to call his troops away from Chanak. Harold Nicolson, in his book on Curzon, says, 'It is sad for any admirer of Lord Curzon to have to admit that he himself can claim no share of this reckless and triumphant gesture. To Mr. Lloyd George and above all to Mr. Churchill is due our gratitude for having at this juncture defied not the whole world merely, but the full hysterical force of public opinion. . . .'

Mr. Churchill was to feel this 'full hysterical force' during his election campaign in Dundee. He was no longer the conquering hero returning from the Boer War. Now he was the political turn-coat, a man who liked 'a whiff of grapeshot', somebody who was against the 'workers' revolution in Russia and ill-disposed to trade unions at home, a military adventurer ready yet again to gamble with men's lives. Churchill had begun to equate Socialism and Bolshevism in his public speeches, forgetting that the Labour Party had only become articulate and organized after centuries during which the working-man was always considered a class apart, first to be exploited and last to be rewarded.

Communists had, of course, begun to infiltrate into trade unions, but their influence was not as widespread as Mr. Churchill alleged.

Shortly before the election Mr. Churchill was taken ill and was rushed off for an operation for appendicitis. His election address had to be sent from a nursing home. It was a terrible ordeal for him to be lying weak and in pain while his political future hung in the balance. With great effort he roused himself from his sick-bed to make a last-minute intervention in the contest. Before a gathering of 4,000 people at Caird Hall in Dundee he was carried in on a sort of improvised 'sedan chair' which was placed on a raised dais on the platform. 'The stopping of the new war in the Near East,' he told them, 'is an achievement which, to my dying day, I shall always be happy to have taken part in.' He apologized for having been kept in London and said he still had two days in which, if strength were granted to him, he would meet every point and every attack.

His speech was long and reasoned and well received. He defended the Coalition's post-war policies, especially the Treaty with Ireland.

But at an eve-of-the-poll meeting the following day, held in the Drill Hall, pandemonium broke out. No quarter was given to the sick man. Abuse, heckling and interruptions rained on him from the beginning and it was impossible for him to get through his speech. The opposition was clearly organized, although only a minority of the five to six thousand audience. Churchill came in wildly cheered by his supporters and booed and hissed by his opponents. Some hecklers were probably Communists, as they raised a counter-cheer for Willy Gallagher, the Communist candidate, and for Mr. Scrymgeour the prohibitionist. Sir Charles Barrie, M.P. for Banffshire, who brought a bouquet of flowers for Mrs. Churchill, was howled down.

With an effort, Mr. Churchill raised himself to speak. A chorus of abuse started. 'The hero of Sidney Street!', 'Good old Gallagher!' During a brief lull he said, 'Ladies and gentlemen (chorus of SHUT UP!!), 'I ask your permission to address you sitting down.' (Cheers and 'give him a hearing' and uproar.) 'I haven't had much chance of prosecuting. . . .' ('Put a sock in it!') 'You might give me fair play. . . .' ('You'll get what you had at Manchester this time!') 'I haven't had much opportunity of prosecuting . . .' (A voice: 'Get on your feet!' Cries of 'Shame!').

'No man is judged unheard in Britain,' Churchill declared, striving for a hearing still, 'and now the election has been in progress for three weeks and I was only able to come here last Saturday, and this is only the second great meeting I have had the chance of addressing. As the poll is on Wednesday . . .' (A VOICE: 'You won't get in.') . . . 'If I am to be at the bottom why should not you at least let me have my last dying kick?'

In vain he appealed for free speech, 'one of the greatest assets of democracy.' Pandemonium broke out again and during a brief lull Churchill said he would not speak unless he was listened to in silence. 'If about a hundred young men and women in the audience choose to spoil the meeting—if about a hundred of these young reptiles' (uproar) . . .

Now Churchill's temper was really up. Stung by their insults, smarting at the utter hooliganism at refusing him his limited hearing, for which he had come prematurely from a sick bed, he would spare them nothing. 'Now,' he yelled, 'you see what the Gallagher crowd are worth! (applause and uproar); now you see the liberty you would have if the country were run by them! (cheers and boos) Ah, boo—no sense, no brain (uproar) just break up a meeting (Boo!) The electors will know how to deal with a party whose only weapon is idiotic clamour. . . .'

As the uproar continued Mr. Churchill leaned back in his seat and said, 'I give way.' Some questions were asked, why a workman should have to stamp his card, why working men were so poorly paid. . . .

'Were you not,' demanded a heckler who got on to the platform and pointed an accusing finger at Churchill, 'were you not one of the British Cabinet that Lord Robert Cecil accused of giving a free hand to the Black and Tans of Ireland to beat the women and children down?'

Churchill, after more interruptions, told the audience, 'I say that when our soldiers and our policemen were shot down and murdered we had the right to strike back to defend ourselves.'

The air was now electric. 'Murderer!' screamed one heckler. Another yelled, 'We got medals for fighting. You got them for running away.'

Wearily, Churchill waited for the dreary wail of 'The Red Flag' to die down, and having told the crowd, 'We will not submit to the bullying tyranny of the feather-heads, we will not be ruled by the mob' he was escorted by police to the back door amidst cheers and catcalls.

The following day Mr. Churchill attacked Mr. Thomson, proprietor of the Dundee newspapers, for refusing an election advertisement. He did not mince his words. 'Here we get in the morning the Liberal Mr. Thomson through the Liberal *Dundee Advertiser* advising the electors of Dundee to be very careful not to give a vote to Mr. Churchill because his Liberalism is not quite orthodox. . . . At the same time you have the Conservative, the 'die-hard' Mr. Thomson, through the columns of the Conservative *Dundee Courier* advising the Conservative electors of Dundee to be very careful not to give a vote to Mr. Churchill . . . behind these two, I say, you get one single individual, narrow, bitter, unreasonable, eaten up with his own conceit, consumed with his own petty arrogance and consumed from day to day and from year to year by an unrelenting bee in his bonnet.' Then, to the reporters present: 'Now put *that* down for the *Dundee Advertiser* and the *Dundee Courier!*'

He complained of 'two years of ceaseless detraction, spiteful, malicious detraction. Anything I have done for this city . . . has been whittled away or crabbed or put in some obscure position in relation . . . I do not speak against the papers . . . but against the man behind the papers, and he is the man I hold up here in the district where he lives to the reprobation of his fellow-citizens. . . .'

It was a foolish, almost an incoherent, speech. How often had Churchill fulminated in print and out of print against people and policies he disliked!

The outcome could be foreseen. Mr. Churchill was beaten. The alcohol-hating Mr. Scrymgeour, after years of fruitless efforts, had won the day (VOTE FOR SCRYMGEOUR AND NO BEER! workers had chalked up on the walls). One of Churchill's supporters ran over and killed a black cat with her car, after which nobody expected much. And so it was, as Churchill put it when in slightly better humour, he found himself 'without an office, without a seat, without a party and without an appendix.'

In the polling 345 Conservatives and 142 Labour members were returned, Mr. Ramsay MacDonald being elected leader of the Parliamentary Labour Party and Bonar Law being Prime Minister. Mr. Stanley Baldwin was Chancellor of the Exchequer. Both were to play an increasingly significant part in the House of Commons. Churchill glowered on the scene with undisguised envy. The House of Commons was his home, and he was determined to return.

How often in history the leading actors steal in from the wings scarcely noticed. Somebody called Mussolini had taken over as Premier in Italy, while the homely pipe-sucking, farmer-type Stanley Baldwin considered Britain's financial position. His negotiations with the United States on the subject of war debts were adjudged a success by some and an abdication by others, but when Bonar Law resigned as Prime Minister in May 1923 on account of ill health (he died the following November) it was Baldwin who was asked by King George V to form a Government. A General Election was held in December, Baldwin deciding that the issue should be protective tariffs to give British trade a respite from foreign competition and so—it was said—alleviate Britain's chronic unemployment problem.

This unemployment problem, and the natural tactics of both Socialists and Communists to gain members by espousing the cause of the unemployed, produced that association between Communism, Socialism and Trade Unionism in Churchill's mind which he never entirely shook off. In these early days there was more substance in his suspicions—or, rather, outspoken aversion—than many imagined. The various unemployed workers' movements were firmly in Communist hands. Communist agitators such as Alexander Zuzenko were inveigled into England with the help of members of the Communist Party of Great Britain (in his case, complete with credentials from Lenin sewn up inside his clothing). Communists operating under Labour Party membership tickets organized Labour support of Communist candidates—Shapurji Saklatvala who won Battersea North for the Communists in 1922 was sponsored by the local Labour Party. European Communist Parties within the Comintern were being urged to whip up class warfare by every means in their power; the revolution in Russia confirmed Lenin's theory that the chaos and confusion of class warfare made a country vulnerable to a bold Communist take-over. In Britain's case the disillusionment of war's aftermath was an added factor.

In this General Election Mr. Churchill stood as Liberal candidate for Leicester West. He was too disgusted even to consider standing for Dundee again. But in supposing that Leicester might prove a better bet he was sadly mistaken. The anti-Bolshevist obsession of his was a good stick with which to beat him; even among many Liberals the illusion that Russia was a workers' paradise persisted; and amongst those who had no illusions about Communism there was the feeling that Churchill was dangerously disposed to get mixed up in another country's internal affairs for the mere pleasure or excitement of it. Dr. Addison, speaking for the Labour Party, raised many a laugh by his references to Churchill 'seeing red'.

But Churchill injected many a laugh into his meetings. At one, he said he had done his best to familiarize himself with the constituency. A voice from the crowd called encouragingly, 'You'll get a place', to which Churchill replied, 'I might get a win or a place.' On Protection, he said that Baldwin claimed it was to be temporary and Lord Derby had said it was to be permanent. (A Voice: 'What does Ramsay MacDonald say?') 'Mr. MacDonald,' Churchill said, amidst roars of laughter, 'has said a lot of things, but I am trying to keep off controversial subjects tonight—it's my birthday.' Churchill made the most of Lord Derby's claim to be a Free Trader but 'not a bigoted Free Trader'. 'It reminds me of the man who was a teetotaller but not a bigoted teetotaller.'

Organized rowdyism was a feature at many of his meetings. 'What about Antwerp?' 'How about the Dardanelles?' were standard interruptions. Children, too, caught the popular anti-Churchill mania. Outside Cristow-street School he was mobbed by children. 'Got a cigarette card, Guv'nor?' yelled one boy, and the question was a signal for a deafening chorus of catcalls, boos and shrieks. Placards outside the Committee Room were kicked down and in true electioneering spirit the youngsters sang in unison:

Vote, Vote, Vote for Pethick Lawrence,
Chuck old Churchill in the sea. . . .

But at this childish exuberance, Churchill grinned broadly.

The rowdiness he experienced in London was more dangerous. Speaking at political gatherings at Finsbury Park, Shepherd's Bush and Walthamstow he encountered pandemonium and actual violence. At Finsbury Park a heckler smashed a window of his car. 'I can't shy a stone at every dog that barks' Churchill growled at one interrupter. He dismissed the 'sheer impudence' of Socialist 'parrot-cries' and declared that it was a delusion to suppose that by shutting out imports more work would be made at home. Imports had to be paid for by exports, produced by sweat and skill. 'What have you done?' yelled a heckler. 'I have made as large a contribution as the Tired Tim and Weary Willie who interrupts me.' After the meeting at Walthamstow Mr. Churchill had to be escorted from the hall to his car by mounted police. 'The whole question of preventing this sort of organized, cold-blooded rowdiness will have to be considered by the new Parliament,' Churchill declared; 'the right of public meeting is one of the most valuable which the British democracy possesses. . . . The interrupters were working to a plan; they asked the same questions and made the same interruptions. They have all been taught in the same centre what they are to do . . .'

At his meetings Mrs. Churchill would support him with cheerfulness and—at times, as necessary—spirited defence. An observer described her as 'tall and slim, with handsome, clear-eyed features and a very sweet lingering smile that every member of the audience feels is personally addressed to him or her.' But she could scarcely feel so sweet-tempered all the time. To hear her husband insulted at Dundee, where he had left a sick bed after a painful operation to address his audience, was not easy. And in this election campaign, she was not going to stand idly by while Winston was attacked.

'Perhaps,' she told a Leicester audience, 'your Free Trade swords have grown rusty with lying by for so long but you must get them out and polish them up. There was a man at one of his meetings who said my husband was not fit to represent the working classes. Well, I am not a politician, but I must say my blood boiled when I heard that. I have consulted Whittaker's and with the single exception of Lloyd George my husband has been responsible for the passing of more legislation for the benefit of the working class than any other living statesman.' She instanced the Sweated Industries Act of 1909, the Labour Exchanges, the Coal Mines Regulation Act and the Shop Hours Act, all of which had removed or mitigated widespread hardship and hazard.

But when it came to the count, Churchill had lost again with his 9,236 votes as compared with Mr. Pethick Lawrence who won the day for Labour, and the Unionist candidate, Captain Instone, who polled 7,696 votes.

The tide of politics was changing course. The Conservatives this time secured only 258 seats in the House, the newly-united Liberals 159 and—significantly—the Labour Party gained 191 seats.

The Liberals felt that, having opposed the Conservatives on the issue of Protective tariffs, they could only side logically with the Labour Party. This wooing was not at all to Churchill's liking, and he broke with the Liberals, declaring himself a Constitutionalist and fighting the Abbey Division of Westminster as 'Independent and Anti-Socialist' in March 1924.

Whatever else could be said of him, nobody could question his astonishing persistence. Rejected and abused in two elections, he came up for more, a chorus of disparagement ringing in his ears. Thundered the *Morning Post*: 'Mr. Churchill has been a political wrecker. He has never served under any chief with wholehearted loyalty . . . he sees himself first and cause and comrades as subordinates. No one has ever felt safe with him.'

Three days later he knew that Westminster was to be no more genteel than Dundee or Leicester. At a meeting convened by the Westminster Branch of the League of Nations at Essex Hall, he was howled down and unable to speak. He was escorted to his car by police, amidst jeers and hisses, and the same day at Pepys Hall, Rochester Row, the same unruly clamour drowned his voice. There were cries of 'Traitor!' 'Sit down, you dog!' and 'We don't want you!' In vain he warned them, 'If you substitute violence and clamour for talk, then you are bound to lose the institutions which have always been the glory of this country.'

Churchill's intense individualism made it difficult for any Party to back him effectively. The *Daily News* grumbled, 'Mr. Churchill appears to be trying hard to make the best of every possible world. He is a Liberal, a Constitutionalist, an anti-Socialist and a pro-Conservative. . . .'

Patiently, often belligerently, he pursued his campaign. His anti-Socialist stand provoked attention and usually hostility. At Drury Lane he was booed, especially by two militant Suffragette-type women and by a young, dark-haired man with a husky voice who repeatedly shook his fist at Churchill. Churchill's anti-Socialist sallies brought yells from 'the gods' (topmost gallery of the theatre). 'One-tenth of the dose of Socialism which ruined Russia (A Voice: 'Liar!') would kill Great Britain stone dead. How well the Socialist Government is doing! How moderate, how gentle they are! How patriotic Mr. Thomas's speeches are! How lofty Mr. Thomas's views of his functions. How pious is Mr. Henderson, how prudent Mr. Snowden—left to themselves Mr. MacDonald and his leading colleagues . . . would be swept away and replaced by those dark figures which in every country are lurking in the background.'

At the Victoria Palace his friend Major-General Seely spoke in defence of Churchill's war record: 'I have seen him, month after month, as a humble battalion commander in the front line. If he had a fault, it was that he was too reckless.' (Loud applause, during which one ex-Service man stood up and yelled, 'Good old Winston!')

With Mrs. Churchill, he drove through Soho, where Jimmy

Wilde, the famous boxer, spoke on his behalf. 'Boys, vote for Churchill is what I am going to do. You do the same.' But as Churchill began speaking he was constantly interrupted. 'Give him a chance,' said Wilde, rubbing his knuckles appraisingly, 'be sports.' It must be confessed that Winston's description of his political orientation was almost all-embracing. 'I stand for a united Conservative Party with a Liberal Wing, both standing on a broad and progressive platform. . . .'

Jerome K. Jerome, the famous author and an Abbey Division voter, sent a telegram of support to the Socialist candidate Fenner Brockway: 'When thieves fall out there is a chance for honest men.' As Mr. Churchill was motoring through King Street, Covent Garden, late at night, several men sprang forward from the shadows and there was a scuffle between them and Churchill's supporters, in which one of Churchill's friends was wounded below the knee with a knife.

WESTMINSTER WANTS WINSTON declared the true-blue posters. But did it? On the day of the count Mr. and Mrs. Churchill waited in the early hours of the morning at Abbey Hall. It was known that the figures would be very close and tension mounted as the scrutineers, at twelve tables, received the totals. It was soon apparent that 100 or even 60 votes could bring victory to one or the other. Churchill showed signs of nervous strain. Whispers went around that Churchill had won; there followed a fierce denial from Mr. Nicholson's supporters. Then, as the last figures were brought up to the scrutineer's table somebody dashed up to Churchill and told him, 'You're in, sir!' Beaming happily, Churchill sought out Mrs. Churchill and told her the good news. It seemed the figures gave him a majority of 130 but the figures were not yet official. Then came an announcement that Mr. Churchill had lost by 33 votes, and congratulations were switched to his rival, Mr. Nicholson. Churchill, still smiling, puffed at his cigar and awaited a checking of the figures. Then, realizing his position, he went very pale and gazed moodily at the floor. The recount confirmed Mr. Nicholson's majority as 43 and not 33 votes. At a subsequent meeting Churchill 'had difficulty in controlling the emotion in his voice'.

For the third time he had been rejected. For the third time the tumult and fatigue of an election campaign had been in vain. Not that there was much sympathy forthcoming. As the *Daily News* put it: 'We cannot pretend to regret the result . . . the only result of the anti-Socialist campaign which Mr. Churchill preached with such strident violence will be, if persisted in, to split the nation into two warring camps.'

But the trend of political balance in Parliament was now proving more favourable to Churchill. He had *nearly* got in at Westminster. Now the Liberals were tired of being the tin can on the end of the Socialist dog's tail. They withdrew their support, and the Labour Party, conscious of its growing strength and tired of the necessity of being propped by a rival and unpredictable political party, was not reluctant to try for even more public support.

MacDonald's Socialism was, inevitably, mild. His short-lived Government had never been self-sufficient, hence his sophistry when reproached with timidity at an Albert Hall meeting: 'One step enough for me. One step! Yes, my friends, on one condition— that it leads to the next step.'

And so, on 27th September 1924 the *West Essex Gazette* carried this surprising intelligence:

'A POLITICAL BOMBSHELL
Mr. Winston Churchill to Stand for Epping.'

The West Essex Unionist Association had adopted Churchill as Unionist and Anti-Socialist Candidate, and at Loughton he defended vigorously his right to change his party: 'The circumstances and conditions under which I have come forward are similar to those which in 1886 caused men like Mr. Joseph Chamberlain, The Marquis of Hartington and other prominent Liberals to think it their duty to stand with the Conservative Party to repel evil and danger to the structure of the British Empire. . . .' He condemned the proposed loan of over £30,000,000 to Russia. 'We are not like the people in Russia, who are only living like maggots in a cheese,' he said, amidst laughter.

A powerful factor in the General Election—particularly in Churchill's case because of his anti-Bolshevism and anti-Socialism— was the publication, four days before the election, of the now-famous 'Zinoviev Letter'. It was alleged to be a 'very secret' communication from Grigori Evseyvich, general secretary of the Comintern or Communist Party International, urging the British Communist Party to infiltrate the Labour Party, the Army and the

Navy to ensure 'complete success of an armed insurrection.' The British Foreign Office protested to the Soviet Government about it and the Conservatives made the maximum propaganda out of it in the course of the election campaign.

But at his first meeting at Waltham Abbey he was asked what he meant by saying he stood as a Constitutionalist and Anti-Socialist— 'Is Mr. Churchill standing as a Liberal or Conservative, or is it merely a question of sending his political garments to the dyers to have them freshly coloured?' But now Churchill proclaimed the complete and final abandonment of his Liberal affiliations: 'I am opposed to the official Liberal Party. I opposed it after the last election, when they put the Socialist Government in power. I stand as an opponent of all who associate themselves with the official leaders of the Liberal Party. . . .' (Boos and counter-cheers.)

The picturesque Countess of Warwick, who sallied forth from Warwick Castle to further the Socialist cause, declared herself in favour of the Russian loan. She had, she said, known Winston from boyhood and they called each other by Christian names. But she felt sorry for him. 'He doesn't care for the Conservatives,' she said, 'but wishes to get into public life again. What he has said in the past about the Conservative Party is unspeakable, but now they welcome him. . . .'

But Lord Birkenhead commended his friend Churchill as 'the greatest House of Commons man now living'. Austen Chamberlain sent his good wishes. And this time, as he rode in a coach drawn by four beautiful black horses to the Church Room where the count was made, he heard the wonderful news. This time he was IN by a sweeping majority of 9,763 over his Liberal opponent, G. G. Sharp, and over 16,000 more than the Labour candidate. Now he was beaming and quipping as cheering supporters pulled his car along with a long, stout rope.

And not only was Mr. Churchill in Parliament; he was in the Government—well in. 'I was surprised, and the Conservative Party dumbfounded, when he (Stanley Baldwin, the Prime Minister) invited me to become the Chancellor of the Exchequer, the office which my father once held,' Churchill writes in *The Gathering Storm*.

He certainly was surprised. 'I can offer you the job of Chancellor,' Baldwin had said. 'Of the Duchy?' asked Churchill, in all serious-ness—it was the ornate but ineffectual sinecure to which he had been relegated from the Admiralty during the war. 'No,' said Baldwin, 'of the Exchequer.'

A year earlier Mr. Churchill had written in *The World Crisis*, 'Looking back with after-knowledge and increasing years, I seem to have been too ready to undertake tasks which were hazardous or even forlorn.' A fourth election campaign after three election campaigns lost amidst a welter of abuse would have seemed a forlorn prospect to most reasonable men. But Churchill by sheer pugnacity and self-faith had won through at last, to fulfil, in the fullness of time, Lord Birkenhead's assessment.

16

The General Strike

The Parliament to which Churchill now accounted as Chancellor of the Exchequer was one in which the Liberals declined in power and prestige and the Labour Party, despite its defeat at the polls, grew steadily in power.

Churchill's first budget, introduced on 28th April 1925, was notable for its measures to restore the Gold Standard, its pensions for widows and a sixpenny reduction in income tax which, it was hoped, might give a fillip to industry and so reduce unemployment. The emergence of new industrial competitors such as Germany and Japan, coupled with the slump in the export demand for coal, had produced widespread industrial unrest.

The return to the Gold Standard, said to be a panacea for all this, proved the opposite. It was hoped that by tying the pound to the dollar London would regain its reputation as the financial centre of the world. What was forgotten was that this well-meant but mistaken attempt to recapture pre-1914 economic glory would actually lead to increased unemployment. The pound would be dearer, British goods abroad would be more expensive, and to compete commercially prices would have to be reduced—and so would wages. But Mr. J. M. Keynes, the eminent economist, was almost alone in warning Britain of the dangers ahead in consequence of this move; in *The Economic Consequences of Mr. Churchill* he warned that by giving the pound an artificial value Britain would price herself out of the world's markets.

Churchill was confident of the wisdom of restoring the Gold Standard. 'We are often told that the Gold Standard will shackle us to the United States,' he told the House. 'I will deal with that in a moment. I will tell you what it will shackle us to. It will shackle us to reality. For good or for ill, it will shackle us to reality.' Lloyd George was bitter in his denunciations: 'At this very hour, coalowners and miners have been driven to the brink of a yawning chasm of strife, largely through this deed of egregious recklessness by the Chancellor of the Exchequer.' Keynes called it 'the deliberate intensification of unemployment.'

However Churchill, now a Tory again, got some praise from unlikely quarters. *The Spectator* considered that he had 'suffered a great deal of undeserved abuse' (forgetting that a decade ago it described him as 'a political adventurer . . . with a want of scruple, want of consideration of public interests, and with a reckless selfishness to which our history holds no parallel . . .').

One part of the Chancellor's speech caused an uproar. He said that it was in the interest of trade unions, as long-established contributors to the Unemployment Fund, to see that there should not grow up a habit of qualifying for unemployment benefit. 'For ingenuity and artistry Mr. Churchill's Budget speech in the House of Commons takes a high place . . . it was highly characteristic of the author, an obviously fertile and resourceful brain had been at work. There is no single proposal that is humdrum just as there is no sentence in the speech that was dull. Mr. Churchill must have worked at his speech as though it were a gem or a piece of mosaic. It was beautifully cut, burnished and adapted. . . .'

One happy aspect of Mr. Churchill's office was that by some irony, Mr. Ronald McNeill, who had once thrown a heavy book in Mr. Churchill's face, was now his assistant. It was pleasant, said the *Daily News*, that the vehicle of national finance should be drawn by a lion and a lamb in harness. There was also a pleasant moment when he saw above the fireplace in the Treasury the same painting under which he had stood as a little boy when Lord Randolph Churchill, then Chancellor of the Exchequer, had taken him there.

In the National Liberal Club, however, from which he had resigned in December 1924, a new sort of comedy was enacted. These changes of party allegiance are highly inconvenient to clubs, who like to hang portraits of their more prominent worthies in conspicuous places. A group of members were talking on what to do with Mr. Churchill's portrait, which was hanging on the wall opposite. 'Send it back to the cellar,' said one member. 'Give it to the Carlton,' said another. 'Why bother?' said another, 'Let it stay, but put a brass plate beneath it, recording his changes:

Conservative
Liberal
Coalitionist

Independent
Constitutionalist
Conservative Chancellor

That would be a perfect revenge!'

Mr. Churchill took a good deal of buffeting in the House in the
debates on the Budget, and on occasions was shouted down. Both
Mr. Snowden and MacDonald belaboured him over his reference
to men wanting to qualify for unemployment benefit. Churchill
maintained he had said a 'certain' habit. They insisted that he had
said 'general' habit. Snowden claimed that whatever good the Prime
Minister had achieved by appealing for a new spirit in industry had
been very nearly destroyed by the Chancellor.

These brushes with Snowden were always guaranteed to fill the
Parliamentary benches. M.P.s can survive most things, but not
boredom. Whatever the merits of the respective contestants, a good
fight is always enjoyed, and a controversial speaker better listened to
than a dull one. Snowden in his memoirs admits that he 'found
Mr. Churchill worthy of my steel. . . . Mr. Churchill, during these
years, gradually developed as a Parliamentary debater. He learnt to
rely less on careful preparation of his speeches and more on spontaneous effort. However much one may differ from Mr. Churchill,
one is compelled to like him for his finer qualities. There is an
attractiveness in everything he does. His high spirits are irrepressible.'

At this time Churchill was under heavy fire from the *Daily Mail*.
In an article MR. CHURCHILL'S DOWNFALL: HE HAS
THROWN AWAY HIS CHANCE, Lovat Fraser said, 'He had
the greatest chance of restoring himself in popular estimation ever
given to a statesman with a record full of blemishes, and he has
thrown it away.' It then proceeded to say that the public had long
forgotten his many 'mistakes' (all the worst of which were studiously
recounted). He was, of course, in a difficult position in 'returning
to a Party which did not greet his political repentance with much
cordiality' and did not feel like making a firm stand against his old
political colleagues.

Churchill's second budget, introduced in April 1926, was mainly
notable for a tax on betting, which produced the novel consequence
of a bookmakers' strike!

Hot on the trail of the budget came the General Strike of 1926.

Its main cause was the slump in the coal industry which Keynes had foreseen. Pending the findings of a Royal Commission, which reported in March, the industry had been subsidized. The Commission recommended a small reduction in wages and a thorough reorganization of the industry. Owners wanted reduced wages and longer working hours. The miners refused both and, as no further subsidy was forthcoming from the Treasury, came out on strike at midnight on 30th April. It became more serious when the printers' chapels of the *Daily Mail* refused to print a leader criticizing the miners' action. It was Churchill who informed the Cabinet of this decision, and it resulted in the T.U.C. delegates being sternly warned to repudiate the act of the printers. The delegates withdrew and went away to draft a repudiation of the strike, but on returning to the Cabinet room they found everything in darkness; Baldwin, the Prime Minister, had gone to bed, and the chance of a last-minute reconciliation was lost.

Soon ten million workers in all fields were on strike. Churchill, on the presses of the *Morning Post*, edited an official publication, *The British Gazette*, which appeared from 5th to 13th May, increasing its sales from less than a quarter of a million on the first day to nearly two and a half millions by the end of the strike. It is easy to see the Churchill hand at work in its bold, forthright headlines:

HOLD-UP OF THE NATION
Government and the Nation
No Flinching

And about its pages, every day, were sprinkled quotations from Kipling:

Keep ye the law—be swift in all obedience
Clear the land of evil, drive the road and bridge the ford
Make sure to each his own
That he reap where he hath sown
By the peace among Our Peoples let men know we serve the Lord.

Once more there was that 'whiff of grapeshot' in Churchill's pronouncements. King George V, through Lord Stamfordham, protested to the War Office at a statement in the *British Gazette* that the Military might be used to put down the strike—'an unfortunate announcement'.

The strike was a failure. Although there was some rioting and disturbance, it was, in view of the issues involved, a mild affair and was broken by the enormous amount of voluntary help. Sir Herbert Samuel worked quietly behind the scenes to bring about peace, but the miners continued their strike until November. Starvation forced them to submit, and they had lost all they had attempted to gain— worsened conditions of employment, vanished savings, impaired health, they faced insecurity and some victimization.

J. H. Thomas, the Socialist who later became a great favourite of Tory businessmen, has recorded in his memoirs, *My Story*, Churchill's reaction to the impending strike:

> How strong Winston felt over the General Strike I have every reason to know. I remember meeting him behind the Speaker's chair a few hours before this great event, and he not only denounced the whole business, but did not hesitate to tell me that a little bloodshed would do no harm!

But to the House itself he said, 'The Trade Union Congress have only to cancel the General Strike and withdraw the challenge they have issued and we shall immediately begin, with the utmost care and patience with them again, the long, laborious task . . . of endeavouring to rebuild on economic foundations the prosperity of the coal trade. That is our position. No door is closed.'

The final word on the strike, and perhaps the only note of humour, was given by Mr. Churchill in a speech to the House of Commons after the collapse of the strike: 'But I warn you—I warn you that if ever there is another General Strike we will let loose another *British Gazette!*'

17

The Twenties

The General Strike had wrought economic havoc and embittered industrial relations still further. There was still widespread unemployment, and 200,000 miners out of work. But Churchill, apart from his work at the Treasury had found time and energy to write two volumes of *The World Crisis*—a series which, when completed, earned him over £40,000 and enabled him to buy Chartwell, his country home which became the Mecca of politicians of all kinds and a mixture of notables from all countries and of every interest. This masterly work is, as it claims to be, an interpretation of world events by Churchill; not everyone agreed with his interpretation and indeed some—including the contributors to *The World Crisis: A Criticism*—considered that he had been inaccurate in many vital particulars and actually unjust to certain people. The criticisms, which are specific, are worth reading in conjunction with Sir Winston's books, although it has to be remembered that many of the contributors, including Col. Lord Sydenham of Combe, had long been critics of Churchill.

Early in 1927 Churchill, complete with paintbox and brushes, went on a holiday to Italy and in the course of it met Signor Mussolini, the Italian dictator with whose anti-Socialist views he sympathized, but about whose repressive methods of government he had obvious reservations.

One of the main concerns of the House of Commons was the Trade Disputes Bill, the Government's answer to the General Strike. Baldwin's object was to make another General Strike impossible, to limit the powers of trade unions, prevent coercion of members into participating in strikes, prohibiting Civil Servants from affiliation to the T.U.C. and ensuring that no trade unionist was compelled to pay a political levy, or draw attention to his unwillingness to do so by having to ask to 'levy out'. There were many—including, of course, the whole of the Labour Party—who felt that the Bill went too far in restricting Trade Union activities. The right

of working men to organize for the purposes of protecting their
interests had been hardly won. Churchill's attitude was summarized
in his speech to the House on 9th February 1927:

> But when the right hon. Gentleman tells us that we are going to
> take away the workers' only bargaining power I must ask him
> one or two questions. Is a General Strike—which, whether
> intentionally or not, is inevitably against the Constitution—a
> necessary part of the workers' bargaining power in trade methods?
> (an hon. Member: 'Certainly!') I do not seem to get a very
> decided answer to that. Is mass intimidation at a works or at a
> man's home an essential part of the reasonable collective bargain-
> ing power of the trade unionists of the country? . . . Is collecting
> money for Socialist candidates from Liberal and Conservative
> trade unionists an essential part of the workers' collective bargain-
> ing power?

To a suggestion that the trade unions should be consulted in the
framing of the Bill, Mr. Churchill told the House of Commons:

> I remember it was the fashion in the Army when a court martial
> was being held and the prisoner was brought in that he should be
> asked if he objected to being tried by the President or to any of
> those officers who composed the court martial. On one occasion
> a prisoner was so insubordinate as to answer: 'I object to the whole
> —— of you.' This is clearly illustrative of the kind of reception
> which, at this stage, consultation of the trade unions by the
> Government would meet with.

Churchill listened approvingly as on one occasion Captain Anthony
Eden, then Parliamentary Private Secretary to Sir Austen Chamberlain, the Foreign Secretary, denounced both strikes and lockouts as
'the scalping knife of the twentieth century, abhorrent alike to
reason and truth . . .' Churchill's 1927 budget was uneventful, but
he managed to get over the problem of a £33,000,000 deficit by
making further raids on the Road Fund.

The main feature of his Budget of 1928 was the announcement
of a scheme for reforming the country's rating system. It was an
immensely involved scheme with enormous ramifications, and
Mr. Churchill's explanation lasted three and a half hours. Even
Churchill's main opponent, Mr. Snowden, congratulated him upon
it. There was, in fact, a curious affinity between these two men, so

utterly unlike in background and temperament. But they had one thing in common, and that was that they were both fighters. Churchill would lambast and belabour an opponent with all the rhetoric and energy at his command, but nobody would be more disappointed than he if the subject of his displeasure acceded mildly to his criticisms. He liked to get as good as he gave. He always acknowledged and respected a doughty opponent and despised a weak one. 'It would be wrong,' he wrote in *Great Contemporaries*, 'to think of Mr. Snowden as the spiteful, vindictive Death's-head of his caricatures; as a sworn tormentor who used the Rack, the Thumbscrew and the Little Ease of taxation with gusto upon his victims. He was really a tender-hearted man. . . .'

Their verbal battles were to become more frequent and more intense when their roles were reversed and Snowden was Chancellor. Snowden, after pulling Mr. Churchill to pieces in a rather violent speech, finished it by saying, 'I am really fond of the right honourable Gentleman, and wish him a Merry Christmas.' The concentrated pugnacity of Mr. Churchill's expression faded; there was the briefest interim of uncertainty, as one could almost see him weighing up whether the compliment was sincere or ironic; then, as the sentence drew to its close and Snowden's tone of sincerity was unmistakable, Churchill was visibly touched.

But there was a tense scene in the House when Snowden declared that 'We have never subscribed to the principle of the Balfour Note', which he thought an 'infamous' one and which a future Socialist Government would repudiate at the first opportunity, if circumstances demanded it. The Balfour Note was a declaration that Britain would not take more in the way of war debts and reparations than needed to be paid to Britain's creditor, the United States. Churchill, taking up the challenge, found Snowden unrepentant over this 'wanton challenge' whilst Ramsay MacDonald preferred to sit on the fence and utter ambiguities which could be construed by some as faint support and others as partial repudiation—as they pleased. 'I commend to the attention of the country,' said Churchill, 'the fact that the Leader of the Labour Party and the ex-Prime Minister of the country is incapable of answering plain and simple questions. He sits there and does not open his mouth.'

Churchill had one eye on the forthcoming General Election of 1929. The results of that election were unsatisfactory. On a basis of proportional representation, the Conservatives would have been

back in power again, for they polled more than 300,000 more votes
than Labour. But Labour, with 288 seats, was the strongest Party
in the House, the Conservatives holding 260 seats and the Liberals
59. It was not a very happy balance of parties, since it gave the
Liberals influence out of proportion to their numbers—they could
weight the scales for either Party.

It was a dull election, the Conservatives urging 'safety first' and
plastering the country with posters of the homely, placid, pipe-
sucking Stanley Baldwin.

Ramsay MacDonald formed a Labour Government, with Snow-
den, Churchill's antagonist, as Chancellor of the Exchequer, with
J. R. Clynes as Home Secretary and—a precedent—Miss Margaret
Bondfield as Minister of Labour and the first woman Cabinet
Minister.

Mr. Churchill was returned to Parliament for Epping, and sat
himself with relish on the Opposition benches.

Was Churchill a success as Chancellor? Trade Unionists never
entirely forgot his attitude during the General Strike (and, alas,
never entirely remembered his lack of vindictiveness afterward; his
aversion to Socialism he never disguised, but beyond ensuring
against a repetition of the General Strike he was entirely uninterested
in revenge). Perhaps Churchill's own assessment of his merits as
a Chancellor will suffice and disarm:

Everybody said I was the worst Chancellor of the Exchequer that
ever was. And now I'm inclined to agree with them.

18

In Opposition

Now Churchill could snipe at the Socialists from the Opposition benches. But the fact is that, to whatever party he had found himself aligned, he would have felt ill at ease. He still glowed with the old-fashioned type of patriotism based on pride of achievement, sense of purpose and sureness of destiny. Try as he might, he found it difficult to make anyone, even any of the Tories, feel as definite about these things. As he put it, in 1930:

> The grand and victorious summits which the British Empire won are being lost, have indeed largely been lost in the years which followed the peace. We see our race doubtful of its mission and no longer confident about its principles, infirm of purpose, drifting to and fro with the tides. . . .

Now for a while the easy-going Baldwin had been replaced by Ramsay MacDonald, who at times was almost incoherent.

The Labour Government, dependent upon Liberal support, was in a weak position. During a debate on the Coal Bill, Aneurin Bevan, the miners' M.P., made an impassioned protest against Lloyd George and Churchill being in 'a temporary re-alliance, which may be carried right through to the division lobby in their capacity as joint executioners'.

In October 1930 the Wall Street slump dragged down the whole of the European economy, bringing a depression to Britain and an unemployment level of two million rising to nearly four million by the end of 1932. Throughout the world there was a fall in prices, and Germany, especially vulnerable, found itself with a growing army of unemployed which reached nearly six million by 1932. In human and financial terms, the army of people living 'on the dole' constituted a heavy burden. Their collective and cumulative bitterness and frustration were a most powerful factor in politics— certainly in Germany, where Communism and Fascism had grown apace, with the latter, scarcely less evil than the former, in the ascendancy. J. H. Thomas, the 'h'-dropping Socialist, was Minister for Dominion Affairs, but Snowden, now Chancellor of the Exchequer, could not spend as freely on social welfare and development schemes as he would have wished. Sir Oswald Mosley, then a Labour M.P., put forward a good scheme for the relief of unemployment and, finding it rejected, broke away to start a new party, later still founding Britain's first Fascist Party.

The year 1931 was notable for Mr. Churchill's drift from his own party, the Tories. Although in sympathy with many of their policies, he was scandalized at their seeming determination to move India nearer and nearer to self-government. He became head of a subcommittee of Conservative Members of Parliament on India and by every means in his power advocated the retention of British rule there. He did not share the admiration which so many Socialists and Liberals felt for Mahatma Gandhi, who had so often been imprisoned by the British for seditious activities: 'It is alarming and also nauseating,' he declared, 'to see Mr. Gandhi, a seditious Middle Temple lawyer, now posing as a fakir, striding half naked up the steps of the Viceregal Palace to parley on equal terms with the representative of the King-Emperor.'

The Round Table Conference was sitting to try and work out a formula by which India could achieve autonomy. Churchill watched the process with alarm. He asked the House of Commons: 'How will the British feel about all this? I am told that from one quarter or another they are worried by unemployment or taxation or absorbed in sport or crime news. The great liner is sinking in a calm sea. One bulkhead after another gives way; one compartment after another is bilged; the list increases; she is sinking; but the captain and the officers and the crew are all in the saloon dancing to a jazz band. But wait till the passengers find out what is their position.'

And he warned the House that all Indians would not automatically love each other if and when British rule weakened or was altogether withdrawn:

Where there have been differences between India and Great Britain, some adjustment has been made by Great Britain giving way; but as to differences between Indians themselves, there has not been one concession, not one difficulty has been solved or surmounted. Nevertheless, on we go, moving slowly, in a leisurely manner, jerkily onwards, towards an unworkable conclusion, crawling methodically towards the abyss which we shall reach in due course.

Churchill's fundamental difference of opinion on the subject of India's future was to have a profound effect upon his political career; ever since his entry into politics he had been distinguished by his insistence on opposing his Party on some big issue. Now, said his critics, he was at the same game again.

By summer 1931 Britain's financial position had become extremely grave. Unemployment had reached 2¾ million, and a potential deficit of £120 million demanded economies of £96 million and new taxation to raise £24 million. The run on the Bank of England's gold reserves necessitated the raising of a loan of £80 million in Paris and New York and even that money was fast draining away.

Ramsay MacDonald hurried back from holiday on 11th August, and on 24th August the King accepted the resignation of the Labour Government. Ramsay MacDonald was invited to form a 'National' or Coalition Government and the new Cabinet, the day afterwards, included Baldwin and Samuel and—amongst the Labour members —Snowden, Thomas and Lord Sankey. Ramsay MacDonald told the public that the new Government had been formed only to meet the emergency, that it would be soon dissolved and followed by a General Election.

On 27th October 1931, a General Election resulted in a sweeping victory for the National Government—417 Tories, 72 Liberals of different groupings and a mere 52 Labour Members. MacDonald continued as Prime Minister, Neville Chamberlain became Chancellor, Sir John Simon went to the Foreign Office. MacDonald, Snowden and Thomas came in for more invective and criticism for their 'betrayal' from their own Labour Party than they had ever endured from Churchill's oratory. Furthermore, the denunciations, unlike Churchill's, were not laced with wit.

Churchill was returned to Parliament again by his constituency, but his political future looked bleak. Until January 1931 he had been a member of the Opposition's 'Shadow Cabinet'—consisting largely of ex-members of the previous Government and, by inference, those who would in the event of an electoral victory, be included in a new Government. But his disagreement with Baldwin on the subject of Indian independence went so deep that Churchill resigned from the 'Shadow Cabinet'—thereby throwing away his immediate political prospects for the sake of a principle. He would not, he declared, 'serve in any Administration about whose Indian policy I was not reassured.'

From the Conservatives and from Stanley Baldwin in particular Churchill could expect no preferment. Least of all was he likely to enjoy the sponsorship of Ramsay MacDonald, whom he had attacked during a debate on the Amendment Bill—a measure introduced by the Socialists to undo some of the restrictions imposed on trade unions by the Trades Disputes Act after the General Strike of 1926. Churchill's wounding words, delivered with a vigour that made them ring through the ancient chamber to the anger of MacDonald's friends and the derision of his critics, went around the world, achieving a permanence for which MacDonald never forgave him.

Churchill had been shocked and disgusted at the action of the Liberals in supporting the amendment. Churchill's conviction that the powers of trade unions needed to be kept within due bounds remained as strong as ever, and having attacked the amendment in general he turned his fire on Ramsay MacDonald in particular:

What is the Prime Minister going to do about it? I spoke the other day, after he had been defeated in an important division, about his wonderful skill in falling without hurting himself. He falls, but up he comes again, smiling, a little dishevelled but still smiling. But this is a juncture, a situation which will try to the very fullest the particular arts in which he excels.

I remember when I was a child being taken to the celebrated Barnum's Circus which contained an exhibition of freaks and monstrosities, but the exhibit on the programme which I most desired to see was the one described as 'the Boneless Wonder'. My parents judged that the spectacle would be too revolting for my youthful eyes, and I have waited fifty years to see the Boneless Wonder sitting on the Treasury Bench.

The *boneless wonder*! Thereafter this was the description applied to MacDonald by all who disliked him.

No wonder Churchill declared, 'I have cheerfully and gladly put out from my mind all idea of public office.'

19

The Years of Drift

We come now to a period which historians will surely adjudge the most cruelly negative in Britain's history. Churchill himself calls them 'the locust years' because the spirit had gone out of Britain. Just as foreign affairs had been neglected before the onset of the First World War, so now both politicians and public did not want to heed the drift of events. Pacifism, it was hoped, would impress other countries by our example. Meanwhile the Revolution had long since consolidated itself in Russia, Italy had become a militarized police state, and Communism in Germany, bred of despair and unemployment, had provoked the blackest reaction and both aristocracy and industry—especially the latter—gave their backing to Hitler's Fascist movement.

Ramsay MacDonald was a weak and vacillating Prime Minister; he had not wanted the job and indeed had told the King that he 'was beginning to feel the strain and had better clear out'. The King told him flatly that he should pull himself together, put duty before self and not presuppose that his King would accept his Prime Minister's resignation even if it were proffered. So now the ex-Socialist, scorned and reviled by the Labour Party as a traitor to the working class cause, accepted with scant grace by the Conservatives whose numbers dominated the Government, had to lead again.

While Germany armed, the British put their trust and hope in the League of Nations. Britain reduced her arms while France increased hers by 150 per cent, Italy by 40 per cent and the United States by 160 per cent.

In this new Government Anthony Eden was given the job of Parliamentary Under-Secretary at the Foreign Office. During the General Election a war had started, the Japanese attacking Manchuria. It all seemed far away and nobody at home bothered much. But it was a blow to the League of Nations, the organization set up at America's insistence (and deserted by her) and which all hoped might end war as an instrument of politics. Britain was committed at the Geneva Disarmament Conference to a dangerous policy of altruism which left her naked before her enemies. The Army was barely more than a police force, the Navy was attenuated, and the Air Force fifth amongst the air powers. The Conference was a fiasco, the broad issues being lost in detail. Russia boldly asked for all-round reduction in armaments, culminating in their abolition—without any intention or willingness to grant facilities to any international body to ensure that her own promises in this respect were kept.

The uselessness of the League of Nations was underlined by Manchuria's fate. When China appealed to the League, it persistently hedged and procrastinated until Japan's victory was achieved and any further argument was academic. And when, later, Japan walked out of the League and made war upon China, the United States—a signatory to the Briand-Kellogg Pact—did nothing about it.

In January 1933, Hitler became Chancellor of Germany and the great terror began there. By fanatical nationalism, sustained by a bullying secret police, all liberal and humanistic movements were crushed and illegal arming began. Later in the year Germany withdrew both from the Conference and the League of Nations.

Churchill was well informed on developments in Germany; it could be said, so varied and influential was his circle of informants, that he possessed his own intelligence service and—unlike some of the official services, which file valuable reports away and let them collect the dust—he gave some of the facts an airing. Germany's frenetic militarism and brutal persecutions spoke for themselves; if Germany's government could organize cruelty against its own people, what would it do to its neighbours in the fullness of time?

It was thoughts such as these which made him intervene, again and again, in the House of Commons when foreign affairs and matters of defence were discussed or involved. When Ramsay MacDonald, who had led the British Delegation to the Disarmament Conference, bored the House with a diffuse and obscure speech on disarmament, Churchill said bluntly that such conferences did more harm than good. He did not mean in all circumstances; he was talking of present conditions. When the burglar approaches you put an extra lock on the door as well as shutting it; you don't leave the door open. And when Anthony Eden rose, with some heat, to defend the Prime Minister, castigating Churchill for what he called 'a mischievous absurdity' the House applauded while Churchill sat there glowering.

Churchill's parliamentary prestige was very low at this time. His 'diehard' speech showed how far he had moved to the right since his Liberal days, and prompted Mr. Lansbury, leader of the Opposition, to describe Churchill as 'a Vicar of Bray' (the Berkshire prelate who between 1520 and 1560 was twice a Papist and twice a Protestant in successive reigns). The Rt. Hon. Earl Winterton, K.G., who first took his seat in Parliament in 1905 and retired after nearly fifty years of unbroken service—unbroken save by active service in the Army—had watched Churchill's erratic parliamentary progress with friendly but critical eyes. In his memoirs, *Orders of the Day*, he shows that Churchill's strong stand over India was doing him political harm:

> Mr. Churchill's parliamentary position temporarily deteriorated. He was accused by his enemies within and without the Party, of having tried, by his espousal of 'Diehardism' over India, to bring off a *coup d'état* which would unseat Mr. Baldwin from the leadership and eventually put in office himself and his followers in both Houses, who included men of great ability, such as Lord Wolmer, M.P. (now Lord Selborne) and the late Lord Lloyd. The fact that the 'Diehards' failed to carry their point was a serious defeat for Mr. Churchill. A 'whispering campaign' about him, sedulously encouraged by, if not originating from Ministers, started in the lobbies of the House of Commons and in the country. He was, it was hinted, another but a lesser Lloyd George, with the same brilliant gifts and powers of oratory, but unstable in character: he would never be in any Government again, because he invariably tried to domineer over his colleagues and persist in wrong courses. . . .

Lord Winterton notes that in accordance with human nature, those who were most vociferous in their denunciations or criticisms of Mr. Churchill at this period were amongst the first to seek favours and preferment from him when the tide of his fortunes turned.

In May 1934 the Disarmament Conference was adjourned—in fact, abandoned. To Churchill, an opponent of disarmament, this was no loss. Even two years earlier he had read the writing on the wall and warned the Commons about Germany—one year before Hitler assumed supreme power.

I have the greatest respect and admiration for the Germans and the greatest desire that we should live on terms of goodwill and fruitful relations with them. But I put it to the House that every concession that has been made . . . has been followed by a fresh demand. Now the demand is that Germany should be allowed to rearm. Do not let us delude ourselves. Do not let the Government delude themselves by supposing that which Germany is asking for is equal status. All those bands of splendid Teutonic youth marching to and fro in Germany with the light of desire to suffer for their Fatherland in their eyes, they are not looking for status. They are looking for weapons, and when they have those weapons, believe me, they will then ask for the restoration of lost territories and lost colonies, and when the demand is made it cannot fail to shake, and possibly shake to their foundations, every country in the world.

Events were swiftly to justify Churchill's warning. In Austria German agents were undermining the State and Dollfuss, the 'pocket Chancellor' of Austria, was assassinated. Anthony Eden made a tour of Paris, Rome and Berlin, seeing Mussolini and Hitler in the process. Hitler was campaigning for the return of territories lost after the World War.

Anthony Eden's statement to the House made the situation seem more hopeful than it was. How could France's natural apprehensions —her need for security in face of Germany's abominable record of aggression—be reconciled with Germany's insistence on arms parity? Eden thought that France and Germany did 'not understand each other's point of view' and spoke of 'mistrustful apprehension' and 'aggravated impatience'. But by what was Hitler's 'impatience' aggravated except by his secret ambitions? What had he, anyway, to be impatient about?

Mr. Churchill, in an earlier speech, had found it 'incredible' that as the war sabres rattled again we should be pressing France to weaken herself.

What happens, for instance, if, after we have equalised and reduced the army of France to the level of that of Germany . . . Germany then proceeds to say, 'How can you keep a great nation of 70 millions in a position in which it is not entitled to have a navy equal to the greatest of the fleets upon the seas? You will say 'No, we do not agree' . . . But what position shall we be in to say 'No' ? . . . Not one of the lessons of the past has been learned, not one of them has been applied, and the situation is in comparably more dangerous. Then we had the Navy and no air menace. Then the Navy was the 'sure shield' of Britain . . . we cannot say that now. This cursed, hellish invention and development of war from the air has revolutionised our position . . .

And now, with the situation deteriorating, there was all this facile optimism. Mr. Churchill was soon on his feet, warning the House that Germany was creating, in violation of the Treaty of Versailles, an Air Force nearly two-thirds as strong as Britain's Home Defence Force.

Hitler was making his final moves towards complete personal power in Germany. Arms factories there were working day and night. Planes were being made in secret. Anti-Semitism was spreading the contagion of hate and racial intolerance and bringing out the streak of evil cruelty that lurks in most people. In June Hitler visited Mussolini in Rome. And on his return Hitler put down an attempted revolution of the thugs who had helped him to power, the Brownshirts, by a night of massacre in which over 7,000 perished. The nature of the man was revealed to the world by this one frightful act—and still the mass of people in Britain hoped that, somehow, it would be nothing to do with them.

In July the Labour Party moved a Vote of Censure against a proposal for strengthening the Royal Air Force, which would have taken five years to complete. Major Attlee for the Labour Party declared, 'We deny the need for increased air armaments.' The Liberals supported Labour in their contention.

All politics are based on power. A weak nation is simply not listened to. The purpose of armaments is depressing and their acquisition expensive, but if a near neighbour is clearly out for trouble, it has to be stopped in its early stages. That, all along, is what Mr. Churchill kept telling the House. If France and Britain had each kept air parity with Germany, that country's air force would have been hopelessly outnumbered and unable to terrorize and threaten Europe.

'Let us remember,' Mr. Churchill warned the House, 'our weakness does not only involve ourselves; our weakness involves also the stability of Europe.'

Hitler had in 1933 taken over Germany as Fuehrer and Reich-chancellor. The concentration camps overflowed with victims, Jews became the object of increasing violence, humiliation and persecution, spying and sabotage by Nazi agents abroad vastly increased, and Fascist propaganda in all its forms poured out from German presses and from radio stations. In March 1935, flouting world opinion in general and the Versailles Treaty in particular, Hitler introduced conscription. Italy launched a cruel and utterly unprovoked attack upon Abyssinia, using all the fearful implements of air warfare against tribesmen equipped with spears and ancient rifles. While the Abyssinian war proceeded a 'Non-Intervention Committee' on which, ironically, Italy the aggressor was a member, talked on and on until Abyssinia was entirely subjugated. Britain, while paying lip service to the League (which was so ineffectual as not to justify even the compliment of lip service) was attempting a line-up of power against Germany, called 'The Stresa Front', which would have included Italy. If collective security could not be made to work, perhaps the old-fashioned military alliances could. The League pronounced Italy an aggressor.

In June 1935 another 'National' Government was formed, Baldwin succeeding Ramsay MacDonald as Prime Minister and Sir Samuel Hoare succeeding Sir John Simon as Foreign Secretary. The possibility was that the Government was not too anxious to press Mussolini over Abyssinia because of the faint hope that he might join the Stresa front against Germany. But when, late in 1935, it was revealed that Sir Samuel Hoare had agreed with Pierre Laval, the French Prime Minister, that huge sections of Abyssinia should be ceded to Italy, the Hoare-Laval Pact, as it came to be known, caused a tremendous outcry of indignation. The British Cabinet had, on 9th December, approved this plan to dismember a peaceful country, leaving the aggressor with the fruits of violence. But the Cabinet, in face of the uproar, had to repudiate its own decision; Sir Samuel Hoare resigned and Anthony Eden became Foreign Minister. It was a very popular choice, for in the public eye Eden had become identified with efforts for collective security and support of the League of Nations. For in this same year eleven million people had signed a 'Peace Ballot' in support of the League and its collective security policy. Everybody longed for peace, which was understandable; what was less explicable was how, in face of constant and sinister warnings, they did not realize that neither Hitler nor Mussolini intended to let anybody have it.

The Hoare-Laval Pact was abandoned but the war in Abyssinia

went on until Italy was the victor. 'Today,' Mr. Churchill told the House, 'Abyssinia is irrevocably, fully and finally Italian alone.' The fact revealed Britain's pose as champion of collective security for what it was.

Churchill had said earlier that he did not seek office nor expect it. At this time, however, he did, and was disappointed when Mr. Baldwin, on assuming the office of Prime Minister, passed him over. 'The growing German menace made me anxious to lay my hands upon our military machine,' Churchill wrote in *The Gathering Storm*, 'I could now feel very keenly what was coming.'

Throughout 1936 Anthony Eden was gaining in stature and Churchill, called by some the parliamentary Jeremiah, stuck consistently to his warnings that war was becoming more of a likelihood and that Britain should be prepared. In January King George V died, to be succeeded by Edward VIII, once known as 'the smiling Prince' and a long-standing friend of Winston Churchill's. On 7th March Germany denounced the Treaty of Locarno and the German Army marched into the demilitarized zone of the Rhineland with no effective protest from anyone. Italy won her war in Abyssinia in May, and Emperor Haile Selassie, after an impassioned though futile appeal to the League of Nations, was a refugee in England. By 18th July Spain was torn by the savagery of civil war in which Russia, Germany and Italy were able, by backing those sides they wished to win, to try out their latest and most fearsome weapons.

By the end of the year tension in Europe mounted and all hopes of peace and collective security receded. In a debate in the House on 12th November Churchill attacked Baldwin for not tackling the country's defences more energetically in face of the long and now rapidly-growing peril. 'The Government simply cannot make up their minds, or they cannot get the Prime Minister to make up his mind. So they go on in strange paradox, decided only to be undecided, resolved to be irresolute, adamant for drift, solid for fluidity, all-powerful to be impotent. So we go on preparing for months or years—precious, perhaps vital, to the greatness of Britain —for the locusts to eat. . . .'

These stinging words provoked 'Honest Stanley Baldwin' into an admission which left the House gasping with surprise, humiliation and dismay.

I put before the whole House my own views with appalling frankness. You will remember at that time the Disarmament Conference was sitting in Geneva. You will remember at that time there was probably a stronger pacifist feeling running through this country than at any time since the war. You will remember the election at Fulham in the autumn of 1933, when a seat which the National Government held was lost by about 7,000 votes on no issue but the Pacifist. My position as leader of a great party was by no means a comfortable one. I asked myself what chance was there—when that feeling which was given expression to in Fulham was common throughout the country—what chance was there within the next year or two of that feeling being so changed that the country would give a mandate for re-armament? Supposing I had gone to the country and said that Germany was rearming, and that we must rearm, does anybody think that this pacific democracy would have rallied to that cry at that moment? I cannot think of anything that would have made the loss of the election from my point of view more certain.

In other words, by his own admission, he had put Party before Country. The winning of an election had been of more moment than to pursue a policy necessary for the country's good, but which at that time the majority of people did not favour. Must leaders always follow the people? Seneca once said that 'human affairs are not so happily disposed that the best things please the most people.' The same might be said of the thirties. And so Baldwin had let things drift until 1935, when he judged it a safer bet to go to the country with a policy of rearmament. His strategy (politically speaking) proved correct, but the admission cost him his reputation.

The Abdication of King Edward VIII was another occasion on which Mr. Churchill risked unpopularity for a principle. Always a staunch and warm-hearted supporter of the Monarchy, he had watched the growing constitutional crisis with distress. Baldwin had so manœuvred matters that the dilemma of a King who wished to marry a woman who had been divorced was never debated in the House. The King sought Churchill's advice in his painful situation and Churchill issued a statement to the Press in which he asked that no decision should be taken until the wishes of Parliament and the nation as a whole had been sounded, and this had not been done.

I plead for time and patience. There is no question of any conflict between the King and Parliament. Parliament has not been consulted in any way or allowed to express any opinion. The question is whether the King is to abdicate upon the advice of the Ministry of the day. No such advice has ever been tendered in parliamentary times.

This is not a case where differences have arisen between the Sovereign and his Ministers on any particular measure. These could certainly be resolved by normal process of Parliament or dissolution. In this case we are in the presence of a wish expressed by the Sovereign to perform an act which in no circumstances can be accomplished for nearly five months, and may conceivably, for various reasons, never be accomplished at all. . . . The Cabinet has no right to prejudge such a question without having previously ascertained at the very least the will of Parliament. . . .

Churchill pleaded for time. His actions at this time aroused widespread suspicion. What was Churchill up to? Trying to start a 'King's Party'? But those who sneered forgot how lonely was the King's position, an isolation which is movingly described in the Duke of Windsor's memoirs, *A King's Story*:

The Prime Minister controlled all the levers of power. He could bargain with the Opposition. He could canvass Members of Parliament. He could exert Party pressure for the support of the newspapers. He could even consult the Dominion Premiers in his own terms. He could do all this and more. Such was the discipline of the Party machine under Mr. Baldwin's control that influential friends upon whom I might otherwise have counted never dared to step forward—perhaps not wishing to risk loss of Party favour. I had to stand silent. How lonely is a Monarch in a struggle with a shrewd Prime Minister by all the apparatus of a modern State!

On 7th December 1936 Churchill, dissatisfied with the Prime Minister's vague and evasive replies on the grave crisis, asked for the second time that no 'irrevocable step' should be taken before Parliament as a whole was consulted. It is sad to record that Churchill was shouted down. The Duke has said, 'I have always regretted this incident, and would give much for the power to erase from the records of that ancient assembly that owes him so much. Yet I am proud, also, that of all Englishmen it was Mr. Churchill who spoke up to the last for the King, his friend.'

In glowing words, when the sad news of the Abdication had been broken to the House, Churchill accepted with sadness a constitutional decision which was plainly irrevocable.

What is done, is done. . . . It was my duty as Home Secretary, more than a quarter of a century ago, to stand beside His Majesty and proclaim his style and titles at his investiture as Prince of Wales amid the sunlit battlements of Caernarvon Castle, and ever since then he has honoured me here, and also in wartime, with his personal kindness, and, I may even say, friendship. I should have been ashamed if, in my independent and unofficial position, I had not cast about for every lawful means, even the most forlorn, to keep him on the throne of his fathers. . . .

20

Appeasement

From 1936 onwards appeasement constituted the main feature of British foreign policy. Lethargy and drift represented easy-going commonsense whilst warnings of impending disaster were denounced as warmongering by the left and pessimism by the right. Churchill, almost alone, irrepressible, impenitent, emphatic and incessant, continued his warnings of impending disaster not only for Britain but for Europe. When Baldwin once reproached him in the House for his continued warnings, dismissing them as 'panic', Churchill reminded him that a man who panicked before the onset of disaster, and kept his head when at last it came, was to be preferred to the drifter who kept his head when he should be losing it, and in the resultant crisis went into a panic.

In a private address to Conservative Members of Parliament in March 1936 he told them:

> For four hundred years the foreign policy of Britain has been to oppose the strongest, most aggressive, most dominating power on the Continent, and particularly to prevent the Low Countries falling into the hands of such a Power. . . . Here is the wonderful unconscious tradition of British policy. . . . Observe that the policy of England takes no account of which nation it is that seeks overlordship of Europe. The question is not whether it is Spain, or the French Monarchy, or the French Empire, or the German Empire, or Hitler's regime . . . it is solely concerned with whoever is the strongest or the potentially dominating tyrant. . . . I am for the armed League of all Natians, or as many as you can get, against the potential aggressor, with England and France as the core of it. . . .

And of Fascist rearmament he told the House on 23rd April 1936: 'I cannot believe that, after armaments in all countries have reached a towering height, they will settle down and continue at a hideous level. . . . Europe is approaching a climax. I believe that climax will be reached in the lifetime of the present Parliament.'

There was at this time, not only amongst a considerable section of Members of Parliament, but especially in British industry, a strong nucleus which was indifferent to the methods of Fascism and its growing power, hoping forlornly that Hitler and Mussolini were a sort of insurance against Communism in Europe. Churchill hated Communism and had never made any bones about it, and for the same reason disliked Socialism because he believed that it softened the national spirit of a country by under-estimating the ruthlessness of Communists once they had gained a secure foothold. But he never made the mistake of thinking one dictatorship preferable to another. 'I will not pretend that, if I had to choose between Communism and Nazi-ism, I would choose Communism,' he told M.P.s in a speech in the House in April 1937. 'I hope not to be called upon to survive in the world under a Government of either of those dispensations.'

His understanding of what Hitlerism meant brought upon him the full fusillade of hate from Hitler's propaganda machine. Goebbels, Hitler's propaganda chief, used every means in his power to influence British public opinion against Churchill, and German protests at Churchill's revelations of German rearmament were even made to the British through diplomatic channels. Similarly Anthony Eden was made the subject of persistent vilification by Mussolini's subservient propagandists; but then Mussolini happened to know more about Britain's attitude to Fascism than Britain realized; a servant in the British Embassy in Rome was consistently handing over to the Italians, for huge sums of money, secret diplomatic documents.

On 27th May 1937 Stanley Baldwin, the Prime Minister, who had been for some time in failing health, resigned. He was succeeded by Mr. Neville Chamberlain. Mr. Churchill seconded his nomination as leader of the Conservatives when the Party met; Mr. Chamberlain however, in forming his Government, passed Mr. Churchill over. There were many who thought this a great pity, for signs were not lacking now that it was Churchill who had correctly forecast the trend of events and his detractors who had been misled or naive.

But Mr. Chamberlain was mentally and—as he saw it—by necessity committed to a policy of appeasement. In the Far East, of course, there was nothing Britain could do, despite the horrors of the war against China which Japan began on 8th July. Soon the Chinese were driven back to the Yellow River and in due course Shanghai, Nanking and (a year later) Canton were to fall. The full enormity of modern bombing was again demonstrated, as it had been manifested in Spain. But the United States had intimated in 1934 that they would not wish to be involved unless Hawaii or Honolulu were attacked. Britain could not 'go it alone' in the Far East.

Piracy in the Mediterranean, for which Italy was largely responsible, was ended by Anthony Eden's adroit steerage of the Nyon Conference in Switzerland, in which Italy participated. As Italian ships had been sinking vessels taking arms to Republican Spain, there was concealed irony in Churchill's tribute to Mussolini: 'I must pay my tribute to Mussolini whose prestige and authority—by the mere terror of his name—quelled the wicked depredations of these marauders.'

Italy had by the end of 1937 left the League of Nations. Nothing remained of the edifice of collective security.

Mr. Chamberlain, meanwhile, had taken to negotiating with the Italians behind the back of his own Foreign Secretary, Mr. Eden, who, on 20th February 1938, resigned in protest at the continued policy of appeasement. The loss to the Government of a Minister of Eden's integrity was a great grief to Churchill. As Mr. Churchill has put it:

> Late in the night of February 20 a telephone message reached me as I sat in my old room at Chartwell . . . that Eden had resigned . . . sleep deserted me. From midnight till dawn I lay in my bed consumed by emotions of sorrow and fear. There seemed one strong young figure standing up against long, dismal, drawling tides of drift and surrender, of wrong measurements and feeble impulses. My conduct of affairs would have been different from his in many ways; but he seemed to me at this moment to embody the lifelong hope of the British nation, the grand old British race that has done so much for men, and had yet more to give. Now he was gone. I watched the daylight slowly creep in through the windows, and saw before me in mental gaze the vision of Death.

The debate on 21st February 1938 was one of the most dramatic for years. Neville Chamberlain entered the chamber from behind the Speaker's Chair. Press and public galleries were crowded to capacity. Diplomats of the world craned forward to catch every word. Eden came in from the other end, took a seat on the third bench from the gangway, sitting next to Lord Cranbourne, Under-Secretary at the Foreign Office, who had resigned with him.

Eden rose to make his 'personal statement'. He outlined his efforts to protect British interests and secure better relations with Italy without loss of principle. 'I do not believe,' he said, 'that we can make progress in European appeasement . . . if we allow the impression to gain currency abroad that we yield to constant pressure. I am certain in my own mind that progress depends above all on the temper of the nation, and that temper must find expression in a firm spirit.'

Mr. Churchill said:

It is with sorrow that I rise today to take part in the debate. Since my Right Honourable Friend became Prime Minister I have tried my best to give him disinterested and independent support. I know the dangers by which we are encompassed: yet I could not sit silent here this afternoon without expressing, in good faith and sincerity, my disagreement with the course he has taken and my increasing concern at the consequences attendant upon it. . . . I must express my keen personal sympathy with the late Foreign Minister, whose policy I admire and whose friendship I enjoy. My Right Honourable Friend has had a long and laborious apprenticeship at the Foreign Office and upon the League of Nations, and he undoubtedly is in possession of a body of knowledge and experience about Europe which no-one else possesses . . . and which no-one else is likely rapidly to acquire. I say that he is an irreparable loss to the Government (cheers) . . . and I feel personally, as an older man, the poignancy of his loss all the more because he seems to be the one fresh figure of first magnitude arising out of the generation which was ravaged by the war (cheers).

But there was much Tory hostility to Churchill's defence. Words were flung backwards and forwards. Britain, said Churchill, had over-estimated Italian strength. Italy had many internal difficulties, whereas British weakness would buoy up their flagging spirits and embolden them to new aggressions. Speaking of Rome's anxiety to get rid of Eden from the British Government, he added, 'This last week has been a good week for the dictators, one of the best they have ever had . . . was it really worth while to throw over Mr. Eden and give Mussolini his triumph before the whole world for the sake of a few kind words from the Italian propagandist wireless station?' Since Eden's resignation 'the friends of England all over the world were dismayed, and the foes of England were exultant.'

Churchill might not have been as popular as other parliamentary figures at this time—but we must remember the reason. He was concerned with realities, and spoke of realities. Not to face unpleasant facts was simply cowardice which, apart from being wholly alien to everything he admired, solved nothing anyway. He saw the situation for what it was; Germany, arming frenetically and secretly, committed to a programme of conquest stated explicitly in Hitler's *Mein Kampf*; France riddled with factions and Communism, changing her Governments every five minutes and pinning all her hopes for defence on the Maginot Line; Russia, a vast power which could neutralize the Fascist menace, but studiously avoided by the British in all matters, thus far, relating to Germany and Italy; and the well-meaning Pacifists in Britain. The latter hoped that by espousing pacifism themselves militarists abroad would throw aside their ambitions and leave them alone. 'The vision of death' which Churchill saw 'in mental gaze' was coming nearer.

Chamberlain's policy rested heavily on Italian friendship. In April 1938 he signed an agreement with Italy recognizing her conquest of Abyssinia, offering her a share in the control of the Suez Canal and agreeing to exchange military and naval information as it affected activities in the Mediterranean and the Red Sea. So the Abyssinians were left to their fate, the millions of Spaniards suffering in the Spanish 'civil' war (in which Italy had 100,000 'volunteers' fighting) were ignored. The fearful indignities and injustices being heaped upon Germany's Jewish citizens were glossed over, and the wholesale inhumanities perpetrated in Germany's concentration camps overlooked.

Churchill despised the attitude of mind revealed in the Anglo-Italian Agreement. He attacked it vigorously in the House, pointing out that placating Italy was a policy of helping her strategically and politically at the expense of smaller or weaker nations. A better policy, he said, would be to organize a defensive system which could resist aggression and so prevent war.

However, Britain was—although now arming energetically—by comparison with Germany weak and unarmed. The economic crisis of the thirties, coupled with the snipings of Socialists and Liberals, who consistently opposed rearmament, coupled in turn with the almost universal hatred of war as expressed in pacifism, had all contributed to this perilous policy of drift. Now Britain's Prime Minister thought of little else except to play for time. But he also had considerable faith in his own intuition—a feeling that he could deal with dictators successfully where others might fail.

Within a few weeks of Churchill's warning that only upon the international foundations of law and order could peace be preserved, Hitler's troops marched into Austria, which became part of the German Reich. A formal protest from Mr. Chamberlain was ignored with disdain.

Churchill, almost immediately afterwards, visited France and conferred with the French Premier, M. Blum, the War Minister Daladier and General Gamelin, Chief of the Defence Staff. He emphasized the need for Britain and France to stick together and act together in face of the growing Nazi menace. He reported on these conversations to Lord Halifax, the British Foreign Minister, on his return. And on his own account he advocated that Britain and France, united in purpose, and themselves constituting 'an enormous force', should approach smaller States which would otherwise, in due course, be overrun by Nazi tyranny and say to them bluntly, 'We are not going to help you if you are not going to help yourselves. What are you going to do about it?'

'If we could rally even ten well-armed States in Europe all banded together to resist an aggression upon any one of them, then we should be so strong that the immediate danger might be warded off and a breathing-space be gained for building later a still broader structure for peace.' He instanced Yugoslavia, Rumania, Hungary and Czechoslovakia as countries which could be 'mopped up one by one' and mentioned the Danubian and Baltic States. And there was Russia:

To the East of Europe lies the enormous power of Russia, a country whose form of government I detest, but which at any rate seeks no military aggression upon its neighbours; a country profoundly menaced by Nazi hostility. We should certainly not go cap in hand to Soviet Russia or count in any definite manner upon Russian action. But how improvidently foolish we should be when dangers are so great to put needless barriers in the way of the general association of the great Russian mass with the resistance to an act of Nazi aggression. . . .

In April and May 1938 Hitler paid visits to Italy. Chamberlain still pursued his hope of separating Hitler and Mussolini, despite every indication that this policy was failing. But there was at this time a strong pro-German movement in Britain; even the Liberal Lloyd George described Hitler as 'a saviour of Germany'. People who have known power themselves are quite often attracted to powerful people, on the same principle that one is inclined to accept as an equal a man you meet in an exclusive club. Many British firms had strong financial connections in Germany, and it was not surprising—even if unedifying—that one prominent thought was the need to avoid either loss of trade with Germany or the loss of property and holdings there.

It was evident that, hot on the trail of his Austrian conquest, Hitler proposed to seize Czechoslovakia, which bestraddles Central Europe with borders with several countries and provides a gateway to Russia through Ruthenia. Hitler prepared the way by a violent propaganda campaign against President Benes and his Government, and by heavily subsidized sabotage and agitation by German agents in the Sudeten territory of Czechoslovakia. Numerous bloody border incidents, obviously organized in advance, were used as flimsy justification.

Chamberlain watched these developments with dismay. France had given Czechoslovakia a guarantee to come to her aid in the event of an attack upon her; Anglo-British obligations would oblige Britain to aid France in such an event. That, he decided, must be avoided. He sent Lord Runciman to Czechoslovakia, ostensibly as an independent investigator. Runciman visited the Nazi agitators as well as the Government of Czechoslovakia. His report, whilst acknowledging that the Sudeten territory was economically a vital if not indispensable part of the country, claimed that so powerful and violent were the Nazi dissidents amongst the Sudeten Germans that only by ceding that territory to Germany could peace be maintained.

By mid-September the campaign of vilification and intimidation of Czechoslovakia had almost reached its zenith. Hitler, in a fiery speech at Nuremberg, declared his patience exhausted.

France was not ready for a war. Daladier was Prime Minister

and Bonnet, an appeaser, was Foreign Minister. Support for Czecho-slovakia in face of a German attack would inevitably have involved France. At all costs France was determined not to honour her pledge, and as the crisis developed Daladier telephoned Chamberlain, told him that the French Cabinet was resolved to leave Czechoslovakia to her fate and asked Mr. Chamberlain to get the best terms out of Hitler that he could.

France's disunity and her dishonourable abnegation of her pledged word meant that Britain would probably stand alone if she cried 'halt!' to Hitler. Churchill's dream of a Franco-British-Soviet *bloc* of resistance to Nazi aggression remained a dream. When, on 18th March, the Russians had proposed a conference to discuss means of making the Franco-Soviet pact effective as part of the League of Nations machinery for ensuring freedom from aggression, they had met with a cool response. So France would not help Czechoslovakia and Russia would not therefore help France.

On 15th September 1938 Chamberlain flew to see Hitler at Berchtesgaden, for talks on Czechoslovakia. His stated object was 'to find out in personal conversation whether there was any hope of saving the peace'. With the good wishes of press and Parliament and public, the elderly British Prime Minister made the tiring seven-hour journey to Hitler's mountain eyrie. That a British Prime Minister should come chasing after him to this obscure spot was to Hitler as surprising as it was gratifying; dissembling his delight, he did not go forward to meet him, but waited on the steps in the manner of a great man waiting to receive a lesser. Hitler demanded an assurance that Britain accepted the principle of 'self-determination' (the right of the Sudeten Germans in Czechoslovakia to 'return' to Germany—a euphemism for Germany's intended seizure of Sudetenland). Playing for time, Chamberlain asked Hitler to hold his hand while he discussed the matter with the British Cabinet, after which they could meet again. A second meeting was agreed.

In the event, France and Britain agreed between themselves to cede Sudetenland to Hitler whether Czechoslovakia liked it or not. France, of course, was jeopardizing her own security by her heartless and ignoble action; she had given Czechoslovakia a pledge, whereas Britain had not. France was an ally, Britain a friend, though in this crisis for survival the former was to prove false and the latter useless.

When Mr. Chamberlain flew to Godesberg to see Hitler again, he did so to tell him that France and Britain accepted Germany's 'self-determination' demands. Hitler's plan, drawn up carefully, allowed for the invasion of the territory by 1st October. Chamberlain's visits were, therefore, a luxury he could well afford; the British Minister thought he was buying time, while Hitler knew he was not. But the considerable concessions by the French and British were not enough for Hitler. Czechs must clear out of the predominately German areas of their country, and a plebiscite held in November. Some areas where the Germans were not the majority might still have a plebiscite. In face of the barrage of hate and threats poured out over the German radio, and the mobilization of German troops along the Czech border, those formalities were simply a smokescreen for invasion.

By 28th September—only two days before the 'D-day' which Hitler, secretly, had set himself—Chamberlain gave the House of Commons an account of the negotiations. In the course of it a scrap of paper was passed to him. Smiling, he told the Members that he proposed to meet 'Herr Hitler' in Munich the next day. 'That is not all. He (Hitler) had also invited Signor Mussolini and M. Daladier. Signor Mussolini has accepted and I have no doubt that M. Daladier will accept. I need not say what my answer will be. . . . I am sure that the House will be ready to release me now to go and see what I can make of this last effort. . . .' There were tears and cheers; order papers were flung into the air. But in the gallery Jan Masaryk, Czechoslovakia's Ambassador in Britain and son of the Republic's founder, listened grimly.

Most people now over forty can remember the newsreel shots of Chamberlain departing for Munich, full of thinly-suppressed excitement. The following day the Munich Agreement was signed, giving Germany everything she demanded and allowing Czechoslovakia not even a voice. The Czechs were deserted and given a *fait accompli*. For them the shock and dismay were unbelievable; many stood in the streets of Prague and wept as the news broke.

There were scenes of rejoicing when Chamberlain returned and waved the agreement with smiling enthusiasm. But relief at the thought of war temporarily averted was soon replaced by a sense of shame at honour lost and obligations deferred. Mr. Churchill listened glumly while the Prime Minister told the House of Commons what had transpired. Pale and unsmiling, chin set with its characteristic forward thrust, Mr. Churchill shocked the House back to a sense of realities:

> ... I am sure it is much better to say exactly what we think about public affairs, and this is certainly not the time when it is worth anyone's while to court political popularity.
>
> I will, therefore, begin by saying what everybody would like to ignore or forget but which must nevertheless be stated, namely, that we have sustained a total and unmitigated defeat, and that France has suffered even more than we have . . . the utmost he (the Prime Minister) has been able to gain for Czechoslovakia . . . has been that the German dictator, instead of snatching the victuals from the table, has been content to have them served to him course by course. . . . I believe the Czechs, left to themselves and told they were going to get no help from the Western Powers, would have been able to make better terms than they have got after all this tremendous perturbation; they could hardly have got worse.

Then, in sonorous phrases that sent a chill through his listeners, with a directness and diction which carried with it all his passion, rage and grief, he put the whole desertion of Czechoslovakia into perspective:

> All is over. Silent, mournful, abandoned, broken, Czechoslovakia recedes into the darkness. She has suffered in every respect by her association with the Western democracies and with the League of Nations, of which she has always been an obedient servant. She has suffered in particular from her association with France, under whose guidance and policy she has been actuated for so long.
>
> I venture to think that in future the Czechoslovak State cannot be maintained as an independent entity. I think you will find that in a period of time which can be measured by years, but may be measured only by months, Czechoslovakia may be engulfed in the Nazi regime. . . .
>
> But we cannot consider the abandonment and ruin of Czechoslovakia in the light only of what happened last month. It is the most grievous consequence of what we have done and what we have left undone in the last five years—five years of futile good intentions, five years of eager search for the line of least resistance, five years of uninterrupted retreat of British power, five years of the neglect of our air defences. . . .

When I think of the fair hopes of a long peace which still lay before Europe at the beginning of 1933, when Herr Hitler first obtained power, and of all the opportunities of arresting the growth of the Nazi power which have been thrown away, when I think of the immense combinations and resources which have been neglected or squandered, I cannot believe that a parallel exists in the whole course of history.

The course events would take, Churchill told the House, could clearly be foreseen. All the countries of Central and Eastern Europe would make the best terms they could with 'the triumphal Nazi power'. Then followed a warning worthy of Pericles:

. . . the terrible words have for the time being been pronounced against the Western democracies: 'Thou art weighed in the balance, and found wanting'. This is only the beginning of the reckoning. This is only the first sip, the first foretaste of a bitter cup which will be proffered to us year by year unless by a supreme recovery of moral health and martial vigour, we arise again and take our stand for freedom as in olden time.

Hitler's policy of 'brinksmanship', his demoniac personal magnetism (one observer once remarked that it seemed impossible that the animal sounds of hate and violence, when he was in a rage, could emerge from a human mouth) and his ability, like an evil hypnotist, to stage-manage vast demonstrations of violent emotion, seemed to paralyse his intended victims into inactivity.

The next sup from 'the bitter cup' was not long in being proffered. Germany consolidated her hold on that part of Czechoslovakia ceded by the Munich Agreement and from 12th March 1939, at 6 a.m., invaded Czechoslovakia in force. Within days the Republic had been utterly subjugated, Hitler proclaiming his 'Protectorate of Bohemia and Moravia' on 16th March. Slovakia, which had been given a spurious autonomy, now became a puppet State.

All indications were that Poland was likely to be Hitler's next victim and Chamberlain gave to that country a pledge of assistance in the event of attack. Yet even at this late stage in the unfolding disaster, Britain's rulers could not throw off the malaise of appeasement and compromise, running cap-in-hand after the dictators. On 27th February Britain and France had recognized Franco's conquest of Spain, and earlier Chamberlain and Lord Halifax had been to

Rome for conversations with Mussolini. On 7th April, despite the Anglo-Italian Agreement, Italy invaded Albania and on 22nd May a military alliance was signed between Germany and Italy.

What of Russia, another giant in this sinister game? Again and again Churchill had pressed for moves to bring Russia into the Western democratic camp. Negotiations had dragged on and Russia did not trust the West. The deadlock was also in substantial part due to the refusal of the Baltic States and other countries having proximity to or boundaries with Russia to come into any mutual security plan; they, for their part, did not trust Russia. But Churchill told the House of Commons that 'A full and solid alliance should be made with Russia without delay. The Russian claim that we shall all stand together in resisting an act of aggression upon the Baltic States seems just and reasonable, and I cannot understand what we have been boggling at all these weeks.'

A bad job was made worse. A British military mission with few powers and headed by a comparative nonentity was sent to Russia. This convinced Stalin that he was wasting his time with the West. He must put a 'buffer' between his vast country and Germany, both to delay the inevitable German attack upon Russia and to ensure, if at all possible, that other countries would be trampled underfoot before the oncoming hordes ever reached the Russian border.

On 23rd August the West was appalled to learn that Stalin had signed a mutual pact of non-aggression with Nazi Germany. This virtual alliance between the immense Communist Empire and the expanding Nazi Empire seemed incredible. Hitler mobilized for an attack on Poland. And on 1st September his armies marched into Poland.

Britain was on the verge of war, and strangely calm about it. There was no parallel with 1914. Reports of the bombing of open cities in China, Abyssinia, Spain, with photographs of what this meant to ordinary civilians, left no room for doubt about what war would mean. There could be no jingoism, no flinging of straw boaters wildly into the air, no hysterical females offering their charms to those they labelled heroes and white feathers to cowards. You could not cheer the boys off at the station and go home to a life normal except for anxiety about husbands, brothers or friends overseas, and the inconvenience of rationing. Everybody was in this war from the beginning. Even Churchill, as he sat on the bench in the House of Commons on the evening of 1st September, was silent as well as thoughtful.

The debates in the House on 2nd September were tense and crowded. A message had been sent to Germany, and ignored; what were we waiting for? We had guaranteed Poland's integrity—now she was being attacked. The truth was that the French had pleaded for more time to mobilize before war was declared. The House was restive. 'Speak for England!' somebody shouted at Chamberlain. Maxton, the Socialist M.P., praised the delay.

At eleven o'clock on 3rd September Chamberlain broadcast to the people that Britain was at war with Germany. Churchill was called to the Cabinet Room, where Chamberlain asked his help in the War Cabinet and, later, the post of First Lord of the Admiralty, in which he had served during the First World War. With few comments and certainly no recriminations—this was no time for such things—Churchill accepted. In the Commons that evening he spoke calmly:

> In this solemn hour it is a consolation to recall and to dwell upon our repeated efforts for peace. All have been ill-starred, but all have been faithful and sincere . . . our hands may be active, but our consciences are at rest. There is a feeling of thankfulness that, if these trials were to come upon our island, there is a generation of Britains, here now, ready to prove that it is not unworthy of the days of yore, not unworthy of those great men, the fathers of our land.

The die was cast. And from Admiralty building flashed a message to the ships and establishments of the Royal Navy: WINSTON IS BACK.

21

The Phoney War

Within minutes of Mr. Chamberlain telling the nation on the radio
that Britain was at war with Germany, an air-raid alert was sounded
in London. At once the whole of the elaborate air-raid precautions
machinery jolted into action; even Mr. Churchill remarked that
Hitler had missed no time—but on this occasion, at least, it proved
a false alarm. Indeed, the opening months of the Second World War
were, so far as Britain was concerned, totally unlike anything that
had been expected.

It has been said that King George VI was surprised at the appointment of Mr. Churchill to the Admiralty, although he greeted him
warmly. I do not think that Mr. Churchill himself was surprised;
he was one of the few men in the Government who had warned the
House consistently of the dangers ahead and emphasized again and
again the urgent need for the nation to prepare for them. Indeed,
he could hardly get to the Admiralty quickly enough; once there, he
felt entirely at home. He found in his old room reminders of his
work there twenty-five years ago. Even an old wooden map frame,
which he had had specially made in 1911, was still there doing
service. It framed a chart of the North Sea.

One of his first steps was to see the First Sea Lord, Admiral Sir
Dudley Pound, whom Mr. Churchill had only recently criticized
severely in the House of Commons. Each greeted the other with
the respect due to a worthy opponent. Indeed, in this national crisis,
from the very first moment, they got on well together. It must be
remembered however that at no time was Mr. Churchill an easy
man to work with. He could think in big terms. His thoughts were
wide-ranging and audacious but his reactions were unpredictable,
and he was impatient. Apart from seeing the picture as a whole, he
could and would interest himself in detail. At any moment he might
ask about anything and everything, a habit which could be highly
disconcerting to his subordinates, sometimes giving them the impression that there was very little left, finally, to their own judgement

and initiative. On the other hand, this love of action—and love of action it certainly was—communicated itself to others, making it abundantly clear to all concerned that no slackness or malingering or defeatism would be tolerated. A dozen times a day he would send a memorandum asking for information on some topic, always beginning 'Pray tell me . . .'.

For good or for ill, the mood of the nation was one of relief that at last they knew where they stood, though few, of course, could imagine the course of events, least of all the Government itself. There was widespread satisfaction that the Admiralty had been entrusted to Mr. Churchill as First Lord, and that Anthony Eden, who had had the courage and integrity to resign from the office of Foreign Minister as a protest against appeasement in 1938, was back again, this time as Dominions Secretary. Only the older generation remembered that when Mr. Churchill was at the Admiralty in the First World War he had lost his job through being accused of responsibility for the failure of the Gallipoli Campaign. To most people he was known as the man who, from the outset, had foreseen the danger of Nazism and had stood up to Hitler and Mussolini.

Britain's transition from peace to war was sudden and dramatic. The blackout came into force as a precaution against air raids. Curtains were drawn, shop windows reinforced (as their owners fondly hoped) by ugly strips of gummed paper, to prevent splintering. Over a million children were evacuated to the country. Hospitals, ambulances, police, fire-fighters and air-raids precaution teams held themselves in readiness. Plans were made to split the country into regions, each capable of becoming autonomous in the event of an invasion, so that the life of the country should not be immobilized by isolation from the normal centre of power.

When Mr. Churchill strode into the House of Commons and took his place on the Treasury Bench he was given a tremendous ovation from every part of the House. This reception—in which members of all Parties took part—typified the relief felt by everyone that one of the country's most vital services had been entrusted to a man of strength and character. On this occasion, without further ado, he had to give the House bad news. On the previous day, on the very outbreak of the war, the *Athenia*, with 1,400 passengers, had been torpedoed by the Germans 200 miles west of Ireland, with the loss of 120 lives. Mr. Churchill told the House: 'She was torpedoed without the slightest warning in circumstances which the whole opinion of the world, after the late war in which Germany concurred, has stigmatized as inhuman.'

It was soon abundantly clear to everybody at the Admiralty and in the Navy that Mr. Churchill worked hard himself and expected everyone else to do so too. Disdaining the usual official residence reserved for the First Lord of the Admiralty, he chose instead to live in a top-floor flat crammed with a variety of telephones and an infinite assortment of gadgets. From it he would emerge at all hours of day and night, often wandering into the war room in his pyjamas and demanding to be informed of the position of every ship, scanning and following the charts with the attention of an expert.

One fixed habit, however, peculiar to Mr. Churchill, was to enable him to carry his immense burden, which increased month by month. Every afternoon he would take a sleep—it could hardly be called a nap—for one or two hours. His day started early, usually at 7 a.m. He would read and dictate in bed, but by three o'clock he had virtually done a full day's work. By 5.30 p.m. however he was refreshed and invigorated by his sleep and ready to work to any hour, well past midnight and beyond. His energy astonished everyone. He could sleep during the day without the ensuing drowsiness which would affect most people, and maintained, with perfect truth, that the habit enabled him to do twice as much work as he would otherwise have been able to achieve. He was once asked how—in a world of chaos, with every type of responsibility on his shoulders—he could sleep at will. His reply was simple. 'I just say "Damn the lot of them" and doze off.'

Mr. Churchill made it his business to visit naval establishments and vessels. One of his first visits was to the anti-submarine school at Portland, where he stayed with the Commander-in-Chief in his flagship *Nelson*. Continuing his tour, he visited Scapa Flow, to see for himself the facilities for docking and servicing vessels and to examine the precautions against enemy attack. On his return from this trip he was met by Admiral Sir Dudley Pound, who conveyed to him the grave news that H.M.S. *Courageous* had been sunk in the Bristol Channel on 18th September with the loss of 560 men. Churchill's reply was not callous—he was never ashamed, as are some Anglo-Saxons, at displays of emotion, and was not infrequently seen in tears at the thought of the sufferings—but now he was simply realistic: 'We can't expect to carry on a war like this without that sort of thing happening from time to time. I've seen lots of it before.'

It could be said that Mr. Churchill was the busiest of all the Ministers. At this time the war, so far as Britain was concerned, was on the sea. Britain's home defences were in a parlous state, and the immediate responsibility of protecting Britain from invasion and ensuring the safe transport of supplies and men to and from our shores rested with the Navy. Fortunately—and much to the bewilderment of many people—Hitler did not choose this moment to invade Britain. He was absorbed with the *blitzkrieg* on Poland; his tanks and outriders roared through that stricken country while his planes unleashed bombs on the undefended cities of Warsaw, Krakov, Gdynia, Poznan and other open towns.

During the first two weeks of war German submarines sank 111,000 tons of British shipping, besides many neutral merchant vessels. With all the considerable energy at his command Churchill stepped up anti-submarine warfare, and the tonnage of German merchant ships captured in the first month of the war proved greater than the shipping losses sustained by Britain. Mr. Churchill was able to tell the House that: 'The whole vast business of our worldwide trade continues without interruption or appreciable diminution. Great convoys of troops are escorted to their various destinations. The enemy's ships and commerce have been swept from the seas. Over two million tons of German shipping is now sheltering in German, or interned in neutral harbours.' But he added a note of warning: 'One must not dwell upon these reassuring figures too much, for war is full of unpleasant surprises.'

One particularly unpleasant surprise was the loss of the *Royal Oak* when a German U-boat slipped inside the boom of Scapa Flow and, having sunk the battleship, escaped undetected and unharmed. Meanwhile, however, the British Expeditionary Force, escorted by naval convoys, had arrived safely in France. Russia had decided to put a buffer between herself and Germany, and on 17th September invaded Poland. By 27th September war in Poland was virtually over, although occupation by the Germans, with the dreaded S.S. and the hated Gestapo following on the rear, was to bring fresh and protracted persecutions and exploitations. Warsaw surrendered. Speaking of Russia's role thus far in the war Mr. Churchill said:

What is the second event of this first month? It is, of course, the assertion of the power of Russia. Russia has pursued a cold policy of self-interest. We could have wished that the Russian armies should be standing on their present line as the friends and allies of Poland instead of as invaders. But that the Russian Army should stand on this line was clearly necessary for the safety of Russia against the Nazi menace. At any rate the line is there and an Eastern front has been created which a Nazi Germany does not dare assail. When Herr von Ribbentrop was summoned to Moscow last week it was to learn the fact and to accept the fact that the Nazi designs upon the Baltic states and upon the Ukraine must come to a dead stop. I cannot forecast to you the action of Russia; it is a riddle wrapped in a mystery inside an enigma: but perhaps there is a key. That key is Russian national interest. It cannot be in accordance with the interest or safety of Russia that Germany should plant itself upon the shores of the Black Sea, or that it should overrun the Baltic States and subjugate the Slavonic peoples of South Eastern Europe. That would be contrary to the historic life interest of Russia. Therefore, to sum up the results of the first month, let us say that Poland has been overrun but will rise again; that Russia has warned Hitler off his eastern dreams, and that U-boats may be safely left to the care and constant attention of the British Navy. . . . Here I am in the same post as I was twenty-five years ago. Rough times lie ahead, but how different is the scene from that of October 1914. Then the French front, with its British Army fighting in the line, seemed to be about to break under the terrible impact of German imperialism. Then Russia had been laid low at Tannenberg; then the whole might of the Austro-Hungarian Empire was in battle against us. Then the brave warlike Turks were about to join our enemies. Then we had to be ready, night and day, to fight a decisive sea battle with a formidable German fleet almost, in many respects, the equal of our own. We faced those adverse conditions then; we have nothing worse to face tonight.

On the loss of the *Royal Oak* Mr. Churchill said:

It is now established that the *Royal Oak* was sunk in the early hours of 14th October by a German U-boat which penetrated the defences of the land-locked anchorage of Scapa Flow. These defences were of two kinds; first, the physical obstructions by nets, booms and blockships, and secondly by small patrolling craft upon the approaches to the various entrances of sounds which are seven in number. Neither the physical obstructions nor the patrolling craft were in that state of strength and efficiency required to make the anchorage absolutely proof, as it should have been against the attack of a U-boat on the surface or half submerged at high water. Measures had been taken and were being taken to improve the physical obstructions and the last blockship required reached Scapa Flow only on the day after the disaster occurred. All the more was it necessary, while these defences were incomplete, that the patrolling craft should have been particularly numerous, but from a variety of causes connected with the movement of the fleet, which was not at that time using the anchorage, these patrolling craft were reduced below what was required.

The extent of British unpreparedness at this grave time is emphasized by the fact that Mr. Churchill, remembering how in 1919 he had caused certain heavy guns to be oiled and kept in storage, demanded that their whereabouts be traced forthwith, their usability assessed and any faulty parts made good so that they could be added as a meagre complement to Britain's defences. Generally, they were usable, although certain parts had to be remade and others refurbished.

A new and ruthless form of warfare which Churchill had actually predicted before the war now came into operation—the use by the Germans of magnetic mines. Six ships had been sunk by magnetic mines in the approaches to the Thames, but by a stroke of good fortune, on 22nd November, one such mine was recovered, examined and in due course, when its mechanism and workings were thoroughly understood, an answer to it was found. It was, basically, a simple method of demagnetizing ships by means of an electric cable. In a statement to the House of Commons on 6th December Mr. Churchill said of the German magnetic mines that they were 'about the lowest form of warfare that can be imagined. It is the warfare of the I R A (Irish Republican Army), leaving the bomb in the parcels office at the railway station.'

Except for the upheaval of people's domestic lives by conscription, rationing and the reorientation of normal commercial life to war production, the 'phoney war' as the Americans called it, or 'the twilight war' as it was known in Britain, seemed a mild ordeal indeed compared with the agonies of Poland, Czechoslovakia and Austria—and indeed of Finland, which Russia invaded on 30th November 1939 and had subjugated by 13th March 1940. Mr. Chamberlain continued to hope great things of Mussolini as a peacemaker, and was more than preoccupied with the possibility of sending British troops to Finland to fight the Russians. The invasion was a tragedy to the Finnish people, but it was fortunate for Britain that Russia's onslaught on that country succeeded so soon—before Britain had a chance to send her force of 100,000 men to Finland. Time was to prove that we had troubles enough without fighting two major powers on two fronts.

There were many who felt that Britain was taking too little initiative, that, war having been declared, it was foolish to pursue a policy of 'wait and see'. In April Chamberlain even went so far—in a speech which nobody forgot or forgave—to say that 'Hitler has missed the bus'. Within weeks Hitler had invaded Denmark and Norway, the lull of quiescence and procrastination ended suddenly. In the small hours of 9 April 1940 troop transports swarmed into the harbours of Norway and a powerful naval fleet, escorted by convoys, sailed up the dark Oslo fiord. German warships glided into Copenhagen and endless swarms of heavily-armed Nazis moved over the Danish frontier. The defenceless Danes surrendered; the Norwegians, by the time they tried to organize themselves for resistance, found that their ports and airfields had been seized and that their country was riddled with traitors organized by the Norwegian Nazi leader Quisling, whose name has passed into the dictionary as a synonym for treachery. In the first and second Battles of Narvik, the Royal Navy took heavy toll of German shipping, and the minefields laid off Norway's western coast on Churchill's insistence were a formidable handicap; but they were not enough to save the day. On 15th April British troops began landings near Narvik—at Namsos on 16th–18th April and at Andalsnes on 18th–19th April. But within three weeks these British expeditionary forces at Namsos and Andalsnes had to be withdrawn. Whatever the gallantry and good intentions displayed, the campaign had been a failure. The lightning competence with which Hitler's forces could assault countries and consolidate their power with every device of secrecy, force and terror was a guarantee that fresh assaults could be expected elsewhere, and that the weak and vacillating leadership in Britain would be useless against Hitler's demoniac energy and insatiable ambition.

Grieved as he was by the unnecessary war brought about by years of drift and irresolution, Churchill was loyal to his Prime

Minister, whose weaknesses he knew too well. He understood well enough that Chamberlain reflected, and did not set the pace for, the defeatism of the thirties; everyone was to blame in some measure and, however absurdly, Chamberlain had tried to save Britain from embroilment in a war for which she was not prepared.

On 2nd May, when the Prime Minister made a statement to the House on the Norwegian campaign, he found an influential and growing number of his own Party highly critical of the conduct of the war. He told Members:

The House will remember that some three months ago we made preparations for the despatch of Allied forces to the assistance of Finland. The possibility of reaching Finland was dependent upon the collaboration of the Governments of Norway and Sweden, and realising that even the acquiescence of Allied troops might involve them in an invasion by Germany we prepared other forces to go to their assistance in that contingency. It did not escape our attention that in such a case Trondheim and other western ports . . . might well be the subject of an attack by Germany and accordingly further forces came and made ready to occupy these places . . . the instructions to the Commanders of those forces provided that they were only to proceed to the occupation on one of two conditions; either that they were invited to do so by the Norwegian Government or that Norwegian neutrality had already been violated.

He continued to explain that permission to send troops through Norway and Sweden was refused, and after a certain period the greater part of the forces which had been accumulated were dispersed since both they and the ships which were allocated for their transport were wanted elsewhere. About a month ago, however, it had been decided that 'certain small forces' should be kept in readiness to occupy Norwegian western ports at short notice in case of an act of aggression by Germany against South Norway. 'It will be noted again that any action contemplated by us on Norwegian soil was conditional upon prior violation of Norwegian neutrality by Germany.'

'It has been asked,' continued Mr. Chamberlain, 'how it was that Germany has been able to forestall us' (hear, hear). 'The answer is simple. It was by long-planned, carefully-elaborated treachery (cheers) against an unsuspecting and almost unarmed people.'

This explanation did little to assuage the growing discontent. Why should Britain, in face of Germany's numerous prior acts of treachery, be so surprised or pained at this new act of aggression? Were mere phrases deploring the fact that Hitler was not a gentleman likely to have the slightest impact?

From 7th–8th May an historic debate raged in the House of Commons, ranking with the most important discussions ever held there. The atmosphere towards Chamberlain was now frankly hostile. Mr. Chamberlain volunteered a long and detailed reply to his critics; he began by saying that, whatever criticisms might be made about anyone else he was sure everyone would agree that the troops who had been engaged in Southern Norway carried out their task with magnificent gallantry; opposed by superior forces with superior equipment, they had acquitted themselves well in every respect . . . no doubt, he said, the news of our withdrawal from Southern Norway created a profound shock both in the House and in Britain (an interruption: 'and abroad'). There were cries from several parts of the House 'and all over the world!' Mr. Chamberlain said that it had not been thought that withdrawal would be necessary, and he saw it was stated that the Ministers were to blame for that (cries of 'they missed the bus').

There were then many interruptions, and the Speaker ordered Members to allow the Prime Minister to continue his statement. It had been suggested, Mr. Chamberlain continued, that the forces assembled for the assistance of Finland should never have been dispersed, and that assistance could have been sent more quickly to the scene, but whatever forces had been at Britain's disposal, the Germans could not have been forestalled unless the Norwegians had either invited the British or allowed them to come in. He did not suppose that anyone would have suggested that Britain should have invaded Norway before Germany did.

Here he had a valid point. Nobody had suggested it. Such a step would have been vehemently opposed by most Members of Parliament and almost certainly by the British public; Russia, of course, was inhibited by no such niceties in her assaults upon Poland and Finland, both undertaken for long-term motives of expansion and self-protection. He was on less sure ground in trying to explain away his disastrous reference to Hitler having 'missed the bus'. He was referring, he said, to the past, not the present or future—but M.P.s recalled that Hitler had not missed the bus in attacking

Austria, Czechoslovakia or Poland. Such cocksure complacencies
could leave Britain defenceless in her mortal danger. Irritably, Mr.
Chamberlain declared the interpretation of his 'missed the bus'
speech an example of prejudice; he had been referring to the folly
of Hitler in not attacking at the very beginning of the war when the
disparity between German and Allied arms was so much in Hitler's
favour. He added that perhaps the phrase was 'a trifle colloquial for
a Prime Minister'—as though anybody was bothered by linguistic
niceties at such a time.

Mr. Chamberlain went on to describe how he had strengthened
the War Cabinet by including Lord Hankey and Winston Churchill
despite the fact that they had heavy ministerial duties; it was right,
he said, that they should be present when decisions affecting their
functions were discussed. He had, for instance, asked Mr. Churchill
to succeed Lord Chatfield as Chairman of the Military Co-ordinating Committee of the Cabinet. Mr. Churchill had accepted, also
representing that it would be a good thing if he were put in closer
contact with the Chiefs of Staff, and accordingly he had been
authorized to give guidance and direction to the Chiefs of Staff
Committee, to prepare plans to carry out the objectives given to
them by him.

Mr. Wedgwood pointed out that because of the drift of events,
all neutrals bordering on Germany would obey Hitler for fear of
what Germany might do. The campaign had proved that with air
power as it was now, an army could not move by day; further,
the fleet could save Britain from starvation but not from invasion. He raised a storm when he said that the British Navy
could perfectly well defend Britain if it had not gone to the other
end of the Mediterranean to keep itself safe from bombing. The
Government, he warned, should realize that the lightning stroke
would always win, and be ready to deliver unexpected blows to the
enemy.

A notable and weighty speaker was Admiral Sir Roger Keyes,
who told Members that he had come to the House in uniform
because he wanted to speak for the officers and men of the Navy,
who were very unhappy. He wished to make it perfectly clear that
it was not their fault that the German ships forced their way into
the Norwegian ports by treachery and were not followed in and
destroyed as they were at Narvik. It was not the fault of those for
whom he spoke that the enemy had been left in undisputed posses-

sion of vulnerable ports and aerodromes for nearly a month and had been given time to pour in reinforcements by sea and air, and to land tanks and heavy armaments and mechanized transport. Everything the Prime Minister had said had reinforced his conviction that the capture of Trondheim was imperative and vital; this, he maintained, could have been effected. The naval hazards would have been 'trifling' compared with others he had overcome. He had approached the Cabinet, and had been 'foolish enough to think his suggestions might be welcome' and been told that it was astonishing that he should think that such matters, with their attendant problems of resources and consideration of what dangers would be involved, had not been thought of.

Sir Roger Keyes added other detailed criticisms which, backed by the authority of his career and competence, helped to weight the scales against Chamberlain and his Government.

Mr. Amery demanded a searching inquiry into the conduct of the war. By whose authority was the indispensable hammer-blow on Trondheim countermanded? There were risks, but war was not won by shirking risks. There must be a supreme war directorate, such as Lloyd George had introduced in the last war. Further, the Government must represent 'all the elements of real political power' in the country. The Opposition must take its share of the responsibility. A Government was needed which would match the enemy in daring, fighting spirit, and resolution. Britain could not go on being led as it was. He would quote Cromwell with great reluctance because he was speaking of those who were old friends and associates and the words were applicable to the present situation. 'Speaking to the Long Parliament when he felt it was no longer fit to conduct the affairs of the nation, Cromwell said: "You have sat too long here for any good you have been doing; depart, I say, and let us have done with you. In the name of God, go!" '

On the following day Mr. Herbert Morrison added his voice of protest. The Prime Minister, he said, presented a new figure to the House. It was obvious as the debate proceeded that Ministers were open to considerable censure for their conduct of affairs. Mr. Chamberlain was not a confident Prime Minister, he was uncertain of the case he was presenting. He asked that Mr. Churchill, as one of the men primarily responsible, should appear as early as possible to give the House all the facts it needed on the conduct of the operations.

'It may well be,' said Mr. Chamberlain, 'that it is a duty to criticize the Government. I do not seek to evade criticism, but I say this to my friends in the House—and I have friends in the House—that no Government can prosecute the war efficiently unless it has public and parliamentary support. I accept the challenge and I welcome it. Now at least we can see who is with us and who against us. I call upon my friends to support us in the Lobbies tonight.'

Whatever Chamberlain may have meant to convey, what he did in fact imply was that for him it was all a personal issue, that personal loyalty to him was the issue at stake, whereas, as Lloyd George was quick to remind him, the House was discussing the interests of the country. 'I say solemnly,' the old war leader declared, 'that the Prime Minister should give an example of sacrifice because I tell him that there is nothing that would contribute more to victory in this war than that he should sacrifice the seals of office.' Lloyd George's speech was bitter and incisive. Britain's promises, he declared, were 'now rubbish in the markets'. When this accusation brought cries of 'Shame!' Lloyd George asked, 'Tell me one neutral country that would be prepared to stand up to the Nazis upon a mere promise by ourselves?'

Everything, he said, had been done half-heartedly, ineffectively, without drive and unintelligently. Then came the war. The tempo was hardly speeded up. There was the same leisurely inefficiency. . . . When he said, in the course of his criticisms of the campaign in Norway, that he did not think the First Lord of the Admiralty wholly responsible, Mr. Churchill was quickly on his feet, determined that he would not draw credit or immunity to himself by deserting his Prime Minister, now under fire. 'I take complete responsibility for everything that has been done by the Admiralty and I take my full share of the burden.' This brought from Lloyd George the good-humoured retort, 'I hope the hon. Gentleman will not allow himself to be converted into an air-raid shelter.' The retort caused loud laughter on all sides.

Perhaps if Mr. Churchill had been given a more prominent part in this two days' debate, and much earlier, the course of events might have been different. But try as he might, his eloquence could not remove the House's conviction that the ship of State was foundering and that its captain had lost his head.

Mr. Duff Cooper spoke for the discontented elements of the Conservative Party when he said that members must at such a time throw away respect for all friendships and Party loyalties and pay attention to two questions—the absolute truth, and the welfare of the country.

He regretted Mr. Morrison's intention to divide the House but he regretted still more the Prime Minister's appeal to the affection of his friends. Since his resignation he had never found it necessary to vote against Mr. Chamberlain but in time of war he felt the issue so urgent that no man had the right to wash his hands like Pontius Pilate and take neither one side nor the other. With the deepest reluctance he would have to vote against the present administration.

Mr. Churchill supported British policy at Narvik and although he sympathized intensely with Sir Roger Keyes' wish to repeat in Scandinavian waters the 'immortal glories of the Zeebrugge mole' he was sorry that 'this natural, honourable impulse should have led the hon. and gallant Gentleman to cast imputations and aspersions on his old shipmates and his own chosen staff officers, Sir Dudley Pound and Vice-Admiral Phillips.' He defended the decision to abandon any plan for taking Trondheim, and warned the House that Britain's limited Air Force could not be dispersed and diverted to such an extent that the English Channel was left undefended; 'There are other waters we have to think of.' Mr. Churchill said that he did not recede from the statement he had previously made that the decision by Hitler to invade Norway had been 'a cardinal political and strategic error'.

Mr. Churchill's outline of the reasons underlying the Navy's strategy thus far was eloquent and detailed. In representing the fall of Denmark and Norway, however, as a circumstance of disadvantage to Germany and implied advantages to the Allies, perhaps he verged on the sophistic. Certainly some Members thought so. The advantages, Mr. Churchill said, rested substantially with the Allies. Hitler had lost ten lives for every one and 'he has compelled a large part of the Scandinavian Peninsula to enter the Nazi empire of hungryland. He has committed an act of self-blockade, and the Government see no reason why our blockade should not become more effective now that the Norwegian corridor exists no longer. Unhappy Denmark, after her food reserves have been devoured, will no longer be a channel of trade communication with the outer world. . . .'

At this a Member shouted 'Oh!'

Mr. Churchill glowered at his interrupter. 'Yes, I dare say the honourable Gentleman does feel like it. He would rather that I had a bad tale to tell. That is why he is skulking in the corner.'

There were immediate and angry shouts of 'Withdraw!' but Churchill was adamant. 'No, I will not withdraw it.' Mr. MacLean, M.P. for Glasgow, asked, 'Is "skulking" a parliamentary word?' to which the Speaker replied, 'It all depends on whether it is used accurately.' There was loud laughter at this but Mr. MacLean stuck to his guns and insisted on continuing his point of order in the face of loud opposition. The uproar grew, and Mr. Churchill rose from his seat and stood shouting at the Labour members—the hubbub was so great that his words could not be heard.

At last Mr. MacLean was able to put his point. 'Are we to understand that a word becomes parliamentary if it is accurate?' and Mr. Churchill growled: 'All day long we've had abuse and you won't even listen.' Order was at last restored.

Mr. Churchill, in supporting Mr. Chamberlain, was espousing a losing cause, and knew it. But it was not the first time, nor was it to be the last, that he was to sponsor an unpopular cause. Every one had made mistakes, and was in part to blame, for the disaster of war, and he could not be bothered at so grave a time, with heresy-hunting. He owed the Prime Minister loyalty, and gave it. Nevertheless he knew that the hour was grave and that more vigorous leadership would be needed.

In the event, he could not save the day. Forty Government back benchers, who would normally have voted with the Government, including Sir Roger Keyes, Mr. Duff Cooper, Harold Nicolson and L. S. Amery, voted with the Opposition, so that when the vote was taken it was found that the Government had secured a majority of only 81 instead, as it should have been, of 200. From the Opposition benches came cries of 'Resign!' and 'For God's sake go!' and as Mr. Chamberlain left the House he was booed by the Opposition while a section of the Government supporters rose and cheered him.

Chamberlain had lost all chance of continuing as Prime Minister, but did not see it. Indeed, when he was received by the King after the first day's debate on 7th May he was in good humour and said that he had not come to tender his resignation. He hoped to reconstruct his Government in a national coalition in which the Labour Party would co-operate.

The King offered to speak to Mr. Attlee, the Labour leader. This, Mr. Chamberlain thought, should wait until the Labour Party's annual conference at Bournemouth, due that week-end, after which Attlee would know the disposition of his members. The King sympathized with Mr. Chamberlain over the rough handling his Prime Minister had had in the House. But the following day's voting on his vote of confidence showed that Chamberlain had over-estimated the number of 'friends in the House'.

The following day Chamberlain still dallied with the idea of re-constructing his Government with himself still as Premier. In the morning he summoned Lord Halifax, Mr. Churchill and Captain Margesson (Government Chief Whip) to 10 Downing Street; again, Chamberlain was not convinced that he would need to resign, but discussed with them who his successor could or should be should his attempts to form a Coalition willing to work under him prove unsuccessful. Halifax did not press his own cause; his peerage, he thought, would be an obvious disadvantage to a Prime Minister whose main business would be in the House of Commons rather than the House of Lords. Churchill said little, and expressed no opinion as to a successor.

Later the same day Chamberlain saw Mr. Attlee and Mr. Green-wood. To them he extended an invitation (which he had also made two months ago) to join a National Government with himself as Prime Minister. Mr. Attlee told Mr. Chamberlain what the latter had already told the King—that such a decision would first of all have to be endorsed by the Party's Executive, then meeting at Bournemouth. But it was made clear to Mr. Chamberlain that there was little likelihood of the Labour Party serving under him.

While these discussions were going on, ominous news came from Holland. Germans were massing for an invasion. Where would the onward sweep of the Nazi legions end? Was Britain united enough to withstand the oncoming storm? Might not German paratroopers come dropping out of the sky upon Britain, in a never-ending cascade, until the ground defenders were exhausted? Would White-hall echo to the rhythmic tread of jackboots and the swastika be unfurled over Buckingham Palace? Would the harmless-looking 'newspaper kiosk' outside the Houses of Parliament be spitting fire at the invader?

On Friday, 10th May, events moved with startling rapidity. At dawn that day Germany invaded Holland, Belgium and Luxem-bourg. Mr. Attlee sounded his Executive and had to tell Chamber-lain that the Labour Party would not serve in a coalition so long as he remained Prime Minister, but would serve in a National Government under another Premier. The Liberals had similarly refused to serve under Chamberlain.

Late that afternoon Chamberlain told of his wish to resign. The King was much disappointed and thought that Chamberlain had been treated most unfairly. The King's preference was for Lord Halifax and to overcome the handicap of the peerage (in presiding over the House of Commons) offered to put his peerage 'in abeyance'. This, Chamberlain knew, would not work; besides, the Labour Party would not be keen to join a Ministry led by a 'Man of Munich', meaning that he had supported the Munich Agreement of 1938, by which Hitler gained his first foothold in Czechoslovakia as a prelude to further expansion.

And so Mr. Winston Churchill was recommended as the man to form a Ministry. King George sent for him, and in *The Second World War* Churchill gives his account of that historic meeting:

His Majesty received me most graciously and bade me sit down. He looked at me searchingly and quizzingly for some moments and then said: 'I suppose you don't know why I have sent for you?' Adopting his mood, I replied: 'Sir, I simply couldn't imagine why'. He laughed and said: 'I want you to form a Government'. I said I would certainly do so.

But at this stage, the King's private attitude towards Winston Churchill was somewhat cool. He was sorry to lose Chamberlain and even more sorry that Halifax could not replace him. Churchill's bitter attack on Chamberlain at the time of the Munich crisis had not been forgotten, while his long-standing reputation as an erratic and unpredictable controversialist must have encouraged a 'wait-and-see' attitude. However, the King did as advised, and before long was recording in his diary that he could not have had a better Prime Minister.

And so, for Winston Spencer Churchill, the hour of destiny had struck. Once rejected, reviled, assailed, ignored and derided, Churchill found himself at the age of sixty-five to be Prime Minister of Britain in the most critical hour of her long history.

Churchill, in his own splendid prose, has recorded for posterity his personal reaction to the immense responsibilities and cares which now faced him:

. . . I went to bed at about 3 a.m. I was conscious of a profound sense of relief. At last I had the authority to give directions over the whole scene. I felt as if I were walking with destiny, and that all my past life had been but a preparation for this hour and this trial.

22

A Fighting Leader

Mr. Churchill lost no time in forming a Cabinet. The criteria of competence, drive, initiative and natural authority were all that concerned him. To his political enemies he showed a magnanimity greater than that which, for most of his life, he himself had received from his political friends.

Churchill had always liked responsibility. There are people who hate it and dodge it, preferring the refuge or ostentation of mere criticism of those in authority. Churchill was glad to have power—because his fervent conviction that Britain was great, and that even at this late hour could save itself and give the world much, could be translated into action. 'Power, for the sake of lording it over fellow-creatures or adding to personal pomp, is rightly judged base,' he declares in *Their Finest Hour*. 'But power in a national crisis, when a man believes he knows what orders should be given, is a blessing. In any sphere of action there can be no comparison between the positions of number one and numbers two, three and four. . . .' Their functions, as he so rightly says, are totally different, and when a subordinate, however highly placed, initiates anything or authorizes anything, he must consider not only his judgement, and that of his subordinates, but that of his boss.

Future generations may be thankful that he accepted cheerfully at this time the crushing load of office, a load which would have daunted most people or, if it did not do that, would have proved them inadequate.

In Churchill's War Cabinet there were only five members: Mr. Churchill combined the offices of Prime Minister, First Lord of the Treasury, Minister of Defence and Leader of the House of Commons. Mr. Neville Chamberlain, as Lord President of the Council, was included; Mr. C. R. Attlee, as Lord Privy Seal, and the Labour leader, was included, together with another Labour colleague, Mr. Arthur Greenwood. Lord Halifax, Secretary of State for Foreign Affairs, was the only member of the War Cabinet with a Department. However, three departmental heads enjoyed Cabinet rank—Mr. A. V. Alexander, Labour, First Lord of the Admiralty, Mr. Anthony Eden, Secretary of State for War and, of course, a Conservative; and Sir Archibald Sinclair, the Liberal Secretary of State for Air. Cabinet meetings were sometimes attended by others whose opinions or guidance were necessary to the discussions or decisions, but the basic responsibility rested on the five Cabinet members, and the ultimate responsibility on Mr. Churchill.

The various political parties were fairly represented in the Government; with disaster lapping on the shores of Britain, party political differences seemed very trivial.

By the time Parliament met for the first time under Churchill's Premiership—on 13th May 1940—Queen Wilhelmina and Princess Juliana of Holland were already refugees in Britain. The German assault on the Low Countries gathered momentum at terrifying speed. There was almost universal relief that a firm leader had been found at last, and when Churchill entered the House in the afternoon he was loudly cheered. He moved:

That this House welcomes the formation of a government representing the united and inflexible resolve of the nation to prosecute the war with Germany to a victorious conclusion.

The Commons had become, for all practical purposes, a Council of State. Labour Members formerly on the Opposition benches now sat on the Treasury bench, facing the official 'Opposition' with friendly mien. Everyone who entered got cheered—Mr. Chamberlain most of all, with order papers being flung in the air. Mr. Eden got his share. So did Mr. Alexander and Mr. Herbert Morrison. But all could feel vibrating through the House a heartfelt thankfulness as Mr. Churchill rose to speak. He leaned forward slightly, as though about to spring upon the presumptuous; his chin was thrust forward, his rubicund features flickering in expression between aggression and ebullience.

The shifting and rustling of papers stopped. He stood like a giant in the debating chamber, every eye upon him, every ear strained. After recounting how he had received the King's Commission to form a new administration, and the considerations with which he had tackled this task at short notice, he uttered, with the dignity and force of argument, with perfect economy of words, a call to duty and endeavour recalling the full glory of Shakespearean English and the splendour of Elizabethan chivalry:

> I would say to the House, as I have said to those who have joined this Government: 'I have nothing to offer but blood, toil, tears and sweat'. We have before us an ordeal of the most grievous kind. We have before us many, many long months of struggle and suffering. You ask, what is our policy? I will say: It is to wage war, by sea, land and air, with all our might and with all the strength that God can give us: to wage war against a monstrous tyranny, never surpassed in the dark, lamentable catalogue of human crime. That is our policy. You ask, What is our aim? I can answer in one word: Victory—victory at all costs, victory in spite of all terror, victory, however hard and long the road may be; for without victory there is no survival. Let that be realised; no survival for the British Empire; no survival for all that the British Empire has stood for, no survival for the urge and impulse of ages, that mankind will move forward towards its goal. But I take up my task with buoyancy and hope. I feel sure that our cause will not be suffered to fail among men. At this time I feel entitled to claim the aid of all, and I say, 'Come, then, let us go forward together with our united strength'.

The mood of the House was almost entirely with Mr. Churchill. Mr. Lloyd George, in particular, speaking as 'one of the oldest friends of the Prime Minister in the House', congratulated Mr. Churchill and added, 'I congratulate the country upon his elevation to the Premiership at this very, very critical and terrible moment. If I may venture to say so, I think the Sovereign exercised a wise choice. We know the right honourable Gentleman's glittering intellectual gifts, his dauntless courage, his profound study of war and his experience in its operation and direction. They will all be needed now. . . . The friends of freedom and of human right throughout the world will wish him god-speed.'

A more critical note was sounded by Mr. Maxton, who felt keenly the frustration of a man whose humanity and ideals made any endorsement of a war on the scale now envisaged—or on any scale—unthinkable. That to turn the other cheek would have been to bring upon British people and their institutions the disaster and degradation that followed inevitably in the wake of the Nazis in no way altered his feelings. 'We are in this position today because of twenty-two years of wasted opportunity', he said, bitterly and sorrowfully. 'For practically twenty of those years the country was under the control of Governments not essentially differing in position or personnel from this one.' And now they said this was going to create an entirely new orientation. The only difference was that the Prime Minister cut out of his speech any reference to the possibilities of peace short of 'wholesale slaughter'. Mr. Maxton and his friends believed that the overwhelming mass of people in the world, Germany included, were against the slaughter. He admitted all the difficulties facing people who held anti-war beliefs, who held democratic beliefs and who believed that the world must be reconstructed on a different social basis, but he stood by those principles of freedom and social equality. Just as Mr. Churchill had got his chance, so the chances of those people who stood by these principles now would come also, and something better would come out of this slaughter and general folly.

Therefore, continued Mr. Maxton—while Mr. Churchill listened respectfully—he opposed the Motion because it conflicted with every political belief that he had ever had. But he congratulated Mr. Churchill on having achieved 'the highest political governmental position in the country'. His personality and courage no one could deny.

His and that of another Independent Labour Member, Mr. Stephen, was the only opposition. Mr. Lees-Smith, spokesman of the Labour Party and Sir Percy Harris for the Independent Liberals, gave the new administration their blessing. There was only one person in the Distinguished Strangers Gallery—the familiar, but now sad, presence of the Belgian Ambassador. Later the French Ambassador arrived and heard part of the short debate. The sitting ended in a division challenged only by Mr. Maxton and Mr. Stephen, and as they acted as tellers their votes were not counted. The division figures were 381 for the Government and none against. The House of Lords later passed unanimously a similar vote of confidence.

A gracious and sagacious gesture of Churchill's was his decision not to lead the Conservative Party which, as Prime Minister of a Conservative Government, it would be usual for him to do. Firstly, partisan politics must rest until peace had been won; secondly, there was his loyalty to Chamberlain. 'When the bull is down,' says the

Spanish proverb, 'everyone is quick with the knife'; but this was never true of Churchill. He had nothing but contempt for cowards who profit, in whatever way, from the misfortunes of others.

Not a minute too soon had Britain's administration been re-invigorated and unified. It is interesting to recall how little use Churchill had for recriminations. The harsh realities of life will defeat a man who repines uselessly over what cannot be altered and so weakens his resolve to combat and overcome the problems that face him in the present. Holland and Belgium—like Denmark and Norway—had maintained an obstinate and unrealistic neutrality despite every indication of imminent and inevitable attack. Two days after Churchill's 'blood, toil, tears and sweat' speech Holland had capitulated; in two more days the Germans had occupied Brussels. But with Rotterdam in flames and thousands buried under the ruins of smoking buildings, and with the terrible onrush of the German forces through France, even to Boulogne, with the King of the Belgians telling his army of 500,000 trained soldiers to capitulate—who could choose such a moment for reproaches? The answer is that many could, and did; but not Churchill. From him, nothing but a factual appraisal of situations and realistic, sturdy, confident plans to circumvent or overcome them.

As Churchill spoke to the House of Commons on 29th May the fury of war lapped even nearer to English shores. The public had read of Brussels, Antwerp and Liège falling to the Germans with deadly monotony, of tanks and motorized columns screaming inexorably across the River Meuse near Sedan and roaring ahead across North-eastern France. The capitulation of the Belgian Army on 28th May exposed the flank and means of retreat of the British forces sent at King Leopold's urgent last-minute appeal when his country was invaded. Calais was under heavy bombardment. Meanwhile, the First French Army and four British divisions were being caught in a German pincer movement and seemed to face annihilation.

On 29th May Churchill said that the British and French forces were in good heart despite the gravity of their situation. They were fighting with discipline and tenacity. The French Prime Minister had spoken with scorn of King Leopold's decision, which was taken without warning the Allied forces; the Royal Air Force was trying to relieve pressure on the Allied lines by bombing military objectives behind the German front:

The House will be aware that the King of the Belgians sent a pleni-potentiary to the German Command asking for a suspension of arms on the Belgian front. The British and French Governments instructed their Generals immediately to dissociate themselves from this proceeding, and to persevere in the operations on which they are now engaged (cheers). However, the German Command has agreed to the Belgian proposals and the Belgian Army ceased to resist the enemy's will at 4 o'clock this morning. I have no intention of suggesting to the House that we should attempt at this moment to pass judgement upon the action of the King of the Belgians in his capacity as Commander-in-Chief of the Belgian Army. His Army has fought very bravely and has both suffered and inflicted heavy losses. The Belgian Government has dissociated itself from the action of the King (cheers) and declaring itself to be the only legal Government of Belgium has formally announced its resolve to continue the war on the side of the Allies (cheers). We had come to the aid of the Belgians at her urgent appeal. Whatever our feelings may be . . . we must remember the sense of brotherhood between the many peoples who have fallen into the power of the aggressor. The situation of the British and French Armies, now engaged in a most severe battle and beset on three sides . . . is evidently extremely grave. The surrender of the Belgian Army in this manner adds appreciably to their grievous peril. But the troops are in good heart . . . meanwhile the House should prepare itself for hard and heavy tidings. I have only to add that nothing which may happen in this battle can in any way relieve us of our duty to defend the world cause . . . nor should it destroy our confidence in our power to make our way, as on former occasions in our history, through defeat, through grief, to the ultimate defeat of our enemies (cheers).

Before the war Mr. Churchill had visited the Maginot Line, the chain of defensive forts and underground labyrinth on which the French had spent a fabulous fortune. It had almost everything, even conveyor belts on which, like flitches of bacon about to be smoked, the corpses of the inevitable casualties could be swept on mechanically to oblivion. But, as everyone knows now, and nobody expected then, the Germans chose to outflank it on the north.

Only three days before making his 'hard and heavy tidings' speech to the House, Churchill had had a sad duty. The British garrison at Calais were outnumbered and in due course must be

engulfed and annihilated; should they evacuate? But if they did,
would the trapped B.E.F. escape destruction? At all costs, to gain
hours, perhaps days, the Germans must be held back. Churchill's
message to Brigadier Nicholson was typical of his grasp of realities:
'Every hour you continue to exist is of the greatest help to the B.E.F.
Government has therefore decided that you must continue to fight.
Have greatest possible admiration for your splendid stand. Evacuation will not (repeat not) take place and craft required for above
purposes are to proceed to Dover.'

This was virtually a message of death for these men, but it helped
to make possible the 'miracle' of Dunkirk. From the coasts and ports
of Britain an endless procession of craft, ranging from pleasure boats
to dinghies, from motor-boats to luxury yachts, from minesweepers
to battleships, made their way to Dunkirk, and from the bomb-
scarred beaches rescued the bulk of the B.E.F. Over 600 little ships
braved German submarines, planes and E-boats while the R.A.F.
gave battle to the *Luftwaffe* in the skies. Eventually, by 4th June,
337,131 French and British troops had been rescued to fight again.
But the B.E.F. had lost staggering and costly quantities of equipment, including 82,000 vehicles, 90,000 rifles, 8,000 Bren guns and
400 anti-tank rifles. From the human and military point of view,
the rescue of the B.E.F. in the nick of time was a matter of profound
thankfulness, but these losses of equipment were a heavy blow. Only
time could remedy the loss; but the need was immediate.

On 4th June Mr. Churchill told the crowded House of this tremendous event, in a silence so profound that a pin might almost be
heard to drop. His speech was a classic of rhetoric which will be
read and which will enthrall hundreds of years from now, so clearly
does it convey the unfolding drama:

I have said that this armoured scythe-stroke almost reached
Dunkirk—almost, but not quite. Boulogne and Calais were the
scenes of desperate fighting. The Guards defended Boulogne for
a while and were then withdrawn by orders from this country.
The Rifle Brigade, the 60th Rifles, and the Queen Victoria's
Rifles with a battalion of British tanks and 1,000 Frenchmen, in
all about 4,000 strong, defended Calais to the last.

The British brigadier was given an hour to surrender. He
spurned the offer, and four days of intense street fighting passed
before silence reigned over Calais, which marked the end of a
memorable resistance. Only thirty unwounded survivors were

brought off by the Navy, and we do not know the fate of their comrades. . . . Thus it was that the port of Dunkirk was kept open.

But Churchill had scarcely hoped, when uttering his forewarning to the House on 29th May, that more than 20,000 or 30,000 men might be rescued. Belgium had, until she was invaded, insisted on remaining neutral. When at last the Nazi hurricane hurled itself upon her, she sent a frantic and urgent appeal to Britain, which was promptly answered, with no recriminations uttered for her obstinacy, which had imperilled Britain as well as herself. And Britain having come to the rescue, Belgium then threw in her hand and immobilized her vast and efficient army without regard for the disaster to which she thus exposed her allies.

Suddenly the scene cleared, the crash and thunder for the moment—but only for the moment—died away. A miracle of deliverance, achieved by valour, by perseverance, by faultless service, by resource, by skill, by unconquerable fidelity, is manifest to us all. . . .
We must be very careful not to assign to this deliverance the attributes of a victory. Wars are not won by evacuations. . . .

He paid his tribute to the tremendous efforts of the British Air Force:

There never had been, I suppose, in all the world, in all the history of war, such an opportunity for youth. The Knights of the Round Table, the Crusaders, all fall back into a prosaic past: not only distant but prosaic: but these young men going forth every morn to guard their native land and all that we stand for, holding in their hands these instruments of colossal and shattering power, of whom it may be said that
      Every morn brought forth a noble chance
      And every chance brought forth a noble knight,
deserve our gratitude. . . .

This was a cause of thankfulness and admiration.

. . . Nevertheless, our thankfulness . . . must not blind us to the fact that what has happened in France and Belgium is a colossal military disaster. The French Army has been weakened, the Belgian Army has been lost . . . the whole of the Channel ports

are in his (the enemy's) hands. . . . We are told that Herr Hitler
has plans for invading the British Isles. This has often been
thought of before. When Napoleon lay at Boulogne for a year
with his flat-bottomed boats and his Grand Army he was told by
someone, 'There are bitter weeds in England' . . . I have, myself,
full confidence that if all do their duty, if nothing is neglected,
and if the best arrangements are made, we shall prove ourselves
once again able to defend our island home, to ride out the storm
of war, and to outlive the menace of tyranny, if necessary for years,
if necessary alone.

No listener could doubt what these words presaged. The heavy
defeats were only, like Munich, 'a foretaste of a bitter cup'. But
with gathering momentum and eloquence, Churchill poured forth
words that imbued his listeners with pride, rather than dismay, at
their being privileged to face the great challenge:

Even though large tracts of Europe and many old and famous
States have fallen or may fall into the grip of the Gestapo and all
the odious apparatus of Nazi rule, we shall not flag or fail, we
shall go on to the end, we shall fight in France, and we shall fight
on the seas and oceans, we shall fight with growing confidence
and growing strength in the air, we shall defend our island whatever the cost may be, we shall fight on the beaches, we shall fight
on the landing-grounds, we shall fight in the fields and in the
streets, we shall fight in the hills; we shall never surrender. Even
if, which I do not for a moment believe, this island or a large part
of it were subjugated and starving, then our Empire beyond the
seas, armed and guarded by the British Fleet, would carry on the
struggle until, in God's good time, the New World, with all its
power and might, steps forth to the rescue and the liberation of
the Old.

These were times when the challenge of grim circumstance was all
that could be foreseen by a people so recently immersed in domestic
thoughts and schemes of social security. No man of this century or
any other has been able to combine dignity, directness and factual
exposition with glowing prose, intermixed with colloquialisms and
even slang, to speak from a height and yet make personal touch with
every listener and every reader of his words.

But for this gift, it is difficult to see how Churchill could have
rallied the British people; for it was not only his example of courage

but his ability to reduce confusion and chaos, uncertainty and surprise, to tangible aims and clearly stated objects. Underlying all his oratory, of which his collected speeches—and even more moving, some of the recordings—provide a rich treasury, is an intuitive understanding of how to 'get over' what he has to say. The tautology and repetition, used with such skill as to be almost hypnotic in its sonorous rhythm . . . 'we shall fight . . . we shall fight . . . we shall fight. . . .' And always his speeches, no matter how tragic or distressing their content, ended on a note of hope.

For most people power implies a loss of humanity and more especially of humour. Churchill always enjoyed power and consciously sought it. To him authority was a pleasure. Difficulties were a challenge to be taken up with zest. He could brush aside people and things which were negative; ineffectuals, woolly-minded people, vacillators, defeatists, double dealers, intriguers . . . with no loss of time or nervous energy. He was the living contradiction of Emerson's dictum: ' "You shall have joy or you shall have power," said God, "but you shall not have them both".' Churchill had joy and power—his combination of offices made him virtually a dictator.

France was weakening rapidly in her resolve to maintain her independence. She had no stomach for a fight. Churchill had no time for reproaches, but tried instead to reinforce her flagging resolve by promises of all help that lay within Britain's power. But France during the inter-war years had become infected by Fascism. Their *Cagoulards* were in influential positions in the armed services, the public and municipal services and the upper and middle reaches of industry. Marshal Pétain, veteran and hero of World War I, was a known admirer of Fascism. Admiral Darlan and General Weygand had little appetite for the struggle. Reynaud, in a broadcast to the U.S.A. on 10th June, begged Americans to 'give the Allies by every means their moral and material support without an expeditionary force. I beg you to do so before it is too late.' He had said that the French would fight before Paris and inside Paris, but by the 12th, when the Germans were at the gates of Paris, the Government declared it an open city and moved to the provinces. The day before 'that jackal', as Churchill, with robust vituperation, described Mussolini, declared war upon France. America could do nothing, for Presidential elections were not far ahead and the American public was still strongly isolationist and disinclined to be caught up in a European struggle which, from their far distance, seemed to have been resolved on the side of disaster already.

The roads of France were blocked by teeming masses of refugees. News of French defeatism reached Churchill, who, together with the Foreign Secretary, Lord Halifax, and Lord Beaverbrook, Minister of Aircraft Production, flew to Tours in a bold attempt to breathe resolution into the French leaders. It was a hopeless task. Weygand, Baudouin, even Reynaud, had given up hope of effective resistance. Reynaud even asked Churchill to release France from her obligation not to negotiate a separate Armistice. '. . . I felt bound to say,' Churchill told Parliament on his return, 'that I could not consent. I saw there would be no use in adding mutual reproaches to the other miseries we might have to bear, but I could not consent.'

The proud boulevards of Paris echoed to the thunder of Nazi tanks. Jewish citizens watched fearfully the strutting S.S. and Gestapo officers, news of whose brutalities had long since gone before them. From the top of the Eiffel Tower the swastika, with all the terror it implied, waved in the breeze. From the cafés came, not the sentimental twang of guitars or wheezy accordions, but the coarse and menacing strains of the '*Horst Wessel*', the S.S. marching song.

America's reply to Reynaud's desperate appeal was cold comfort. So long as France stayed in the struggle, America would send 'ever-increasing quantities of materials', but this implied no military commitment—'Only Congress can make such commitments'.

It was clear to Churchill that the French were contemplating giving up the struggle. He could not prevent them from inquiring from the Germans on what terms they might be granted an armistice, but emphasized that Britain would not be associated with it and would herself continue the fight. As a last resort he made a bold and unprecedented offer of union with France, suggesting a declaration that ' . . . The two Governments declare that France and Great Britain shall no longer be two nations but one Franco-British Union. Every citizen of France will immediately enjoy citizenship of Great Britain, every British subject will become a citizen of France . . .' On 16th June the offer was rejected; Reynaud resigned, to be replaced by the willing German puppet, 84-years-old Marshal Pétain—but it must be remembered that he typified, and did not initiate or promote, the defeatism of the majority of French people. 'It is with heavy heart,' the Marshal told France with quavering voice, 'that I say we must cease to fight. I have applied to our opponent to ask him whether he is ready to sign with me . . . a means to put an end to hostilities.'

The collapse of French resistance was a terrible blow. Britain would be left alone to carry on the fight, within easy striking distance of German aircraft. And the French Navy? Throughout Churchill had its fate constantly in mind. Our air force was smaller than the German; if the French vessels fell into German hands the balance of sea power would also be affected and Britain would be in the most mortal danger—she was already in considerable danger as it was, but for the moment her fleet was a match for the German.

By 17th June the evacuation of the British Expeditionary Force from France was completed. General de Gaulle, the courageous, temperamental, egotistical and austere Under-Secretary for Foreign Affairs, had arrived in England, to carry on resistance, not only with the Germans but not infrequently with Mr. Churchill himself ('Everyone has their cross to bear,' Mr. Churchill once said, with a chuckle. 'I have my Cross of Lorraine').

Mr. Churchill followed his admirable—and necessary—practice of telling the British public what was afoot, so that they should be aware of the dangers threatening the country and steel themselves to deal with them. Broadcasting that evening he said:

The news from France is very bad and I grieve for the gallant French people who have fallen into this terrible misfortune. Nothing will alter our feeling towards them or our faith that the genius of France will rise again. What has happened in France makes no difference to our actions and purpose. We have become the sole champions now in arms to defend the world cause. We shall do our best to be worthy of this high honour. We shall defend our island home and with the British Empire we shall fight on unconquerable until the curse of Hitler is lifted from the brows of mankind. We are sure that in the end all will come right.

The following day, 18th June, Members of the House of Commons crowded into the Chamber to hear one of the most historic pronouncements ever uttered there. All were conscious that this was a moment of destiny; the appalling forecasts which Churchill had made and for which he had once been attacked by friend and foe alike for making, were now vindicated by events. In this situation Churchill proved what a master he was of the art of being a parliamentarian.

Firstly, he outlined the course of recent events succinctly giving the facts without repining or reproaching. When the French High Command failed to withdraw the Northern Armies from Belgium at the moment the French front was broken at Sedan the delay meant a loss of fifteen or sixteen divisions and the near-annihilation of the British force, which was snatched from the jaws of fate only in the nick of time, but with the loss of all their precious equipment. Those missing divisions might have turned the scale; as it was only three British divisions had been able to fight with the French, although following Dunkirk every man and piece of equipment possible was sent to their aid.

I am not reciting these facts for the purpose of recrimination. That I judge to be utterly futile and even harmful. We cannot afford it. I recite them in order to explain why it was we did not have, why we could have had, between twelve and fourteen British divisions fighting in the line in this great battle instead of only three. Now I put all this aside. I put it on the shelf, from which the historians, when they have time, will select their documents to tell their stories. We have to think of the future and not of the past. This also applies in a small way to our own affairs at home. There are many who would hold an inquest in the House of Commons on the conduct of the Governments—and of Parliaments, for they are in it, too—during the years which led up to this catastrophe. They seek to indict those who were responsible for the guidance of our affairs. This would be a foolish and pernicious process. There are too many in it. Let each man search his conscience and search his speeches. I frequently search mine. . . .

At once Churchill had struck the right note. This was his first rallying-cry for unity in Parliament, where precious time and energy could not be wasted in mutual recrimination, a digression which could help none but the enemy. 'If we open a quarrel between the past and the present, we shall find that we have lost the future. Therefore, I cannot accept the drawing of any distinctions between members of the present Government. It was formed at a moment of crisis in order to unite all the parties and all sections of opinion.

It has received the almost unanimous support of both Houses of Parliament. Its Members are going to stand together, and subject to the authority of the House of Commons, we are going to govern the country and fight the war. It is absolutely necessary at a time like this that every Minister who tries each day to do his duty shall be respected; and their subordinates must know that their chiefs are not threatened men, men who are here today and gone to-morrow, but that their directions must be punctually and faithfully obeyed. . . .'

These were words of real statesmanship. The name-calling could have continued indefinitely—'you opposed rearmament!'—'and *you* said Hitler was a good fellow!'. M.P.s closed their ranks behind Churchill, their chosen leader, a man of strength anyone could respect, politics apart.

With the ease of a master-strategist, Churchill then proceeded to summarize the chain of events and the respective roles of the three armed Services. He did this, leaving aside certain details which would be reserved for a secret session so that the House could discuss vital matters 'without having everything read the next morning by our dangerous foes'. (Ireland was neutral throughout the war; British newspapers made their way there and thence to Germany, where their contents were analysed, filed and co-ordinated.)

Throughout, Churchill sounded the constructive note. There would be Local Defence Volunteers on guard against invasion; industry would be mobilized; and its resources immensely increased by an intake of new labour; the Dominions were with us. The Navy was in good fettle—its activities were limited in Norway because of lack of air support, whereas its actions in the North Sea and the Channel would have it.

And even in this grave hour Churchill's humour did not desert him. Faces wreathed in smiles at his quiet tilts at the Italians, emboldened by Hitler's lightning successes to strike at France when she had no more fight left in her: 'We are told that the Italian Navy is to come out and gain superiority in these waters. If they seriously intend it, I shall only say that we shall be delighted to offer Signor Mussolini a free and safeguarded passage through the Straits of Gibraltar in order that he may play the part to which he aspires. There is a general curiosity in the British Fleet to find out whether the Italians are up to the level they were in the last war or whether they have fallen off at all. . . .'

He dealt with possible invasion: 'This brings me, naturally, to the great question of invasion from the air and of the impending struggle between the British and German air forces. It seems quite clear that no invasion on a scale beyond the capacity of our land forces to crush speedily is likely to take place from the air until our Air Force has been definitely overpowered. In the meantime, there may be raids by parachute troops and attempted descents by airborne soldiers. We should be able to give those gentry a warm reception, both in the air and on the ground, if they reach it in any condition to continue the dispute. . . .' As for bombing, 'I do not at all under-rate the severity of the ordeal that lies before us; but I believe our countrymen will show themselves capable of facing up to it.'

With complete sureness of timing and exposition, he made his way through the long explanation, every word clearly delivered, changing mood from grave to gay as the context dictated, stressing the things that mattered most and giving other facts as a sort of aside. And then, with a flow of Shakespearean prose, he heartened and emboldened the entire House with a fitting climax of disciplined emotion:

I expect that the Battle of Britain is about to begin. Upon this battle depends the survival of Christian civilisation. Upon it depends our own British life, and the long continuity of our institutions and our Empire. The whole fury and might of the enemy must very soon be turned on us. Hitler knows that he will have to break us in this island or lose the war. If we can stand up to him, all Europe may be free and the life of the world may move forward into broad, sunlit uplands. But if we fail, then the whole world, including the United States, including all that we have known and cared for, will sink into the Abyss of a new Dark Age made more sinister, and perhaps more protracted, by the lights of perverted science. Let us therefore brace ourselves to our duties and so bear ourselves that, if the British Empire and its Commonwealth last for a thousand years, men will say, 'This was their finest hour'.

It is not my object to recount in any sort of detail the war which spread like a prairie fire. The memoirs of war correspondents and of principal participants such as Lord Ismay, Lord Chandos, Field-Marshal Montgomery—and, most of all, the subjective but masterly account of not less than a million and a half words, written by Sir

Winston Churchill himself, are a Pandora's box of woe and wonder for those who want to re-live those days.

But from the standpoint of Churchill as a parliamentarian, they were the most fateful days of his life. He reached the zenith of his achievement as a statesman, but also became The Great Commoner, holding the reins of Government by sheer force of personality and with due regard for the traditions of the Parliament he loved. It was there that he accounted to the nation for his conduct of affairs; it was in that chamber that his eloquence made all hearts beat as one and quickened the pulse of the nation. It was there he inculcated a sense of purpose and resolve, by his own magnificent and never-wavering dedication to work, to struggle and to victory. And it was a victory not simply for England but for Europe; for the moment England was the only free spot left, the only springboard from which a campaign for the liberation of the enslaved countries could be mounted.

On the day of Churchill's 'Finest Hour' speech to the House General de Gaulle broadcast to the French people from English soil. Four days later France signed an Armistice with Germany and two days after that an armistice with Italy. Thereafter hostilities ended in France.

Next came the saddest decision Churchill had to make. What of the French Navy? France was given every possible alternative to allowing the French ships to fall into German hands. They were asked to make for British waters, or, with an attenuated crew, to make for ports where they could be interned, or to scuttle their vessels. 'Never in my experience,' declared Churchill, 'never have I seen so grim and sombre a question as to what we were to do about the French Fleet discussed in a Cabinet . . . every member of the Cabinet had the same conviction about what should be done . . . the three Service Ministers, as well as men like the Minister of Information (Mr. Duff Cooper) and the Secretary of State for the Colonies (Lord Lloyd), particularly noted for their friendship with France . . . were equally convinced that no other decision than that which we took was possible. We took that decision, and it was a decision to which, with aching hearts but with clear vision, we unitedly came.'

The decision which, despite the most desperate and urgent negotiations with the French until the last moment, had to be taken, was indeed grim: to sink the French fleet at Oran.

Admiral Somerville's task was, as Churchill rightly described it in a message to him via the Admiralty 'one of the most disagreeable and difficult tasks that a British Admiral has ever been faced with . . .' But all negotiations being fruitless, and the Men of Bordeaux proving totally indifferent to the fate of Britain, her ally until a few days ago, the French fleet was attacked and sunk. The *Bretagne* was blown up, the *Dunkerque* grounded, the *Provence* beached and other vessels sunk or burned. That was on 3rd July. Three days later the British attacked the French battleship *Richelieu* at Dakar. French vessels berthed at Portsmouth and Plymouth were taken and only in the case of the *Surcouf* was there actual fighting, in the course of which two British officers and a leading seaman were killed and a seaman wounded.

Mr. Churchill reported to Parliament on the action taken and the reasons for it on 4th July. 'A large proportion of the French fleet has, therefore, passed into our hands or has been put out of action or otherwise withheld from Germany by yesterday's events. . . . I leave the judgement of our action, with confidence, to Parliament. I leave it to the nation, and I leave it to the United States. I leave it to the world and to history.'

The battle of France was over and the battle for Britain was imminent. Apart from the infinite detail of defence, Churchill was concerned constantly to raise the spirits and morale of the people and not least of those who led them. Churchill was well aware that there were some faint-hearts about, some within uneasy proximity of himself. Rather than reproach or expose them, he preferred to exhort them to courage and set an example himself. But to avert panic, defeatism and idle rumour, he issued a directive to civil servants and also read it to Parliament:

On what may be the eve of an attempted invasion or battle for our native land, the Prime Minister desires to impress upon all persons holding responsible positions in the Government, in the Fighting Services or in the Civil Departments their duty to maintain a spirit of alert and confident energy . . . the Prime Minister expects all His Majesty's servants in high places to set an example of steadiness and resolution. They should check and rebuke the expression of loose and ill-digested opinions in their circles, or by their subordinates. They should not hesitate to report, and if necessary remove, any persons, officers or officials who are found to be consciously exercising a disturbing or depressing influence, and whose talk is calculated to spread alarm and despondency. Thus alone will they be worthy of the fighting men who, in the air, on the sea, and on land, have already met the enemy without any sense of being outmatched in martial qualities.

His speech, listened to in silence, sparked off a storm of cheering from all sides. Here was a leader who thought and acted as a leader, and the House responded to a man.

The British reaction to France's defection was 'at least we know where we are'. A known enemy is sometimes less danger than a false friend. 'Personally I feel happier now that we have no allies to be polite to and to pamper,' the King wrote to Queen Mary. Our politeness in waiting correctly whilst neutrals waited to be overrun was poorly rewarded. But as Churchill told the British public in a broadcast, 'We shall not waste our breath nor cumber our thought with reproaches. When you have a friend and comrade at whose side you have faced tremendous struggles, and your friend is smitten down by a stunning blow, it may be necessary to make sure that the weapon that has fallen from his hands shall not be added to the resources of your common enemy. But you need not bear malice because of your friend's cries of delirium and gestures of agony. You must not add to his pain: you must work for his recovery. The association of interest between Britain and France remains. The cause remains. Duty inescapable remains. . . .'

Hitler had hoped to conclude a separate peace with Britain (which he would have broken when it suited him) and was not to give up hope for some time yet. He would have liked to secure his borders to the east and then devoured what remained of the west. However, seeing that Churchill was determined to continue the battle and resist invasion, the German air force (which had for weeks been bombing provincial towns, killing 336 and seriously injuring 476 people during the last two weeks of June) turned its fury on the Royal Air Force and radar stations in south-east England. The Germans knew that they must smash the air force before they could hope to land an invasion force in Britain. Daylight raids on Britain were intensified.

There was talk of the King and his family going to Canada—but never in royal or governmental circles. He would not hear of it, neither would the Queen.

The King preferred to improve his marksmanship on his private
8*

shooting range in the Palace grounds—an improvised affair—while both Queen Wilhelmina and King Haakon of Norway warned him that Hitler had tried hard to capture them, and would certainly make determined efforts to make the King and Queen his prisoners if and when he had the opportunity. Churchill carried a pistol, determined to give a good account of himself if paratroopers dropped from the skies: 'I will always get one or two before they can shoot me down!' he declared.

The Battle of Britain had begun. The attempt to smash the R.A.F. was a moment of enormous menace for Britain. If that battle were lost, it could be the last battle.

The young airmen proved equal to the challenge, although outnumbered; pilots went up again and again, often dashing away in the midst of drinking a cup of tea as the warning again sounded. Churchill liked to go to the operations room of No. 11 Group, Fighter Command, to watch the progress of the battle. Lord Ismay has described one of these visits:

There had been heavy fighting throughout the afternoon; at one moment every squadron in the group was engaged. There was nothing left in reserve, and the map table showed new waves of attackers crossing the coast. I felt sick with fear.

As the evening closed in, the fighting died down, and we left by car. Churchill's first words were, 'Don't speak to me. I have never been so moved.' After about five minutes he leaned forward and said, '*Never in the field of human conflict was so much owed by so many to so few.*' The words burned into my brain, and Churchill, as everyone knows, used them in a speech that was heard throughout the world.

Hitler's 'Operation Sea-Lion' was scheduled for 15th September. But the *Luftwaffe* sustained crippling and unexpected losses in the Battle of Britain. German records later revealed that between 10th July and 31st October, 1940, 2,376 German planes had been accounted for—no less than 1,733 entirely destroyed and 643 seriously damaged.

It was with heartfelt sincerity that Churchill told the Commons that 'The gratitude of every home in our island, in our Empire, and indeed throughout the world, except in the abodes of the guilty, goes out to the British airmen who, undaunted by odds, unwearied in their constant challenge and mortal danger, are turning the tide of world war by their prowess and their devotion.' He referred with admiration and thankfulness to the dynamism of Lord Beaverbrook, Minister of Aircraft Production, who was achieving 'astounding increase in the output and the repair of British aircraft and engines' by 'a genius of organization and drive. . . .'

The first bomb in the London area had hit a ploughed field at Addington in Surrey on 18th June, but there had been raids on provincial towns such as Middlesbrough. The air-raid casualty figures told their own story (although, of course, not published at the time): June, 336 killed and 476 seriously injured; July, 258 killed and 321 seriously injured; August, 1,075 killed and 1,261 seriously injured; September, 6,954 killed and 10,615 seriously injured.

The peace feelers put out by Hitler having failed, the full-scale terror of day and night raids on London was stepped up. High explosives, oil bombs, fire bombs, mines, were dropped and all pretence of concentrating on military targets was abandoned. Hospitals such as St. Thomas's, churches such as St. Bride's in Fleet Street and St. Clement Danes in the Strand, famous Livery halls in the City, St. Paul's Cathedral, Buckingham Palace—all suffered. So, too, did countless homes. 'We can take it' became a slogan of pride. For the time being Churchill gave up sleeping at No. 10 and moved to a Government building by Storey's Gate, known then simply as 'the annexe'. Often he would go up on the roof, indifferent to the thud of bombs and the whizzing shrapnel to watch the dog-fight in the skies, once nearly suffocating the staff beneath by sitting on the smoke vent!

But while keeping up his own spirits and insisting that everyone else do the same, Churchill was never indifferent to the sufferings of the people. He knew that air raids meant people, including women and children, being buried under the débris of fallen buildings, trapped and burned in fires or fearfully mutilated by débris or explosive. He was often seen on the scene of a bombing incident, striding through the piles of glass and masonry, chin out, cigar in mouth, walking-stick in hand. His personal military adviser, General (afterwards Lord) Ismay often accompanied him and recalls how, on visiting the London Docks after an especially heavy raid, he found an air-raid shelter where forty people had been killed. The crowd surged around, proud of the man who in what would be the eventide of life for most men, could lead them through such terrors.

At the sight of the suffering and carnage, he broke down and wept. He was never ashamed of emotion. An old woman who saw him remarked, 'You see, he really cares—he's crying.'

Those around the Prime Minister marvelled at his energy. His day would start at 8 o'clock with a pot of tea and the newspapers. Breakfast would follow, capped by a cigar. At Downing Street his staff would be preparing; Ismay, Professor Lindemann, now Lord Cherwell, his scientific and technical adviser. The efficient but off-hand Desmond Morton would be assembling papers and making appointments, while Brigadier Harvie Watt, M.P., his unpaid parliamentary private secretary, would be noting what questions were on the order paper and preparing any other matters concerning the Parliamentary aspects of the Premier's immense job. Supplementing them all were a private secretary, three typists and a typing pool. There were always plenty of labels—Churchill was fond of affixing them to anything he wanted done—ACTION THIS DAY. At about nine o'clock his secretary would bring him 'the boxes'—despatches from the Service departments, Ministries and Dominions. These he would read thoroughly but quickly. At half past nine he would see Captain James Stewart, M.P., the Chief Whip.

Sometimes Churchill would take a walk by way of exercise, Inspector Thompson, his personal detective, following up the rear, but he preferred a glass of whisky and a cigar to exercise as such. 'The Churchills always die young,' he once said, 'so why should I bore myself to premature death with exercise?'

In the House of Commons much latitude was allowed to him. He loved Parliament and respected its traditions and routines, accepting limitations only when they were for the purpose of security; for example certain matters relating to defence or forth-coming plans were discussed only in secret session. Thus questions on the order paper were often kept until Churchill could appear—everyone knew that his day's work would kill many a younger man. The Speaker would call the question, the M.P. asking it would state the number of the question and then proceed 'Will the right honourable Gentleman tell us . . .' Churchill, briefed in advance, would proceed to do so, and then wait for the ball to be shot back into his court. A supplementary question would probably follow and for this, too, he would be prepared. In answering questions he would never take it for granted that his answer would be accepted uncritically. He was too old a hand for that. He came amply briefed to answer additional questions on matters of fact. Far from wanting to see Parliament's powers whittled away because there was a war on, he wanted to see Parliament's privileges zealously guarded, as they were part of the way of life to preserve which the war was being fought. The questions over, Churchill would go to the smoking-room for a cigar and after lunch to the Cabinet room where most of his work was done.

From three o'clock until five he would sleep the sleep of the just, not altogether with the enthusiasm of his staff, to whom this routine meant an adjustment of their own work schedules and working until very late. Conferences and discussions would often go on until midnight and it was certainly his happy habit of an afternoon nap which kept up his vitality. The clock meant nothing to him. If a problem had to be solved, especially requiring action, somebody would hear his gruff voice on the telephone, saying, 'If it is not inconvenient to you I would like to see you.' So far as is known, nobody ever had the temerity to say, 'I'm afraid, Prime Minister, it is *not* convenient.' There was a war on, and the convenience of individuals, most of all in the public service, did not matter.

His appearance in the War Room, the underground labyrinth beneath London, covering nearly six acres, was often bizarre—a zipper 'siren suit', slippers embroidered with dragons, cigar clenched in his mouth. He had a habit of throwing his cigar butts away without looking away from the person he was speaking to, or without taking his eyes from a document; somehow the butts never misfired.

The blitz put a stop to most theatrical performances in London, although ironically Cocteau's *Infernal Machine* was one of the last to shut down.

In the Commons Churchill denounced 'These cruel, wanton, indiscriminate bombings of London' which were part of Hitler's invasion plan. 'He hopes, by killing large numbers of civilians and women and children, that he will terrorize and cow the people of this mighty Imperial city and make them a burden and anxiety to the Government, and thus distract our attention from the ferocious onslaught he is preparing. Little does he know the spirit of the British nation or the tough fibre of Londoners, whose forebears played a leading part in the establishment of parliamentary institutions, and who have been bred to value freedom far above their lives.

'This wicked man, the repository and embodiment of many forms of soul-destroying hatred, this monstrous product of former wrongs and shames, has now resolved to try to break our famous island spirit by a process of indiscriminate slaughter and destruction. What he has done is to kindle a fire in British hearts here and all over the world which will glow long after all traces of the conflagrations he has caused in London have been removed. . . .'

The brilliant thing about so many of Churchill's speeches to Parliament is that they had to serve several purposes at once. In language appropriate to the dignity and importance of the subject, he had to explain the war situation to Members of Parliament, allowing for any misgivings they might have and giving them as much information as could be given without aiding the enemy; they were addressed in part to the public, who would read them, and were intended to be truthful, informative and inspiring. They were also for the delectation of foreign countries; they contained references to Germans and Italians which were intended to reach the populace over the heads of their Fascist rulers, while, at the same time, they were intended to strengthen President Roosevelt's hand in his attempts to aid Britain by means other than intervention. With Roosevelt himself, of course, he was in correspondence from the outset of war, and an early triumph was the Anglo-American Agreement of 3rd September 1940, under which Britain leased overseas bases to the United States in return for fifty obsolete—but useful—destroyers.

The scope of the war widened all the time. Lithuania, Latvia and Estonia became incorporated into Soviet Russia; the Italian Army crossed the Libyan border into Egypt; Germany, Italy and Japan signed a three-power pact; Italy invaded Greece; Britain's shipping losses became heavier, with the loss of 198,000 tons in the last week of October. Air raids on Berlin were followed by British raids on Italy.

On 9th November 1940 Neville Chamberlain died. He had been much reproached for the Munich Agreement, but Churchill paid him a moving tribute in the House. 'It fell to Neville Chamberlain in one of the supreme crises of the world, to be contradicted by events, to be disappointed in his hopes and to be deceived and cheated by a wicked man. Those hopes, those wishes, that faith that was abused was surely among the most notable and benevolent instincts of the human heart—the love of peace, the toil for peace, the strife for peace and the pursuit of peace even at great peril and certainly to the utter disdain of popularity or clamour.' The benevolence of this tribute can be appreciated when one remembers Churchill's sad, solemn and prophetic denunciation of the Munich Agreement.

23

A New Phase of War

A few days before Chamberlain's death President Roosevelt had been re-elected to his third term of office as President of the United States. Like Churchill, he was a great believer in personal freedom, and although his approach to world affairs was very different from Churchill's, he increased by degrees, according to his knowledge of what Congress and the American people would find acceptable, American help to Britain short of actual participation in the war. On 6th January he proposed to Congress what became known as the 'Lease-Lend Scheme' by which ships, guns, tanks and necessary equipment were supplied without the necessity of paying for them in dollars at that time.

Much else had happened. There was the three-power pact between Germany, Italy and Japan and the opening of the Western Desert offensive. Incidentally, it is just as well that Anthony Eden, sent by Churchill to consult in Cairo with General Wavell and Maitland Wilson, resisted Churchill's incessant bombardment of urgent telegrams. Italian motorized forces were being massed for an attack on Egypt from Libya, then an Italian colony. Churchill wanted forces to be sent to defend Crete following Italy's attack on Greece, but Eden could scarcely tell Churchill what the truth was by telegram—that the British Army commanders were planning an offensive. Churchill, in his own words, 'purred like six cats' when Eden told him, on his return, but had the Prime Minister had his way the desert forces at Britain's disposal might have been weakened.

Such misjudgements must be weighed against the greater number of sound judgements and actions for which Churchill was responsible. One can avoid mistakes, I suppose, by sheer inaction, but Churchill had to make decisions, often of a momentous kind, every hour of every day—in many cases being faced with a choice of equally unpleasant alternatives.

One aspect of Churchill's brilliance as a statesman and parliamentarian was his ability to conform to and enliven parliamentary tradition and yet remember the harsh realities of war which made some erosion of these traditions essential to survival. Furthermore, few realize, as I have mentioned earlier, that he had to address several publics at once, achieving some useful purpose with each.

He loved the cut-and-thrust of vigorous parliamentary debate. He was frank to the House about both the limitations on his parliamentary appearances—his immense responsibilities took him everywhere—and upon what he could say.

I should like to put rather frankly to the House a difficulty which I feel about making frequent statements on the war situation . . . there is a danger, if one gives full and frank and frequent statements revealing one's own point of view, or the point of view of the Government, or of those who are charged with the strategical and tactical decisions, that the enemy may gain an advantage. Certainly it would be very convenient if Herr Hitler or the important chiefs in Germany were to give us, every fortnight or so, an honest-to-God—if they were capable of it—statement. I am sure we would immediately set a dozen active and agile Intelligence Officers to study not only what was said but what was not said, and to read not only the lines but between the lines. . . . Therefore I hope the House will be indulgent with me if, although always at their service, I choose the occasions somewhat rarely. . . .

He understood the temper of Members of Parliament. They had not studied and struggled and worked to get into Parliament simply to be used as rubber stamps. But this was war, and their ranks must be closed.

His pronouncements in the House on Italy show his extraordinary capacity to cope with the present with one wary eye on the future. That the Italians could expect to receive as determined attention from the British as the Germans, he left no doubt. Equally he made it clear that he regretted the reckless vainglory of their dictator Mussolini and sympathized with the humble Italians so uselessly caught up in frightful suffering. Here again, we see him with his capacity for addressing several audiences at once; he was too sensible to offend the immense and influential Italian sections in the United States by hurling insults at the Italian people themselves; knowing the Italian temperament, he did not believe they could have much appetite for this war, and decried their soldiering and seamanship in carefully-chosen words, intended to reach the ears of the Italian people over the heads of their rulers, and reach the ears of their German allies so that the Germans would come to distrust and dislike the Italians. 'One cannot say,' Churchill told M.P.s, 'that the Italians have shown a high fighting spirit, or quality, in this battle. In other periods of Italian history, we know, they have shown great courage; and I am certainly not going to frame a charge of lack of military qualities against a people with whom up to this time we have had—and God knows we did not seek it now—no quarrel. But perhaps their hearts are not in their work. Perhaps they have been so long controlled and disciplined and ruled, and so much relieved of all share in the government of their own country, that they have not felt those virile emotions. . . .'

The Battle of the Libyan Desert was proceeding at the time, and a few days later, on 23rd December 1940, Churchill broadcast directly to the Italian people. It was a magnificent piece of rhetoric, cunningly conceived—to wean the Italians from Mussolini, play on their unwillingness to fight with Germany and emphasize their cultural and historic background, disgraced by these latest follies.

I speak to the Italian people, and I speak to you from London, the heart of the British Islands and of the British Commonwealth and Empire. I speak to you what the diplomatists call words of great truth and respect. We are at war—that is a very strange and terrible thought. Whoever imagined until the last few melancholy years that the British and Italian nations would be trying to destroy one another? We have always been such friends. We were the champions of the Italian Risorgimento. We were the partisans of Garibaldi, the admirers of Mazzini and Cavour. All that great movement towards the unity of the Italian nation which lighted the nineteenth century was aided and was hailed by the British Parliament and public . . . we have never been your foes until now. In the last war against the barbarous Hun we were your comrades . . . and now we are at war: now we are condemned to work each other's ruin. Your aviators have tried to cast their bombs upon London; our armies are tearing and will tear your African Empires to shreds and tatters . . . how has it all come about? Italians, I will tell you the truth. It is all because of one man. One man, and one man alone has ranged the Italian people in deadly struggle against the British Empire . . . against the Crown and the Royal Family of Italy, against the Pope . . . against the Italian people. . . .

It was a masterly oration, glowing with passion, warm in its admiration of all that was good in Italian history. And brilliantly he sowed the seeds of division between Italy and Germany, warning the Italians that Mussolini had called in 'Attila over the Brenner Pass, with his hordes of ravenous soldiery and his gangs of Gestapo policemen to occupy, hold down and protect the Italian people, for whom he and his Nazi followers cherish the most bitter and unspoken contempt that is on record between races. . . .'

As 1940 drew to a close the desperate desire to crush Britain before turning east was made clear. On 29th December in a large-scale raid on the City of London the Guildhall and nine city halls were destroyed by fire-bombs. By 5th January the Italians had surrendered at Bardia, 30,000 prisoners being taken. Indeed on 17th January Churchill was able to say that 'The offensive in the Middle East has succeeded beyond our wildest dreams. . . . 80,000 prisoners have been taken.' But as usual he added a warning note against complacency. 'Do not suppose that we are at an end of the road. . . .'

On 21st January Ernest Bevin, Minister of Labour, submitted to the House of Commons his scheme for mobilizing and directing labour, on which occasion Winston Churchill made a witty supporting speech. The next day the House listened to him describing the administrative machinery of Government (a speech any aspiring civil servant might read with profit) and at the same time assuring the House that despite secrecies and circumspections inherent in wartime utterances, Parliament remained for him the inspiration and the medium through which the healthier ideas of democracy would triumph over Nazism.

To try to carry on a war, a tremendous war, without the aid and guidance of the House of Commons, would be a superhuman task. I have never taken the view that the debates and criticisms of this House are a drag and a burden. Far from it. I may not agree with all the criticism—I may be stirred by it, and I may resent it; I may even retort—but at any rate, debates on these large issues are of the very greatest value to the life-thrust of the nation. . . .

In February he brushed with Earl Winterton over a proposal to alter the law relating to 'offices of profit under the Crown' to enable Malcolm MacDonald to go to Canada as High Commissioner without losing his parliamentary seat. Winterton has described Churchill as being in 'a curious and truculent mood', accusing him of trying to form an opposition with the Socialist Shinwell.

The day and night bombing continued. In the first month of 1941 1,500 were killed and 2,012 seriously injured; in February 789 killed and 1,068 injured, in March 4,259 killed and 5,557 injured, The raids, of course, were not simply on London but included Cardiff and Swansea, Bristol, Plymouth, and Birmingham. Few equalled in ferocity the terrible air raid on Coventry in November 1940, when Churchill lost no time in going to the spot himself to see the devastation. The air raids on London, Bristol and Plymouth in March 1941 were particularly heavy.

The flow of supplies from America from March 1941 offset to some extent the gloom over the Allies' immense shipping losses; before the end of 1941 nine million tons of Allied and neutral shipping were sunk.

By April the German offensive in Libya and the evacuation of Benghazi by the British, followed by the arrival, on the 17th, of German forces on the Egyptian frontier and the siege of Tobruk, were causing uneasiness in Parliament, the mood being not dissimilar, although perhaps nor so vehement or organized, as during the great Dardanelles controversy in the First World War. On 6th May Anthony Eden opened the debate with a somewhat dull speech, followed by some penetrating sallies from Hore-Belisha, former Minister for War, and Shinwell. Lloyd George criticized the administrative machine, bringing from his old friend Churchill the cruel and insulting retort that 'it was the sort of speech with which, I imagine, the illustrious and venerable Marshal Pétain (the aged and pro-Hitler puppet dictator of France) might well have enlivened the closing days of M. Reynaud's Cabinet.' Such words should not have been used against the aged statesman, then 78 years old and heartbroken by the recent loss of his wife. Perhaps Churchill remembered, with nausea, Lloyd George's adulation of Hitler, describing him as 'a great and wonderful leader'. But had not Churchill, when he assumed office as Premier, lectured the House on the need for unity, and the need to abjure name-calling and recriminations about the past, since none were guiltless of misjudgement? Lloyd George never forgave the insult; Churchill also attacked Hore-Belisha for alleged incompetence when in office, again in contradiction of his previous appeal to forget the past in the interests of present unity. And, perhaps just for luck, he implied that Earl Winterton had been a failure at the Air Ministry.

Never before in his life had Churchill such scope for his oratory. Here was the role he loved: plenty of action, drama, urgency, challenge. The occasion brought his oratory to a peak of perfection to which he had been steadily winning his way in the few years before the war. America, in particular, liked his forthright way, which enabled them to forget that he was an aristocrat. Although traditionally anti-Colonialist, and both distrustful and jealous of British power and its Empire, they felt he understood America as few Englishmen did (in which I think they were right) and remembered that his mother had been an American. '*Give us the tools, and we will finish the job!*' he said—and the phrase rang from end to end of the American continent, helping Roosevelt to implement his idea of lease-lend. They were words every American could understand. And Churchill's reference to Mussolini as 'the crafty, cold-blooded, black-hearted Italian, who had thought to gain an Empire on the cheap by stabbing fallen France in the back' was welcome invective.

The ferocity of the air raids in April (6,065 people were killed), culminating in the large-scale raid of 10th May 1941, when the Debating Chamber of the House of Commons was destroyed, marked what Hitler hoped might be a significant phase. If only Britain would stop fighting, enable him to attack and defeat Russia and then turn on Britain and deal the *coup de grâce*! Certainly Britain owed no gratitude to Russia, whose pact with Germany had helped to make the Second War inevitable and added to the agony of Poland by stabbing her in the back. But when Deputy-Führer Rudolf Hess flew from Germany in a plane piloted by himself and descended by parachute in Scotland in a fantastic peace effort, Churchill knew what was really afoot.

The world could make no sense of it. Had Hess gone mad? Or had Hitler really asked him to go? Hess hoped, by contacting pro-Nazi circles in Britain, to negotiate a separate peace. He forgot that after Hitler's crimes against Europe in general and Britain in particular, the British would not compromise, and that most of the Nazi sympathizers were behind bars or detained in the Isle of Man under Regulation 18b (though this did not imply that they had been guilty of an offence; it was a precaution which the urgency of the times demanded).

What Churchill *did* learn from the questionings of Hess was that Hitler was planning an invasion of Russia, his ally. This information was passed on to Stalin.

When Churchill visited the shattered House of Commons Chamber he could not contain his grief. The Chamber where Disraeli, Keir Hardy, Gladstone, a whole host of legislators, had come and gone . . . and now, the fire, followed by high explosive, had left a heap of rubble. It was a scene of indescribable desolation. Desultorily, he poked with his walking-stick amongst the historic wreckage. A tear trickled down his plump cheek, to be followed by another and another until he was simply weeping, while Beaverbrook, who was with him, knew better than to utter words of consolation. Churchill disdained to use a handkerchief and let the tears dry in the wind.

He had warned the House, when he became Prime Minister, that this could happen. Parliament is a conspicuous, an inescapable target on the river which, from the air, is a brilliant silver streak. 'On the other hand,' says Churchill in his own memoirs, 'we can be thankful that the Chamber was empty.' Indeed we can be; an afternoon raid might have blown up the whole Government, a Guy Fawkes act in reverse.

As a precaution against this very eventuality, the Ministry of Works had long ago 'mocked up' a sort of debating chamber in Church House, the administrative headquarters and debating centre of the Church of England. Officials had tried to simulate as nearly as possible the layout of the original chamber, but as it was never meant to be anything but an improvisation, there was a skimpy and insubstantial look about it all. However, there were benches covered in green, in parallel rows, facing each other; and instead of the intricately carved and decorative speaker's chair, which in Parliament is a sort of throne, with canopy, there was an ordinary armchair.

There was also an improvised House of Lords, reflecting but faintly the warm, mellow glow of the real place, with its red leather and chandeliers and richly fretted stone.

It was the sentimental and historical aspect of the destruction, not any thought of personal discomfort, that grieved Churchill. Not a day's work, he decided, would be lost by it—and so it proved.

On 10th June Mr. Churchill faced a more critical Commons. The Germans, dissatisfied with the fighting prowess of the Italians, had reinforced Italian forces in Libya and flung a network of spies, agents and *agent provocateurs* into Syria, Iraq and Persia. Bulgaria, under pressure, joined the Axis. German troops marched on Greece and Prince Paul of Yugoslavia acceded to Nazi terms; his cowardice so incensed his people that he was straightway flung out. Prince Peter in his place was entrusted with rallying his country against alien invasion.

Seizing this advantageous moment, Churchill applauded Yugoslavia's brave stand, adding a promise: 'Great Britain will give all the aid in her power to those who are defending their native lands, the heroic Greeks, the Turks if they are attacked.' General Wavell must have heard these promises with less enthusiasm; his men had been doing well in Libya, but some of his troops had been diverted from their onward push to take part in the Balkan campaign.

A fierce German blitz, with bombing of Belgrade and the loss of thousands of men, women and children, followed. Through Hungary and Bulgaria the Germans swarmed into Greece. Soon the Greeks and British were overwhelmed by the unequal odds, and although Crete held out a little longer, British troops had eventually on 1st June 1941 to evacuate in circumstances reminiscent of Dunkirk. 'Wars are not won by evacuations' Churchill had said then; now it was his turn to be reminded of it—not that he needed it.

Punch described Churchill as looking 'worried and wary'. He came under fire from Leslie Hore-Belisha, Earl Winterton and from M.P.s of all parties who were demanding a debate on Crete. Winterton told Churchill that it was a bit late in the day for him to blame his predecessors for lack of arms. Some reminded him that a month earlier he had said that Crete would be defended to the end, and that any thought of retreat was unthinkable.

Churchill, never a man to retire before criticism, warned of the dangers of such demands in time of war.

I think it would be a mistake if the House got into the habit of calling for explanations on the varying episodes of this dangerous and widespread struggle and asking for an account to be given on why any action was lost or any part of the front was beaten in. In the first place, no full explanations can possibly be given without revealing valuable information to the enemy, information not only about a particular operation which is over, but about the general position and also about the processes of thought which are followed, such as they may be, by our direction and our high command. There is always a danger that a Minister in my position may supply the enemy with some essential, with some seemingly innocent fact, about which the enemy is in doubt, and thus enable the enemy to construct a comprehensive and accurate picture of our frame of mind. . . . The heads of the Dictator Governments are not under similar pressure to explain or excuse any ill-success that may befall them. Far be it from me to compare myself or the office I hold with those of these pretentious and formidable potentates. I am only the servant of the Crown and Parliament, and am always at the disposal of the House of Commons, where I have lived my life.

Hitler, he said, would not be asked why the *Bismarck* had been allowed to go to her doom, nor Mussolini held to account for 200,000 Italians being taken prisoner.

Once again he accused one speaker, Hore-Belisha, of negligence as War Minister. 'The state in which our Army was left when the right honourable Gentleman had ended his two years and seven months' tenure of the War Office, during the greater part of which he was responsible for production and supply, was lamentable. We were short of every essential supply. . . .'

Churchill gave a very long and detailed explanation but in somewhat aggrieved vein. Some questions, he said, he could answer, 'but I do not propose to discuss tactics here, because I am sure it is quite impossible for us to fight battles in detail, either beforehand or afterwards from Whitehall or the House of Commons. His Majesty's Government in their responsibility to Parliament choose the best generals they can find, set before them the broad strategic objects of the campaign, offer them any advice or counsel that may seem fitting, ask searching questions . . . and then support them to the best of their power in men and munitions. . . .'

Churchill's speech that day was about a quarter the length of a full-length novel. He was working at the time about twelve hours a day; the fact-crammed exposition, a model of lucidity, was to him just an extra task. He had won the day with flying colours.

Slowly, gradually, Roosevelt was leading America on to the side of the Allies. German and Italian money was frozen in the U.S.A. On 16th June he ordered the closing of German consulates and the expulsion of their staffs, who were in close league with dangerous subversive groups in America.

But it was on 22nd June that an event occurred which shook the world and changed the course of history. Germany invaded Russia. Their Panzer divisions, motorized columns, guns, supply vehicles and lorry-loads of fanatical troops roared over the 1,800-mile frontier hell-bent on destruction. In Britain and America there was a sharp intake of breath. What now? For over twenty years Churchill had made plain his hatred for Bolshevism. Communism was feared and hated in America. What would they do? For Churchill it was the moment for a supreme act of statesmanship. The two countries, Britain and Russia, might not like each other, but they were united by a common hatred—of Germany. They were fighting the same foe; why not side by side? Churchill's answer was an alliance with Russia. In a broadcast he broke all records in uninhibited vituperation:

Hitler is a monster of wickedness, insatiable in his lust for blood and plunder. Not content with having all Europe under his heel or else terrorized into various forms of abject submission, he must now carry his work of butchery and desolation among the vast multitudes of Russia and Asia . . . so now this bloodthirsty guttersnipe must launch his mechanised armies upon new fields of slaughter, pillage and devastation. . . .

But how reconcile his lasting hatred of Communism with the present situation? Churchill's words were direct and unequivocal:

The Nazi regime is indistinguishable from the worst features of Communism. It is devoid of all theme and principle except appetite and racial domination. It excels all forms of human wickedness in the efficiency of its cruelty and ferocious aggression. No one has been a more consistent opponent of Communism than I have for the last twenty-five years. I will unsay no word that I have spoken about it. But all this fades away before the spectacle which is now unfolding. The past, with its crimes, its follies and its tragedies, flashes away. I see the Russian soldiers standing on the threshold of their native land, guarding the fields which their fathers have tilled from time immemorial. I see them guarding their homes where mothers and wives pray—ah, yes, there are times when all pray—for the safety of their loved ones. . . . I see advancing upon all this in hideous onslaught the Nazi war machine, with its clanking, heel-clicking, dandified Prussian officers. . . . I see also the dull, drilled, docile, brutish masses of the Hun soldiery plodding on like a swarm of crawling locusts. . . .

'Any man or State who marches with Hitler is our foe. Any man or State who fights on against Nazidom will have our aid . . . it follows, therefore, that we shall give whatever help we can to Russia and the Russian people. We shall appeal to all our friends and allies in every part of the world to take the same course. . . .'

The last statement was made in the knowledge that, almost simultaneously, President Roosevelt would promise aid to Russia Five days after Churchill's speech a mission headed by Sir Stafford Cripps, the upright, austere, religious Socialist, arrived in Moscow with the British Military Mission. No time was lost, for Britain had been expecting the German attacks, which thrust towards the strategically vital towns of Leningrad, Moscow, Kiev and Odessa, and were to penetrate 600 miles into Russia before the onset of a cruel and pitiless winter.

There were realities to be faced. The Russians, Churchill knew, were no friends of Britain. They had stood aloof while London was in flames and had no word of criticism for Nazi crimes throughout Europe; the Communist *Daily Worker* had been docile and silent about Fascist crimes, dismissing the conflict as another 'capitalist war'. Churchill had to swallow many a slight in order to encompass the destruction of Nazism, his first and main concern. Churchill wrote a friendly and encouraging letter to Stalin on 7th July 1941 promising all support which Britain's resources would allow, following this up by a further message conveyed through Sir Stafford Cripps. Stalin did not reply to either until 18th July and straightway proposed a front in Northern France—the proposal for a Second Front, impossible then for reasons of equipment and manpower, was to be constantly reiterated. Little was said in the Soviet press of Britain's efforts in sending help, and the losses suffered by British convoys to Russia were virtually ignored by the Russians. 'The Soviet Government had the impression,' Churchill commented afterwards, 'that they were conferring a great favour on us by fighting in their own country for their own lives. The more they fought the heavier our debt became. This was not a balanced view.' He protested at the ill-usage of British sailors who had brought desperately-needed equipment to Russia at risk and discomfort. But he allowed for the 'pressures under which Stalin and his dauntless Russian nation lay'.

It looked like a long war (and was to prove so), and with America becoming increasingly involved, and certain to be concerned with post-war policies in Europe and elsewhere, a meeting to agree on broad principles became necessary. Harry Hopkins, President Roosevelt's envoy, was sitting with Churchill in the garden of 10 Downing Street on a July afternoon when he told him that President Roosevelt would like to meet him. A few trusted newspapermen knew of Churchill's intention of sailing to meet the President somewhere in the Atlantic; in America the secret was less well kept, the departure from Washington of almost all of Roosevelt's Cabinet attracting attention. The Atlantic was teeming with German U-boats, and there was much anxiety amongst Churchill's friends. His loss would have been a tragedy for Europe at such an hour, but it was a risk he took cheerfully. It meant the vessel dodging U-boats and often steaming ahead in total darkness. Major Attlee, in particular, feared that the *Tirpitz* might be sent to sink the *Prince of Wales*, on which Churchill and his staff travelled. Lord Beaverbrook, now Minister of Supply, was asked to join the discussions on supply of aid to Russia. The rendezvous was in Placentia Bay, Newfoundland; and on Sunday, 10th August, President Roosevelt came aboard the *Prince of Wales* with his Staff officers and considerable entourage of experts. The Stars and Stripes and Union Jack were draped on the pulpit, and American and British chaplains conducted a service in which both Americans and British worshipped jointly. It was a moving and significant occasion.

There was much to discuss; joint attitudes to Russia and aid to her; Japan, whose warlike preparations had been noted—though not sufficiently noted; American supplies to Britain; political co-operation. One outcome of the meeting was a statement of war aims, an eight-point declaration known as the Atlantic Charter. It embodied 'certain common principles in the policies of the two countries on which they base their hopes for a better future of the world'. President and Prime Minister sent a joint message to Stalin assuring him of aid and support.

The formal bulletins conveyed little of the human drama, an omission hastily and ably remedied by Mr. Churchill when he returned. With the enthusiasm of the born story-teller he said, 'In a spacious, land-locked bay which reminded me of the west coast of Scotland, powerful American warships, protected by strong flotillas and far-ranging aircraft, awaited our arrival and, as it were, stretched out a hand to help us. Our party arrived in the newest, or almost the newest, British battleship, the *Prince of Wales*, with a modest escort of British and Canadian destroyers. There for three days I spent my time in company, and I think I may say in comradeship, with Mr. Roosevelt, while all the time the chiefs of staff and naval and military commanders, both of the British Empire and of the United States, sat together in continual council. President Roosevelt is the thrice-chosen head of the most powerful State and community in the world. I am the servant of both King and Parliament, at present charged with the principal direction of our affairs in these fateful times. . . . Therefore this meeting was bound to be important. . . . The meeting was therefore symbolic . . . this was a meeting which marks for ever in the pages of history the taking up by the English-speaking nations amid all this peril, tumult and confusion, of the guidance of the fortunes of the broad, toiling masses in all the continents. . . .'

Churchill's broadcast to the people of Britain was certainly intended as much for the ears of American listeners as for those at home. 'Three-and-a-half years ago I appealed to my fellow-countrymen to take the lead in weaving together a strong defensive union . . . but none would listen. All stood idle while Germany rearmed. Czechoslovakia was subjugated. A French government deserted their faithful ally and broke a plighted word in that ally's hour of need. Russia was cajoled and deceived into a kind of neutrality or partnership while the French Army was annihilated. The Low Countries and the Scandinavian countries, acting with France and Britain in good time, even after the war had begun, might have altered its course . . . the Balkan States had only to stand together to save themselves from ruin. . . .

'Why is Hitler striking at Russia and inflicting and suffering himself, or rather making his soldiers suffer, this frightful slaughter? It is with the declared object of turning his whole force upon the British Isles. And if he should succeed in beating the life and strength out of us, which is not so easy, then is the moment when he will settle his account . . . with the people of the United States and generally with the Western Hemisphere. . . .'

In other words, he was saying to the United States, it may be your turn next. 'One by one . . . there is the process. . . . I rejoiced to find that the President saw in their true light and proportion the extreme dangers by which the American people, as well as the British people, are now beset.'

On 9th September, reviewing the war situation, Churchill remarked on some of the salient points discussed with President Roosevelt, being careful however not to elaborate on points whose significance the Americans would decide for themselves in the course of time; he had no wish, in other words, to prod and harry them forward when they had chosen their course and were going at a good pace. It was encouraging for him to be able to tell the House that German and Italian shipping losses were three times those sustained by the Allies, whose hazards were greater because they were spread over a wider area.

In Russia one of the mightiest battles in all history was raging. In August the Russians evacuated Smolensk and began to withdraw across the Dnieper. The German attack on Leningrad intensified. Novgorod, then Dnieprotrovsk were evacuated; then Kremenchug, Orel, Briansk, Odessa. By October Moscow was in a state of siege. Kharkov fell.

Elsewhere there was war, intrigue and turmoil. The *Ark Royal* was sunk off Gibraltar. On 17th November British commandos raided the German H.Q. in Libya and two days later General Auchinleck opened the Battle of Sidi Resegh. By 22nd November the Germans had captured Rostov and three days later opened a fresh offensive on Moscow. On 27th November 10,000 Italians at Gondar garrison in Abyssinia surrendered to the British, proving, as Churchill had said, that the Italians had no heart in the fight.

America, step by step, had moved nearer to war with the Axis. The Neutrality Act had been revised in October to permit American ships to sail to British ports with lease-lend materials. When the U.S. destroyer *Kearney* was torpedoed the American Navy was ordered to shoot on sight.

On 7th December came the Japanese attack on the American Fleet in Pearl Harbour, the Hawaian base, and on other bases in the Philippine Islands; the attack took place while the Japanese envoy, Kurusu, was engaged in negotiations with the American Secretary of State, Mr. Cordell Hull. The war launched on the United States and Britain, whose bases were attacked simultaneously, was confirmed after the event by a quaintly worded note from Emperor Hirohito: 'We by the grace of heaven, Emperor of Japan, seated on the throne of a line unbroken for ages, enjoin upon you, our loyal and brave subjects: We hereby declare war on the United States of America and the British Empire.'

Churchill responded with a brief note. Japanese forces having attempted a landing on the coast of Malaya, bombing Singapore and Hong Kong, with no declaration of war or ultimatum, he had been 'instructed to inform the Imperial Japanese Government, in the name of His Majesty's Government in the United Kingdom, that a state of war exists between the two countries," finishing his note, with proper formality:

'I have the honour to be, with high consideration,
   Sir,
            Your obedient servant,
               WINSTON S. CHURCHILL.'

The thought of Mr. Churchill, at such a time, being the obedient servant of the Japanese Emperor is a droll one.

Now the war was on a global scale. Not only the defence of Britain and liberation of Europe, but the whole Asian theatre had to be considered. There was little enough Churchill could tell Parliament by way of comfort on 8th December: 'The ordeal to which the English-speaking world and our heroic Russian allies are being exposed will certainly be hard, especially at the outset, and will probably be long, yet when we look around us over the sombre panorama of the world, we have no reason to doubt the justice of our cause or that our strength and will-power will be sufficient to sustain it. We have at least four-fifths of the population of the globe upon our side. . . .'

Two days later it was Churchill's painful duty to give the House the terrible news that the *Prince of Wales* and *Repulse* had been sunk by the Japanese. He had received the news while opening despatch boxes in bed, and was thankful that nobody was present to see the effect of the shock upon him. 'I have bad news for the House which I think I should pass on to them at the earliest moment,' he said that morning, 'A report has been received from Singapore that H.M.S. *Prince of Wales* and H.M.S. *Repulse* have been sunk while carrying out operations against the Japanese in their attack on Malaya . . . both ships were sunk by air attack.'

On 12th December in the course of his war review his tone was confident, but he recognized the grave threat of the Japanese onslaught. True, the English-speaking world was now united in its resistance to Fascism; the Libyan offensive was not taking the

course its authors intended, but would achieve its intended object
in time; it was a prolonged battle, but served to divert German
forces from the Russian front. Then came a tribute to Russia:

Six weeks or a month ago people were wondering whether Moscow would be taken, or Leningrad in the north, or how soon the
Germans would overrun the Caucasus and seize the oilfields of
Baku. . . . Since then a striking change has become evident. The
enormous power of the Russian armies and the glorious stead-
fastness and energy with which they have resisted the frightful
onslaught made upon them have now been made plain. On top of
this has come the Russian winter and on top of that the Russian
Air Force. Hitler forced his army into this barren and desolated
land. He has everywhere been brought to a standstill. On a large
portion of the front he is in retreat; the sufferings of his troops are
indescribable; their losses have been immense. The cold snow,
the piercing wind which blows across the icy spaces, the ruined
towns and villages, the long lines of communication assailed by
dauntless guerilla warriors, the stubborn, unyielding resistance
with which the Russian soldiers and the Russian people have
defended every street and every house, every yard of their soil,
all these facts have inflicted upon the German armies and the
German nation a bloody prop, almost unequalled in the history
of war. . . .

The House rang with cheers. It was a graphic, and a true picture;
Next he dealt with the 'cold-blooded, calculated, violent, treacherous
attack upon the United States and ourselves. . . . It seems to be quite
certain that Japan . . . counted on the active support of the German
Nazis and the Italian Fascists. It is, therefore, very likely that the
United States will be faced with the open hostility of Germany,
Italy and Japan. . . . I know that I speak for the United States as
well as for the British Empire when I say that we would all rather
perish than be conquered (loud cheers). And on this basis, putting it
at its worst, there are quite a lot of us to be killed (laughter)'.

There were uneasy questions about the sinking of the *Prince of
Wales* and *Repulse*. Sir Roger Keyes asked whether the ships had
been protected by fighters, a question which Churchill parried with
the true but irrelevant statement that Admiral Sir Tom Phillips was
a most skilful officer who had acted on 'sound naval lines'. Sir A.
Knox, reverting to the original question, asked, 'Have we adequate
aircraft for the Navy?' To this Churchill could only state that 'We

have only a certain amount of aircraft to meet the many engagements we have to face'. He added that he could give no guarantee that ships might not have to engage without carrier-borne or shore-based air support.

Just before Christmas, under conditions of great secrecy, Churchill—accompanied by Lord Beaverbrook—crossed the Atlantic in the *Duke of York* to meet President Roosevelt in Washington. He stayed at the White House and engaged immediately in discussions on the co-ordination of the allied war effort. It was a visit without precedent; never before had a Prime Minister of England conferred with a President of the United States while the two countries were facing a common foe. Now Churchill had to think in global, rather than European terms. He had placed Burma under Wavell's command to resist the inevitable Japanese advance towards Burma and India; he followed the progress of the desert war—on Christmas Eve came the splendid news of the capture of Benghazi by Auchinleck's troops, but on Christmas Day itself came the heartbreaking news of the surrender of Hong Kong after days of bitter fighting.

The two leaders got along well. Churchill's part-American ancestry certainly helped them in their relationship, although he could not get the President to share his glowing enthusiasm for the British Empire (Commonwealth seemed to him a mealy-mouthed euphemism, a compromise) while he, for his part, felt that the President took too hopeful a view of Stalin's post-war intentions. However, for the moment, the problem was the survival of their respective states.

On Boxing Day Churchill addressed Congress. The Senate Room was bursting at the seams with notabilities—Congressmen, diplomats, judges; and as Churchill entered, escorted by Senator Barkley, the roar of cheering was deafening. With felicitous timing, Churchill reminded his hearers of his American ancestry: 'The fact that my American forebears of so many generations played their part in the life of the United States and that here I am, an Englishman, welcomed in your midst, makes the experience one of the most moving and thrilling in my life. . . . I wish indeed that my mother, whose memory I cherish across the vale of years, could have been here to see me. By the way, I cannot help reflecting that if my father had been American and my mother British, instead of the other way round, I might have got here on my own. In that case, this would not have been the first time you would have heard my voice. In that case I should not have needed any invitation, but if I had, it is hardly likely that it would have been unanimous. . . .' The sally brought the House down with laughter. Churchill, with unerring judgement, had struck the right note of informality. Then followed a passage epitomizing his love of Parliament:

I am a child of the House of Commons. I was brought up in my father's house to believe in democracy. 'Trust the people'—that was his message. . . . Therefore I have been in harmony all my life with the tides which have flowed on both sides of the Atlantic against privilege and monopoly, and I have steered confidently towards the Gettysburg ideal of 'Government of the people by the people for the people'. I owe my advancement entirely to the House of Commons, whose servant I am. In my country, as in yours, public men are proud to be the servants of the State and would be ashamed to be its masters. But any day, if they thought the people wanted it, the House of Commons might by a simple vote remove me from my office. . . .

On 1st January 1942 the President was wheeled into Mr. Churchill's apartment with a draft; Churchill got out of his bath to read it. It was a joint declaration by twenty-six countries, including the United States and Britain, pledging mutual aid and support in the fight for freedom. A few days later, in bitter weather but amidst scenes of wild enthusiasm, Churchill delivered a great speech to the Canadian Parliament in Ottawa—a joint session of the Canadian Senate and the House of Commons. At one point in his war review he broke into French to pay a tribute to France and his confident hopes of France's resurgence. He sounded a note of general hope:

Now that the whole of the North American continent is one gigantic arsenal, an armed camp; now that the immense power of Russia is gradually becoming manifest; now that the long-suffering, unconquerable Chinese sees help approaching; and now that the outraged and subjugated nations can see daylight at the end of the tunnel, it is permissible to take a more forward look of the war.

But the cares of office, the work of consultation, the incessant travel and these extra labours were quite a heavy burden for a man of sixty-seven. Even Churchill felt the strain: '. . . these great occasions imposed heavy demands on my life and strength, and were additional

to all the daily consultations and mass of current business'. Churchill
was also uneasy in his mind about Russia. Circumstances made us
allies, but he was disturbed at reports of Russian purges and persecutions in the Baltic States, whose political leaders were killed,
deported or cruelly maltreated. Looking ahead, as was his habit, he
wondered whether Russia had any intention, in the name of international decency, of reverting to her original frontiers when the
war was ended; he doubted it, but told Anthony Eden that the 1941
frontiers of Russia were never recognized, having been 'acquired
by acts of aggression in shameful collusion with Hitler'.

The unity of the English-speaking peoples had been achieved,
and his speeches, as the greatest parliamentarian, in these two great
Parliaments of the Western hemisphere had brought everyone closer.
But at home, and especially in Parliament, Members were growing
restive. The outlook in the Far East was grim. In the Indian Ocean
and the Pacific only the remnants of America's vanquished fleet
remained to prowl the seas. Victory in the Western Desert still
eluded the Allies. Taking leave of the President on 14th January he
flew to Bermuda, addressed the Assembly there and then, instead
of travelling home by sea, flew in a Boeing flying-boat which got
off course and only narrowly escaped being shot down by German
batteries at Brest, changing course just a few minutes before they
would have been a target. The arrival at Plymouth was hardly less
dramatic. Coming from an unaccustomed direction, the plane was
assumed to be an enemy aircraft and six Hurricanes of Fighter
Command were ordered into the air to shoot Churchill's plane down.
Fortunately it landed in time. It would have been a cruel irony and
a blow for Europe if Churchill had been shot down, at this crucial
time (or any other) by his own people.

The atmosphere of the House of Commons on his return, however, was much cooler than the two he had recently addressed.
What, M.P.s were saying, is the good of a Prime Minister who
assumes all the most important jobs and is away for weeks on end,
with Britain tottering on the edge of a precipice? Everything seemed
to be going wrong everywhere. There were mutterings that the need
for keeping the enemy in ignorance was a rather useful way of
keeping M.P.s in ignorance too. But the feeling was not so much
against Churchill as a person as against his judgement in picking
his team. Things were going wrong to a greater degree than the
hazards of war would appear to warrant; and that implied something

wrong in the administration. *The Times*, in particular, reflected in a spirited article the trend of opinion, public and Parliamentary.

Churchill asked that his speech to the Commons should be broadcast simultaneously. His motive, I am sure, was to save the labour of a separate broadcast. But the House would have none of it, and Hore-Belisha, sniping as usual, reminded him acidly that Parliament was a deliberative assembly, not a place for the projection of personality to the nation. *The Times* added its own weight to this opposition, implying that Churchill was unduly influenced by what he had observed of the President's powers in America. At a later sitting Churchill withdrew his request, and also promised a three-day debate during which all grievances could be aired.

This debate opened on 27th January and the full reports of it occupy the space of a whole book. It was significant at the time, though some issues seem remote (being resolved) now; it is worth study by any history student. It was inaugurated by the technique of a confidence motion, moved by Mr. Attlee, Lord Privy Seal:

That this House has confidence in His Majesty's Government, and will aid it to the utmost in the vigorous prosecution of the war.

There was a fine speech by Sir John Wardlaw Milne. Although anxious that the world would know that Britain was united in its determination to fight for victory, he was concerned that parliamentary procedure might imply that everyone was satisfied with the Government. He looked with some misgivings to the Treasury Bench and asked why the Ministers, senior and junior, were carrying the same responsibilities after nearly two years of war. Loyalty to one's colleagues was all very well, but loyalty to the people and the nation was greater still.

The Prime Minister had no reason to be surprised at the dissatisfaction, he said. There was a feeling almost of horror that we had been found unprepared. If the military and other authorities were aware of the inadequacy of the preparations in Singapore, why did they indulge in flights of fancy? He referred to the ludicrously complacent—and misleading—communiqués issued respecting both Libya and the Far East. 'One would think,' he said, 'that duststorms fall only on British troops and that it is somewhat below the belt for the Japanese to land in sampans. I appreciate that the Far Eastern question is primarily one of sea power. We are entitled to

look to the United States for naval control in the Pacific. I have no
doubt that in the end we shall not be disappointed. It will not be of
any value to say what took place at Pearl Harbour. After all, the
Americans at least had the excuse that they were not at war. We
are, and we were caught napping. . . .'

A letter from a Defence Security Officer in Malaya, which he read,
was a devastating exposure of military incompetence. The defence
of Singapore consisted entirely in preparations against attack from
the sea. The naval base lay between Singapore and the Malayan
mainland. Even in the State of Johore, north-west from the open
roadstead, there were no defences, no troops, scarcely police even; a
long coastline, unprotected, unpatrolled except by occasional aircraft.

What about the half-a-million Japanese soldiers in Indo-China?
What preparations had we made? Was it true that to the very end
the authorities scouted the idea of an attack? What was the cause
of all this dangerous drift? *Was the Prime Minister trying to do too
much?*

A solemn note of warning was sounded by Mr. R. Richards,
Labour M.P. for Denbigh. The campaign in North Africa was going
badly. Somebody must be blamed. How was it that when we undertook an object we never somehow carried it off? How was it that
we had so many of these apparent failures? There had been inadequate preparation in the Far East. Was this generation to witness
the disintegration of the British Empire?

Beverley Baxter, Unionist M.P. for Wood Green, said, 'The
Government is emerging into a one-man Government. Even Napoleon had his marshals. Mr. Churchill, by a combination of despotism
and paternalism, is reducing his Ministers to lieutenants. There are
no marshals among them, except perhaps Lord Beaverbrook, who
had made himself a marshal.' But Baxter defended Churchill against
criticisms of his absence. 'In spite of all, Mr. Churchill has given
to this country a renaissance, a new vision of the heroic part we
have to play in history. He may take too much on himself but
throughout the world he looms up like a giant, the personification
of the centre of a Grand Alliance. . . .'

Emanuel Shinwell, once a fire-eating Socialist, raised cheers by
congratulating Mr. Churchill as having earned gratitude by his
adventurous voyage, and for cementing relations between the two
great English-speaking peoples. Colonel Elliot thought the restive-
ness of the House was due more to events than individuals.

Earl Winterton likened Churchill to the Victorian cricketer, W. G. Grace, who, at the end of the first-class cricketing season, was in the habit of going into the country district of Gloucester and choosing a team among the village players. They then went to different places. Grace went in first and invariably remained until the last wicket was down, and he bowled the whole of the time. The other players were quite satisfied to serve under such a grand master. Several of the players in the present team had played for a good many other sides, and they would be equally ready to play for any other side that was formed.

This sally brought some badly-needed laughter to a solemn House.

At last Churchill rose to wind up the debate. 'No one can say,' he said, 'that this has not been a full and free debate. No one can say that criticism has been hampered or stifled. . . . In no country in the world at the present time could a Government conducting a war be exposed to such a stress. No dictator country fighting for its life would dare allow such a discussion. . . . The House of Commons is master all the time of the life of the administration. . . . Therefore, I say, the House of Commons has a great responsibility.'

They must either, he said, produce an effective, alternative administration by which the King's Government could be carried on, or sustain the existing Government in its enormous tasks. 'I feel myself very much in need of that help at the present time, and I am sure I shall be accorded it in a manner to give encouragement and comfort as well as guidance and suggestions.' (Hear, hear.) He was ready to profit from suggestions, even from hostile quarters. 'I shall not be like that saint . . . who refused to do right because the devil prompted him,' he added with a chuckle, and the House roared with laughter. 'Neither,' he added, for the benefit of those who criticized him for changes of views, 'shall I be deterred from doing what I am convinced is right by the fact that I have thought differently about it in some distant, or even in some recent past.' There was renewed laughter. The House was with him already. He then reviewed the war in all its aspects. He dismissed as 'mischievous' the allegation that the Naval Staff wished to send an aircraft carrier in defence of the *Prince of Wales* and *Repulse*. The fact was that it had always been intended that any large ships going to the Far East should have aircraft-carrier support. But 'through a succession of accidents' not a single one was available and all, except one with the

Home Fleet, were under repair. In deciding to join issue with the Japanese, his friend Admiral Phillips had acted gallantly; the stakes of both sides were high. 'The prize was great if gained; if lost, our danger was grievous. Admiral Phillips was fully aware of the risk . . . the prize might have been 20,000 drowned in the sea and a relief to the whole catalogue of misfortunes which have since come upon us and have still to come. I have finished. I have done. . . . I offer no apologies, I offer no excuses. I make no promises. . . . I have finished. Let every man act now in accordance with what he thinks is his duty in harmony with his heart and his conscience.'

There were loud and prolonged cheers. Sir Roger Keyes hoped that the House would give a unanimous vote, to show the world they were solidly behind the leader. 'We are grateful to the Prime Minister,' he concluded, 'for the great inspiration he has given us in our blackest hour.' The House divided and voted: 464 Members voted for the Motion and only one against, giving a majority of 463 —an overwhelming victory. The tension lifted. Faces wreathed in smiles, the Chamber rang with cheering and Mr. Churchill, lurching slightly forward in familiar stance, strode slowly from the Chamber.

24

Still Under Fire

Churchill had won that battle. But 1942 offered more than its share of reverses and until well into autumn he was under fire from critics at home. By the middle of February his forewarnings of graver news were amply fulfilled, inspiring more dismay at their truth than gratitude for the prior notice. Withdrawal after withdrawal, disaster after disaster, was the story from the Far East, culminating in the fall of Singapore, a calamity which seemed to symbolize the impending fate of the British Empire. Singapore, by all except those who knew it, had been regarded as impregnable. Certainly the awful story was mitigated by acts of heroism; but it was a defeat, strategically, morally and politically.

On 15th February the Prime Minister announced Singapore's capitulation, 'the greatest disaster to British arms which our history records.'

The nation in general and the House of Commons in particular were mortified and humiliated by the escape of the German warships *Scharnhorst*, *Gneisenau* and *Prinz Eugen* from Brest. They were sighted at 11 a.m. on 12th February off Boulogne and made their way through the English Channel to German waters. It is true that the bombs of the R.A.F. at Brest had made that place untenable, but that the German warships should successfully have run the gauntlet was humiliating.

Once more his administration—and he himself—came under fire. On 17th February the House was tense and restive. Nor was it a feeling confined to any side of the House. In so subjective a mood, it seemed to Churchill that an immediate debate would serve little purpose. 'It would ill become the dignity of the Government and the House,' he said, 'and would render poor service to the Alliance of which we are a part, if we were to be drawn into agitated or excited recriminations at a time when all our minds are oppressed with a sense of tragedy and with a sorrow at so lamentable a misfortune.'

Of the escape of the three German warships, he reminded those who expected Britain to keep ships constantly on patrol that if they had been, they would have been liable to the same scale of attack as the German ships at Brest. He also tried to make it look like a blessing in disguise. 'Though it may somewhat surprise the House and the public, I should like to state that in the opinion of the Admiralty, with which I most cordially concur, this abandonment by the Germans of their position at Brest has been decidedly beneficial to our war situation. A threat to our convoy routes has been removed and the enemy has been driven to leave his advantageous position. The diversion of our air bombing effort which, although necessary, was so wasteful, is over and the heavy-scale attack on Germany is now possible, in which the near misses will hit German and not French dwellings.'

Sir John Gordon (Conservative, Kidderminster) said the purpose was not to find fault with individuals but to examine the whole conduct of the war and those conducting it, and the House of Commons was the proper place for that to be discussed. He asked that if the matter could not be debated right away, there should be a promise that it would be debated soon.

Churchill agreed to a debate, although after the detailed three-day defence of war policy at the end of January it was a burden which, in the worsening situation, he could have done without. 'The House is absolute master,' he said, 'if its confidence is not extended to the Government, if it does not believe that the war is being well managed, if it thinks it can make arrangements which would lead to the war being better managed, then it is the duty and the right of the House to express an opinion, as it can do in a proper and constitutional manner. I do not know whether it can all take place in public; I am absolutely certain that I could say things to this House which would arouse honourable Members to the seriousness of the situation. Let us say there will be a debate; I was only deprecating that it should be held as it seems in a mood of anger and panic. . . .'

There were angry cries of 'No!' and 'Withdraw!'

Churchill would not apologize, although Members were irked at the implication that they needed reminding of 'the seriousness of the situation'. It was precisely because they were aware of it that they were pressing for an examination of the effectiveness of the Administration. In a world of harsh realism, they were judging by results. 'I think,' Churchill continued, 'that a very excited debate, taking place here today, when all our minds are oppressed by what has happened, might easily have the effect of causing a very bad and unfavourable reaction all over the world.'

This was true. Churchill never forgot that what was said in the House was disseminated everywhere—to the enemy, to wavering neutrals (of which few remained) and to friends, especially the U.S.A., whose support was measured by their assessment of British resolution. For the Americans were now thoroughly in with Britain. They had agreed to their bombers joining in heavy raids on Germany. His broadcast to the nation on the fall of Singapore was a masterly oration intended not only to stiffen resistance at home but cement the Anglo-American alliance. He had told how British resources had been stretched to the utmost. Britain had fought alone for a year against Hitler and Mussolini, and had to send massive help to Russia. 'In these circumstances,' he told listeners, 'we British had no means whatever of providing effectively against a new war with Japan.'

This was true—so far as it went. This was not the time to admit that the assumption that an enemy would invade Malaya and Singapore in the most difficult way, ignoring the unprotected back door was naïve; that a complacent and old-world-colonial type local administration had been caught napping. 'It would never have been in the power of Great Britain while fighting Germany and Italy— nations long hardened and prepared for war—while fighting in the North Sea, in the Mediterranean, and the Atlantic, to defend the Pacific and the Far East single-handed against the assault of Japan. We have only just been able to keep our heads above water at home . . . only by so little have we held our own in the Nile Valley and the Middle East. The Mediterranean is closed, and all our transports have to go round the Cape of Good Hope, each ship making only three voyages in the year. Not a ship, not an aeroplane, not a tank, not an anti-tank gun or anti-aircraft gun has stood idle . . . we are struggling hard in the Libyan desert where perhaps another serious battle will soon be fought. . . . We have to provide for the safety and order of liberated Abyssinia, of conquered Eritrea, of Palestine, of liberated Syria and redeemed Iraq, and of our new ally Persia. . . . Tonight the Japanese are triumphant . . . we are taken aback. . . . The overthrow for a while of British and United States sea power in the Pacific was like the breaking of some mighty dam. . . . I must warn you, as I warned the House of Commons before they gave their generous vote of confidence a fortnight ago, that many misfortunes, severe torturing losses, remorseless and gnawing anxieties lie ahead. . . . I speak to you all under the shadow of a heavy and far-reaching military defeat. . . . This, therefore, is one of those moments when the British race and nation can show its quality and genius. . . . Here is the moment to display that calm and poise, combined with grim determination, which not so long ago brought us out of the very jaws of death . . . we are no longer alone . . . three-quarters of the human race are now moving with us. . . . Let us move forward steadfastly together into the storm and through the storm.'

Churchill had read perfectly the mood of the House. He believed in its collective wisdom and respected its supreme authority; no man ever loved any institution more. His mind, as he played for time before agreeing to fix a debate, was already made up. Clearly, there *must* be a Cabinet and Government reshuffle. Even good men might be replaced by better men; the best men must be given their authority and heads irrespective of Party or popularity. Strength, integrity, drive and ability alone must count. . . .

Within days Churchill had achieved a drastic reshuffle. Mr. Attlee became Dominions Secretary and Deputy Prime Minister; Sir John Anderson Lord President, Oliver Lyttleton Minister of State for Production, and, most interesting appointment of all, Sir Stafford Cripps emerged as Lord Privy Seal and Leader of the House. These, besides Churchill himself, Anthony Eden (still Foreign Secretary) and Ernest Bevin (Minister of Labour and National Service) constituted the new Cabinet which was now also smaller and more compact. Lord Beaverbrook had been dropped from the Cabinet and assigned to Washington for the co-ordination of supply problems. The dour Lord Reith, once the able and puritanical chief of the B.B.C., was replaced. In effect, the new War Cabinet now had seven members, three of them having no Departmental duties.

A happy thought was the inclusion of Sir Stafford Cripps, whose ambassadorship in Moscow had proved a brilliant success, and whose political situation was unique. Expelled from the Labour Party for being too individualistic, regarded with misgivings by the right for being ultra-left, he had qualities which, in the jargon of the period, were 'in short supply'. He was of unimpeachable integrity, an ascetic, a fervently religious man, a believer in human equality and lover of fair play. He was also a lawyer of acute and tireless intellect.

How wise Churchill had been to postpone the debate on the war situation until he had done what he knew the House would have demanded anyway, was proved by the ensuing debate.

Churchill reminded the House of the last war. 'It is now the fashion to speak of the Lloyd George Cabinet as if it gave universal satisfaction and conducted the war with unerring judgement and with unbroken success,' he said, having outlined his plans and paid tribute to retiring colleagues. 'On the contrary, complaints that were loud and clamant, such as the slaughters of Passchendaele, the destruction of Caporetto in 1917, and the destruction of the Fifth Army in 1918, befel that rightly famous Administration. It made numerous serious mistakes, and no one was more surprised than its members when the end of the war came suddenly in 1918.' The House roared with laughter. Now it was relaxed, catching his mood of sober optimism.

Of the appointment of Cripps as Leader of the House, Churchill explained that he himself had never expected to undertake this job, onerous in itself; he had had to take it on because his proposal that Neville Chamberlain should take the whole of the House of Commons work off his hands was unacceptable. 'I must admit,' he said, 'that this parliamentary task has weighed upon me heavily. During the period for which I have been responsible I find, to my horror, that I have made more than twenty-five lengthy speeches to Parliament, in public or in secret session, to say nothing of answering great numbers of questions and dealing with many current emergencies. I have greatly valued the honour of leading the House, which my father did before me'—here the House rang with cheers—'and even in very rough periods I have taken most particular care of their rights and interests.'

Churchill's summary of a war leader's inescapable quandary could hardly be bettered:

If I were to dilate upon our hopes these might soon be falsified, and I might be mocked at by those who prove themselves wise by our failures. If, on the other hand, I painted the picture in its darkest hues, very great despondency might be spread among our ardent and growing forces, and the enemy might be encouraged.

Though long forgotten, this debate is no less historic than that following Dunkirk. Only a master-Parliamentarian could have handled such a situation. Having satisfied them that he had a strengthened Cabinet, outlined the progress of the war, explained his own functions, he quoted from a speech he made when he resigned from Asquith's Government on 15th November 1915:

> There is no reason to be discouraged about the progress of the war. We are passing through a bad time now, and it will probably be worse before it is better. But that it will be better if we only endure and persevere I have no doubt whatever. . . .

'I find comfort in the passage,' Churchill declared, amidst renewed cheers, 'which comes back to me like an echo from the past, and I commend it respectfully to the consideration of the House.'

Churchill had won the day—not simply by his eloquence but by his action. He was in no need of the New York *Herald-Tribune*'s warning that 'the incomparable leader of a magnificent people' should understand that the urgent problem was to destroy the enemy and not his critics.

Of the changes King George VI commented: 'I am glad Winston has been prevailed upon to make them before and not after the debate. The House of Commons wants Winston to lead them; but they don't like the way he treats them. He likes getting his own way with no interference from anybody and nobody will stand for that sort of treatment in this country.'

The disasters at which Churchill had hinted were multiplied. Dutch bases in the Netherlands East Indies, Java, and Batavia fell to the Japanese. Malta reeled under perpetual aerial bombardment. Rangoon was evacuated to the Japanese. The Germans recommenced their offensive in Russia. Against this there were heavy Allied raids on Germany, production at home was getting into its stride, and the road to India protected by the seizure, at great cost in time and men, of the Vichy-held base of Madagascar, which was then occupied by the Free French. In India, Sir Stafford Cripps endeavoured to get Indian approval to a proposed new constitution granting the country Dominion status after the war. But although Congress Party, the most powerful, was at first predisposed to the idea, they yielded to the fanatical promptings of Gandhi, who favoured discussions with the Japanese, and rejected the proposals. At all times Churchill had been fully determined to defend India, but his outspoken opposition to Indian self-government in earlier years and his contemptuous dismissal of Gandhi as 'nauseating' were not forgotten, least of all by Gandhi himself. Cripps left India on 13th April.

The intransigence of the Hindu Congress Party, and the determination of Gandhi, under the pretext of non-violence, to maintain a revolutionary movement which by obstruction could sabotage the defence of India against Japanese invasion, posed serious problems for Churchill. A minor irritation—but a recurrent one—was Stalin's continual insistence on the opening of a Second Front, which would have been of benefit to Russia but a potential disaster to Britain whose ordeal—when bombs were raining on London—was a matter of total indifference to them. The Second Front agitation was carried on in Britain largely by members of the Communist Party and their 'fellow-travellers'.

Aneurin Bevan, who was hob-nobbing with Communists and lending his support inside and outside of Parliament for the creation of a Second Front, was forever sniping at Churchill in the House. Bevan disliked 'the concentration of hero-worship on one individual' (although continually anxious to draw the limelight upon himself).

Churchill's refusal to be stampeded into large-scale offensives for which men and resources were lacking was based on his understanding of Russia's expansionist plans. Under conditions of great secrecy, Mr. Molotov, who had signed the Soviet pact with the Nazis, came to London seeking promises from the Allies that Soviet annexation of the Baltic States, of Eastern Poland and Bessarabia, as well as her new frontier with Finland, would be recognized when war was over. Molotov went from London to Washington and back to London and thence to Moscow, taking with him no promise regarding frontiers but a twenty-years Anglo-Soviet Treaty of Alliance. To have given Russian *carte blanche* to keep the spoils of war would have been contrary to the Atlantic Charter, which Stalin had signed.

On 10th May 1942 Churchill broadcast to the nation. It was his second year as the 'King's First Minister'. He reviewed the progress of the war, spoke of the mounting aerial attack on Germany and warned Hitler that if rumours of German intentions to use poison gas in Russia were proved, Britain would retaliate with the same weapon against the Germans. Of the Second Front agitation, he parried with a subtle blow—a paean of praise for those who demanded it. 'Is it not far better that in the thirty-second month of this hard war we should find this general desire to come to closest grips with the enemy than that there should be any signs of war weariness? Is it not far better that demonstrations of thousands of people would gather in Trafalgar Square demanding the most vehement and audacious attacks than that there should be weepings and wailings and peace agitations . . . we shall not fail them, either in daring or in wisdom. . . .'

Meanwhile the Russians were claiming that a Second Front in 1942 had been promised them, and there were indications that President Roosevelt was even toying with the idea. Churchill knew that Roosevelt and his aide Stettinius were inclined to under-estimate Russian expansionist intentions. Had not Roosevelt once said to the Polish leader, Mikolajczyk, 'But of one thing I am certain, *Stalin is not an Imperialist*'? Anglo-American talks at top level were urgently necessary, to co-ordinate campaigns all over the world, to discuss present and future economic and political problems, including the pattern of the post-war world.

Before leaving for Washington, Churchill lunched with the King who asked, prudently and with that shrewd grasp of practical detail he had shown from the outset of the war (his counsel was more valuable than many appreciate, as he was totally objective), who could succeed Mr. Churchill in the event of his untimely death? Mr. Churchill gave thought to this possibility and submitted 'with his humble duty' that 'In the case of my death on this journey I am about to undertake, I avail myself of Your Majesty's gracious per-mission to advise you that you should entrust the formation of a new Government to Mr. Anthony Eden, the Secretary of State for Foreign Affairs, who is in my mind the outstanding Minister in the largest political party in the House of Commons and in the National Government over which I have the honour to preside and who, I am sure, will be found capable of conducting Your Majesty's affairs with the resolution, experience and capacity which these grievous times require.'

On 17th June 1942 Churchill visited the United States to discuss strategy and war plans. Admiral Leahy, then United States Ambas-sador to Vichy France and later Chief of Staff to the Commander-in-Chief of the United States Army and Navy, later went on record as saying of Roosevelt that 'I believe history will record that he exercised greater skill in the direction of our global war effort than did his gallant and brilliant contemporary, Winston Churchill.' Leahy suggested that the Chiefs of the British armed forces 'were loyally supporting the views of the Defence Minister only because it was their duty and because they were carrying out orders. On our side, we never laboured under any such handicap. There were differences of opinion, of course, but, due to the mutual confidence and daily contact between the President and his military chiefs, these differences never became serious.'

The underlying inference is that they were serious as between Churchill and his colleagues. Certainly he was a powerful personality, fond of authority and inclined to overshadow subordinates. But the differences were never serious. At home it was a different matter. Twice, at home, he had had to placate a restive Parliament, and now, while he was away, it was all boiling up again. Churchill read banner headlines in the American press telling of discontent with his administration at home; it was hardly calculated to strengthen his hand. But within days of his departure the campaign in the Western Desert had taken a turn for the worse. On 17th June British forces had withdrawn to the very frontiers of Egypt, itself now threatened with German invasion; they withdrew to Mersah Matruh on the 24th, the enemy advance being held at El Alamein on 1st July. On 21st June Tobruk fell, with 25,000 Allied soldiers taken prisoner.

It was too much. This time it was Winston Churchill and not simply his administration which came under fire. Sir John Wardlaw-Milne gave notice of a motion of censure on the Government, which was debated on 1st and 2nd July. A great battle was raging in North Africa as Auchinleck fought desperately to hold back the Germans. Some M.P.s were ashamed at belabouring the old man who had travelled thousands of miles and nearly killed himself with work and would have delayed the censure resolution. Churchill would not have it. The die had been cast; the world had been told that Parliament and public were dissatisfied with the leadership—the issue must be decided, and at once.

And so the motion was put: 'That the House, while paying tribute to the heroism and endurance of the Forces of the Crown in circumstances of exceptional difficulty, has no confidence in the central direction of the war.' Churchill had been angry and contemptuous of the criticisms he had read in America, and of such headlines as CHURCHILL TO BE CENSURED. Sir Stafford Cripps, on Churchill's return, had warned him of 'a very grave disturbance of opinion both in the House of Commons and in the country'.

Sir John, an influential back-bencher and who had been a supporter of the Munich Agreement, rose, rather diffidently, to the attack. He had tried to back out—at least temporarily—but Churchill, figuratively speaking and with a glum look that boded no good to anybody, beckoned him forward. He was in no mood to be challenged and then permit his opponent to withdraw as though thereby he was conferring some concession.

Wardlaw-Milne's speech was dull, if painstaking. The Prime Minister's optimism had proved consistently misleading, he declared. 'We have almost got to the stage when if my right honourable friend comes down to the House to tell us that we are going to win, or makes an optimistic statement elsewhere, one becomes afraid of what we shall hear next.' Why were our tanks inferior? Why were we outgunned in Libya? But from the moment he suggested that the Duke of Gloucester should be appointed Commander-in-Chief of the British Army, nobody took him seriously.

Sir Roger Keyes, who spoke for the vote of censure, obviously hoped his own words would be ineffective. He had no stomach for this particular fight. 'It would be a deplorable disaster if the Prime Minister had to go!' he declared, but Earl Winterton was not so diffident. 'Are you prepared, if these disasters continue,' he asked the House, 'whatever happens, to say that right up to the end of the war, however long it lasts, we must never have another Defence Minister or Prime Minister? That he is the only man who can win the war?'

By the second day of the debate few had appetite for the attack. They remembered Churchill's truthful sally earlier in the year: 'When I was called upon to be Prime Minister . . . there were not many applicants for the job. Since then perhaps the market has improved.' But it had not. There was not one man of even approximate calibre in experience, courage, audacity and shrewdness, and they knew it. It was left to Aneurin Bevan to keep the debate going. In bitterness and hostility it exceeded anything said before. But he was entitled to ask searching questions about the availability of weapons. Nor did he spare the military hierarchy, who must, he said, be held responsible for the drift of the country's military fortunes. If Rommel had been in the British Army he would still be a sergeant—'The fact of the matter is that the British Army is ridden by class prejudice. You have got to change it. If the House of Commons has not the guts to make the Government change it, events will. Although the House may not take any notice of me today, you will be doing it next week. Remember my words next Monday or Tuesday. It is events which are criticizing the Government.' Churchill mistook 'verbal felicities for mental inspirations'. 'The Prime Minister has been fighting rearguard actions against the House of Commons all the while to buy off the political situation, not to create a machine for war-making.' He added a passionate plea for the opening of a Second Front.

At last Churchill rose to answer, a pile of notes under his arm. The debate had been 'a remarkable example' of parliamentary freedom in time of war. 'Everything that can be thought of or raked up has been used to weaken confidence in the Government; has been used to prove that Ministers are incompetent and to weaken their confidence in themselves; to make the Army distrust the backing it is getting from the civil power; to make the workmen lose confidence in the weapons they are striving so hard to make; to represent the Government as a set of nonentities over whom the Prime Minister towers, and then to undermine him in his own heart and if possible in the eyes of the nation—all this poured out by cables and radio to all parts of the world, to the distress of all our friends and the delight of all our foes.'

The accusation came clear and vibrant, filling the chamber as each challenging word was spoken. He looked around, few having the courage to return his gaze direct. And then the old magic worked. Cheers echoed again and again through the chamber. Churchill had won, but he had more to say yet—plenty more.

I am in favour of this freedom . . . and I must now make my appeal to the House of Commons to ensure that it does not end there. Although I have done my best—my utmost—to prepare a full and considered statement to the House, I must confess I have found it very difficult, even during the bitter animosity of the diatribe of Mr. Aneurin Bevan, with all its careful and calculated hostility—I have found it very difficult to concentrate my thought on this debate and to withdraw it from the tremendous and most difficult battle now raging in Egypt.

He turned to Tobruk. We had lost 50,000 men, mostly as prisoners, and immense quantities of precious stores. Rommel had advanced 400 miles in the desert and was speeding towards the Nile Valley, menacing Turkey, Spain and French North Africa. The fall of

Tobruk meant the loss of its garrison of 25,000 in a single day and was unexpected 'by the public, by the War Cabinet and even by the General Staffs.' He spoke of the 'bitter pang' the telegram of Tobruk's fall brought to him when he was with the President of the United States. 'Some people assume too readily that because a Government keeps cool under reverses its members do not feel as keenly the public misfortune as do its critics. On the contrary, I doubt whether anyone feels greater sorrow or pain than those who are responsible for the general conduct of our affairs.'

Once more he explained, chapter and verse, the mighty drama now grown so complicated that one could follow all superficially or only a tiny part in detail. Then he invited the House to decide:

I undertook the office of Prime Minister and Minister of Defence . . . when the life of the British Empire hung upon a thread.

I am your servant, and you have a right to dismiss me when you please. What you have no right to do is to ask me to bear responsibilities without the power of effective action. . . .

The Government received a vote of confidence of 475 votes to 25.

Bevan's quarrel with Churchill enlivened parliamentary proceedings whenever the two were in the House together. They were poles apart. Bevan represented militant Socialism, which Churchill detested in any degree. Bevan challenged almost everything Churchill said. Churchill liked authority; Bevan questioned it. Churchill believed in his strategic skill. Bevan regarded him as an amateur and a dangerous amateur at that, 'a man suffering from petrified adolescence'.

Such rebuffs could often be answered only by a statement of intentions—which Churchill could not and would not make. Actually, he had agreed with President Roosevelt to step up the Allied attack in the Western Desert, but could not say so. Meanwhile, during the summer recess he visited Stalin in Moscow, visiting Cairo and calling in on troops at El Alamein on the way. A tremendous battle was raging in Russia as Churchill told Stalin that Britain and America could not yet agree to a Second Front in Europe. Churchill was accompanied by Field Marshal Brooke, C.I.G.S., Air Marshal Tedder, Chief of the Middle East Air Command, Sir Alexander Cadogan of the Foreign Office, and—later—by General Wavell who came from India. Averill Harriman represented President Roosevelt and Major-General Macwell, C.-in-C.

of the American Forces in Egypt, was present. They told Stalin of plans for Anglo-American landings in North Africa; he was not impressed.

Churchill returned on 17th August, the day of the first all-American bombing raid on Europe and two days before the nine-hour combined operations raid on Dieppe. On 8th September he reported to the House on his long tour. With commendable candour he told M.P.s that 'the Russians do not think that we or the Americans have done enough so far to take the weight off them. This is not at all surprising in view of the terrific onslaught they are enduring. . . .'

Churchill added a eulogy of Stalin intended, no doubt, as much for his ears as for the House of Commons. Stalin, he reported, was 'a man of massive outstanding personality, suited to the sombre and stormy times in which his life has been cast; a man of inexhaustible courage and will-power and a man direct and even blunt in speech which, having been brought up in the House of Commons, I do not mind at all, especially when I have something to say of my own. . . .' Such bluntness was not always to prove acceptable to Churchill, as on one future occasion he pointedly refused to accept a communication from Stalin, so offensive were its insinuations. But for the moment, despite differences in ideologies, the Allies were fighting a common enemy and must remain united.

The tide of war seemed, at last, to be turning. On 23rd October, General Montgomery hit back at Rommel; his superb co-ordination of land and air forces and the fine morale resulting from his leadership led to the victory at El Alamein and was followed on 8th November by the great Anglo-American invasion of French North Africa, landing in Morocco and Algeria and either taking over supine Vichy garrisons unwilling to fight or crushing them without much difficulty. General Eisenhower was given supreme command of the operations, although the main weight of naval support rested with the British, whose First Army was to break the German resistance in Tunisia. The American action in permitting Admiral Darlan, the pro-Hitler Frenchman (who had somehow heard of the operation and arrived in North Africa) to negotiate the submission of certain garrisons was a blunder of the first water. The Americans did not realize how Darlan was hated and despised by the Free French and those underground workers who, at risk of life and limb, were working against their Nazi occupiers. The assassination of Darlan, later, removed the distrust and horror which his adoption by the Americans had inspired.

In comparison with many sombre sessions, that of 11th November 1942 was a happy occasion. When the King had opened the new session with a minimum of pomp and ceremony, Churchill was able to tell the House, 'I have . . . to tell the House about the great Battle of Egypt, which is a British victory of the first order—and also about . . . the United States and British intervention in North Africa.' This time the House cheered him for the good news, and not simply for sustaining their spirits in adversity. He told the House of how (at the age of nearly 68) because Roosevelt could not leave America or Stalin Russia, he had to make 'journeys in each direction, carrying with me to and fro the most important military authorities'. The Russians, he said, had rendered 'incomparable service to the common cause' by killing or putting out of action far more millions than Germany had lost in the last war. But respite would be coming. 'We are entitled to rejoice only upon the condition that we do not relax' he told the House. The prolonged cheering did not cease until he had left the Chamber.

The bells rang throughout Britain, a brilliantly-timed piece of heart-warming symbolism. Until then, there had been little enough to rejoice about. It was the turn of the tide, but there was no room for complacency, only sober optimism. It was not, Churchill said, the beginning of the end but 'the end of the beginning'.

25

The Turn of the Tide

At Casablanca in French Morocco, Churchill attended on 13th January 1943 an Allied Conference on supreme war strategy and post-war aims. Roosevelt, despite his invalidism, journeyed there but Stalin was too absorbed with the mighty battle devastating his country to attend. De Gaulle came, haughty, aloof, suspicious; and so did General Giraud. One momentous decision was that only the 'unconditional surrender' of the Axis powers could mark the end of the war. Schemes and dates for future offensives were settled in principle, and all-out support for Russia agreed. General de Gaulle's temperamental testiness and initial unwillingness to attend prompted Roosevelt to ask Churchill: 'Who pays for de Gaulle's food?' 'Well, the British do,' said Churchill. 'Why don't you stop his food and maybe he will come?' asked Roosevelt. De Gaulle was bitterly jealous of any other Frenchman presuming to be a leader in any field, and his intractability was a constant headache for Churchill.

Churchill then visited Turkey, where he saw the President and his top political and military chiefs. On his return he gave the House, on 11th February 1943 a summary of the decisions reached and the progress of the war. Changes in the Mediterranean commands would bring British naval, army and R.A.F. leaders under General Eisenhower, and linking his name with General Alexander, Churchill said, 'In them you have two men remarkable for selflessness of character. Leave them alone and it is quite possible that one fine day the bells will ring again.'

He gave some facts of the turn of the tide. Sinking of enemy shipping had vastly increased; the United Nations merchant fleet was 1,250,000 tons bigger than six months ago. Heavily-escorted troop convoys suffered scarcely any losses, the Navy's protection having safeguarded the movement of 3,000,000 men with the loss of only 1,348—he was talking, as one had to in war, in statistical and not human terms. Half a million men had been landed in North-west Africa, less shipping being lost than had been gained. In

Burma, operations were confined to keeping open the Burma Road. The defeat of Hitler would have priority over the defeat of Japan.

Churchill was in fine form, buoyant and stimulating, delighting the House with his description of his visit to the Desert Army and the orderly morale of the British soldiers. He was loudly cheered as he entered the Chamber and in the galleries could be seen the Lord Chancellor, the Archbishop of York, and the Ambassadors of Russia and Turkey and diplomatic representatives of Poland, Belgium, Holland, Sweden, Brazil and Argentina. His speech was constantly interrupted by cheers and exuberant laughter. 'On arrival in Cairo,' he said, 'I found that the enemy who had boasted that he would enter Alexandria and Cairo, and cross and cut the Suez Canal, and had even struck a medal to commemorate the event, of which I was handed a specimen, had been rolled back 1,500 miles, and it is probably 1,600 miles by now.' He praised the desert soldiers with a soldier's pride: 'I have never in my life, which from my youth up has been connected with military matters, seen troops with the style and air of those of the Desert Army. (Cheers.) Talk about "spit and polish" (cheers and laughter) The Highland and New Zealand Divisions paraded after their immense ordeal in the desert as if they had come out of Wellington Barracks.' And he paid a tribute to Montgomery, 'this vehement and formidable General . . . a Cromwellian figure, austere, severe, accomplished, tireless, his life given to the study of war, who has attracted to himself in an extraordinary measure the confidence and devotion of the Army.' The biggest laugh came when he read the instructions he had given the Desert Commanders and the message he received from Montgomery couched with terse economy of phrase:

Sir,
    The Orders you gave me on August 15, 1942, have been fulfilled. His Majesty's enemies, together with their impedimenta, have been completely eliminated from Egypt, Cyrenaica, Libya and Tripolitania. I now await your further instructions.

Amidst the loud and prolonged cheers and laughter Churchill, with an impish grin, was heard to add, 'Obviously, we shall have to think of something.'

There was a more sombre note in his warning that 'justice must be done upon the wicked and the guilty, and, within proper bounds, justice must be stern and implacable.' The warning, as we know, fell upon deaf ears; the torture and killing of prisoners of war, the oppression of the populations of occupied countries and the appalling massacre of millions of Jews continued unabated in all its senseless fury. But retribution was already being visited, in some measure, upon the German people, punishing as is inevitable in war, the innocent with the guilty. Cologne had been virtually destroyed in a heavy air raid of 2nd February and savage air attacks on German towns continued.

On 21st March Churchill spoke—after a severe bout of influenza which 'but for science might have had awkward consequences'—of post-war prospects for a better world. He was thinking ahead, he said, not committing Ministers, who should never be 'pledge-bound delegates'. He thanked the House, in a voice full of emotion, for 'the trust and confidence . . . placed in me during long, dark and disappointing periods. I am absolutely determined not to falsify or mock that confidence by making promises without regard to whether they can be fulfilled or not. . . . At my time of life I have no personal ambitions, no future to provide for. And I feel I can truthfully say I only wish to do my duty by the whole mass of the nation and of the British Empire as long as I am thought to be of any use for that. . . . However, it is my duty to peer through the mists of the future to the end of the war. . . .'

The United Nations, headed by the three victorious great powers, the British Commonwealth, the United States and Soviet Russia, would be the basis of the United Nations as a world organization. He ranged the whole field of both foreign and domestic policy, of social and economic advance. He envisaged a Council of Europe, and at home of expanded social insurance, including a national health service. It was, incidentally, he who had encouraged Lord Beveridge to produce his historic report on social insurance. It was an agreeably surprising, and a very Liberal speech, showing that amidst all the cares of war, and a burden of duties which had several times endangered his health, he could look ahead to problems of peace and reconstruction. He painted a picture of a peace worth fighting for. Many of the reforms he advocated were to come to pass, although he was to receive little credit for his part in them.

The mighty German armies were taking a beating in Russia. In January the siege of Leningrad had been raised; in early February Kursk, Krasnodar, Rostor, Voroshilovgrad and Kharkov were captured by the Russians; but the Germans still found time and energy for such enormities as the total destruction of the Warsaw Ghetto and the murder of 56,000 of its inhabitants including starving women and children, old men and infants—many perishing in buildings deliberately set on fire.

Churchill had no less than five conferences with President Roosevelt in 1943. On his second visit, between 11th and 25th May, Churchill was invited to address the United States Congress, reviewing the war situation, stressing the unity of interest and endeavour of the two great countries and—incidentally—answering the anti-British fulminations of Senator 'Happy' Chandler who enjoyed a large following of isolation-minded Americans.

Considerable (I do not say unnecessary) security precautions were taken; an American Guy Fawkes is not an impossibility. Squads of Secret Service men searched the building from top to bottom, poking around in attics and basements, combing telephone booths, cupboards, committee rooms and lavatories. Two great air ducts were guarded lest they should unleash poison gas on the assembly, over the Speaker's Chair. Against the possibility of an assassin—and it would not be the first time that an assassin's bullet had altered the course of history—272 military, city and capitol police, 90 detectives and 60 Secret Service men moved restlessly around and inside the building. The Governor of North Carolina was sent packing for want of a ticket and Henry Morgenthau, Secretary of the Treasury, was almost thrown out by a burly policeman.

In the President's gallery over the Speaker's rostrum the Duke of Windsor and his wife appeared, to be greeted with deafening cheers. The members of the Cabinet entered and took their seats. The doorkeeper then, conscious of the historic moment, announced in a ringing voice: 'Mr. Speaker! The Right Honourable Winston Churchill, Prime Minister of Great Britain!'

His speech was long and masterly, every word followed with rapt attention. '. . . I am proud,' he said, 'that you should have found us good Allies, . . . for my part, I will say . . . after our long and, for a whole year, lonely struggle, I could not suppress in my heart a sense of relief and comfort that we were all bound together by a common peril, by solemn faith and high purpose, to see this fearful quarrel through at all costs to the end. . . .' He promised full British support in the war on Japan: 'It may not have escaped you that I brought with me to this country and to this Conference Field-Marshal Wavell and the other two Commanders-in-Chief in India.

They have not travelled all the way simply to concern themselves about improving the health and happiness of the Mikado of Japan,' he said, amidst roars of laughter. The loudest laugh came when he said, 'The proud German army has once again proved the truth of the saying "The Hun is either at your throat or at your feet".'

The final ovation burst like a thunderclap, rising and falling in crescendo after crescendo, and he sparked off yet another when he turned and bowed graciously to his one-time King, whose good name and office he had so stoutly and impenitently supported.

The speech was broadcast, reaching fourteen million people, and made a tremendous impression. 'By all indications the Prime Minister's triumph was the greatest of his career,' commented the *New York Times*. Senator 'Happy' Chandler was not so happy, and issued a critical communiqué of his own. At the succeeding luncheon Churchill devoured with delight prodigious quantities of fresh spring onions and seemed surprised when the creamed chicken and peas followed; but these he tackled 'manfully'.

On 8th June 1943 Churchill could give the House of Commons at home an increasingly hopeful picture. He did not of course underestimate the hazards inherent in future operations, which would be on a large and costly scale—in terms of men and money. Long-range aircraft had been thrown into the U-boat struggle; the balance-sheet of ship sinkings and buildings was the best for a long time. Britain's bombing capacity had increased. Stalingrad and Tunisia were 'the greatest military disasters that have ever befallen Germany'. There were 'brighter and more solid prospects'. But victories meant sacrifices. British losses in Tunisia had been severe —the Eighth Army since they crossed the frontier from Tripolitania had sustained 11,500 casualties and the First Army about 23,500 casualties; but the enemy in Tunisia had lost 248,000 prisoners and 50,000 dead. And, as always, he finished on a note about his love of Parliament, 'an instrument for the waging of successful war and for the safety of the State never surpassed in modern or ancient times.'

A reminder of Churchill's political vicissitudes came on 22nd July 1943 when he spoke at the unveiling of his restored portrait in the smoking-room of the National Liberal Club. It had been consigned to a cellar when he fell into disfavour with the Liberals following his political defection, and it had been damaged by bombing in 1941. But now the Liberals were proud to acknowledge and honour him again. Churchill made a felicitous speech praising the role of

Liberalism in Britain's development and saying that he looked forward to Liberal activities playing an important part in reconstruction. So the picture was unveiled in its place of honour, and the Liberals sang, as Mr. and Mrs. Churchill smiled happily, 'For he's a jolly good fellow'.

More and more the initiative was seized by the Allies. On 9th July had come the Allied invasion of Sicily. The Russians launched new offensives north and east of Orel. American planes bombed Rome. On 25th July Mussolini resigned and was confined in a winter sports hotel high in the Abrazzi Mountains. In August the Russians captured Orel, Bielgorod, Kharkov, Taganrog and many other big cities. A huge Allied convoy crossed the Atlantic without damage from the enemy.

Speaking to the House of Commons on 27th July 1943, Churchill foresaw the end of Fascism in Italy, although not disposed to await it passively. 'The keystone of the Fascist arch has crumbled. . . . The guilt and folly of Mussolini have cost the Italian people dear. It looked so safe in May 1940 to stab falling France in the back and advance to appropriate the Mediterranean interests and possessions of what Mussolini no doubt sincerely believed was a decadent and ruined Britain. . . .' The rest of the speech was intended primarily for Italian ears. The Allied forces stood 'at the portals of the Italian mainland' bringing, if the Italians so decided, 'relief from war, freedom from servitude and—after an interval—a respectable place in the new and rescued Europe.' Otherwise, as he put it in expressive if inelegant metaphor: 'Let them stew in their own juice—we will hot up the fire.'

From 9th to 19th August Churchill visited Canada and the United States, and at the Quebec Conference, which lasted from 11th–24th August, plans for the invasion of Europe were drawn up. By 17th August enemy resistance in Sicily had ceased and on 20th August there was rebellion in Denmark, some Danish warships escaping to Sweden. In Russia, the tide of war was stiffening against the Germans—the Russians captured Novorossisk, Bryansk, Poltava, Smolensk, Kremenchug, and completed the liberation of the Donetz Basin. On 3rd September allied forces landed on the toe of Italy and on the same day the Italian armistice (announced by General Eisenhower on 8th September) was signed. On 9th September the Allied Fifth Army landed near Salerno; the next day the Italian fleet sailed into Malta Harbour, six more warships arriving three days later. As Churchill knew when he made his speech on Italy, the Italians had little time for their German allies. On the 12th German parachute troops rescued Mussolini. In the Balkans the Germans reeled under the utterly unpredictable blows of the Yugoslav guerillas.

Throughout 1943 Churchill was forever travelling vast distances in order to co-ordinate and cement relations between the Allies. We know from the many memoirs available that this was far from an easy task. American suspicions that Britain was 'Empire-minded'; De Gaulle's vanity and impossible temperament; Russia's pressure and abuse over her desire for a Second Front in Europe; bitterness between Ernest Bevin and Lord Beaverbrook over Labour problems; Beaverbrook's continual clamour for a Second Front, which for a strange limited period found him in step with the Communist Party—all these things, too, made demands upon Churchill's patience and vitality. It is interesting, and amusing, to reflect how much patience he showed under sore trial, and how he could explode over trivialities, such as when he once emerged from his bedroom in his underground war room and, stubbing his toe against a battery of milk bottles which were always left standing around, flung them one at a time against the walls, the crash of breaking glass almost drowned by a volley of vehement protest.

On 22nd September Churchill was able to assure the House that the *Luftwaffe* had been driven increasingly to the defensive; that our help to Greece and Yugoslavia, so far limited to air-borne supplies and money, would take a different form with the collapse in Italy; the Russian armies had since autumn 1942 advanced on 1,000 miles of front from the Volga almost to the Dnieper, driving before them with prodigious slaughter the hordes of Germans that invaded their country and inflicted indescribable barbarities upon its inhabitants. 'For a whole year we and our great allies have had almost unbroken success by land, sea and air,' he said, and in damnatory phrasing warned the Germans that Nazism and Prussianism must be crushed. Italy, he made it clear, was not in the same category as Germany. 'I cannot touch upon the matter of Italy without exposing myself to the question . . . "Would you apply this line of argument to the German people?" ' he told the House, 'I say that the case is different. (Hear, hear.) Twice within our lifetime, and also three times in that of our fathers, they have plunged the world into their wars of expansion and aggression. They combine in the most deadly manner the qualities of the warrior and the slave. They do not value freedom themselves, and the spectacle of it in others is hateful to them. Whenever they become strong they seek their prey, and they will follow with an iron discipline anyone who will lead them to it. . . . Let us aim every gun, and let us set every man who will march in motion against them. Satellite States, suborned or overawed, may, perhaps, if they can help to shorten the war, be allowed to work their passage home (laughter).'

Churchill had some difficulty convincing the House that the Italians should be excused some of the rigours of conquest, but he was able to assure Members that 'the Italian forces and population have everywhere shown themselves unfriendly and hostile to the Germans'. They had shown themselves willing to obey the new Government; there was no doubt that Italian sympathy was with the Allies. As for the Second Front, it existed, and the time would come 'at what we and our American allies judge to be the right time'.

One Member who was not happy about Churchill's nostalgia for the Italian monarchy was Aneurin Bevan. 'The Prime Minister has got very many virtues and when the time comes I hope to pay my tribute to them, but I am bound to say that political honesty and sagacity have never been among them,' he declared, amidst murmurs of astonishment and anger. He quoted some of Churchill's long-forgotten references to Mussolini, whom he had once admired because of the Duce's anti-Bolshevist fervour, which gave them something in common. On a visit to Rome in 1927 he praised the dictator's 'gentle and simple bearing', his statesmanship and vision in saving Italy from Bolshevism. But that was an initial reaction—Churchill was foremost in warning Britain and the House of the dangers of Fascism, Italian or German.

In the great Coal Debate of 13th October 1943, when Churchill rejected nationalization of the coal industry in time of war, he pointed out that such an issue would probably be preceded by a break-up of the present administration and the separation of the political parties into the lines of regular battle. There was a bigger and more real war to be thought of—'the bloodiest fighting has yet to come'. But he made the encouraging or discouraging forecast, according to the disposition of his respective listeners: 'As soon as the war is over the soldiers will leave off fighting and the politicians will begin.'

There was certainly much unrest in the mining industry, but

Churchill maintained that against an output of coal of 200,000,000 tons in the last twelve months, only 750,000 tons had been lost by strikes and stoppages. At this point, to the amusement of the House, he sought refuge in arithmetic. 'The loss by strikes and stoppages,' he said, 'has not been more than two-thirds of one half of one per cent.' Members wrinkled their brows, and he went into decimals: 'Point ·05,' he explained, 'you may say two-thirds of ·05.' He began to get flummoxed and M.P.s laughed. 'Neither I nor my father was any good at figures,' he explained. The figure should have been ·005.

There had been some bitter debating. Seymour Cox, M.P. for Broxtowe, said, 'The state of feeling among the miners at the moment is not placid, it is developing into a raging maelstrom, a foaming Niagara of discontent.' Pleading for unity at so crucial a time in the war, Churchill said he hoped national unity might be preserved after the war, but that he would not be at all alarmed for Britain's future if there was a return to Party Government; 'for my part,' he added, to Labour cheers, 'I must say that I feel I owe a great debt to the Labour Party, who were a most stalwart support to me when I first undertook the burden which I am still permitted to bear. We must just see how things go after the war, and how we feel. . . .'

Members of Parliament had soon grown tired of the mocked-up and insubstantial Chamber at Church House. By permission of the Lords they met in the Lords' Chamber, which was undamaged by the air raid of 1941. With its noble proportions and rich adornments, its stained windows and statuary, magnificent gilded throne under its gilded canopy, its Gothic grandeur, murals, mellow timber and red leather benches, it had dignity and tradition . . . but it was not *their* home, the M.P.s' proper meeting-place.

It was with pleasure, therefore, that Churchill, on 28th October 1943, moved: 'That a Select Committee be appointed to consider and report upon plans for the rebuilding of the House of Commons and upon such alterations as may be considered desirable while preserving all its essential features.'

The occasion was one for which Churchill described the nature of the British House of Commons in a perfectly balanced speech.

On the night of May 10, 1941, with one of the last bombs of the last serious raid, our House of Commons was destroyed by the enemy, and we now have to consider whether we should build it up again, and how, and when. We shape our buildings, and after-wards our buildings shape us. Having dwelt more than forty years in the late chamber, and having derived very great pleasure and advantage therefrom, I, naturally, would like to see it restored in all its old form, convenience and dignity. . . .

There are two main characteristics of the House of Commons which will command the approval and support of reflective and experienced members. They will, I have no doubt, sound odd to foreign ears. The first is that the shape should be oblong and not semi-circular. (Hear, hear.) The semi-circular assembly, which appeals to political theorists, enables every individual or every group to move round the centre, adopting the various shades of pink, according as the weather changes. (Cheers and laughter.) But I am a convinced supporter of the Party System in preference to the Group System. I have seen many earnest and ardent parliaments destroyed by the group system. The party system is much favoured by the oblong form of the Chamber. It is easy for an individual to move through those insensible gradations from left to right, but the act of crossing the floor requires serious consideration (loud cheers and laughter). I am well informed on this matter—(loud laughter)—because I have accomplished that difficult process not once but twice.

The second characteristic of a Chamber formed on the line of the House of Commons is that it should not be big enough to contain all its members at once without overcrowding—(laughter) —and that there should be no question of every member having a separate seat reserved for him. The reason for this has often been a puzzle to uninstructed outsiders. . . .

The reason was, Churchill explained, that if the House were big enough to contain all its members, nine-tenths of the debates would be conducted in the depressing atmosphere of an empty or half-empty Chamber. 'The essence of good House of Commons speak-ing,' he explained, 'is a good conversational style . . . the conversa-tional style requires a fairly small space, and there should be on great occasions a sense of crowd and urgency. . . . We wish to see our Parliament a strong, easy, flexible instrument of free debate. For this purpose a small Chamber and a sense of intimacy are indis-pensable . . . the vitality and the authority of the House of Commons, and its hold upon the electorate based upon universal suffrage, depend to no small extent upon its episodes and great moments, and upon its scenes and rows, which, as everyone will agree, are better conducted at close quarters' (laughter). Then, in phrases which will always be remembered, and especially by those privileged to hear him then, he epitomized the glory and achievement of the Mother of Parliaments:

> The House of Commons has lifted our affairs above the mechanical sphere into the human sphere. It thrives on criticism, it is perfectly impervious to newspaper abuse or taunts from any quarter, and it is capable of digesting almost anything—(laughter) —or almost any body of gentlemen, whatever be the views with which they arrive. There is no situation to which it cannot address itself with vigour and ingenuity. It is the citadel of British liberty; it is the foundation of our laws; its traditions, its rules and its privileges are as lively today as when they broke the arbitrary power of the Crown and substituted that Constitutional Monarchy under which we have enjoyed so many blessings (hear, hear).

There would be a Committee of more than fifteen Members of the House, drawn from all parties. A new House would be built upon the old foundations, which were intact and its shattered walls utilized. The First Commissioner of Works had submitted a scheme, which should take eighteen months, but it would be prudent to allow longer. The last House of Commons, set up after the fire of 1834, was promised in six years and took twenty-seven years to build. At this point Mr. Maxton intervened, 'There was not a bricklayer Prime Minister then.' The work was essential and there must be no hiatus in the continuity of parliamentary life.

He finished on a delightful note, a gracious compliment to the Lords whom he had berated so soundly during the Parliament Act controversy of 1911:

> We owe a great debt to the House of Lords for having placed at our disposal this spacious, splendid hall. We have already expressed in formal resolution our thanks to them, but we do not wish to outstay our welcome. We have been greatly convenienced by our sojourn on these red benches and under this gilded, ornamented, statue-bedecked roof. I express my gratitude and appreciation of what we have received and enjoyed, but
> 'Mid pleasures and palaces though we may roam
> Be it ever so humble, there's no place like home.'

And as he spoke of the House, his spiritual home, in terms of such pride and truth and humour, the hearts of the M.P.s warmed to him as one man, and there came a thunder of cheers. Wise and cherubic, humorous and determined, he stood there, listening to the plaudits, which as nobody could doubt came from the heart. He seemed a symbol of the House and the freedoms it embodied.

26

In God's Good Time

'Until, in God's good time, the New World, with all its power and might, steps forth to the rescue and liberation of the Old. . . .'
These had been Churchill's words after the fall of France in 1940. That day was now drawing near. But an immensity of planning, most of it in secrecy, lay ahead.

Towards the end of October, Anthony Eden, at Churchill's urgent behest, went to Moscow. Relations between Britain and Russia had become badly strained because of the delay—as Stalin saw things—in opening a 'Second Front', an entirely misleading term, anyway, as Britain had long been engaged on many fronts. Stalin had sent to Churchill a note so offensive that the Prime Minister had no choice but to refuse to accept it.

The Conference of Foreign Ministers having done its work in Moscow, Churchill now embarked on a most gruelling round of conferences concerned with the planning of the war and the reconstruction period that would follow it. First he went to Cairo to meet President Roosevelt and General Chiang Kai Shek, where they discussed broad principles while their political and military advisers worked out the detail of the war against Japan. Thence to Teheran, where the three world leaders, Churchill, Roosevelt and Stalin, met and where the Russian security precautions were fantastic. Churchill did not entirely approve of the well-intentioned efforts of the Russian security guards to use Eden as a decoy for any intending assassins, bundling him into the most expensive and conspicuous car which was taken on the obvious and most hazardous route, while Churchill was pushed protesting into a mousy and dejected vehicle which went on a circuitous and unlikely route.

The announcement after the Teheran Conference declared that 'We came here in hope and determination. We leave here friends in fact, in spirit, and in purpose.' Not much in that for a spy to bite upon! Then back to Cairo, for long and detailed conferences with President Roosevelt and President Ineunu of Turkey and his entourage. The endless hours, the arguments, the speeches, the detail, the incessant travel—to all of these Churchill, who celebrated his sixty-ninth birthday on 30th November, at a memorable banquet in Teheran, had stood up wonderfully. But even his iron constitution began to feel the strain, and on 16th December 1943 Britain and her Allies were shocked by the news that Churchill had been stricken by pneumonia (the one illness to which he was prone all his life). Mr. Attlee made the understatement of the day when he told a quiet House of Commons, 'The House will be sorry that the Prime Minister is in this condition', and there were cheers when he spoke of the House sending Churchill good wishes. For days it seemed touch and go, and his medical advisers and nurses had anxious moments; he was a restless patient, though appreciative. 'Clemmie', his wife, flew out to be at his bedside. The fate of millions had something to do with that huge bulk of a man gasping and fighting for breath. At last he rallied and recovered but, weakened by the virus disease, he convalesced in the sunshine of Marrakesh in French Morocco, whose Moorish scenery had inspired some lively paintings from his brush on a pre-war holiday.

General Eisenhower, on 24th December, was appointed Supreme Allied Commander in Europe. January 1944 saw the stepping up of allied air raids upon Germany. Berlin, Cologne, Frankfurt, Nuremberg, Bremen and the great industrial centres suffered a hundredfold the agonies which Hitler's planes had brought upon the defenceless cities of Europe. By day and night, by British and American bombers, the attacks continued, reaching a crescendo of carnage and terror. Vital installations on the Continent were also attacked by air as a preliminary to invasion at a later stage.

Furthermore, one of Churchill's most outlandish and ambitious schemes was rapidly nearing fruition—the construction of the fantastic 'Mulberry' harbours. Realizing that the Channel ports were heavily fortified and manned, two artificial harbours—each as large as Dover Harbour—weighing over 3,000,000 tons and including miles of piers, breakwaters and so on, were being constructed in bits and pieces. It seemed impossible, but a peremptory note from Churchill on 30th May 1942 had jolted and hustled the technical waverers: 'They *must* float up and down with the tide. The anchor problem must be mastered. . . . Let me have the best solution worked out. Don't argue the matter. The difficulties will argue for themselves. W.S.C.'

If this seems brusque, one should try and imagine the mountains of documents which made their way to Churchill's desk. It was essential, so forbidding was the mass of detail, that there should be no persiflage. 'Prof: ten lines please' Churchill would scribble in a note attached to a vast sheaf of papers and send the lot to his scientific and economic adviser, Lord Cherwell. Somehow Cherwell managed this prodigious paraphrase. And this grasp of essentials was often vital. In mid-1943 Churchill noted that Britain's debt to India was rising at the rate of £1,000,000 a day. Why? he asked. The Treasury couldn't tell him specifically. 'The Prof.' discovered that we were not only paying for India's petrol, but paying *import duty into India* on every gallon!

In mid-January 1944 Churchill returned to England bronzed, fit and full of energy. In Russia, the Soviet were on the offensive and by the end of January the blockade of Leningrad had been lifted. On 21st April Churchill talked to the House of his favourite subject —the might and continuity of the British Empire.

Then, this war broke out. The Mother Country—I must still ask leave to use this name; anyhow, I think it is rather dangerous to plunge into new nomenclature and I am not sure that anything like 'The Elder Sister Country' would be a very great success . . . the Mother Country I say, was geographically involved, once again, in the struggles of Europe. . . . Instantly, from all parts of the British Empire, with one lamentable exception . . . came the same response. . . . When the signal came, from the poorest Colony to the most powerful Dominion, the great maxim held: 'When the King declares war, the Empire is at war.' Did anyone flinch? Was there one cry of pain or doubt or terror? No, Sir, darkness turned into light, and into a light that will never fade away. What is this miracle . . . that called men from the uttermost ends of the earth, some riding twenty days before they could reach their recruiting centres, some armies having to sail 14,000 miles across the seas before they reached the battlefield? . . . You must look very deep into the heart of man, and then you will not find the answer unless you look with the eye of the spirit. . . .

Militarists will long debate amongst themselves the Allied strategy of mid-1944. This is no place to do it. It should be said, however, that the plan as it unfolded was not that which Mr. Churchill would have preferred. He had hoped to liberate Europe by moving victoriously from the Mediterranean to the Balkans, there meeting the great Russian armies and bringing Turkey in on the side of the Allies. At the Quebec Conference of August 1943 the United States got its way—for an invasion of Western Europe. 'Operation Overlord', as it was called, was planned with considerable secrecy—surprising secrecy, as southern England was thick with British and American troops and the build-up of stores and equipment was tremendous. But even if the Germans anticipated an invasion of Europe by the Allies in 1944, they could not know when, where or how it was to take place. General Smuts was sorry Churchill's original plan had been dropped, and said so vehemently to King George VI; the King was at that stage more in favour of Churchill's rejected plan than the new 'Overlord'. But Churchill now supported Eisenhower's preference and the plan for 'Overlord' went forward.

The night of 5th June 1944 was dark, dismal, squally and wet. It was everything the planners had hoped it would not be; but the vast armada having been assembled, it had to proceed. In any case the very weather was calculated to make the Germans think a frontal attack unlikely. And sure enough, as dawn broke and the armada swooped in on the Normandy shore, the enemy was taken by surprise. And they were further deceived by a 'feint' at the Pas-de-Calais.

On 6th June a crowded House of Commons awaited with admirable patience. Churchill, perhaps on the principle of saving the good wine, dealt first of all with the Allied liberation of Rome on 4th June, 'a memorable and glorious event which rewards the intense fighting of the last five months in Italy. The original landing, made on January 22nd at Anzio, has, in the end, borne fruit. . . .' He described the fighting which preceded the liberation, said that developments in that theatre of war must be awaited, and then came to the announcement of the greatest military operation in history:

I have also to announce to the House that during the night and the early hours of this morning the first of the series of landings in force upon the European Continent has taken place. In this case the liberating assault fell upon the coast of France. An immense armada of upwards of 4,000 ships, together with several thousand smaller craft, crossed the Channel. Massed airborne landings have been successfully effected behind enemy lines, and landings on the beaches are proceeding at various points at the present time. The fire of the shore batteries has been largely quelled. The obstacles that were constructed in the sea have not proved so difficult as was apprehended. The Anglo-American lines are sustained by 11,000 first-line aircraft, which can be drawn upon as may be needed for the purposes of battle. I cannot, of course, commit myself to any particular details. Reports are coming-in in rapid succession. So far the Commanders . . . report that everything is proceeding according to plan. And what a plan! This vast operation is undoubtedly the most complicated and difficult that has ever taken place. . . . The battle which has now begun will grow constantly in scale and intensity for many weeks to come, and I shall not attempt to speculate upon its course. This I may say, however. Complete unity prevails throughout the Allied armies. There is a brotherhood in arms between us and our friends of the United States. There is complete confidence in the Supreme Commander, General Eisenhower, and his lieutenants, and also in the Commander of the Expeditionary Force, General Montgomery. . . . The outstanding feature has been the landings of airborne troops, which were on a scale far larger than anything that has been seen so far in the world. . . .

As a final word, he asked M.P.s to maintain morale and to 'give strong warnings against over-optimism, against the idea that things are going to be settled with a run, and that they will remember that although great dangers lie behind us, enormous exertions lie before us.'

Within a week Eisenhower had landed 326,000 men on a fifty-mile bridgehead. By 2nd July there were nearly a million combatants in France. Churchill, of course, lost no time in visiting Normandy—he arrived within a week of D-Day and would, indeed, have landed with the invading forces had not the King, with no little difficulty, dissuaded him. In mid-August General Patch's American army landed together with French contingents, in the south of France. Soon there were two million allied soldiers in France. At the same time the German armies south of the Seine found themselves trapped round Falaise; but although much valuable equipment was captured by the Allies, many Germans escaped. There was bitter fighting, although not comparable with the protracted and routine mutual slaughter of the 1914–1918 trench warfare—and soon the German armies were driven back towards what had been the Siegfried Line, to the very borders of Hitler's Reich.

Incidentally, Churchill's well-known obstinacy with friend and foe alike, once his mind was set upon a course, did not exclude his contacts with the King. Churchill had done everything he could—

effectively—to prevent the King from landing with his troops on D-Day but had no intention of applying this prohibition to himself. The King, for his part, was advised that it would be little short of disastrous if he had the headache of finding a new Prime Minister in the middle of 'Overlord'. But if Churchill was persuaded by the King not to land with the troops, he nevertheless did no more than postpone his visit—and the King too, in due course, visited his armies in France, Italy and the Low Countries.

Meanwhile a new terror was unleashed against the civilian population of Britain—the Flying Bomb. Launched from France, these weapons, looking for all the world like huge, black evil birds belching fire from the rear, brought widespread death and destruction. But Churchill could tell the House of Commons on 6th July part of the dramatic story behind this attack, for it was only achieving a small proportion of its intended impact. Churchill, while not underrating the seriousness of the attack, could tell the House that, but for the bravery and brilliance of the Intelligence Service, the attack would have come much sooner, and been far heavier. Early in 1943 it was known that the Germans were planning to bombard London with long-range missiles of some kind. '. . . as a result of searching investigations by agents and by reconnaissance, we had by July 1943 succeeded in locating at Peenemunde, on the Baltic, the main experimental station both for the flying bomb and the long-range rocket. In August the full strength of Bomber Command was sent out to attack those installations. The raids were costly, on account of the great distances into Germany which had to be flown, but very great damage was done to the enemy and his affairs, and a number of key German scientists, including the head scientist, who were all dwelling together in a so-called Strength Through Joy establishment, were killed. About this time we had also located at Watten, in the Pas-de-Calais, the first of the large structures which appeared to be connected with the firing of a long-range rocket.'

Reconnaissance was stepped up, for the threat to Britain was deadly serious. Over a hundred smaller sites were found along the French coast; experts pronounced them to be firing points for some jet-propelled missile and they were subject to heavy bombing by British and American planes. In fact, 50,000 tons of bombs were unloaded on flying bomb and rocket targets. '. . . the House will, I think, be favourably surprised to learn that the total number of flying bombs launched from the enemy's stations have killed almost exactly one person per bomb . . . the latest figures are 2,754 flying bombs launched and 2,752 casualties sustained.' There was a 'substantially larger number of injured'.

'The flying bomb,' Churchill said, 'is a weapon literally and essentially indiscriminate in its nature, purpose and effect . . . as to evacuation . . . everyone must remain at his post and discharge his daily duty. The House would be affronted if any suggestion were made that it should change its location from London. . . .'

Churchill did not want a debate, and some members were restive. One asked what facilities there would be for bringing to the attention of Ministers points affecting the lives of the people, their welfare and their safety. Another asked for a debate, which Churchill refused as it might help the enemy to gauge the effectiveness of their fire. When Edgar Glanville, M.P., asked about the use of tape on glass windows Churchill dismissed the query with 'Really, these are not questions for me to answer.' Mr. Glanville snapped: 'They save people's lives. Apparently that does not matter to some hon. Members,' and the Prime Minister replied, 'The hon. Gentleman has no right to suggest that other hon. Members do not care about saving other people's lives, or that he has any monopoly of human charity—or any marked pre-eminence in human genius.'

In Russia the Soviet armies moved inexorably forward, rolling across Poland to the very suburbs of Warsaw, where the heroic Polish underground army, who had persisted in resistance to tyranny at terrible cost and in anticipation of this day, were left to their fate on Stalin's orders. Stalin knew they were not Communists—and so the anti-German patriots, so far as he was concerned, were enemies to be exterminated, as well by Nazis as anybody else.

By 22nd August the Germans were in full retreat in north and south France. The following day Paris was liberated by the underground movement, and in the resultant joy and Mafeking celebrations there were also group and individual acts of vengeance, some deserved and others actuated by mere spite or hysteria. On 26th August General de Gaulle headed a victory procession through Paris, and on 27th August General Eisenhower entered. As Russian troops neared Rumania, that country judiciously broke her alliance with Germany and declared war on her; Bulgaria quickly followed her example. Hungary sought Russian help to throw off the Nazi yoke. By 20th August the Russian troops had advanced as far as Belgrade in Yugoslavia; the German grip on the Balkans was lost and—more important omen still—Russians were coming closer and closer into Europe.

The war still offered plenty of preoccupations, but Churchill was still looking ahead. Where would the balance of power lie? What would be the shape of post-war Europe? What Governments or administrations were to take over in all the countries involved in the war when they were liberated? Such problems imposed as many headaches as the war itself, for in Parliament Members tended to support factions abroad whose ideologies appeared to be similar to their own—in other words, they would equate the integrity, efficiency and ideas of the Left in another country, with the Left in Britain, and so on through all the grades of colour from red to blue. Events were to show that the problem was not so simple, but Churchill was to come under constant fire on this issue.

In October Churchill visited Stalin to discuss many problems, including that of Poland, and on 31st October he asked for the prolongation of Parliament for another year, adding, 'I doubt very much whether the Parliament will last so long.' But he felt the Coalition between parties should not be broken until Nazism was smashed. 'This was the purpose for which we came together in the present Parliament and it is still the supreme purpose.' He asked the House to assume, say, that the war with Germany might end in March, April or May, and that some or all of the Parties in the Coalition recalled their Ministers out of the Government, or wished to end the Coalition then. Some would regret it, but it would not be a matter of ill-feeling between political opponents in the House.

What he was saying was that as soon as danger to the country and Empire had passed, normal political controversy and tussle must be restored. He was against a 'coupon' election such as followed the First World War, when voters were asked to show confidence in the existing coalition by returning members on a general policy. 'The people have the right to choose representatives in accordance with their wishes and feelings, and I cannot think of anything more odious than for a Prime Minister to carry on with a Parliament so aged . . . without being refreshed by contact with the people.'

As a last desperate resort, Germany began the bombardment of Britain with long-range rockets. Churchill had warned Parliament of this possibility. They were a vicious and terrifying weapon, going sixty or seventy miles up into the stratosphere and travelling faster than sound. Fortunately, they had been launched too late to save Hitler's crumbling empire. On 11th November Churchill visited Paris as the guest of de Gaulle for the Armistice celebrations. Churchill's 'Cross of Lorraine' paid generous tribute to Britain's war leader: 'We should not have seen an Armistice Day like today had not our old and brave ally, Britain, with all her Dominions, under the inspiring leadership of him whom we are greeting here today, displayed the extraordinary determination to gain victory and the magnificent courage which saved the freedom of the world.' Churchill responded with equal charm and a spicing of humour. 'Happily, you have at your head an incontestable leader, General de Gaulle. From time to time I have had lively arguments with him about matters relating to this difficult war, but I am absolutely sure you ought to rally round your leader and do your utmost to make France united and indivisible.'

Early in August Churchill visited the Italian front. A visit from the P.M. was always a delight to Servicemen. On his visits to Normandy he made his headquarters on board the *Enterprise*, and after dinner one night came down to the wardroom and led the sailors in singing 'Rule Britannia'. On his visit to the Fifth Army in Italy he was presented with the Union Jack that had been raised at the liberation of Rome. He personally fired a shell at an enemy gun position—with no luck. It was a ranging shot and fell short, but a small correction in elevation by the gunnery officer and within two rounds the enemy position was destroyed. In Rome he had a busy round, and decided that the Italians had 'worked their passage' and ought not to be as demoralized as they were by food shortages and impossible transport.

In early September Churchill was in Canada, there to meet Roosevelt (but not Stalin, unwilling to leave Russia) where the future conduct of the war was discussed. On his return the House of Commons gave him a fine reception, and cheered loudly as he paid tribute to the Warsaw fighters. He promised that Nazi war criminals would be firmly dealt with and that every effort would be made to prevent their escape to neutral territories. He was able to tell a jubilant House that 'Brest, Havre, Dieppe, Boulogne and Antwerp are already in our hands' and that all the Atlantic and Channel ports, from the Spanish frontier to the Hook of Holland would soon be in Allied possession. He gave a masterly review of the war situation—a detailed, factual account infused with glowing phrase and a sense of drama. Such speeches took him from six to eight hours' hard work to prepare but they were worth it—they made, and were intended to make, his listeners feel 'in the picture'.

Back to Quebec again, this time for a second conference; President Roosevelt was there and there were long and detailed discussions on war policy and peace plans. At this time a Sunday newspaper invited readers to say what reward they would like to see Churchill receive. One felt that the nation should open three accounts for Mr. Churchill—with a firm of paint-makers to supply him with artist's colours for life; with a bricklaying firm and an importer of Havana cigars. Another (with no idea of Churchill's restless disposition) suggested that he should 'spend the rest of his life in hobbies and tobacco smoke, with no responsibilities and worries'. Another thought he should be given a house, forgetting that the Prime Minister had already refused the gift of a house in Devonshire. Yet another thought the best reward would be 'an overwhelming majority for himself and his supporters at the next General Election'. Time was to tell whether this last ambition would be achieved.

At this time (on 17th September) airborne troops were dropped at Nijmegen and Arnhem in Holland, but bad weather and the alerting of the German defenders by a spy made it less than the success that was hoped.

December brought acute political problems. Relations between Russia and Poland had deteriorated, Stalin was hostile to the exiled Polish Government, and had no intention of relinquishing the half of Poland taken by force in 1939. Churchill's speech to the House on 15th December contained a warning that the 'words of hope reinforced by confidence' on this subject no longer held good. The Russians had formed a 'Polish National Committee of Liberation' at Lublin, one result, Churchill thought, of the delay of Mr. Mikolajczyk of the Polish Government in London, to reach agreement on the new Russian-Polish frontier.

This rift in Russian-Polish relations was particularly unwelcome at a time when the main issue was to defeat Germany.

All these burdens were additional to the endless complications and details of a global war.

On 30th November, Churchill's seventieth birthday, the feeling of the House towards him was especially warm. 'Seventy not out!' shouted old Will Thorne, the Socialist M.P. Everyone cheered him cordially. He sported a bright buttonhole, and everything about the sprightly leader was a warning to the speculative gossips who were saying that when the war ended he would retire from public life.

Any satisfaction over the improvement in the Allies' fortunes in war was overshadowed by the complications of liberation. In December 1944 events in Greece were sombre and dark. Britain had dealt with King George of the Hellenes when he was in exile, but the Republicans in Greece identified him with the pre-war dictatorial régime of General Metaxas and his ruthless suppression of an uprising in Crete in July 1938. The King asked Papandreou to form a Government, in which he included some Leftists. But no sooner were the Germans cleared out than Royalists and Republicans set about each other with the utmost ruthlessness, their mutual atrocities being hardly less horrifying than those perpetrated by their former oppressors. E.L.A.S., the resistance movement which, despite what Churchill later said about it, had fought the Germans so long and well and courageously to assist in their country's liberation, would not surrender the arms supplied by the Allies for use against the Germans. Communists had infiltrated the resistance movement and were determined to use those arms to gain power for themselves. Civil war broke out, and as neither the Greek Army nor the police were sufficiently integrated or organized to keep the peace, the unenviable task of preventing sheer anarchy fell to the British troops on the spot, who at that time had been getting food supplies to the starving population. It was a tragic mess.

On 8th December Churchill was under fire in the House for his handling of the Greek tragedy, and to his alleged preference for old and reactionary governments in other countries. In his long reply, he berated critics who considered any 'Left' government invariably a democracy. 'It takes all sorts to make a democracy, not only Left Wing, or even Communist. I do not allow a party or a body to call themselves democrats because they are stretching farther and farther into the most extreme forms of revolution. I do not accept a party as necessarily representing democracy because it becomes more violent as it becomes less numerous. The last thing that resembles democracy is mob law, with bands of gangsters, armed with deadly weapons, forcing their way into great cities, seizing the police stations and key points of Government, endeavouring to introduce a totalitarian régime with an iron hand. . . .'

Willy Gallagher, the Communist M.P., was getting more and

more impatient. 'The hon. Member,' said Mr. Churchill, 'should not get so excited, because he is going to have much the worse of the argument. . . . I was for eleven years a fairly solitary figure in this House and pursued my way with patience, and so there may be hope for the hon. Member. . . . We have to assume many thankless tasks, and in undertaking them to be scoffed at, criticized and opposed from every quarter. . . .'

There was trouble in Belgium too; the Resistance Forces would not lay down their arms and were attempting to seize power by force. Aneurin Bevan asked, 'Is it not a fact that the military authorities in Belgium are satisfied that the Belgian Prime Minister unwarrantedly asked for the intervention of British troops?' to which Churchill made the rejoinder: 'I should think it was hardly possible to state the opposite of the truth with more precision. . . . He need not get so angry because the House laughs at him: he ought to be pleased when they only laugh at him. As I said . . .' Several M.P.s were besides themselves with mirth. Bevan waited, cold and glowering. It was not easy to get the better of Churchill in verbal repartee, although sometimes Bevan came rather nearer than most.

Italy came under fire, too. There had been the temporary use of Marshal Badoglio, who had used gas against the natives of Abyssinia, and Churchill was reminded of his praise of Mussolini in the early days of Italian Fascism. He was not put off by this. 'I am not a bit afraid of anything I have said in a long political life. I certainly thought, at that particular time, that the kind of régime which was then set up in Italy was better than a general slump of Italy into the furious Bolshevik civil war which was raging in many other parts of Europe. I never see the slightest good in going back on what one has said . . .'

As for an interjection from Emanuel Shinwell, he disposed of him in a few words: 'I do not challenge the hon. Gentleman when the truth leaks out of him by accident from time to time.'

The Government won the day, but the *Manchester Guardian* reflected a growing feeling that Churchill's right-wing political orientation might be unhappily translated into partisan preference for right-wing political leaders abroad. 'Must we be schoolmasters or policemen to countries in incipient revolution?' it asked. He had denounced Sforza because when he got to Italy he did not stick to Badoglio. 'Mr. Churchill seemed to regard it as a crime that the Italian people had turned Badoglio out. If that is the measure of

Mr. Churchill's judgement one can only shudder. But there it is; the Prime Minister has the defects of his great qualities. Reluctantly we shall have to assume that he may be an uncertain, even a dangerous, guide in our passage through the European maelstrom. Let us hope he does not wreck us.'

27

Victory

Christmas 1944 found Churchill not at his own fireside but in war-torn Athens, to call an all-party conference of the Greek factions and end a civil war which had caused 10,000 Greek deaths and over 2,000 casualties amongst British troops. His negotiations—conducted against a background of distant gunfire and a nearly-successful attempt to blow the Grand Hotel Bretagne up, together with the Greek Government, General Scobie and his staff—were successful.

In January 1945 the Russians began their mighty winter offensive and like a giant steam-roller crushed the Nazi defences as they rolled nearer and nearer—through Poland, into Silesia—to Germany. On 15th January the first civilian boat-train since May 1940 left London.

On 18th January Churchill addressed the House at length on the war situation. The most controversial issue—Greece—he dealt with first. British action there had been the subject of much bitter criticism, not simply from left-wing newspapers and journals but from the staid *Times*. Speaking of the Greek underground movement, Churchill said: 'I have been told that I made a mistake in under-rating the power of the Communist-directed E.L.A.S. I must admit that I judged them on their form against the Germans . . . of course, it was not against the Germans they were trying to fight to any great extent. They were simply taking our arms, lying low, and awaiting the moment when they could seize power in the capital by force or intrigue and make Greece a Communist State with the total liquidation of all opponents. I was misled by the little use they were against the Germans, especially once the general victory of the Allies became probable, in spite of the arms we gave to them. I certainly under-rated them as a fighting force. If I am accused of this mistake, I can only say, with M. Clemenceau, on a celebrated occasion, "Perhaps I have made a number of other mistakes of which you have not heard".'

Churchill outlined the circumstances that had led to civil war in Greece and then gave factual accounts of the many brutalities inflicted in the course of it.

The Times agreed that Churchill recounted 'a dreadful tale of brutalities' but regretted his depreciation of the role played by E.L.A.S. in the liberation of Greece.

Members of Parliament who sympathized with E.L.A.S. got a trouncing from Churchill, and Aneurin Bevan earned a special rebuff. 'I know very well that the hon. Member for Ebbw Vale would not stand for anything of this kind' (the forced march of 800 hostages, resulting in the death of 200 within ten days) 'but would rather throw away great advantages in an argument than stand for one moment for inhumanity.' He did not suppose that 'the hon. Gentlemen opposite would associate themselves with atrocities' and was therefore taking great pains to give the truth, 'in order that they may carefully watch their steps, and choose their language in such a way as to keep themselves clear of all taint of approbation.'

Churchill, whose heavy cold gave extra resonance to his speech, was cheered half-way through for a full minute—not for years had the House of Commons heard such a prolonged ovation.

After an hour's break for lunch Churchill continued with a long survey of the war. Sparks began to fly when the only Communist M.P., Willy Gallagher, interrupted Churchill with an inaudible remark.

Churchill swivelled round upon him like a mighty gun, grabbed the despatch box with both hands, peered appraisingly at him from over his spectacles and said, 'Every two or three minutes the hon. Member, who receives exceptional courtesy from this House thinks it necessary to assert himself by making half audible and occasionally partially intelligible interruptions.' The House laughed while for a moment Gallagher's defiant mien deserted him.

'Let us be of good cheer,' Churchill told M.P.s, '. . . both in the east and the west overwhelming forces are ranged on our side.' American correspondents who heard his speech declared it to be one of the greatest of his career. Mr. Aneurin Bevan declared himself shocked and surprised by the speech, which he described as 'the speech of a swashbuckler'. The speech would make the situation in Greece more bitter and could result in more British lives being lost. The picture drawn of E.L.A.S. forces bearing down on Athens to massacre the population he called 'a characteristic piece of Churchillian rubbish'. Eye-witnesses of the massacres did not.

Churchill finished: 'Whatever happens, the British nation and

Commonwealth may rest assured that the Union Jack of Freedom will forever fly from the white cliffs of Dover.'

On 4th February 1945 Belgium was liberated, and the historic conference between Churchill, Roosevelt and Stalin opened at Yalta in the Crimea. Its two main purposes were the formation of final plans for the overthrow of Hitler and to settle the pattern of the post-war world. The military problems were agreed upon; the political proved more intractable. A joint statement spoke of the three signatories helping liberated nations to peaceful conditions, to bring relief, to establish interim governments which would last only so long as was necessary to get essential services going and then organize free elections on 'democratic principles'. Time was to prove that 'democracy' has different meanings for different peoples; but for the moment the Yalta Declaration sounded like a clarion call of hope.

To Greece. Here Churchill was given a magnificent reception by the people. A street was named after him and a crowd of 25,000 in Constitution Square cheered him to the echo. 'I could not help recalling', Mr. Churchill later told the House, 'the grave conditions of my visit only seven weeks before, when the cannon were firing close at hand and bullets shook the walls, and the people were killed and wounded in the streets not far away.'

To Egypt, for further talks with President Roosevelt. To Ethiopia, there to meet Haile Selassie, The Lion of Judah; to Saudi Arabia to meet the autocratic, fabulously rich Ibn Saud. To Syria, to see President Shukri. This latter move aroused profound suspicions in the mind of De Gaulle, smarting already because of his exclusion from the Yalta Conference. But the basic purpose of these long and exhausting visits was Churchill's perpetual hope of world co-operation and unity between the big powers.

On 27th February Churchill gave what *The Times* called 'a masterly survey . . . illuminated by a cordial tribute . . . to the qualities of the Foreign Secretary (Sir Anthony Eden)'. 'The Crimea Conference,' Churchill said, 'leaves the Allies more closely united than ever before, both in the military and in the political sphere. Let Germany recognize that it is futile to hope for division among the Allies, and that nothing can avert her utter defeat.' As for unity, and the future, Churchill said:

I am sure that a fairer choice is open to mankind than they have known in recorded ages. The lights burn brighter and shine more broadly than before. Let us walk forward together.

There was at this time a furious argument between Lord Winterton, 'Father of the House of Commons', and Churchill over the former's request for a Select Committee to inquire into charges that there had been illegal use of farm produce from land owned by the Air Ministry. Lord Winterton had wanted a Select Committee to inquire into the allegations, suggesting a rule by which one would automatically be convened if a Minister was impugned. Churchill would have none of it. 'If this principle were adopted,' he said, 'it would be open in future for any single Member, however irresponsible, however mischievous, to bring any charge, however ill-founded, however worthless, against any Minister; and thereupon, automatically, the whole ponderous machinery of a Select Committee would be set in motion. I can imagine that in days of Party strife and faction, when feelings run high and a score against the Government is a good thing to bring off, there might be a regular racket among half a dozen Members to bring charges against half a dozen Ministers, or to fling insults against them; and then, automatically, there would be half a dozen Select Committees sitting upstairs, investigating the charges and insults which had been made. Such a procedure would bring the whole principle of Select Committees into contempt. . . .'

It was in this speech that Churchill made a crack at Winterton which forced him to join in the general laughter: 'Let my noble friend be careful that he does not reach senility before he attains old age.'

In March Churchill—for the first time since he became Tory leader four and a half years ago—spoke at the Conservative Party Conference. 'We have been too busy for party politics in any form,' he declared, hinting that the truce must end soon. However, the patriotic restraint would last as long as the National Coalition lasted. But when the Coalition ended 'We must prepare ourselves for the loss of many loyal and capable workers in the Administration, and the full clash of party principles and party interests. . . . It will fall to us as the largest party in the existing House of Commons to arrange for a General Election which will be conducted with British fair play and, I trust, with a minimum of party and personal rancour. . . .' This last plea for moderation and freedom from personal rancour is worth recalling in the light of the course the General Election did take, and the things that Mr. Churchill said.

On 28th March Churchill made a comparatively brief, but moving, tribute on the death of Earl Lloyd George. He reviewed the great leader's spectacular (and controversial) career, 'his power, his influence, his initiative . . . unequalled in the land. He was the champion of the weak and the poor. Those were great days. . . . When the calm, complacent, self-satisfied tranquillities of the Victorian era had exploded into the world convulsions and wars of the terrible twentieth century, Lloyd George had another part to play . . . although unacquainted with the military arts, although by public repute a pugnacious pacifist, when the life of our country was in peril he rallied to the war effort. . . . As a man of action, resource and creative energy he stood, when at his zenith, without a rival. . . . He was the greatest Welshman which that unconquerable race has produced since the age of the Tudors. . . .'

A few weeks later, before a solemn, sober and silent House, Churchill rose to move 'That an humble address be presented to His Majesty to convey to His Majesty the deep sorrow with which this House has learned of the death of the President of the United States. . . .' He spoke of their long friendship and continual correspondence—no less than 1,700 messages had passed between them, many lengthy and detailed. He told how Roosevelt had 'urged forward with all his power such precautionary military preparations as peace-time opinion in the United States could be brought to accept; of how impressed Roosevelt had been by Britain's bearing when she stood alone; of how Roosevelt had sent in his own hand the famous lines of Longfellow:

> '. . . Sail on, O ship of State!
> Sail on, O Union, strong and great!
> Humanity with all its fears,
> With all the hopes of future years,
> Is hanging breathless on thy fate!'

He spoke of Roosevelt's physical affliction, and how wan and ill he had been at Yalta—but nothing altered his sense of duty. 'For us,' he concluded, 'it only remains to say that in Franklin Roosevelt there died the greatest American friend we have ever known, and the greatest champion of freedom who has ever brought help and comfort from the new world to the old.'

The weather in March 1945, by a happy providence, was fine. The spring offensive had gained momentum from the start. Cologne had fallen on 8th March. The American 1st and 3rd Armies, the British and Canadians, pushed on into Germany. On 6th March the Americans had captured Cologne. Vienna was liberated on 13th April; by 23rd April it was possible to lift the hated blackout in our big cities, the enemy being too winded to fight any more in the air; by the 26th April the Russian and American armies had met at the Elbe; on the 28th Mussolini and his mistress were captured by Italian partisans near Milan; by 29th April the Germans surrendered unconditionally in Italy. The end—in Europe, at least—could not be far. It was a classic understatement when Churchill told the House on 1st May: 'I have no special statement to make about the war position in Europe, except that it is definitely more satisfactory than it was this time five years ago.' But he spoke cautiously of preparations for VE (Victory in Europe) celebrations for which the Government departments were making preparations. When Mr. Bevin asked that the fact that a large number of troops were still engaged in the Far East should exercise a 'sobering restraint' Churchill replied: 'I hope that soberness and restraint, for which my hon. Friend is renowned, will always be maintained with propriety in all parts of the country; but soberness and restraint do not necessarily prevent the joyous expression of the human heart.'

Once the Germans had seemed well-nigh invincible, the war endless. Now the Nazi empire, with all its ruthlessness and strength, was cracking everywhere, with astounding suddenness. The mighty Russian armies moved relentlessly from the east; they reached the suburbs of Berlin, a ruined, demoralized and wrecked city. By 2nd May Berlin had surrendered to the Russians. On 3rd May the Fourteenth Army entered Rangoon. Hitler committed suicide in his bomb-proof cellar at the Chancellery. And on 7th May the German forces surrendered unconditionally.

At three o'clock on 8th May Churchill went to the microphone to tell them the news.

Yesterday morning at 2.41 a.m. at General Eisenhower's head-quarters, General Jodl, the representative of the German High Command, and Grand-Admiral Doenitz, the designated head of the German State, signed the act of unconditional surrender of all German land, sea and air forces in Europe to the Allied Expeditionary Force, and similarly to the Soviet High Command. . . .

We may allow ourselves a brief period of rejoicing, but let us not forget for a moment the toils and efforts that lie ahead. Japan, with all her treachery and greed, remains unsubdued. We must now devote all our strength and resources to the completion of our tasks, both at home and abroad. Advance Britannia! Long live the cause of freedom! God Save the King!

Through wildly cheering crowds Churchill made his way via White-hall to the House of Commons. The Chamber was crowded, with only the slight buzz of conversation as the Prime Minister's arrival was awaited. Then, suddenly, he was amongst them, bending slightly forward, chin out, a cherubic grin suffusing his face. A scene such as the House has never witnessed ensued. The cheers seemed never to end. Order papers were flung into the air; some stood on the benches. Churchill looked around at them all, smiling still but tears trickling perceptibly down his cheeks. This was the moment he had longed for. This was the moment he had worked for. To achieve this he had had to rally the faint-hearts, jettison the inadequate, repel traducers, silence the squabblers and plan constantly against the greatest threat to civilization the world has ever known.

Churchill read to the House his broadcast statement. 'I have only two or three sentences to add. They will convey to the House my deep gratitude to this House of Commons, which has proved itself the strongest foundation for waging war that has ever been seen in the whole of our long history. . . . I wish to give my heartfelt thanks to men of all Parties for the way in which the liveliness of Parliamentary institutions has been maintained under the fire of the enemy.' He remembered how, a quarter of a century ago, in a similar situation, Parliament had no appetite for debate 'but desired to offer thanks to Almighty God, to the Great Power which seems to shape and design the fortunes of nations and the destiny of man; and I therefore, Sir, with your permission to move:

> That this House do now attend at the Church of Saint Margaret, Westminster, to give humble and reverent thanks to Almighty God for our deliverance from the threat of German domination.'

The Speaker led the House to church, as another Speaker had a quarter of a century ago.

The streets of London were filled with surging crowds which, on the whole, were well behaved. The balcony of the Ministry of Health was bedecked with flags, and when Mr. Churchill appeared on it with members of his Government, Ernest Bevin led the crowd in singing 'For he's a jolly good fellow' followed by three rousing cheers.

Later he appeared again. Buildings were floodlit, and he led the crowds in singing 'Land of Hope and Glory'. And on the balcony of Buckingham Palace he appeared with the King and Queen and the two princesses. How fit and happy he looked! As well he might. Courageous, audacious, shrewd, possessed of a phenomenal physique for a man of seventy, he had yet pushed his wonderful gifts to a dangerous extent. At times recently, in his underground war head-quarters beneath Storey's Gate, St. James's Park, he had been so physically weary that after Cabinet meetings there he had to be carried upstairs in a chair by Marines. Incidentally his combined bomb-proof bedroom and office, where so much of his work was done, and from whence so many of his war-time speeches were broadcast, was of almost Spartan simplicity. A simple bed such as one would find in the average low-priced commercial hotel; a Ministry of Works reading lamp with its green glass shade, by the bedside; a hideous, antiquated large-faced Government-issue wall clock. Attached was a very small dining-room and Mrs. Churchill's bedroom, which she often shared with her daughter Mary.

What did the future hold for Churchill now? Retirement, with the greatest trophies it is possible for a statesman to earn? But with the plaudits of the entire nation ringing in his ears, could their gratitude to him be expressed in any other way than a mandate to lead the nation in peace as in war? For although the war with Japan remained to be won, the most imminent and worst menace in Europe, Nazi Germany, had been vanquished.

We know from his Parliamentary utterances that Churchill did hope to lead the nation in the immediate post-war years. When, as he anticipated, the Labour Party felt the time had come to assert their identity as a political party and get out of the Coalition, Churchill had no choice but to accept, and to form a 'caretaker' government pending a General Election.

28

His Majesty's Opposition

The war in Europe had been won, but there still remained the struggle with Japan. The Labour Party was willing to continue to serve in the Coalition until the autumn of 1945, and indeed until victory over Japan had been achieved, but Churchill would not accept that. He proposed instead the cumbersome and very un-English idea of a 'referendum' on whether the life of Parliament should be prolonged. Major Attlee, the Socialist leader, had reason to be aggrieved at Churchill's strange anxiety for a General Election so soon after victory in Europe.

Of course, the existing Parliament had had a very long life, but the threat to the nation's very existence had transcended most Party and domestic political issues. Could not that Coalition, which had pulled the country through the worst crisis in its long history, have continued until Japan had been defeated—and perhaps even into the post-war period? Were there not bound to be birth pangs as the democracies of Europe took form again; would there not be terrible economic burdens and stresses, bringing in their wake discontent and instability?

The Labour Party made it clear that if there had to be a General Election, their members would stand as candidates for their Party and not for a Coalition.

On 23rd May the Coalition Government broke up and a 'caretaker' Government formed with Churchill again as Prime Minister. This interim administration was predominately Conservative, with only a sprinkling of Liberals and eight Independents.

The handling of the General Election, both on the part of the Conservative Central Office and by Churchill himself, was maladroit and disastrous. It was assumed that a leader with the status of a national—indeed, international—hero must necessarily lead his Party to victory at the polls. But Churchill had led a Coalition. The Conservatives were identified with appeasement in the minds of young people, who had to do most of the fighting. The rank-and-

file of the fighting services were Socialist in outlook; throughout
the war the *Daily Mirror*, consistently left-wing and in any event
anti-Tory, had been the most widely read newspaper in the Forces
at home and overseas. Its cumulative political effect was considerable.

From hoardings all over Britain the face of the great war leader
looked down. Mr. Churchill's personal status as a war leader was
never in question, but the assumption that it could carry the Tories
to victory was to be upset.

Certainly, in the course of his election campaign, Churchill
received a tumultuous reception. 'I must not say until Nomination
Day whether I shall be a candidate,' he told constituents at Woodford, 'but you never know.' At South Woodford Station cheering
crowds packed the railway bridge. His theme was that only friendship with America and Russia could assure that peace would be
kept; that a long, strong pull was needed to end the war in the
east; and at the end of the tour he told them, 'I am certainly looking
forward to be returned to Parliament as your Member. For eleven
years I was a prophet in the wilderness. You never deserted me.'

But in his first election broadcast of 4th June 1945 Churchill's
common sense and fairness appeared to have deserted him. Within
the context of a long speech were absurd and spiteful references to
the colleagues of other parties who had served him so loyally and
effectively through the war. 'Our Socialist and Liberal friends felt
themselves, therefore, obliged to put party before country,' he told
his listeners.

Later came a polemical attack on the Socialists:

Socialism is, in its essence, an attack not only upon British
enterprise, but upon the right of the ordinary man or woman to
breathe freely without having a harsh, clumsy, tyrannical hand
clapped across their mouths and nostrils. A Free Parliament—
look at that—a Free Parliament is odious to the Socialist doctri-
naire . . . no Socialist system can be established without a political
police . . . no Socialist Government conducting the entire life and
industry of the country could afford to allow free, sharp or
violently-worded expressions of public discontent. They would
have to fall back on some form of *Gestapo*, no doubt very humanely
directed in the first instance. . . .

In the first instance. Who could doubt the innuendo? The *Gestapo* with its wholesale tortures and murders was the most hated word in the language of humanity then. To imply that men such as Major Attlee, Ernest Bevin, Herbert Morrison and Sir Stafford Cripps would lend themselves to anything even remotely comparable with a Gestapo was an unworthy libel on loyal colleagues, and did Churchill and his cause irretrievable harm. And to refer to the Socialist opposition as 'Our present opponents or assailants' was more worthy of a rabble-rouser than a statesman. It dismayed not only Socialists and Liberals but quite a few Conservative supporters. As for the Commonwealth, much indignation was aroused. The New Zealand Labour Party and the Federation of Labour, representing 500,000 organized workers, said, 'We feel that his attack on the Labour Movement is a particularly unfair and bitter one, especially as the blood of millions of members of the great Labour Movement is still wet on the battlefields of Europe. His attack . . . is an insult to those thousands of men in the fighting forces of New Zealand and Australia. . . .'

At a meeting at Walthamstow Stadium there was organized booing —offset, of course, by cheers from supporters. He told his hecklers that the Socialists 'will get a thrashing such as your party has never received since it was born. . . .' As though determined to make a bad job worse, he said of 'Herb' Morrison, the Cockney newspaper boy who served as Home Secretary, 'Of all the colleagues I have lost, he is the one I am least sorry to see the last of. . . .' Morrison's comment was, 'The speech he has made is vindictive and spiteful,' while Ernest Bevin declared, 'I claim that during the dark hours no man served a leader more loyally than I did.' As to Churchill's references to France, Belgium and other countries as 'sliding into Communism', Bevin pointed out that for the Prime Minister to refer to them in terms like that was not helpful to world peace or the forthcoming Berlin Conference.

The General Election of 5th July 1945 was unique in that the voters were so scattered, even as far away as Burma and India. Not until three weeks had elapsed could the results be seen. And the results, when they were known, were outstanding. The 'thrashing' which Churchill had promised the Socialists had happened in reverse; the Labour Party was returned with an overwhelming majority. There were 393 Labour Members against 210 Conservatives and National Liberals. The decline of the Liberal Party appeared complete—of 300 candidates, only 11 were returned.

Studying the results on the blackboard of the War Room, he could hardly believe his eyes. 'It may well be a blessing in disguise,' said Mrs. Churchill, to which he answered, 'At the moment it seems quite effectively disguised.'

By the evening of 26th July it was obvious that the Tories had lost. Churchill bundled into his car, cigar in mouth, making the V-sign to cheering and often puzzled onlookers, and drove to Buckingham Palace. It would be difficult to say now who at this meeting felt most sad, the King or Mr. Churchill. The King told Churchill that he thought the people were very ungrateful after the way they had been led in the war. Churchill agreed to be Leader of the Opposition. The King, anxious to confer on the great statesman the highest honour within his power, asked him to accept the Order of the Garter. But Churchill, determined to refuse honours at this stage, said to a friend, 'Why should I accept the Order of the Garter from His Majesty, when the people have just given me the order of the boot?' 'I have . . . laid down the charge which was placed upon me in darker times. I regret that I have not been permitted to finish the work against Japan,' Churchill declared in a dignified statement, adding his thanks to the British people for their support and 'the many expressions of kindness which they have shown towards their servant'.

While awaiting the results of the General Election, Churchill had attended the Potsdam Conference with President Truman and Marshal Stalin, at which Major Attlee, Anthony Eden, J. Byrnes, Admiral Leahy and Molotov were also present. Proposals for the speeding-up of the end of the war were agreed upon, including a decision by Russia to declare (belated) war on Japan. America was planning to drop the atomic bomb, annihilating in a split second fighting men, ordinary men, women, children and infants, the halt, the blind, any and every living thing. Its use was said to be justified by the lives saved by the fact of the war being brought to an earlier end, a hypothesis incapable of proof; whatever the merits of it, it was a human tragedy beyond description and an ominous precedent. The first nuclear weapon had been used against civilians by a Christian democracy. Since then mutual fear, and increased potentialities in mass and instantaneous destruction, has alone kept the hands of the angry or ambitious from the trigger of disaster. Nine days after the bombs on Nagasaki and Hiroshima, Japan surrendered unconditionally.

The Potsdam Conference was a great anxiety to Churchill. America, always critical and jealous of British Imperialism, was also dangerously complacent about Russian aggression. Little support was accorded Churchill in his attempt to secure justice for the Poles, for whom Britain had originally, in theory at least, gone to war.

At the continuation of the Potsdam Conference, Churchill's place was taken by Major Attlee, while Ernest Bevin sat in Anthony Eden's former place. The demilitarization of Germany, reparations, war with Japan, were all discussed. Admiral Leahy observed that the Soviet Union emerged at this time as the unquestioned, all-powerful influence in Europe. Britain and the United States had to accept many unilateral decisions taken by Moscow since Yalta. . . . This was especially true of Poland. . . . The truth was that England in victory was prostrate economically and compared with America, relatively impotent militarily. By this time Russia had set up puppet régimes in Hungary, Bulgaria, Rumania and part of Poland. Ironically, it was by American insistence that the Russians had been allowed to reach Prague first. Now the truth emerged—in getting the Germans out of Europe the Allies had let the Russians in.

On 15th August 1945 the new Parliament was opened by the King. It was VJ Day (Victory over Japan) and London was wild with rejoicing. I watched the scene from the Strangers' Gallery as the new Commons assembled. The Government benches were crowded with Socialists, while the old Government sat glum and glowering on the opposite benches. Somebody, I am not sure who, started to sing *The Red Flag*; the tune was taken up, one M.P. shuffling to his feet, then another, until all were standing and singing. Into this strange scene Churchill now advanced, rather pale, chin out, stooping slightly forward, his expression half glum, half impish, as though to say, 'You haven't seen the last of me yet!'

He soon had the House of Commons roaring with laughter. 'A friend of mine, an officer, was in Zagreb when the results of the late General Election came in. An old lady said to him, "Poor Mr. Churchill! I suppose now he will be shot." My friend was able to reassure her. He said the sentence might be mitigated to one of the various forms of hard labour which are always open to His Majesty's subjects.' It was the beginning of five years of Opposition which he and often his opponents were to relish.

Churchill, although critical of nationalization schemes and other measures, was quite moderate in his opposition to the new Government. Domestic affairs, in the consideration of which he had engaged for over forty years, had little appeal for him. It was the general problem of the social reconstruction of Europe which absorbed him, and this, he knew, would face Britain whatever Party was in power. For a man of his restless nature and polemical gifts, the opposition was moderate.

The social welfare schemes had been framed and prepared by the Coalition Government of which he had been Premier. He had no objection to the nationalization of the Bank of England, which had for long worked hand-in-glove with the Treasury anyway. He was more concerned with spread of police dictatorships in the Balkans and in the Soviet-dominated part of Poland. In certain regions of Poland between eight and nine million Germans had dwelt; now, according to the new Polish Government, there were still 1,500,000 not yet expelled. Some of those millions had taken refuge behind British and American lines, but there were enormous numbers unaccounted for. Where had they gone and what had been their fate?

The post-war years were a period of austerity hardly less stringent than the years of war. Industries keyed up to war production had to be switched to civilian production. Markets abroad had to be found for goods, when they could be produced—and enough markets were needed to produce foreign exchange sufficient to feed forty-eight million people, and import raw materials sufficient to provide employment. Many of Britain's old customers were themselves disrupted and insolvent. Sources of raw materials such as rubber and tin were swept away. American Lease-Lend ended.

Britain's financial situation was so bad that America agreed to lend 3,750 million dollars, made available between 1945 and the end of 1951. The object was to re-establish British industry and make Britain self-supporting, but the social welfare schemes seemed over-lavish to many Americans, who visualized the British people living idly on American handouts.

Churchill criticized the agreement, pointing out that the proposal to make the pound sterling convertible into dollars within fifteen months was contrary to the decision reached at the Bretton Woods conference, which had envisaged a five-year wait before such convertibility could be introduced. But in international matters, he explained, he had little wish to divide the House. 'It would be a great pity and would weaken us for future tasks, which are heavy, if we were to vote in different lobbies on this question,' he added.

Amidst laughter and cheers Sir Waldron Smithers, Conservative Member for Orpington, asked 'Why?'

Mr. Churchill: The hon. Gentleman asks 'Why?' I should have thought even the most simple process of ratiocination should have enabled him to apply the answer to that (loud and prolonged laughter). Therefore, we thought it better and wiser to abstain as a body. (Cries of 'Why?') For these reasons, that we thought it better and wiser to abstain as a body, and that is the course we intend to pursue.

Mr. Bevin: How can you pursue when you are sitting still? (loud laughter).

Mr. Churchill: We are discussing the movements of the mind and not the much more bulky shifting of the human body.

This brought renewed laughter in which Mr. Bevin and the Government Front Bench joined.

No amount of heckling or interruption could inhibit Churchill's repartee. To Ministerial cries of 'Why?' and 'Shame' he said he did not want advice from the Opposition on the advice he should give his own supporters. 'Let them keep their advice for their own statesmen, arrayed there in an uncomfortable line.' There was loud laughter at this, for the overwhelming Labour majority created something like a human traffic jam on the benches.

Churchill was indignant to hear that Britain was supposed to owe £1,200,000,000 sterling to the Government of India and £400,000,000 to the Government of Egypt. Everything had been charged against Britain without the slightest recognition of the common loss. 'In the case of Egypt,' he said indignantly, 'she would have been ravaged and pillaged by the Italian and German armies and would have suffered all the horrors and indignities of invasion and subjugation had it not been that we had defended her with our life-blood and strong right arm.' Was not Britain entitled to say, 'Here is our counter-charge, which we set forth for having defended you from the worst of horrors'?

Churchill in the ensuing months visited Belgium, France and Greece, being given a hero's welcome and granted honours wherever he went. But on 1st January 1946 it was evident that he had not overcome his previous unrelenting opposition to honours, by the revelation that he had declined the King's offer of the Order of the Garter.

The first three months of 1946 Churchill spent in the United States, where the rejection of Churchill's government had created bewilderment and disappointment. On a visit to President Truman at the White House Churchill showed—as a courtesy—the speech he was to make at Westminster College, Fulton, Missouri, on 5th March. This speech, which was given worldwide coverage, appealed for unity among the English-speaking peoples, warned of the sinister trend of Russian expansion and Communist subjugation in Central Europe and elsewhere, introduced the now famous phrase 'the iron curtain' and warned against the return of tyranny 'on the gleaming wings of science'.

The British public was rather bewildered. For five years they had heard of Russian heroism and resistance to the Nazis. Now there was this sombre note in Anglo-Russian relations. Stalin characterized Churchill's speech as 'a call for war with the U.S.S.R.' That it was not; it was a warning, based on fact, that countries which had hoped for liberation from the Germans found themselves in the stranglehold of Russian-supported Communist dictatorships, with all the apparatus of secret police and the liquidation of political opposition associated with occupation.

'I felt it was necessary for someone in an unofficial position to speak in arresting terms about the present plight of the world,' Churchill said a few days later, as a storm raged about his head. 'I certainly will not allow anything said by others to weaken my regard and admiration for the Russian people or my earnest desire that Russia should be safe and prosperous and should take an honoured place in the van of world organization,' he declared. 'Whether she will do so or not depends only on the decisions taken by the handful of able men who under their renowned chief hold all the 180,000,000 of Russians and many more millions outside Russia in their grip. . . .'

For most of the year Churchill travelled in Europe, and on a visit to Zurich University urged the creation of a United States of Europe and a strong United Nations organization. He considered that Britain could be part of this unified Europe, play her role as a senior member of the United Nations and remain the centre of the Commonwealth.

Although Churchill intervened on many domestic issues in the

House, his greatest contribution at this time was as an international statesman. What he had said at Fulton needed saying, although most people were no more anxious to listen than they had been to his warnings of the menace of Nazism, in the inter-war years. It was a grief to him that countries which had suffered under the German heel should now be subjected to similar alien tyranny.

But when the bull is down—as some hoped he was—everyone is quick with the knife. While Europe applauded Churchill for his great acts of courage and deliverance, critics were not lacking. Ralph Ingersoll, editor of the New York newspaper *P.M.*, alleged in a book *Top Secret* that Roosevelt and Churchill broke their friendship over the final drive that occupied Germany, that Churchill often interfered with the normal function of strategy and said 'the quick defeat of Germany be damned, the British Empire wanted British troops in Berlin before the Russians got there. . . .' More amazing still Mr. Arthur Greenwood, Lord Privy Seal, told a Birmingham audience that Churchill was 'the great appeaser'—a strange accusation: '. . . as the war wore on, and he became Prime Minister, who was then the great appeaser?—the British Prime Minister. His appeasement was to promise to the Big Powers everything they wanted. He did it with the United States and he did it with Moscow.'

There was little about Mr. Attlee's statement on India to please Churchill. It was, he told the House, 'an able but melancholy document'. He recalled that as head of the wartime Coalition he committed himself to an offer to India at the time of the Cripps mission in 1942—that they should have Dominion status, with the right of secession, subject to certain provisions, such as the existence of sincere agreement between the main Indian parties and the proper and honourable treatment of minorities. 'I was personally induced to agree to them,' he told the House, 'by the all-compelling war interests, trying to rally all the forces in India to the defence of their soil against Japanese aggression, with all the horrors that would have followed. The Cripps mission failed. The answer Mr. Gandhi gave at that moment of mortal peril was "quit India". We persevered with the war and toiled on. Eventually the tide turned and India emerged successfully, protected against external violence by the power and the diplomacy of the British Empire, including the valiant contributions of the Indian Forces themselves. We still persisted in the offer turned down in 1942. . . .'

Now, it seemed, the object was not Dominion status and eventual secession but 'direct and immediate independence'. This short-circuiting had come as a surprise to him.

He acknowledged the sincerity and earnestness with which the Minister and Viceroy had laboured. 'They have worked,' he said, 'with a zeal that would have been natural if it were to gain an Empire and not to cast it away.'

It is interesting to compare assessments of Winston Churchill as a parliamentarian in 1946. Derek Walker-Smith, M.P., wrote that 'on the grand theme of world relationships he is still incomparable. Mr. Churchill, like his great ancestor Marlborough, is a good European. . . .' But Sir Hartley Shawcross, speaking in the Battersea North bye-election in July, said of Mr. Churchill: 'It is a very sad thing to see how that great leader has stooped to base practices in the House in recent months. . . .' For minutes he was unable to continue amidst a chorus of cries: 'Who won the war?'

1947 was a year of crisis. Britain had emerged from the war victorious but insolvent. The 'dollar gap' became an acute problem, for American Lease-Lend ended and it was a condition of the American loan that sterling currency should be freely convertible. British factories, geared so long to war, desperately needed re-equipping; raw materials were needed to supply the manufacturing industries. Somehow, the Socialist Government had to find means of feeding half the population—a matter of twenty-four million people—with an empty cash-box.

Thus food rationing continued, there were severe restrictions on spending abroad, and the export emphasis was on goods and services to the dollar area. Even bread and potatoes were rationed. To add to the hardships, a winter of Arctic severity was accompanied by fuel and power cuts.

Presiding over the Treasury was the austere, puritanical Sir Stafford Cripps; his severe, clinical, almost humourless personality tended to conceal his unusual virtues—absolute probity, a deep Christian conviction that class was nonsense and that all men were equal, and an unremitting capacity for hard work. Much as Churchill might twit him in the House, he knew that Cripps was a man whose disciplined personality was just what was needed at this time. To the credit of the Labour Government, it was not afraid to impose controls even when these would be unpopular and an almost sure way of losing votes in a future election. The export drive, mercifully, was a success.

Churchill was not against the general conception of the 'welfare state'—in the course of his Parliamentary career he had often initiated and supported legislature for social betterment—but was apprehensive that too much social molly-coddling might deplete the nation's vigour and encourage a 'soup kitchen' mentality. And he loathed Whitehall jargon. He ridiculed the phrase 'accommodation unit' which kept recurring in debates. At a public meeting Churchill, in a voice not especially musical, began singing 'Home, Sweet Home' as it would sound in Socialese:

> Accommodation Unit, sweet accommodation unit,
> Be it ever so humble
> There's no place like accommodation unit. . . .

He assailed the Ministry of Food for employing snoopers who persuaded shopkeepers to sell them food illegally and then prosecuted them. 'Does the Minister deny that to employ at public salaries a considerable number of persons in order to try to provoke breaches of the regulations is a despicable procedure?' he asked, angrily. And the powers of Inspectors were eroding long-founded liberties. They were entering homes arbitrarily on suspicion that some food undertaking was being conducted there; 'Do these powers not exceed those wielded by the criminal law under the long built-up principles of social life in this country?' he demanded.

In 1947 Britain's mandate in Palestine—inherited from the League of Nations—was becoming increasingly impossible to administer under threat of outrages against the British troops and administration there. 'No country in the world is less fitted for a conflict with terrorists than Great Britain,' he told the House, 'not because of weakness and cowardice, but because of our restraint and our virtues.' He was against the commutation and abolition of sentences imposed on Jewish terrorists because one British major and three British sergeants had been kidnapped and flogged. 'How should we have got through the late struggle,' he asked, 'if we had allowed our will power to be relaxed in that way?'

One trouble was that Jews and Arabs would simply not agree on the country's future. In these circumstances, Britain's unenviable role of unpaid policeman ought, the Government felt, to end, and

Ernest Bevin, the Foreign Minister, told Parliament that the matter would be referred to the United Nations, who on 29th August recommended the ending of the Mandate and the partitioning of the country—a proposal to which Britain, in due course, agreed. Churchill, incidentally, was not advocating staying in Palestine indefinitely. He was protesting at the outrages of terrorist gangs against the British troops who were administering the League of Nations mandate.

Generally Churchill's interventions were good-humoured, but woe betide a Member or Minister who over-stepped the mark of politeness. When Hugh Dalton, Chancellor of the Exchequer, was explaining why part of the American loan was being used to pay for the import of American tobacco into Britain, Dalton said, '. . . In spite of the very heavy tax which Mr. Churchill knows we impose on that practice, the demand has gone on until we are now consuming 130 per cent of the pre-war figure,' to which Churchill was quick to respond, 'You always try to make a joke by turning a personal point against me. I have the utmost contempt for your taunts. May I ask you a question which relates entirely to your public duties . . . ?'

When Mr. Attlee told the House of Commons that Britain would evacuate India and transfer power to the people there by June 1948, and that Lord Mountbatten would succeed Field-Marshal Wavell as Viceroy, Churchill was bewildered and infuriated by the change. 'Will you indicate what differences or divergencies or disagreements have arisen between the Viceroy and the Government?' he asked. Attlee responded with a curt 'No, sir.' But Churchill was not having it. Throwing his voice so that the whole House could hear, and banging the despatch box angrily, he demanded, 'What is the reason which has led to the dismissal of a Viceroy in full conduct of Government policy?' The Prime Minister, however, refused to be drawn. Wavell had not been appointed for any fixed term, he said, and a change in the Indian situation seemed a good time to terminate the appointment.

'There must be some reason,' Churchill continued. 'Why conceal it from the House? The Prime Minister surely did not wake up one morning and say "Oh, let's get a new Viceroy".' There were choruses of 'Answer!' 'Answer!' and at last Attlee, flushed and angry, turned towards Churchill. 'You made many changes both in military and civil appointments when you were Prime Minister (long Governmental cheers). I am not aware that you ever thought it an obligation to come here and explain why.'

But the battle did not last long. Together, as they walked out, they continued argument, but at last their faces wreathed in smiles, peace reigned again, and the two members of Britain's most famous wartime Coalition were friends again.

However, on the general question of handing over India, painful as the dismemberment of the old British Empire was to him, he was too much a realist to object. But he was not happy about the minorities and depressed classes in India who, he said, would be 'left to fend or to fight for themselves as best they can'. As to Mountbatten's mission, he did not think that the fourteen months' time limit gave the new Viceroy a fair chance. Was this 'Operation Scuttle'? 'By their fourteen months' time limit the Government have put an end to all prospect of Indian unity,' he warned; 'I have never myself believed that that could be preserved after the departure of the British *Raj*. But the last chance has been extinguished by the Government's action. How can you expect that the 1,000-years' gulf that yawns between Muslim and Hindu will be bridged in fourteen months? Here are these people, of the same race in many cases, charming people, congregated together in all the streets and bazaars—and yet no inter-marriage. Religion has raised a bar which not even the strongest impulses of human nature can over-leap . . . how can we walk out of India in fourteen months and leave behind us a war between 90,000,000 Muslims and 200,000,000 caste Hindus, with all the other tribulations which would fall on a helpless population of 400,000,000? Would it not be a terrible crime to allow the population of one-fifth of the globe to fall into chaos and carnage?'

Before long Churchill's attacks on the Socialist Government became more biting, more ironic, more pitiless. Criticizing controls, he accused them of converting Britain into one vast 'Wormwood Scrubbery'. He berated them for their class warfare—'One would think that the ten million people who voted for or with the Conservative Party were hardly fit to live in the land of their birth . . . an unbroken stream of scorn and hatred have been poured out upon them.' Most of them had given a lot for the national victory. He reminded them of the war years. '. . . what is so particularly odious and mean and what has caused this deep schism in our island life is that this sacrifice, so nobly made for victory . . . should be used

and exploited for party purposes and for the institution of a system
of Socialism abhorrent to the mass of the nation, destructive of the
free life we have known here for so long. . . .'

Later, he attacked the Government for the 'hideous waste and
extravagance' and accused the Government of living on the American
dole.

The atmosphere in Churchillian interchanges on the floor of the
House can be gauged by his quick repartee: the occasion was a discussion on the appointment of Lord Citrine as chairman of an
organizing committee to nationalize the electricity industry. Mr.
Shinwell had been reported as saying that he did not care 'a tinker's
cuss' about opponents to nationalization.

> Mr. Churchill: Will the committee . . . address itself to the
> interests of the nation as a whole (Ministerial cries of dissent) or
> will they be told that the only thing is to look after organised
> labour and not to care a tinker's cuss for anyone else? (Opposi-
> tion cheers.)
> Mr. Shinwell: Not for the first time, and I deplore the fact, the
> right hon. Gentleman is barking up the wrong tree. (Opposition
> cries of 'Why?' and 'Answer the question.') He has a facility,
> almost an infantile facility, for believing what he reads in the
> newspapers . . . as for the ability and functions of this organising
> committee, the names are themselves an indication of their
> capacity for undertaking work in the interests of the whole nation.
> (Ministerial cheers.)
> Mr. Churchill: I quite understand that the right hon. Gentleman
> feels up a tree. (Opposition cheers.) I did not rely only on the
> newspaper press. I took the trouble to procure the best reports
> available of certain remarks attributed to him. If he wishes to
> explain that he did not use those remarks, no one will be more
> pleased than me, and no one will be more ready to accept the fact
> that he disengages himself from this business.
> Mr. Shinwell: I am amazed that the right hon. Gentleman should
> put himself so completely out of order on this question.
> Mr. Churchill: I presume we are to await a personal explanation
> from the right hon. Gentleman that he has been misreported.

Members on the Government side called out 'Why?' and there
were ironic cheers. Mr. Gallagher, the Communist M.P., made
some interjection and Churchill turned like a tank on a well-oiled
swivel and growled at him: 'Shut up, Moscow!'

Meanwhile, his programme of private and recreational activities was such as would have exhausted many younger men. There were public luncheons, dinners, meetings, family gatherings; there was his prodigious output of writing; there were five hundred acres of farmland, attached to Chartwell, to be cultivated, there was his racing stable, and—of course—his painting.

With all this Churchill could still follow world events with the closest interest, advising and warning without regard to his personal popularity. At the Conservative Party Conference at Brighton he delivered a brilliant and devastating speech in October 1947 claiming that the first step to national recovery was to get rid of the Socialist Government. But instead of his previous rather negative rallying-cry, he adduced a programme of action—the establishment of a minimum standard of life for all; prevention of monopolistic abuses; reduction of Government expenditure; reduction of wasteful expenditure abroad—to be secured by withdrawing from Palestine and making the Germans keep themselves (nearly half the American loan was being spent to feed the Germans and maintain our forces there); and support for a United Europe combined with strong fraternal ties with the U.S.

On 28th October 1947 he moved the official Opposition amendment to the King's Speech, attacking the Government's export policy, its extravagance at home, its restrictions and its slur on the United States as 'shabby moneylenders'. At the time there was a fuel shortage and the public was exhorted to use little hot water:

'Mr. Gaitskell advocated a policy of fewer baths,' said Mr. Churchill. 'I must read the words he used. They constitute, I believe, almost a record. He said:

"Personally, I have never had a great many baths myself. I can assure those in the habit of having a great many that it does not make a great difference to their health if they have any. As to your personal appearance, most of that is underneath and nobody sees it." ' (Loud laughter.)

Soon the House was rocking with laughter as Churchill, face straight, his delivery dry and exaggeratedly formal, added: 'When Ministers of the Crown speak like this on behalf of His Majesty's Government the Prime Minister and his friends have no need to wonder why they are getting increasingly into bad odour. . . .'

Churchill, his pink features now expanding into the broadest of smiles, turned to the Speaker and remarked: 'I wondered, when meditating upon this point, whether you would admit the word "lousy" as a Parliamentary expression—I refer to the Administration—provided, of course, that it was not intended in a contemptuous sense but purely as one of factual narration.'

Turning 'from this new Utopia to wider and far more tragic scenes' Mr. Churchill turned to the riots convulsing India and costing over 500,000 lives, following the withdrawal of British power. He quoted John Morley on the subject forty years ago in the House: 'There is, I know, a school of thought who say that we might wisely walk out of India, and that Indians can manage their own affairs better than we can. Anyone who pictures for himself the anarchy, the bloody chaos which would follow, might shrink from that sinister decision. . . .'

Mr. Herbert Morrison, Lord President of the Council, dismissed Churchill's speech as a plea for *laissez-faire*; it was a plea from the Manchester School of the nineteenth century; it was a plea for economic anarchy. It was 'a dreadfully reactionary speech'.

On 11th November he entertained the House, despite a severe cold, with a brilliant attack on the Government's proposals to amend the Parliament Act so that the Lords' delaying powers should be limited to one year (Churchill had himself been largely responsible for curbing the powers of the Lords in 1911). They were aiming, said Churchill, at a single-chamber government at the dictation of Ministers. 'As a free-born Englishman,' he told the House, 'I would hate to be at the mercy of anyone, or in anybody's power, be it Hitler or Attlee.'

He was in fine form. He frankly admitted that he liked 'this old controversy'. He liked to think that what he thought right thirty-six years ago, the great party which he now led and the great party which he then served—(laughter)—and the mass of the nation, thought right now. Of democracy and the Government's motives, he said:

In these confused and baffling times it is right to regard the broad general principles. The spirit of the Parliament Act and the purpose of the Act were to secure the intimate, effective and continuous influence of the will of the people upon the conduct and progress of their affairs. That was the purpose—not the will of the Governors or Governesses of the people—(laughter)—but the will of the people.

He warned against the erosion of the principles of freedom:

> A thousand years scarce serve to form a State,
> An hour may lay it in the dust.

But it was with a parody of the famous poem, *The Charge of the Light Brigade*, that Churchill combined brilliant invective with timely histrionics:

Of Mr. Morrison's position, he said:

> Crippses to right of him,
> Daltons to left of him,
> Bevans behind him
> Volley'd and thundered

(Loud laughter.) It must have been very harassing. (More laughter.)

> Not though the soldier knew
> Someone had blundered.

(Renewed Opposition laughter.)

There was one more line a little farther on in the poem which might not be irrelevant:

> Then they came back, but not,
> Not, not the four hundred.

It was a reference, of course, to the election chances of the Socialists in any forthcoming General Election. Mercilessly, Churchill pressed for a General Election. He attacked Mr. Morrison's 'unconcealable, well-known relish for petty dictatorship'. 'Why are you so afraid of appealing to the people,' Churchill stormed, 'the Government has brought us low, and it is bringing us to ruin.'

In 1948 the million and a half words which were to be written for his six volumes on the Second World War took form at the rate of about eight thousand words a day (an output few younger authors could equal on factual subjects). It is true that a small army of secretaries, researchers and indexers assembled and codified the basic material, but only a master-mind could have known what he wanted and range over such an immense area of complex activity.

But Parliament was not forgotten. Nor was his determination to see the Socialists out of office although, to do them justice, they could hardly have come to office at a more difficult time in the country's history, inheriting a government with an empty treasury, a tired people and a bankrupt island trying to re-assert itself in a changed and largely hostile world. The export drive was stepped up, productivity was improved, enforced financial economies at last redressed the dangerous imbalance.

On the other hand, the underlying assumption, behind much of the Government's foreign policy, that 'left could talk to left' and that with the Socialists in the saddle we should have better relations with Russia, proved a sad illusion. Indeed, in the countries behind the Iron Curtain the Socialist parties were the first target of the secret police. And now all of Europe was under the threat of Soviet expansion, of conquest by Communist infiltration backed by Soviet might; in Europe alone since 1939 the Soviet Government had annexed 179,649 square miles of territory from friend and foe alike, enclosing 21,418,502 people. It included 69,000 square miles of Eastern Poland, the Baltic States of Lithuania, Estonia and Latvia, Bessarabia from Rumania, Karelian Territory from Finland, East Prussia, and Ruthenia, the eastern section of Czechoslovakia. In addition, with the help of Soviet armies, the U.S.S.R. engineered Communist takeovers throughout Central and Eastern Europe, bringing within her Empire the satellite countries of Bulgaria, Albania, Rumania, Hungary, Czechoslovakia, Eastern Germany and Poland. In the Far East she had acquired with the agreement of the Allies the southern half of Sakhalin and the important Kurile Islands. In 1946 she organized a rebellion in Azerbaijan, Northern Persia, withdrawing her occupying forces only with reluctance.

Only the atom bomb, Churchill felt, kept Russian forces from spilling over to the Channel coast. Only European Unity and the strongest ties with America could preserve Western civilization. The danger was, that wearied by the last war and bored by the numerous post-war restrictions, people might ignore the Russian menace until it was too late.

But first, recovery at home and co-operation between free peoples. 'I am sorry,' Churchill said, 'that certain elements in the Socialist ranks are trying to make the cause of a United Europe a monopoly of the Socialist Party. An important conference of supporters of the European cause is being held at The Hague in May. This event has been welcomed by all parties, other than the Communists, throughout the countries of Western Europe. Alone, the British Labour Party has decided to discourage its members from attending. When I proclaimed this idea at Zurich in 1949 I earnestly hoped that it might be at once all-party and above party. . . .'

On 7th May Churchill opened the Congress with a memorable and heartfelt speech. 'How little it is that all the millions of homes in Europe represented here today are asking: a fair chance to make a home, to reap the fruits of their toil, to cherish their wives, to bring up their children in a decent manner, and to dwell in peace and safety. The freedom that matters most today is freedom from fear. Why should all these hard-working families be harassed first, as in bygone times, by dynastic and religious quarrels; next by nationalistic ambitions, and finally by ideological fanaticism?'

In October, at Llandudno, Churchill once again warned of the Russian menace and pleaded that America should not be so foolhardy as to share her atomic secrets with Russia. He called for national unity under the threat of war. Not only did the speech bring upon his head a shower of invective from Soviet radio stations and newspapers, but from critics at home. The *Daily Worker* called Churchill an 'Atom Gangster'. Mr. Shinwell declared, 'Mr. Churchill is a great war leader. Of course he is. That's why he wants another war. . . .' This brought cries of 'Shame', and Shinwell added a rider, 'Mr. Churchill has been bad-tempered since the General Election. He is like a prima donna who won't go off the stage unless he's allowed to be explosive. Mr. Churchill is a danger to peace. Churchill is an intellectual giant and a great political figure. There is no doubt about that. He doesn't like us, that's the trouble. . . .' Mr. Aneurin Bevan declared that Churchill's speech had done 'deadly harm, and it can be regarded only as a national and international calamity. Mr. Churchill is one of the most reckless speakers in British political history. He does not seem to appreciate that when he is addressing advice to the Soviet Union . . . they recognize him as being the leader of reactionary forces in Great Britain and leader of the party which sold European peace in 1938 and connived at Hitler's rise to power. . . .' The latter reference, of course, was a malicious distortion of the facts. Churchill was not leader of the Party in the days of appeasement, and warned the country of the danger of Hitler.

The *Daily Mail*, appropriately enough, pointed out that when the Russians were let into Berlin Britain's was not the dominant voice in the war alliance. 'The power, the wealth—and the authority —had passed to America. The last word, therefore, rested with Eisenhower, Marshall and Roosevelt. Is it the fault of one or all of these that Asia has advanced to the Elbe? In an article in the magazine *Life* Mr. Bullitt, a former American Ambassador in Moscow, says, in effect, that Roosevelt was as helpless and confused in the jungle of European diplomacy as was President Wilson. He says that Roosevelt tried to appease Stalin in every possible way in the hope that he would be persuaded into the ways of Christianity, democracy and peace. Churchill, says Mr. Bullitt, "constantly worried about the consequences of letting the Red Army into Central and Eastern Europe". To prevent this he wanted an Allied thrust through the Balkans, but General Marshall refused and Roosevelt supported him. . . . It supplies a political reason for Montgomery's failure to punch through Northern Germany to Berlin when the way lay open, and for the halting of the British and American armies.'

Mr. Churchill was to see so many of his ambitions for Europe realized; the creation of the North Atlantic Treaty Organization in 1949 drew Britain to the U.S.A. and to ten other countries in mutual defence against aggression. In the Pacific area ANZUS, creating a defence alliance between the U.S.A., Australia and New Zealand served a similar purpose. Churchill approved the attitude of Ernest Bevin, Foreign Minister, in these matters but was bitterly critical of his handling of the Palestine problem. He would mince no words on 'the vile, wicked brutalities and manœuvres of Communism' and referred ironically to the Dean of Canterbury for 'eulogizing the humanistic virtues of Soviet Communism, while all the time at least twelve million prisoners are being toiled to death as slaves in Soviet concentration camps'. He did not mention the Dean by name, but as 'one of Mr. Ramsay MacDonald's bishops—or perhaps his only bishop'. Such an example of moral and mental obliquity, he said, on the part of a prelate deserved at least the passing notice of thinking men. As that might be considered to reflect upon a member of the other House, he would avoid rebuke by not pursuing the topic or the prelate any further. This simulated restraint caused loud laughter. Churchill's motion protesting against the Government's handling of the Palestine problem was defeated by 383 votes to 193.

11*

But this meant that the Government's majority was down to 90—the lowest it had been on a major issue.

Nobody could hope to slip anything past Churchill, even if he was seventy-five years old. Uproar ensued in the House when Mr. Morrison, Leader of the House, announced casually that there would be a one-day debate in a few days' time to discuss 'a few supplementary votes'. It sounded so unimportant, but it was indeed to raise an extra £58 million to pay for the National Health Service and £50 million to cover Mr. Strachey's food trading. Altogether the Government was asking for £221 million, 'one quarter of a pre-war Budget' as Churchill put it. Again and again Mr. Aneurin Bevan kept shouting at Churchill, but the old man stood his ground: 'Don't shake your finger at me,' he bellowed at him, 'I can quite understand how touchy you are.'

There were many such scenes, but for all the generated heat, no man commanded such respect from all quarters. The chamber seemed strangely empty without him; everyone, Tory or Socialist, brightened perceptibly when his bulk loomed into the chamber, shoulders thrust forward, eyes a-twinkle or glowering with presage of stormy words, sometimes grinning puckishly, at other times wearing a smile of victory anticipated, as though to say 'And now I'll deal with *you!*' 'Here comes the old boy', they would say, and all knew that clichés and platitudes, half truths and evasions, woolliness and weariness would not be tolerated while Churchill was there.

In Brussels on 27th February 1949 Churchill was given a rousing welcome at the new European Unity organization, despite some Communist barracking. 'One half of Europe is in prison today, and the other half is on its guard and justified in taking precautionary measures,' he told them. In April he told 14,000 people crowded into Boston Garden, U.S.A., the same thing—within the context of a masterly survey of the first half of the twentieth century. The atom bomb in U.S. hands had saved Europe, he declared. 'It is certain that Europe would have been Communized and London under bombardment some time ago but for the deterrent of the atomic bomb in the hands of the United States.' He did not advocate violent or precipitate action but vigilance. The West sought nothing but goodwill and fair play, but 'thirteen men in the Kremlin, holding down millions of people and aiming at the rule of the world, feel that at all costs they must keep up the barriers'. Zaslavsky, one of Stalin's mouthpieces, described Churchill's speech as 'flashy rhetoric, egocentric vanity and unrestrained hatred for all progressive ideas'.

Later in the year Churchill and Morrison exchanged angry words in a corridor at the Assembly of Europe in Strasbourg. Mr. Morrison threatened to cut off the delegate's allowance of francs to Mr. John Foster, M.P. for Northwich, Cheshire, who was the Tories' 'reserve man' there. The British team consisted of eleven Socialists, six Tories and one Liberal. Mr. Foster would take Mr. Churchill's place when he left and was drawing a paltry Treasury allowance of £2 a day to defray his expenses there. Mr. Morrison went up to Churchill as he walked along the corridor surrounded by friends and asked him, 'When are you going to leave?' 'I do not know,' said Churchill. 'I thought it was only two or three days that you were to be in Strasbourg,' Morrison continued, to which Churchill replied, 'I say I don't know.' To this Morrison snapped, 'Well, in that case I will have to consider cutting off the special allowance of your reserve man John Foster, if you are both going to be here,' to which Churchill growled, 'You can keep your money in your pocket,' adding, as Mr. Morrison walked away, 'I don't want to talk to you any more on this. If there is any further communication it had better be in writing.' He at once asked Mr. Foster not to claim the allowance.

The tension between Morrison and Churchill was to some extent due to Churchill's unshakable reputation as 'Mr. Europe'. His mere presence made the Government representatives look like pygmies. 'If a God had arrived to sit in the Assembly he could not have been given more homage,' wrote Bill Grieg in the *Daily Mirror*, adding that Churchill was using his popularity, perhaps unthinkingly, to belittle Morrison's status as Deputy Prime Minister and Britain's spokesman.

There was something sad and a little contemptible at the jealousy which Churchill's hard-earned stature excited.

Churchill felt deeply the gratitude of the European peoples. When he was cheered by 10,000 French people at Strasbourg and presented with the freedom of the city, the tears streamed down his face. 'I shall treasure this honour for what is left to me of life,' he told them, brushing away the tears with the back of his hand.

In September 1949 a financial crisis occurred on which Churchill was quick to take political advantage. America was saving Europe from financial collapse by Marshall Aid, which led to the creation of a special organization for administering it—the Organization for European Economic Co-operation (O.E.E.C.). But despite a healthy trade balance, the pound had to be devalued from four dollars and three cents to two dollars and eighty cents—a drastic drop, and one that could have brought inflation.

On 28th September 1949 Mr. Churchill moved an amendment in the House welcoming the Washington agreement but regretting that, 'as a result of four years' financial mismanagement, should not be brought to a drastic devaluation of the pound sterling. . . .'

He pressed for a General Election. He attacked the Government's aversion to 'profits' as though running a business successfully was some sort of crime. 'Large incomes are virtually confiscated. . . . Every capital reserve we had has been gobbled up. As has been well said, we ate the Argentine Railways—£110 million—last year as a mere side dish. Our reserves of gold and currency, which at the end of 1946 were £650 million, have been drained away until only £300 million of the old rate is left . . . we are now brought to the edge of national and international bankruptcy. . . .' An interruptor: 'Sell your horse!' Churchill replied with glee, 'I could sell him for a great deal more than I bought him for' (causing the House to roar with laughter), and adding, 'I am trying to rise above the profit motive.'

'Only an appeal to the people,' Churchill told the House, 'and a new Parliament can relieve the existing tension. If at this moment the Government were to drop steel nationalization and their other extreme plans, it would certainly enable the approaching General Election to be conducted in an atmosphere much less dangerous to the underlying national unities on which fifty million in this island depend for their survival. . . . It is my duty and that of those whom I lead to warn the country in good time of its dangers. I thank God that in my old age I preserve the invincible faith that we shall overcome them.'

And so, at the age of seventy-five—fifteen years after many men have retired—Churchill both organized and faced the rigours of another General Election in February 1950. The results showed a sharp decline in Labour power; Labour gained 315 seats and the Conservatives and the handful of Liberals and Independents 298. Thus Labour secured a tiny working majority which, allowing for sickness and the inevitable absence of some Members abroad on

Governmental business, meant that the Labour Government could not hope to remain long in power.

It was during the election, at Cardiff, that Churchill nailed the lie that as Home Secretary he had sent troops to the Rhondda in 1910. 'When I was Home Secretary in 1910 I had a great horror and fear of having to become responsible for the military firing upon a crowd of rioters or strikers. At that time there were many disputes and much violence in the Cambrian Coal Trust Collieries and the Rhondda Valley. The Chief Constable of Glamorgan sent a request for the assistance of the military and troops were put in motion in the usual way. But here I made an unprecedented intervention. I stopped the movement of the troops and sent instead 850 Metropolitan Police from London with the sole object of preventing loss of life. I was much criticized for this so-called weakness in the House of Commons but I carried my point. The troops were kept in the background and all contact with the rioters was made by our trusted and unarmed London police. . . .'

Churchill kept up his attacks on Government policy and expenditure, and the internal strains to which the Labour Party was subjected in 1950 were severe. The outbreak of war in Korea meant rearmament and heavier taxes at home. Hugh Gaitskell, who succeeded Sir Stafford Cripps at the Treasury, insisted that the cost of spectacles and dentures should be shared between patients and the National Health Service instead of being paid entirely by the latter, and in protest at this deviation from the original idea of the service, Aneurin Bevan and Harold Wilson resigned, in April 1951. Still Churchill warned of the Russian peril—Russian armies, he told the House in August 1950, outnumbered the Western Powers by six, seven or eight to one. 'I pray we may wake up in time,' he said. 'Let us not cast away the remaining chances of all the free democracies to avert a new world war and of not being wiped out if it comes.' The only way to deal with Communist Russia, he declared, was by having superior strength in one form or another and then acting with fairness and reason. There had been delay in sending an expeditionary force to Korea; Russian inspectors had been allowed inside British factories where confidential production was going on; machine tools, diesel engines and similar machinery were being exported to Russia and her satellites; hundreds of jet fighters had been sold to Egypt and the Argentine, although the establishment of a U.S. bomber base in East Anglia put Britain in the firing line. Five months after Mr. Churchill had raised the matter, the Government were at last making plans for inviting German aid in the defence of Western Europe. 'The supreme peril is in Europe,' he said. 'We must try to close the hideous gap on the European front.'

The 24th October 1950 was marked by a more homely but not less historic scene—when Churchill rose in the newly built House of Commons Chamber. His speech was marked with urbanity and humour, reflecting his great love of the legislative holy of holies; he was loudly greeted with cheers as he rose:

I feel, in rising today at a somewhat mature time in my life to make my maiden speech here—(laughter) I ought not to conceal from you that I have a past (loud laughter). I have many memories of the aired space in which we are sitting, now enclosed afresh in its traditional garments. I think I was the last person to speak here until today, and I have a lively recollection of the support and stern enthusiasm with which my remarks were often received. There has, no doubt, been some change in the seating arrangements. So far as my memory serves, I sat on the other side of the House (laughter). The Prime Minister and his principal colleagues sat beside me there. It seemed to me a very good and satisfactory way of carrying on our affairs (laughter).

The Chamber was crowded with Speakers from many Commonwealth countries and representatives of their Governments. They will remember how Churchill praised the efforts with which the Chamber had been rebuilt, and how, in a voice in which humour and emotion were intermixed, he spoke as the greatest commoner of them all:

I was a child of the House of Commons, and have been here—or there, I am not quite sure how it is—(laughter)—I believe longer than anyone. I was much upset when I was violently thrown out of my collective cradle. I certainly wanted to get back to it as soon as possible. Now the day has dawned, the hour almost come. I am grateful to His Majesty's Government for the persistence and vigour and efficiency which they have shown in the task of rebuilding—(cheers)—in so short a time and amid so many other competitive preoccupations (laughter). It excites world wonder in the parliamentary countries that we should build a chamber, starting afresh, which can only seat two-thirds of its members. It is difficult to explain this to those who do not know our ways. They cannot easily be made to understand that the intensity, passion, intimacy, informality and spontaneity of our debates constitutes the personality of the House of Commons and endows it at once with its focus and its strength. . . .

The House of Commons has ever been the controller, and, if need be, the changer, of the rulers of the day and of the Ministers appointed by the Crown. It stands for ever against oligarchy and one-man power. All these traditions which have brought us into being over hundreds of years, and carrying a large proportion of the commanding thought of the human race with us, all these traditions received new draughts of life as the franchise was extended until it became universal. The House of Commons stands for freedom and law, and this is the message which the Mother of Parliaments has proved itself capable of proclaiming to the world at large. . . .

As Churchill sat down, to the resounding cheers of the entire House, there were many eyes that were not dry—including his own.

On 31st October 1950 a dinner party was given to Churchill at the Savoy Hotel by 300 Conservative peers and M.P.s who had served with him in the House of Commons during the fifty years that had passed since he was first elected to the House as Conservative M.P. for Oldham in October 1900. He had sat under the four kings who had reigned since Queen Victoria, and been an M.P. under nine Prime Ministers—Lord Salisbury, Balfour, Campbell-Bannerman, Asquith (whose statue he unveiled in the Members' Lobby a few weeks later), Lloyd George, Ramsay MacDonald, Baldwin, Chamberlain, and Attlee. The menu reflected his incredible career—*sherry Oldham, Les galettes de Dundee* and so on. Was the Parliamentary saga ended for him? Hardly. The Government had gained a majority of a mere six in the recent steel debate. A General Election soon was now a certainty—and Mr. Churchill would be back again. . . .

29

Prime Minister Again

Although Gallup Poll figures showed a marked preference for Anthony Eden over Winston Churchill as head of a Conservative Government, Churchill longed for and fought for one more chance as Prime Minister. 'We have lost our rightful place in the world,' he told his Woodford constituents, 'anyway, we are going to have a General Election. Then the people will have a chance to express their will.'

The pre-election debates in the House were often heated, at other times marked by comedy. To Shinwell, Minister of Defence, Churchill snapped: 'Be quiet; hold your tongue. Go and talk to the Italians. It is all you are fit to do.'

The implications of this retort were not appreciated by the Italians, even if Mr. Shinwell was to them a legendary figure. Indeed a Signor Vanni Teodorani Fabri Serbelloni wrote challenging Mr. Churchill to a duel! In response to Italian protests Churchill apologized for the remark made 'in the heat of debate'. 'Ever since the fall of Mussolini I have done my best to help them regain their honourable position in Europe, and this is shown not by words only but by actions.' The duel did not take place.

This was Churchill's eighteenth election campaign. He had begun his political career in the days of the two-horse landau, now he campaigned in a world of jet-planes, radio and television. In a piece on 'Election Memories' he conveyed vividly his own zest in such elections—even to the rowdyism:

Of course there are rowdy meetings. They are a great relief. You have not got to make the same old speech. Here you have excited crowds, green-eyed opponents, their jaws twitching with fury—shouting interruptions, holloaing, bellowing insults of every kind, anything that they think will hurt your feelings, any charge that they can make against your consistency or public record, or sometimes, I am sorry to say, against your personal character; and loud jeers and scoffs arising now on all sides, and every kind of nasty

question carefully thought out and sent up to the chair by vehe-
ment-looking pasty youths or young short-haired women of
bulldog appearance . . .

He advised all candidates to smile, and remain detached from
vulgar clamour. 'After all, nothing is so ludicrous as a large number
of good people in a frantic state, so long as you are sure that they
are not going to hurt you.'

But the General Election of October 1951 was a different matter.
Britain was in peril—as much from her Allies, very often, as from
her enemies. The country was bankrupt. Here was a last challenge
to render service to his country while he had yet a few years with
sufficient strength. The old man, standing on the hillside in the
Plymouth which was once mercilessly bombed, stretched out his
arms towards the vast crowd and spoke as intimately as if each
were his lifelong friend, words that came from the heart and brought
tears to many eyes:

This is the last prize I seek to win—to bring nearer that lasting
peace settlement which the vast masses of the people of every
race and in every land fervently desire. All the day-dreams and
ambitions of my youth have not only been satisfied, but have been
surpassed. I pray indeed that I may have this final opportunity. . . .

On the day of the election, 25th October, the *Daily Mirror*
featured on its front page its now famous 'Whose finger on the
trigger' appeal for Labour support, implying—since a picture of
Churchill was included—that Churchill was a 'warmonger'. This
was made the subject of legal action on behalf of Mr. Churchill, the
matter being settled out of court and the agreed damages being given
to charity.

Mr. Churchill got his wish. The Conservatives won with a
majority of seventeen over all other parties, and on 26th October
Mr. Attlee resigned and Mr. Churchill, at Buckingham Palace, was
invited by King George VI to form a Government.

Churchill's Cabinet included Anthony Eden as Secretary of State
for Foreign Affairs and R. A. Butler as Chancellor of the Exchequer.
The situation called for drastic economies and discipline all round;
to economize *and* rearm, which was what Britain had to do, was
not easy. As an example, Churchill cut the salaries of Cabinet
members, issuing this statement:

During the period of rearmament or for three years, whichever ends first, Ministers who are entitled to a salary of £5,000 a year will draw £4,000 a year. During the same period the Prime Minister will draw £7,000 instead of his statutory salary of £10,000. It is also intended to effect large reductions in the use of Ministerial motor cars. . . .

With an external debt mounting at the rate of £700 million a year, with shrinking gold and dollar reserves and shortages of fuel and housing, there was a real prospect of widespread unemployment due to lack of raw materials which could only be imported from abroad. We were involved in war in Korea and with anti-Communist operations in Malaya.

Churchill, in the House, deplored the 'cruel ungrateful charge' of warmonger and the deep and painful divisions which had split the nation: 'We are met together here with an apparent gulf between us as great as any I have known in fifty years of House of Commons life. What the nation needs is several years of good steady administration . . . what the House needs is a period of tolerant and constructive debating on the merits of the questions before us, without every speech on either side being distorted by the passions of one election or the preparations for another. Whether we shall get it or not is, to say the least, doubtful. We ask no favours in the conduct of Parliamentary business. . . .

'This country produces food for only three-fifths of its fifty million people and the rest has to be earned from oversea by exporting manufactures for which raw materials must also be imported. No community of such a size and standing has ever been so precariously poised economically.' He promised a secret session for the discussion of defence and hoped again for some *modus vivendi* between East and West. 'There is not much comfort in looking into a future where you and the countries you dominate plus the Communist parties in many other States, are all drawn up on one side, and those who rally to the English-speaking nations and their associates, or Dominions on the other,' he had written to Stalin in 1945. 'A long period of suspicions, of abuse and counter-abuse, and of opposing policies, would be a disaster . . .' he had said then, and since then, Churchill told the House, it had all come to pass with 'horrible exactitude'.

Churchill's moderate tone was governed by the slender majority his Government held, which made them more administrators than governors. The warmonger campaign had done the Tories great harm. Although the Conservatives had a majority of eighteen seats over all the other parties combined, 13,877,922 people voted Labour, 13,665,595 voted Conservative, 710,934 Liberal and 198,149 in other ways.

Some thought that at seventy-seven Churchill could not carry the immense weight of Premier. He proved them wrong. His long statement on defence on 6th December 1951 showed his grasp of detail and capacity to see the broad picture were as vigorous as ever. 'Deterrents rather than the idea of danger' was the key to his policy —hence the calling up of 250,000 men, the strengthening of the Royal Observer Corps and an arms programme of £1,250 million.

Broadcasting before Christmas, Churchill tried to instil that sense of national unity and purpose which had brought the country through trials before:

> This is not the time for party brawling. . . . The differences between parties in this island are not so great as a foreigner might think on listening to our abuse of one another. There are underlying unities throughout the whole British nation. These unities are far greater than our differences. In this we are unlike many countries and, after all, it has been pretty well soaked into the British nation that we all sink or swim together. Take the social services. They have been built up during the past 100 years by each succeeding Conservative, Liberal, and, latterly, Socialist Government. Take foreign affairs and national defence. Nine-tenths of the British people agree on nine-tenths of what has been done and what is being done and is going to go on being done.
> I paid my tribute in the House of Commons to the work of the Labour Government in their resolute defiance of Communism, in their establishment of National Service, and in their attempt to form a solid front in Europe against aggression. We respect the memory of Ernest Bevin for the work he did, and I am certain he could not have done his work without the help and guidance, in some degree, which the Conservative Party gave him. . . .

Abroad, and in America in particular, there was widespread satisfaction that Churchill was back as leader of the British people. There was, too, a quickening of spirit at home. Slowly, life and prosperity began to gain their old momentum.

In January 1952 Churchill visited America to talk over international affairs with President Truman. Britain and America had been drifting apart, with neither admitting it. There were many divergencies of British and American policy. Truman was an entirely different man from Roosevelt; the former permitted much more autonomy and delegated responsibility more whereas Roosevelt centralized so much more power in himself and could promise more confidently to see certain results achieved. There was irritation in America over Britain's attitude to American bases on British soil; this, Churchill maintained, put Britain 'in the very forefront of Soviet antagonism'. 'No doubt,' Americans were saying, in effect, 'but you've always said that only our atom bomb keeps the Soviet at bay; what's the good of a deterrent that can't be delivered? Most of our strategic air force consists of medium-range bombers which couldn't hit at Russia from Canada or America. . . .' There was resentment over Britain's recognition of Communist China. The diplomatic tradition that 'recognition' ought to be accorded a *de facto* Government, and that this doesn't imply approval of it, cut no ice with Americans. 'Didn't you recognize De Gaulle and ignore Marshal Pétain?' they asked. The Foreign Office felt that America was intriguing against Britain in the Middle East; America's approach was one of exasperation—in the words of Senator Vandenberg, the United States should be 'in at the take-offs as well as the crash landings'.

After speaking in America and Canada on such themes as NATO and European Unity, Churchill addressed Congress. 'Defence of the Suez Canal has become an international responsibility,' he told them. 'Britain is not seeking to be master of Egypt; we are there as servants of the commerce of the world. It would aid us enormously if even token forces of the other partners (in the Middle East Command) were stationed in the Canal Zone as a symbol of the resolution of purpose which inspires us.' These words, we now know, fell upon stony ground. On Korea he gave a bold and, some felt at home, injudicious undertaking. Britain and the U.S.A. were agreed that if a truce, once signed, was broken, Britain's response would be 'blunt, resolute and effective'. In other words, she would go to war again with the Americans. He was right to tell Americans that after the war Britain, unwisely and contrary to American advice, accepted as normal debts £4,000 millions sterling of claims from countries which she had supported or protected from invasion. Britain had accepted this instead of making counter-claims which would have reduced the burden on her own shoulders. He spoke for thirty-seven minutes and was interrupted by applause fifteen times. His voice was strong, his delivery perfect, his manner proud yet relaxed; at the end he received a standing ovation from the entire Congress. Their reaction was summed up in the comment of Senator Wiley, the senior Republican on the Foreign Relations Committee—'A grand performance by a grand man.'

Back in the House, sparks flew over the Government's economy measures, particularly as affecting the National Health Service. Aneurin Bevan, his silver locks flying, red in the face, spoke in support of the Opposition's 'no confidence' challenge, which failed on a Government majority of 31 votes. Churchill smiled at him imperturbably: 'You are trying to repay me the remark I made of you in the war, that you were a squalid nuisance,' he said. 'You called me a squalid nuisance then—I say you are betraying your trust now!' snapped Bevan. It was like a paper dart aimed at an elephant; Churchill, smiling good-humouredly, shrugged his shoulders.

On 6th February 1952 King George VI died after a long period of poor health and a lung operation in September. Dedicated to his country, dignified yet democratic, courageous though shy and modest, his loss was keenly felt. Churchill's memorable broadcast tribute was not only a masterpiece of English but a heartfelt 'farewell' that moved the nation deeply. Nobody will forget the feeling, the love and the strength of the old man's voice as he paid tribute to the fifth Monarch under whom he had served. And in a voice of mounting fervour he greeted the sixth:

I, whose youth was passed in the august unchallenged and tranquil glories of the Victorian era, may well feel a thrill in invoking, once more, the prayer and the anthem . . . GOD SAVE THE QUEEN!

In the House of Commons nothing could be done until the oath of allegiance had been taken to the new Sovereign, and this could not be done until, in the evening, Queen Elizabeth had been proclaimed Sovereign by the Accession Council. Nothing more could be done, Mr. Churchill told the House, looking very sad, than to record a spontaneous expression of their grief. Gone were all thoughts of controversy; back had come the national unity which mystifies Britain's friends and incenses her enemies. As Big Ben

chimed 2.30 the Speaker entered, moved past the standing members
to his chair, and then called on Mr. Churchill, who, in grave tones
announced the death of the King. The following day, in the wintry
blast, Mr. Churchill stood bareheaded on the tarmac at London
Airport to pay his respects to the new Queen as she descended from
the B.O.A.C. Argonaut *Atalanta.* The old man bowed deeply,
gravely. Now he was to serve his sixth Sovereign:

> She comes to this throne at a time when tormented mankind
> stands uncertainly poised between catastrophe and a golden age.
> That it will be a golden age in art and letters we can only hope.
> Science and machinery has its part to play. It is certain if a true
> and lasting peace can be achieved, and if the nations of the world
> will only let each other alone, immense and undreamed-of
> prosperity and culture, and leisure even more widely spread can
> come more easily and more swiftly. . . .

Mr. Churchill was a Member of the House when Mr. Balfour spoke
of the death of Queen Victoria. He had heard Mr. Asquith speaking
with breaking voice of the death of King Edward VII; he had been
there, frock-coated as now, to hear Mr. Baldwin record the passing
of King George V. And now Mr. Churchill spoke of George VI—
'No British monarch in living memory has had a harder time,' he
said, and who was more competent to make comparisons than this
old (but mentally and physically virile) leader, the faithful and loving
servant of the British people and of humanity? Three Motions were
approved—a humble address to the Queen, a message of condolence
to the Queen Mother and one to Queen Mary. In deadly silence the
Speaker in his gold and black robes rose and moved in procession
from the House. The motion was put 'that this House do now
adjourn' and the corridors echoed to the unanswered cry: 'Who
goes home?'

Finding himself under fire from the Socialists for his pledges
to the U.S.A. over Korea, Churchill confounded them by proving
that the Socialists themselves had even gone so far as to guarantee
to take military action against China 'not confined to Korea'. All
eyes turned on Mr. Herbert Morrison and Socialist M.P.s were
astounded. Their renewed charge of 'warmongering' fell very flat,
and their motion of no confidence against Mr. Churchill failed.
Whether the rule of secrecy which normally applies to Cabinet dis-

cussions should have been broken in this instance is now an academic question. It has been a rule of practice, though not of law, that Cabinet discussions are secret. True, challenged to produce the documents on which Churchill based his allegation, he refused to do so—he merely summarized them.

In the summer of 1952 Churchill was heavily attacked in the House for his policy in Korea. Socialists claimed that Britain was the tin can on the end of the mad dog's tail; that America had jumped the gun and made war in Korea without consulting Britain, then asked Britain to fight in that war, which could in turn lead to war with the Chinese. This was a matter of defending principles, and with youthful energy and zest, with complete clarity in the marshalling and delivery of his factual arguments, Churchill routed his detractors. The vote of censure was that the Government had failed to secure consultation on the Yalu River bombing. But Dean Acheson, American Secretary of State, had admitted Washington's muddle and had given an off-the-record talk to M.P.s of all parties in Westminster Hall a few days ago. It was, said Churchill, 'a frank and generous statement', and he quoted from it. Acheson had said, 'I am sure you are wholly inexperienced in England with Government errors. Unfortunately, we have had more familiarity with them' (loud laughter from the M.P.s) 'and due to the fact that one person was supposed to do something and thought another person was to have done it, you were not consulted. If you ask whether you had an absolute right to be so consulted, I should say No, but I do not want to argue about absolute rights. I want to say: You are a partner of ours in these operations, we wanted to consult you, we should have done so, and we recognize the error.' 'I don't remember any occasion in international affairs when a more candid and manly course has been taken by a public man,' Churchill declared. The vote of censure was not carried.

There was one argument which his most vehement political opponents could not adduce against him—that his burdens were too heavy. Somehow he thrived on burdens. It seemed impossible to believe that he could be seventy-seven years old. The cigars, the brandy-and-sodas, work, conversation, argument, speeches, memoranda, painting, writing, reading, broadcasting, television appearances—all these he took in his stride. 'When do you think you will retire?' a reporter asked him. 'Not until I am a great deal worse and the Empire a great deal better,' Churchill replied. But there was Anthony Eden, kept waiting in the wings. 'By the time you retire he'll be too old for the job,' Churchill's friends used to joke, to which Churchill once replied, 'When I want to tease Anthony I remind him that Gladstone formed his last administration at the age of eighty-four.' Sometimes his hearing was a trifle defective, yet he never needed to hear anything twice. If he appeared inattentive, it was not necessarily fatigue. The speech of one M.P. seemed interminable and Churchill slumped low in his seat, eyes closed. '*Must* you fall asleep when I am speaking?' cried the angry M.P. Dreamily, but in a perfectly clear voice, and without opening his eyes, Churchill answered, 'No, it is purely voluntary.'

Few members of the Cabinet could out-argue him. 'He still has far more imagination than anybody else in the Government. There are times when he seems to have the physical energy of a front-line regiment,' wrote Hugh Massingham at the time. There had been old Premiers before—Gladstone, Palmerston, Earl Russell and Disraeli. Not one had a tithe of his energy or brilliance; nor had they Churchill's grievous problems, especially in international affairs. There was the burden of rearmament in a world as unsettled as ever. Communist terrorism had broken out in Malaya and Churchill had appointed General Sir Gerald Templer as High Commissioner there, with a mandate to restore and maintain order and prepare the way for that country's self-government. In Kenya the Mau Mau, a vicious secret society, was inflicting as atrocious barbarities upon its own people as upon the white settlers it was hoping to eject. There was the headache of protecting the Suez Canal.

On 23rd October 1952, in a voice of matter-of-fact, almost bored restraint (for Churchill was a master of understatement too, when he chose to be) he announced to the House the 'successful outcome' of the first test of a British atomic bomb which had generated a heat of one million degrees and vaporized a ship in the Monte Bello islands on 3rd October.

When Mr. Churchill unveiled a panel in the library of the Press Gallery, he occupied Mr. Gladstone's chair—an inspiriting experience, said Mr. Churchill, but the precedent of the age at which Gladstone retired might well, if he did not use some word of reassurance, have a serious effect on morale in many places.

The year closed with an ugly scene in the House—and one for which Churchill himself was to blame. Pressed by Mr. Shinwell on information about the projected appointment of a Supreme Commander for the Mediterranean, Churchill lost his temper and wagging a finger at Mr. Shinwell said, 'I would warn Mr. Shinwell not to be too prophetic about the way in which things are going. They may not be as unfortunate for this country as he would no doubt wish.' The Opposition took this to imply a reflection on the former Minister of Defence's patriotism, and uproar at once ensued, with cries of 'Withdraw', 'Shame' and 'You wicked old man!' On an appeal from Mr. Michison the Speaker ruled that to accuse a Member of unavowed motives was out of order, but, pressed to demand that Mr. Churchill withdraw his remarks he said, 'What I heard did not in my judgement amount to that.' Amidst cat-calls, hisses, taunts and cries Mr. Churchill tried to speak over the din. Reminded of previous tributes he had made to Mr. Shinwell ('I have always felt and always testified, even in moments of party strife, to the right hon. gentleman's sterling patriotism and the fact that his heart is in the right place where the life and strength of our country is concerned') he admitted that, but added that his appreciation had been 'inroaded' in recent months. This caused a tremendous outburst of booing—ugly enough anywhere but especially in the House of Commons. Churchill asked the Chair to rule whether booing was in order; the Speaker pronounced it 'grossly out of order'. 'What else can you say to a goose?' snapped Mr. Ross, to be ordered by the Speaker at once to withdraw his remark. Herbert Morrison rose to argue with the Speaker on why 'goose' should be so offensive while an imputation of lack of patriotism be deemed harmless. Eventually Mr. Churchill indicated that the word 'goose' did not worry him in the slightest, and tempers at last subsided.

Meanwhile, on 4th November 1952, General Eisenhower was returned as President of the United States. Anxious to ensure the continuity of Anglo-American co-operation, and to keep abreast of American policy, Mr. Churchill left for America on New Year's Eve, speeded on his way by a goodwill message from Sir Tom O'Brien, President of the Trades Union Congress, saying, 'You carry with you the goodwill of the workers of Britain and the Commonwealth. . . .'

On 5th January 1953 Churchill arrived in the U.S.A. for informal talks with President Eisenhower, who was sworn in on 20th January.

And on 5th March Joseph Stalin died, to be succeeded as Chairman of the Council of Ministers by Mr. Malenkov. Mr. Churchill had little to say of the Russian dictator whose military co-operation had been welcome in the war, but whose pre-war and post-war enormities—the liquidation of the Kulaks in the thirties, the enslavement of the Baltic and Central European States in the decade following the Second World War—made his passing no occasion for panegyrics.

Nor was the appearance of a new leader a matter for precipitate rejoicing but rather of hope. Churchill still longed for an East-West understanding and pressed for a top-level four-power conference in the hope of easing tension and lightening the mounting burden of rearmament and defensive measures. In America there was a hardening of opinion towards Russia; it was for Russia, Eisenhower felt, to cease her 'cold war' tactics before anyone could accept her good faith sufficiently to parley on matters of life and death.

At home, political capital was being made out of Churchill's age. The *Daily Mirror* group was foremost in this campaign, to which it reverted again and again. CHURCHILL IS MISSING THE BUS proclaimed the *Sunday Pictorial* in one-inch type on its front page, and then asked a lot of questions which it answered itself. 'What is the matter with Mr. Churchill? Why is he numbed and overwhelmed by the pressure of events? When is Britain going to speak up and plainly tell the world exactly where we stand on European and Far Eastern affairs? When are we going to demonstrate that the British Commonwealth is the third world power and not merely a satellite of the United States? The Premier's latest speech, full of platitudes and pious hope, indicated all too clearly that he has little or nothing to contribute to this vital juncture of history. *Winston,—now seventy-eight—is missing the bus.*' It urged a change of American and Russian attitudes to the cold war, and in Asia a recognition that mere anti-Communism was not enough; there would need to be a recognition of resurgent nationalism there and the demand for a better life.

Well, it was free speech, which all his life Churchill himself had used freely—and not always fairly—enough. 'Here we can assert the rights of the citizen against the State, or criticize the Government of the day, without failing in our duty to the Crown or our loyalty to the Queen', he told the Honourable Artillery Company. 'Our weakness,' he added with a chuckle, 'is that there are always a number of English people who wake up every morning—very brainy they are—and they look all round and they think: "Now what is there we can find that belongs to our country that we can give away? Or what is there we can find that has made our country great that we can pull down?" . . . Nothing can save England if she will not save herself. If we lose faith in ourselves, in our capacity to guide and govern, if we lose our will to live, then, indeed, our story is told. . . .'

On that day—24th April—Churchill went back to the House in his white tie and tails, fortified by a good dinner and good company, and happy with a secret of his own. 'I was hoping we should find ourselves in a friendly atmosphere tonight,' he told the House, grinning wickedly. 'Nonsense!' snarled a few Opposition Members, but his good humour mellowed them, and as he left the Chamber Conservatives and Labourites called 'Good night!'

Looking for all the world like an ageing Puck in fancy dress, Churchill blew the House a kiss as he left.

A Court Circular the following day revealed his secret. He had accepted from Her Majesty the Queen the honour which King George VI had been anxious to confer upon him in 1945. She conferred upon him the honour of the Order of the Garter at Windsor Castle. The old man knelt before the young Queen, who touched him lightly on each shoulder with the ceremonial sword, saying, 'Rise, Sir Winston.'

Sir Winston! It would take a lot of getting used to. For all of his life he had been plain Mister. He loved uniforms and dressing up and queer hats and the power of office, but he remained always a Commoner, the Great Commoner, the Greatest Commoner. No honours could be conferred upon him greater than the love and respect he had won for himself in the hearts of the people; nevertheless, this honour was conferred at the Queen's especial wish, and how could he possibly refuse, as a lover of the institution of monarchy, this signal honour? The Queen handed him the Insignia of the Order—the collar seven inches deep, the medallion called 'The George' showing St. George in armour on horseback spearing the dragon. He already possessed the Order of Merit, an extremely high order for services in any sphere, but carrying no rank or precedence. Thus he became the only Prime Minister to receive the Order of the Garter in this century while still in office. Balfour, Asquith and Baldwin were not actually in office when they received the K.G., and further were elevated to the peerage, making it impossible for them to sit any more in the House of Commons. The award meant that he would be entitled to a stall in St. George's Chapel, Windsor, with his banner hanging there, and could appear at the forthcoming Coronation in the Garter robes—a dark blue mantle and crimson velvet surcoat over his Privy Councillor's uniform.

A few weeks later Churchill found himself speaking not only as Prime Minister but Deputy Foreign Minister, for Anthony Eden was ill. In the Diplomats' Gallery were the American and French Ambassadors and—uneasily juxtaposed—the Egyptian and Israeli envoys. He spoke of the necessity for and problems of defending the Suez Canal, of the boastful and threatening speeches emanating from Cairo and of attacks by saboteurs. If the attacks continued, he said, 'we are entirely capable of doing this.' Of Franco-German relations and European unity, he said, 'There is no hope of the safety and freedom of Western Europe except by the laying aside for ever of the ancient feud between the Teuton and the Gaul. It is seven years since, at Zurich, I appealed to France to take Germany by the hand and lead her back into the European family. We have made much progress since then. Some of it has been due no doubt to the spur to resist the enormous military strength of Soviet Russia. But much is also due to the inspiring and unconquerable cause of United Europe.'

Churchill had been trying to arrange 'Big Three' talks in Bermuda as a prelude to a top-level conference to end East-West tension. But on 27th June came the sad news that his doctors had ordered him a month's rest. The bulletin said:

> The Prime Minister has had no respite for a long time from his very arduous duties and is in need of a complete rest. We have therefore advised him to abandon his journey to Bermuda and to lighten his duties for at least a month.

The *Daily Mirror* in one-inch type on its front page asked SHOULD CHURCHILL RETIRE? 'How long,' asked the *Mirror*, 'can Britain's position in the Cabinet of nations be sustained by an old man's spurts of energy, an old man's flashes of brilliance, an old man's moments of wisdom, and an old man's bursts of activity? . . . He owes it to himself, his family, and to his country to retire from the Premiership. . . .'

The gardens at Chartwell, which were to be opened in aid of charity, were closed so that Churchill could rest completely—something he always found difficult, being an intensely active man. His illness sparked off much speculation. On 17th August the United Nations was to meet at Lake Success to discuss the Korean problem; the Conservative Party Conference was due to open at Margate on 8th October; Parliament would reopen on 20th October. Would Churchill achieve his ambition of the three-power talks that would guarantee the peace of the world? This, everyone knew, was his dearest wish, his most coveted laurel. WHAT IS THE TRUTH ABOUT CHURCHILL'S ILLNESS? demanded the *Mirror*, busy with its one-inch type again. It quoted the *Observer*'s comment that friends emerged either glowingly confident or alarmingly reticent. It quoted Mr. Stewart Alsop of the New York *Herald-Tribune* as saying that Churchill had had a stroke in June, had made a 'near-miraculous recovery' but would never again be able to resume active leadership. IS THIS TRUE? demanded the paper, scarcely expecting that any of its readers could answer the question. A. J. Cummings in the *News Chronicle* took a less excitable view. 'Why should he keep going at full tilt? His energy is colossal but it is not unlimited. He is in his seventy-ninth year. . . . He should take a large view of what may be regarded as parliamentary routine and leave that to others. . . . I should be sorry indeed if Sir Winston made any decision to retire in the immediate or near future from the Premiership. He is still the Tory Party's chief asset.'

On 18th August Churchill presided again over a Cabinet meeting. Forty years after he had declared—following the loss of his job at the Admiralty—'I am finished', Churchill was still far from finished. He attended the Conservative Party's annual conference at Margate and told them, 'If I stay on for the time being, bearing the burden at my age, it is not because of love for power or office. I have had an ample feast of both. If I stay on it is because I have the feeling that I may, through things that have happened, have an influence on what I care about above all else—the building of a sure and lasting peace.' The audience was unusually silent. Were they demanding too much of him? He seemed assured, poised, his voice determined and resonant. He took a sip of some water, beamed at them and assured them that it was 'an austere refreshment to which I do not normally resort'. At last there were smiles again.

Towards the end of 1953 Churchill was back in his old form,

though disappointed by Eisenhower's view that some change of heart must be actually demonstrated by the Soviet Union before he would talk with Malenkov. This meant, inevitably, the shelving of the four-power meeting for some months. But the velvet-glove treatment allowed for a short spate after Churchill's illness was soon forgotten on 22nd November, when Tory M.P.s were outraged by his refusal to increase the pensions of surviving officers of the First World War. Brigadier Peto went so far as to say that the Government's decision was a betrayal of the trust these officers had placed in Sir Winston. Churchill responded with dignity; the cost could not be borne; he knew the decision would be unpopular; therefore he had given the information himself rather than leave it to a departmental Minister. At Harrow, his old school, he joined with the white-collared Harrovians in singing their song 'Forty years on, when afar and asunder, Parted are those who are singing today', but sang 'Sixty years on . . . ,' and in December the *Mirror* group, through its *Sunday Pictorial*, inquired with renewed solicitude: How Long Can the Old Boy Keep It Up?

On 21st January 1954 Churchill slipped into the House of Commons Chamber, took his seat on the Treasury bench, and listened attentively. Mr. Geoffrey Lloyd, Minister of Fuel and Power, was moving the second reading of his Mines and Quarries Bill, which sought to consolidate all existing legislation relating to safety in mines, and to introduce new safety measures which took account of new techniques and machinery.

Churchill was there because it was he who, as Home Secretary in 1911, introduced the comprehensive mine safety measures which had been the basis of legislation ever since.

A few days later the *Daily Mirror*—using two-inch type this time—was back at its campaign for Churchill's retirement. Churchill, 79, said the screaming headline, Too Old and Too Tired. 'When will the Prime Minister realize that he is too old, too ailing, too tired for the job? When will the Old Man retire?' it asked, trying hard to mix political manœuvre with the necessary minimum of face-saving eulogy. 'The time has come for him to make his last great decision. He must surrender office and retire to the rest he has so richly deserved.' The truth was that Churchill, with his incredible status and popularity, was such an asset to the Conservative Party that the Socialists and of course newspapers supporting the Socialists, such as the *Daily Mirror*, would have liked to see him pruning rosebushes. Such rumours, declared some correspondents, damaged Britain's status abroad, where Churchill was so highly regarded. 'When he does decide to retire,' said the *Daily Sketch*, 'we have a hunch it will not be out of deference to the wishes of the mongrels. The mongrel pack is yapping at Sir Winston's heels.' Lord Alexander criticized in the House of Lords the *Daily Mirror*'s campaign. The *News of the World* predicted his retirement in May. Cartoons made capital out of the Prime Minister's alleged decrepitude. But in subsequent debates, and at question time, the Churchillian star shone as brightly as ever. On 23rd March 1954 his speech on the need to raise judges' salaries, in which in vivid language he described their role, was as concise and forceful and colourful as anything he had said. And his transparent sincerity, as he spoke of the need to keep cool heads and a realistic outlook in a world of atomic and hydrogen power, made a deep impression. On the subject of judges' salaries, and making the point that, in the nature of their vital work, they should be above financial strain, he set the House laughing by asking, 'What would be the thought of a Lord Chief Justice if he won the Derby?'—referring to the more modest success of his own stable. A crowded House followed him enrapt—not the reception normally accorded to a tired old man. The atomic and hydrogen bomb experiments naturally evoked apprehension, but Churchill had a point when he mentioned that nobody had seen fit to protest when the Russians made similar experiments. In 1943 Churchill had reached a secret agreement with Roosevelt by which Britain would be consulted before the U.S.A. used the atomic bomb. But Washington's reaction to Churchill's speech in Parliament was that the 1943 agreement had become void.

Churchill's revelations of this secret agreement aroused a storm in the House on 5th April. Churchill maintained that the failure of the previous Socialist Government to disclose the terms of the Agreement had made possible the McMahon Act which ruled out collaboration with Britain in that field. Churchill stood, calm and unruffled, as shouts of 'resign!' and 'getting down to the gutter' and some boos flew over his head.

For Churchill to have made a party issue out of the awful question of the hydrogen bomb was almost certainly a mistake. Everyone, Socialists, Conservatives, Liberals, wanted discussions at top level and agreement for restraint and control in the use of this terrible weapon. 'More than once,' said Mr. Attlee, 'British courage and

British initiative have saved Europe; British initiative may yet well save civilization.' 'The Prime Minister's sense of occasion,' *The Times* commented, 'deserted him sadly.' The debate had degenerated into 'a sterile, angry and pitiful party wrangle'. The *News Chronicle* thought Churchill's handling of the debate 'one of the biggest misjudgements of his long career'. The New York *Herald-Tribune* felt that Churchill had wrecked all chances of securing a two-party foreign policy while he remained Prime Minister.

In June Churchill and Eden visited Washington to discuss with President Eisenhower and Secretary Dulles a common policy on co-existence with Russia. At a Press Conference Churchill replied heatedly to suggestions in the American press that Britain's policy towards Russia was one of appeasement. It was worthwhile, he said, to see if co-existence could not be made to work, never forgetting that the watchword of the West must be 'Peace through Strength'.

In Canada he saw Mr. St. Laurent, the Canadian Prime Minister, and his Cabinet, and in a farewell talk to Canadians reminded them that fifty-three years had passed since he came to lecture to them on the Boer War. 'Do not forget the Old Land; do not forget that little island lost among the Northern mists . . . ,' he said.

Back in the House on 7th July, Sir Winston was asked by Mr. Warbey to name the enslaved countries mentioned in the Churchill-Eisenhower declaration, and replied, 'When President Eisenhower and I drew up our statement we were very conscious that some countries would be offended by being included in the list and some by being excluded. There was a maxim which I was taught as a young officer which occurs to me now—"No names, no pack drill".' The House enjoyed a good laugh. Churchill's mood was sprightly and confident, and as he had entered the Chamber from behind the Speaker's chair, a wave of cheers rolled towards him. With his usual mixture of Puckishness and old world courtesy, he bowed to the Chair before taking his seat. Churchill was happy to hear President Eisenhower's affirmation that hopes of world peace depended upon 'peaceful co-existence between East and West' and hoped that this passage would reach the ears of Moscow.

On 23rd November, speaking at a meeting in his own constituency of Woodford, Essex, Churchill made a surprising admission which had instantaneous repercussions in many countries. He revealed that when the Germans were surrendering in their hundreds of thousands, he telegraphed to Lord Montgomery 'directing him to be careful in collecting the German arms, to stack them so that they could easily be issued again, to the German soldiers whom we would have to work with if the Soviet advance continued.' This 'vast reversal' of opinion towards the Germans was brought about 'by Stalin, the dictator, who was carried away by the triumphs of victory and acted as if he thought he could secure for Russia and Communism the domination of the world'. When Russia broke the agreement she made at Yalta, and moved steadily towards the West, it was hardly surprising that there should be misgivings in the Western camp.

On 30th November Churchill celebrated his eightieth birthday amidst the plaudits of friends and enemies. Twenty years had passed since he was in the political wilderness. Now he was the best-known man in the world. He still worked twelve hours a day. He ate and drank with appetite and gusto. He could recall the past yet look with perceptive eyes into the years ahead. And Cassandra of the *Daily Mirror*, perhaps the greatest polemical journalist of this period, yet free of bigotry and malice, paid a handsome birthday tribute, in the course of which he dissociated himself from the campaign to secure Churchill's retirement. 'There are those who urge the retirement of Sir Winston Churchill,' he wrote, 'I AM NOT AMONG THEM. The campaign is too much like stubbing your toe on history—and a pretty large and unyielding chunk of history at that . . . he has been magnanimous, sentimental, sardonic, ferocious, humane, witty, cherubic, corrosive, statesmanlike and, withal, I think a very lovable old chap. Many happy returns from the other side of the hill.'

Does anybody really suppose that love of office kept Churchill in politics in his eightieth year? All his life, it is true, he had been a man of action; if there were hardship or struggle or risk, he wanted to be there, accepting the challenge, risking everything he had to risk to get good from a bad situation. 'Old Man' he might be—but old enough, since no living statesman could compare with him in experience, to know the peril that faced humanity.

'Surely no man has done more to strengthen Parliament. During the war, when Authoritarianism might have been easy, he kept Parliament in the centre of things and treated it as his master. For over fifty years his life has revolved round the House of Commons. The House has seen him in all his phases. Impulsive, emotional, steely in resolve, fertile in idea and expedient, sombre and yet gay to the point of impudence, sensitive artist of word and colour, passionate but magnanimous, above all courageous—as odd a mixture as any British public character (as the old phrase goes) has ever seen. . . .'

His eightieth birthday was the occasion for a tribute by Parliament such as has never been accorded any man in its long history. In the vast Westminster Hall, before Lords and Commons, the Grand Old Man of Parliament was presented with a presentation volume in green Levant morocco, inlaid in chocolate and pink and hand-tooled in gold, containing the inscribed names of nearly all the Members of the House of Commons; a portrait by Graham Sutherland and an interim cheque for £150,000 for his birthday fund, initiated as a charitable trust in his honour.

It was an emotional gathering. Behind the banked flowers, on the carpeted platform behind which rose the carpeted stairs and the stonework and mellow stained glass windows, amidst politicians of every party, Churchill soon had everyone roaring with laughter and —in some cases—brushing away a furtive tear.

It started with the drummer in the Guards' orchestra beating upon a drum the 'V' in Morse as Sir Winston and Lady Churchill appeared from St. Stephen's entrance. As the signal became clearer, the medieval hall quivered with cheers. He shook hands with members of the Parliamentary Committee which had organized the tribute, including the doughty protagonists Miss Jennie Lee and Aneurin Bevan. They came down the staircase, taking their places on either side of the Speaker (Mr. W. S. Morrison) in his full-bottomed wig and robes—the Lord Chancellor, Lord Kilmuir, being similarly dressed. Softly, the red-coated orchestra played *Pomp and Circumstance*.

The Speaker made a brief but affecting speech. Parliament sees so much of changing fortune that it regarded the achievements and personalities of any single generation 'somewhat aloofly, knowing that so much has happened and much yet to come. But the generation which has lived through the last fateful fifteen years with Sir Winston Churchill demands—and will not be denied—its own voice of affection and gratitude.'

It fell to Mr. Attlee to present the portrait. 'The House of Commons is a family, and we are paying a tribute of esteem and affection to the most distinguished member of the parliamentary family,' he began. He would not outline Churchill's career—'I come not to bury Caesar but to praise him. Caesar indeed—for you have not only carried on war but have written your own commentary. . . . In 1940 the hour of destiny struck. You became the leader of the nation in the most critical days it has ever faced. You have always been a figure of controversy. You are one who kindly gives and takes hard knocks. It can only be a very youthful Member of Parliament who has not disagreed with you, and most of us at one time or another have been violently opposed to you. Yet, it was found in 1940, in the hour of peril, that members of all Parties were glad to serve under you and recognized you as the daring pilot in extremity through the storm that had struck Britain required. . . . We greet you today especially as a great Parliamentarian, the last of the great orators who can touch great heights. . . . May I hope that you will live to see the beginnings of an era of peace in the world after the storms which it has been your lot to encounter.' The curtain covering the portrait swung away. There are mixed views about the portrait itself; Churchill is said to have commented on it, 'It makes me look half-witted, which I ain't.' Lord Hailsham, in a voice audible to the artist, who was standing near, exclaimed, 'It's disgusting.'

Churchill was in the happiest of moods. 'This is for me,' he said, in his rich, resonant voice, 'the most memorable public occasion of my life. No one has ever received a similar mark of honour before. There has not been anything like it in British history and indeed I doubt whether any of the modern democracies abroad have shown such a degree of kindness and generosity to a party politician who has not yet retired'—there were roars of laughter at this—'and may at any time be involved in controversy.'

'I am sure that this is the finest greeting any member of the House of Commons has yet received and I express my heartfelt thanks to the representatives of both Houses for the gifts which they have bestowed on me in their names. The portrait is a remarkable example of modern art (there were cheers and loud laughter at this). It combines force and candour. These are qualities which no active member of either House can do without or should fail to meet. (Laughter.)

'I have lived my life in the House of Commons, having served there for fifty-two out of the last fifty-four years of this tumultuous and convulsive century. I have indeed seen all the ups and downs of fate and fortune there, but I have never ceased to love and honour the Mother of Parliaments, the model of legislative assemblies of so many lands. . . .'

There were smiles everywhere. Nobody would admit that this occasion had something about it of a farewell—a presage of the inevitable parting. Deliberately, the light touch was kept throughout. And then Churchill dealt with his most glorious years:

'I have never accepted what many people have kindly said, that I inspired the nation. Their will was resolute and remorseless and it proved unconquerable. It fell to me to express it and if I found the right word you must remember that I have always earned my living by my pen, and by my tongue.' (Laughter.)

'It was the nation and the race dwelling all round the globe that had the lion's heart. I had the luck to be called upon to give the roar.' (Laughter.) 'I also hope that I sometimes suggested to the lion the right place to use his claws.'

But a few eyes misted at his closing words. 'Ladies and gentlemen, I am now nearing the end of my journey. I hope I still have some services to render. However that may be, and whatever may befall, I am sure I shall never forget the emotion of this day.'

Lord Salisbury, Leader of the House of Lords, added a tribute from the Lords whose powers Churchill had, in 1911, helped to curtail. 'The Prime Minister belongs to Parliament as a whole, and I have been asked to say a few words of warm congratulation to him on behalf . . . of all parties in the House of Lords. . . .' Eight hundred years ago 'this venerable hall was first built by the workmen of a Plantagenet King among the sedges and marshes of the River Thames. These last eighty years have had crammed into them more revolutionary changes in the life of man than all the centuries that went before.' That was the framework in which Sir Winston Churchill's life must be set. What an immeasurable debt he was owed! He had served them, he had led them, in fair weather and foul, leading them safely through the greatest national crisis. 'It has been the privilege of this generation to see him and know him for themselves. That is something, I believe, for which we shall always be envied by those who come after.'

An audience with the Queen . . . a television appearance . . . a reception in the House of Lords to receive gifts from party adherents . . . but one small, intimate touch at the Westminster Hall ceremony summed it all up; a birthday cake with eighty candles, with pink and white sugar and white roses, and around the centre posy a quotation, truly prophetic:

> *He is a man, take him for all in all,*
> *we shall not look upon his like again.*

The end of Churchill's tremendous parliamentary career was in sight. His knighthood, and the landmark of the eightieth birthday, made it inevitable. In March 1955 it was known to be imminent, yet his speech to the House on 1st March had all the mastery, all the passion and never-failing idealism of Churchill at his best. He spoke of the grave issue before mankind, mankind's survival or annihilation; how, owing to the breakdown in the exchange of nuclear information between Britain and the United States, Britain had started independently on her own—'We have started making the hydrogen bomb, too' and, making the point that in fundamental science the West outstripped Russia in her stockpile of atomic bombs, he banged the despatch case to illustrate a point:

It is now the fact that a quantity of plutonium probably less than would fill this box here on the table (Churchill banged the box as he spoke)—it is quite a safe thing to store—would suffice to produce weapons which would give indisputable world domination to any great Power which was the only one to have it. There is no defence—no absolute defence—against the hydrogen bomb.

'What ought we to do?' he asked, passionately, 'which way can we turn to save our lives and the future of the world?' His voice took on the timbre of deeply-felt emotion: 'It does not matter so much to old people. They are going soon, anyway, but I find it poignant to look at youth in all its activity and ardour, and, most of all, to watch little children playing their merry games, and wonder what would lie before them if God wearied of mankind. . . .'

The advance of Communism in Europe and Asia had bound the N.A.T.O. powers together, sweeping away, because of new and fearful prospects, the nightmare memories of Hitlerism. 'But for American nuclear superiority,' he declared, 'Europe would already have been reduced to satellite status . . . unless a really trustworthy and universal agreement upon disarmament, conventional and nuclear alike, can be reached and an effective system of inspection

is established and is actually working, there is only one sane policy
. . . defence through deterrence.'

And what when everybody possessed these terrible weapons? He
foresaw that possibility, too. The 'saturation' point would be
reached, at which, although one power might be stronger than the
other, they could wreak mutual annihilation.

He pleaded that Britain should have nuclear weapons and not
rely solely upon American protection. 'Personally, I cannot feel that
we should have much influence over their policy or actions, wise or
unwise, while we are largely dependent, as we are today, upon their
protection . . . there is time and hope, if we combine patience with
courage, that the deterrents will improve and gain authority
throughout the next ten years.'

The House was so tense and silent that a pin could be heard to
drop. Everybody seemed frozen into immobility, as they hung upon
every word. And surely enough, since it was Churchill who was
speaking, he ended on a note of hope:

> The day may dawn when fair play, love for one's fellow man and
> respect for justice and freedom will enable tormented generations
> to march forth serene and triumphant from the hideous epoch in
> which we have to dwell. *Meanwhile, never flinch, never weary,
> never despair.*

It was a tremendous, awe-inspiring speech, a cry from the heart of
a man who had seen more of the unfolding drama and tragedy of
mankind's destiny than any other man alive.

Despite a newspaper strike of London daily newspapers, the
country knew, on 4th April 1955, that Churchill was retiring. He
gave a farewell dinner at No. 10 Downing Street, in honour of the
Queen and the Duke of Edinburgh, and the party of fifty included
many of Sir Winston's closest wartime colleagues and members of
the existing administration. Field-Marshal Montgomery was there,
Viscount Bracken, Lord Cherwell (wartime scientific adviser), Sir
Anthony and Lady Eden, and Mr. and Mrs. Attlee. As the Queen
left, Sir Winston, portly but courtly, wearing the Order of the
Garter, stood in the chill night air to hold open the car door.

The following day crowds waiting outside Downing Street saw
Churchill emerge in black frock coat, top hat, carrying his gold-
topped cane; he acknowledged their cheers, drove to Buckingham
Palace, smiled back at the waiting crowds as he drove away soon

afterwards, with their cheers ringing in his ears. He resigned his office of Prime Minister at 4.30 p.m. and half an hour later a bulletin was issued from Buckingham Palace:

The Right Honourable Sir Winston Churchill had an audience of the Queen this evening and tendered his resignation as Prime Minister and First Lord of the Treasury, which Her Majesty was graciously pleased to accept.

The occasion was marked by tributes in both Houses of Parliament. Mr. Attlee said: 'Today we are parting with a Prime Minister who led this country through some of the most fateful years in our history . . . and in history, as one of the greatest of all Prime Ministers, his place is assured.'

In the House of Lords the Lord Chancellor, Lord Kilmuir, spoke movingly of all Churchill had done for his country, for Anglo-American accord and towards a united Europe. 'Whatever the future may bring,' he said, 'no one can take away the fact that we have heard the rustle of the wings of greatness in the years when Sir Winston Churchill has played so great a part in our lives.' From all over the world, and from leaders of the Commonwealth, tributes poured in.

Leaving No. 10 Downing Street was a wrench. He stood on the doorstep, tears in his eyes, his cigar stuck defiantly in his mouth; his staff, lined up inside the doorway, clapped him, but one or two were in tears too. From the crowd outside the cry went up, 'Good old Winnie.' With tremendous effort at self-control, for his lips were trembling, Sir Winston stuck up two fingers in the famous V-sign for victory. A raucous yell went up from another man in the crowd, 'You gave 'em wot for in your time, Winnie!' Good-humouredly, but firmly, the struggling police kept the crowds back. Photographers' bulbs flashed. Somehow it seemed Churchill could not wrench himself away—then, making up his mind, he got into the car, and it moved slowly away, to Chartwell, with his pets and his goldfish and his painting and stables and gardens, and most and best of all, to dear 'Clemmie', his closest and dearest companion through all his struggles and trials.

30

Journey's End

Anthony Eden succeeded Sir Winston as Prime Minister on 6th April 1955 and also became leader of the Conservative Party. Sir Winston said of him, 'He will, I am sure, sustain the highest interests and tradition of Britain, and uphold the cause of Tory democracy which Lord Beaconsfield proclaimed, which Lord Randolph revived and which I have tried to serve. . . .'

On Eden's first day in the Commons as Prime Minister, Mr. Attlee, leader of the Opposition, rose to pay a graceful tribute to the retiring Premier. He spoke with emotion of the lustre which Churchill's oratory, mastery of facts and superb confidence had given to Commons debates. 'We shall miss these witty replies. . . . Above all, we shall miss the familiar figure. . . .' The familiar figure . . . yes, he would be missed. He had only to appear and somnolence, complacency, defeatism and disorder were banished by his presence; the whole Chamber seemed suffused with warmth because of him, an alertness and interest and often a sense of drama tensed the atmosphere; he was so intensely *alive*, standing there, in his frock coat, the heavy gold watch-chain over his ample stomach, his great bulk seeming to heave slightly forward like a bull half wondering whether he should charge, his round, pink features, in their expression, suggestive of a mixture of pugilist and impish schoolboy. Yes, he would be missed.

Mr. Attlee wished Mr. Eden health and strength in his office, 'but not, of course, a long tenure', he added, amidst laughter, in allusion to the inevitable General Election.

Churchill did not retire from Parliament. He became the greatest backbencher of all time. He threw himself with zest into the General Election campaign and—not surprisingly—was returned as M.P. for Woodford. He sat on the corner seat on the front bench below the gangway, thus being near the Ministers—the seat he had occupied for so long while in political exile between the wars. On the swearing-in of the new Parliament on 8th June 1955 a tremendous ovation greeted his appearance. Normally the Ministers of the Treasury Bench take the oath and subscribe the roll, then those on the Opposition front bench, then Members of the Privy Council. But Mr. Attlee, leader of the Opposition, waiving his turn, came forward to his old Tory opponent, greeted him warmly and, taking him by the hand, motioned him to precede him. The gesture touched the heart of all M.P.s and brought roars of approval from the public gallery.

Pruning rose bushes and reading *The Times* was not Sir Winston's idea of retirement. He wrote away as hard as ever, revising and editing the first two volumes of his *History of the English-Speaking Peoples*, published in 1956. He had his six mares, six foals and two yearlings. There were his dogs and his tropical fish. There was his painting. There were social engagements innumerable, and visits abroad, including his beloved Riviera. A constant procession of friends old and new made their way to Chartwell to meet him. His political pronouncements were few, and by limiting his appearances and utterances he took care not to overshadow his successor. But there was poignancy in his reflections of what the political shape of the post-war world might have been 'if our American friends had listened to the appeals I made'. This was with reference to autumn 1944 and spring 1945. If the Americans had heeded him, he declared, 'it is probable that *we*—I repeat, *we*—would have taken Berlin and would have gained a great footing in the whole of the conquered territory . . . there is no doubt that had Field-Marshal Montgomery been allowed to take the course he advocated and which I sustained to the best of my ability, we should have been in a position to deal with the situation when we met our friends who came from the other side—to deal with it better than we have in fact been able to do.' After being in direct contact with Stalin, Eisenhower, as Supreme Commander, withdrew the Ninth Army from Montgomery's command and the full force of advance was diverted southwards from the road to Berlin, striking towards Leipzig and Dresden. The Russians were given a foothold in Western Europe which has been a complication ever since.

One wonders how Churchill would have handled the problem of the Middle East, where Egyptians, Russians and Americans were all working in their different ways to end British influence in that area. Britain, France and America had entered into a pact to keep the peace between Israel and her Arab neighbours; Nasser, Egypt's

12*

ruler, was aiming at domination of the recently-formed Arab League; Russia, hoping to oust Britain and so jeopardize her oil supplies, vital to defence, was pouring arms and technicians into Egypt and Syria as a prelude to attack. When Israel decided not to wait for the blow to fall, but to scotch the conspiracy before it was too late, a menacing situation developed. Israel's capture of Egyptian arms dumps showed conclusively that they were mostly Russian— that Egypt was plotting an invasion of Israel with Russian help. But unless Britain and France stopped the conflagration from spreading, Russia might have moved in troops.

Britain's action at Suez will be long debated. Israel obeyed a summons to cease fire, the Egyptians did not, and Britain and France moved in—but too slowly—to restore order. But America, whose oil companies had long been intriguing against Britain in the Middle East, did not support Britain in her action and even threatened sanctions. Churchill, in a letter to his Woodford constituents, approved of Eden's action. He was aggrieved when Eden's health collapsed under the strain, causing him to resign on 9th January 1957. He was consulted by the Queen on Eden's successor and approved the idea of Macmillan's appointment as Prime Minister.

Gradually Sir Winston's appearances in the House of Commons became fewer and fewer with the passing years, and each visit was regarded by the House as something precious. He had about him the dignity of a fine old tree, indifferent to the howling of gales and the cruel chill of winter. On his television set, he watched his son Randolph receive for him President Kennedy's unique honour —which made Churchill the first honorary citizen of the United States; he watched it 'live' because it was being relayed by satellite to the B.B.C. He heard the words of the proclamation: 'A child of the House of Commons, he became in time its father. By adding his name to our rolls, we mean to honour him—but his acceptance honours us far more. For no statement or proclamation can enrich his name—the name Sir Winston Churchill is already legend.' In 1958 Churchill had declined the honour but in 1963 informed Representative Francis B. Walter of Pennsylvania that 'due to the changed situation from 1958' he would be delighted to accept.

In 1964, as he neared ninety, Churchill announced that he would not stand for Parliament again. It had to come—everyone knew that—yet the sight of this grand old man fading visibly was a pro-tracted grief to all who loved him. Nobody wanted to lose him, nobody could imagine England without him . . . he *was* England, the embodiment of all that was clean and courageous, bold and imaginative. And now, due to the fact that his left leg, fractured in 1962, would not take his great weight without intense pain, he spent much of his time in a wheel chair.

When he visited the House, in those last days, everyone, some-how, knew when he was coming. The hum of business would cease and everyone waited in silence for the huge swing doors to be flung open by the Parliamentary Messengers. Two Members would advance to the chair. He would heave his weight out of it with their help and stand on his feet—nothing would persuade him to enter the Chamber he loved so well except on his feet. Slowly, with calculated effort, he moved forward, one step at a time; amazingly upright except for the familiar forward lurch of the shoulders. Passing the Speaker, as custom enjoins, he would bow, slowly, gravely, as though paying homage at the symbol of tradition and history itself. With relief, he would sink his bulk on to the green leather bench, while friends hurried to explain the day's business. Sometimes, leaning heavily on his gold-topped cane, with a look that said 'Help me if you dare!' he would walk alone while M.P.s watched with admiring yet agonized concern. Sometimes he would turn, moving his head around slowly to take in every detail of the great Chamber, the House that had claimed most of his life, the great heart of a great nation. Then back into his wheel chair. The great doors would close, and the House seemed strangely empty.

On 28th July 1964 Churchill's seat was empty. The previous day Churchill had made a brief appearance. The spirit was there, but age was taking its toll. And on the 28th, probably because the strain of a formal and final parting would be too great even for his fine spirit, he stayed at home.

Sir Alec Douglas-Home moved a motion in honour of the greatest Parliamentarian that institution has ever known. Harold Macmillan told the House: 'There have been great administrators in times of peace, like Walpole, and great leaders of the nation in the hour of peril—Chatham, Pitt, Lloyd George. Others have nearly equalled but not surpassed Sir Winston's immense span of Parliamentary and public life—Palmerston, Disraeli and Gladstone. There have been debaters and orators of equal power, but few with that gift of puckish and mischievous humour which so endears him to us.

'The life we are honouring today is unique. The oldest among us can recall nothing to compare with him, and the younger ones among you, however long you live, will never see the like again. If I were to try to sum up his whole character, I can think of no words more appropriate than those which he himself has written:

> In War: Resolution
> In Defeat: Defiance
> In Victory: Magnanimity
> In Peace: Good will.'

Nevermore, the packed House knew, would the man who was the embodiment of history walk, even with faltering tread, through the Churchill Arch, the memorial to his greatness erected during his lifetime.

Now, with the flame of life flickering but feebly in his great frame, Churchill was entitled to do what his political enemies a decade earlier had so cruelly and unjustly accused him of doing—living in the past. And *what* a past! Too vast, too grand to permit anything but nostalgic glimpses, giving new reality to his words: 'History with its flickering lamp stumbles along the trail of the past, trying to reconstruct its scenes, to revive its echoes, and kindle with pale gleams the passion of former days.' With his family, or old friends such as Lord Ismay and Field-Marshal Montgomery, some pale gleams were kindled.

It was on his eighty-second birthday that a photographer said he hoped he would be able to take another picture of him at the age of ninety. Churchill surveyed the photographer with serious mien: 'I see no reason why you shouldn't, young man. You look hale and hearty enough.' And now came his ninetieth birthday, on 30th November 1964. The crowds outside his house at Hyde Park Gate in London cheered him to the echo, and he came to the open window to return their greeting, his eyes brimming with tears, a smile of happiness on the pale, yet still strangely young, face. Still a lover of unorthodox clothing, he wore a generously cut—loose for comfort—velvet zippered jacket and the inevitable spotted bow tie. At the very end of his journey, he was left in no doubt that amongst all generations, young or old, the majority respected, admired and loved him. He was deeply moved.

On Friday, 15th January 1965, the world was shocked to hear that Sir Winston Churchill was gravely ill. He had suffered a stroke and, because of his great age an operation, which sometimes removes the obstruction which keeps blood from reaching the brain, could not be considered. Nor, from his grievous condition, could he be moved from his home in Hyde Park Gate to hospital.

A long ordeal began and the nation held its breath. Little crowds gathered outside, mostly silent, tense, anxious and sympathetic. There were Americans and Kenyans, Chinese and Scots, New Zealanders and English—just people of every kind, grieved because the 'old man' was ill and fighting his last great battle.

His family came for the last, sad vigil. Flowers and telegrams of sympathy arrived. Cameramen and television operators clustered outside, until, because of the distraction of flashing bulbs, they were asked to wait a little distance away, which they did with respect and understanding. Lady Churchill took a brief motor ride to break the unbearable tension and get a little fresh air. Lord Moran came and went, grave, discreet, parrying anxious questioners as politely as he could. A nurse, Helen Cooke, handed in a bouquet, and called, 'God Bless You.' Miss Sophia Galitzine, a pretty child who always took flowers on Sir Winston's birthday, handed a posy to a policeman.

On radio and television and in the newspapers, the world watched and read of the approaching end. 'He is slipping into deeper sleep...' 'Sir Winston has had a peaceful day but he has lost ground;' 'He is a little weaker...'; 'Sir Winston has had a restless night, and his condition has deteriorated....'

A cold drizzle was falling on the morning of Sunday, 24th January. The watchers had seen Lord Moran drive up at 7 a.m. and leave a quarter of an hour later, grave and sad. Other members of the family arrived. And at 8 a.m. the news the world feared was announced:

'Shortly after 8 a.m. Sunday, 24th January, Sir Winston Churchill died in his London home.'

From all over the world, messages of sympathy and tributes to his wonderful life poured in. The message of Her Majesty the Queen said:

The whole world is the poorer by the loss of his many-sided

genius, while the survival of this country and the sister-nations of the Commonwealth in the face of the greatest danger that has ever threatened them will be a perpetual memorial to his leadership, his vision and his indomitable courage.

The Prime Minister, Mr. Harold Wilson, said, 'He is now at peace after a life in which he created history and it will be remembered as long as history is read.

'Each one of us owes it to him that we are alive and free, for it was Winston Churchill above all others, with his passionate hatred of evil, who rallied the nation against tyranny and who, by his will-power and courage, swung the balance in war from defeat to victory. He was the greatest of all leaders.'

'The world in which we live,' said Mr. Grimond, the Liberal leader, 'is a dangerous place. But for the life of Winston Churchill it might have been one in which none of us would have wished to live. There can be none of us who did not feel a sense of personal loss when we heard that the greatest heart in England had ceased to beat.'

The world seemed at a loss to express fully its sense of gratitude and grief. The State Bell at St. Paul's Cathedral, 'Great Tom', tolled; the lights of Piccadilly Circus were dimmed; from offices and embassies and buildings—most of all the Houses of Parliament —the Union Jack flew at half-mast. Some of his greatest speeches, which Lady Violet Bonham Carter said 'deserve to rank with those of the immortal orators of Greece and Rome, and will live as long', came over on television and radio, and it seemed impossible that Churchill, 'the lovable, fallible man' as the *Spectator* described him, was no longer with us.

There was nothing more the nation could do than to let the remains of The Greatest Commoner lie in State in Westminster Hall, bear them in due course, with all the moving if macabre pomp of a State funeral to St. Paul's, and with every observance of respect possible from State and its people, watch his body borne in State down the Thames, and thence to the little country churchyard at Bladon in Oxfordshire.

The long file of people who passed his grave wept unashamedly, as he himself had wept at times of great emotion. But no man lives more in the memories of the people of the world; and for those near to him, whose loss was beyond words, there remained the remembrance of his tremendous achievement, his endless humanity and his thoughts on death: 'Only faith in a life after death in a brighter world where dear ones will meet again—only that and the measured tramp of time can give consolation.'

Bibliography

AMERY, L. S., *My Political Life* (3 vols.), Hutchinson, 1953–1955.
AMERY, Julian, *Life of Joseph Chamberlain*, Macmillan, 1932.
ASQUITH, Hon. J., *Moments of Memory*, Hutchinson, 1937.
BACON, Sir R. H., *The Life of Lord Fisher*, Hodder and Stoughton, 1929.
BARDENS, Dennis, *Portrait of a Statesman—the Personal Life Story of Sir Anthony Eden*, Muller, 1956.
BEAVERBROOK, Lord, *Politicians and the War*, Oldbourne (re-issue), 1954.
BIRKENHEAD, Earl of, *Contemporary Personalities*, Cassell, 1924.
BOLITHO, Hector, *Edward VIII*, Eyre and Spottiswoode, 1937.
BUTLER, David, with Jennie FREEMAN, *British Political Facts*, Macmillan, 1963.
CARTER, Lady Violet Bonham, *Winston Churchill as I Knew Him*, Eyre and Spottiswoode, 1965.
CHURCHILL, Winston, *Mr. Brodrick's Army*, Humphreys, 1903.
— *The World Crisis* (6 vols.), Thornton Butterworth, 1923–1931.
— *Great Contemporaries*, Thornton Butterworth, 1937.
— *The Second World War* (6 vols.), Cassell, 1948–1954.
— *Liberalism and the Social Problem*, Hodder and Stoughton, 1909.
— *Step by Step 1936–1939*, Thornton Butterworth, 1939.
— *War Speeches* (3 vols. Ed. Charles Eade), Cassell, 1952.
CLYNES, J. R., *Memoirs*, Hutchinson, 1937.
COLE, G. D. H., *The British Labour Movement*, Allen and Unwin, 1948.
— *A History of the Labour Party from 1914*, Routledge and Kegan Paul, 1948.
COOTE, Colin R., *Sir Winston Churchill—a Self-Portrait*, Eyre and Spottiswoode, 1954.
DALTON, Hugh, *Call Back Yesterday*, Muller, 1953.
DANGERFIELD, George, *The Strange Death of Liberal England*, Constable, 1961.
DERBYSHIRE, Taylor, *King George VI*, Hutchinson, 1937.
FEILING, Keith, *The Life of Neville Chamberlain*, Macmillan, 1946.
GALLAGHER, W., *The Chosen Few*, Lawrence and Wishart, 1939.
GARDINER, A. G., *Prophets, Priests and Kings*, Dent, 1917.
GARDNER, Sir J. T. A., *Some Parliamentary Recollections*, Barrow, 1927.
GREY, Sir Edward, *Twenty-five Years*, Hodder and Stoughton, 1928.
GUEDALLA, Philip, *Mr. Churchill, a Portrait*, Hodder and Stoughton, 1941.
HAMILTON, Sir Ian, *Gallipoli Diary*, Arnold, 1920.
KEYES, Sir Roger, *Narrow Seas to Dardanelles*, Butterworth, 1934.

KILMUIR, Lord, *Political Adventure*, Weidenfeld and Nicolson, 1964.

LANSBURY, George, *My Life*, Constable, 1928.

— *Looking Backwards-and Forwards*, Blackie, 1935.

LEE, Jennie, *Tomorrow is a New Day*, Penguin, 1956.

LLOYD GEORGE, Rt. Hon. David, *War Memoirs*, Nicholson and Watson, 1933–36.

MASTERMAN, Lucy, *C. F. G. Masterman*, Nicholson and Watson, 1939.

MUGGERIDGE, Malcolm, *The Thirties*, Hamilton, 1940.

NICHOLSON, Harold, *George V—His Life and Reign*, Constable, 1952.

OWEN, Frank, *Tempestuous Journey*, Hutchinson, 1954.

RIDDELL, Lord, *Lord Riddell's War Diary*, Nicholson and Watson, 1933.

SIDEBOTHAM, H., *Pillars of State*, Nisbet, 1921.

SIMON, Lord, *Retrospect*, Hutchinson, 1952.

SIMON, Sir J. A., *Comments and Criticisms*, Hodder and Stoughton, 1930.

SNELL, H., *Daily Life in Parliament*, Routledge, 1930.

SNELL, Lord, *Men, Movements and Myself*, Dent, 1936.

SOMERVELL, D. C., *Life of King George V.*, Faber and Faber, 1935.

TEMPLEWOOD, Viscount, *Nine Troubled Years*, Collins, 1954.

THOMAS, J. H., *My Story*, Hutchinson, 1937.

THOMSON, Davis, *England in the Twentieth Century*, Penguin, 1965.

WEBB, Sidney and Beatrice, *History of Trade Unionism*, Longmans, 1894.

WEDGWOOD, Rt. Hon Josiah C., *Memoirs of a Fighting Life*, Hutchinson, 1940.

WILDING, Norman with Philip LAUNDY, *An Encyclopaedia of Parliament*, Cassell, 1958.

WINDSOR, Duke of, *A King's Story*, Cassell, 1951.

WINTERTON, Earl, *Orders of the Day*, Cassell, 1953.

WRIGHT, Arnold, with Philip SMITH, *Parliament Past and Present*, Hutchinson, 1900.

YOUNG, Sir Malcolm, *Stanley Baldwin*, Hart-Davis, 1925.

Index

A

Abdication of Edward VIII, 183–5
Abyssinia, 181–2, 300
Acheson, Dean, 343
Adamson, Mr., 140–1
Addison, Dr., 117, 155
Aitken, Max, *see* Beaverbrook, Lord
Albania, 197
Alexander, Gen., 277
Alexander, A. V., 217, 218, 351
Algeria, 275
Alsop, Stewart, 349
Amery, L. S., 209, 212
Amiens, Battle of, 123
Amritsar, 141–2
Andalsnes, 205
Anderson, Sir John, 266
Antwerp, 89, 90, 91, 220, 297
Anzio, 292
ANZUS, 329
Ark Royal, H.M.S., 253
Armenian massacres, 149
Armistice Day 1918, 125–6
Army discontent, 133–5
Arnhem, 298
Ashanti, 37
Asquith, H. H., 49, 53, 95, 97, 100, 107, 112, 113, 125, 126, 129, 132
Athenia, S.S., 200

Athens, 302, 303
Atlantic Charter, 251, 269
Atomic bomb, 344, 352
Attlee, C. R., 180, 212–13, 216, 251, 259, 266, 290, 310, 312, 313, 314, 318, 321, 325, 337, 351, 354, 358, 359, 360
Attlee, Mrs. C. R., 358
Auchinleck, Gen. Sir Claude, 253, 256, 271
Australia, 329
Austria, 179
Azad Mohammed Singh, 142
Azerbaijan, 327

B

Bacon, Sir Reginald, 80
Badoglio, Marshal, 300
Baku, 255
Baldwin, Stanley, 150, 154, 155, 156, 161, 168, 174, 175, 178, 181, 182, 183, 184, 186, 187
Balfour, A. J., 97, 132, 133
Banbury, Sir F., 77–8
Barclay, Senator, 256
Bardia, 243
Barnes, George, 120
Barrie, Sir Charles, 152
Battle of Britain, 230, 233, 234–6
Baudouin, M., 226
Baxter, Beverley, 260

Beatty, Rear-Adm. Sir David, 75–76, 84
Beaverbrook, Lord, 107, 113, 117, 133, 226, 235, 246, 251, 256, 260, 266, 283
Belgium, 213, 300, 304
Belgrade, 247, 295
Benes, President, 192
Benghazi, 244, 256
Berchtesgaden, 193
Beresford, Adm. Sir Charles, 116
Berlin, 290
Bermuda, 258
Betting tax, 165
Bevan, Aneurin, 172, 269, 272, 274, 284, 300, 303, 328, 330, 333, 341, 354
Beveridge, Sir William, 58, 67, 279
Bevin, Ernest, 243, 266, 283, 309, 312, 314, 316, 321, 329
Bielgorod, 282
Birkenhead, Lord, 49, 65, 79, 110, 111, 112, 133, 146, 161
Bliss, Gen., 123
Blood, Sir Bindon, 19
Blum, L., 191
Blunt, Wilfred, 68
Bondfield, Miss M., 171
Bonham Carter, Lady Violet, 366
Bonnet, G., 193
Booth, Gen., 67
Borthwick, O., 30
Bottomley, H., 144
Boulogne, 222, 297
Bracken, Viscount, 358
Bremen, 290
Brest, 263, 264, 297
Brest-Litovsk, Treaty of, 135
Bretton Woods, 315
Brighton, 324
British Gazette, 166, 167
Brockway, Fenner, 159
Broderick, W. St. J., 42–3
Brooke, F.-M. Sir Alan, 274

Brown, J. S., 131
Brussels, 220, 330
Bryansk, 253, 282
Budget League, 59
Bulair, 96
Bulgaria, 247, 295, 314
Bullitt, Mr., 329
Burma, 256
Burns, John, 49
Butler, R. A., 337
Byles, W., 51
Byrnes, J., 313

C

Cadogan, Sir Alexander, 274
Cairo, 278, 289
Calais, 220, 221, 222
Campbell-Bannerman, Sir Henry, 48, 49, 53
Canada, 257, 340
Canterbury, Dean of, 329
Carden, Adm., 103, 104
Cardiff, 333
Carson, Sir Edward, 101, 111, 113, 127
Casablanca, 277
Cecil, Evelyn, 117–18
Cecil, Lord Hugh, 44
Cecil, Lord Robert, 153
Chamberlain, Sir Austen, 73, 79, 80, 97, 161, 169
Chamberlain, Joseph, 30, 41, 42, 47, 59–60
Chamberlain, Neville, 174, 187, 188, 190, 191, 192, 193, 194, 196, 198, 199, 204, 205, 206, 207, 208, 209, 210, 211, 212, 213, 214, 216, 217, 219, 238, 267
Chanak, 149, 151
Chandler, Senator Happy, 280, 281
Chandos, Lord, 230
Chartwell, 168, 324
Chatsfield, Lord, 208

Cherwell, Lord, *see* Lindemann, Prof.

Chiang Kai Shek, 289

China, 340, 342, 343

Churchill, Lady Randolph, 15–16

Churchill, Lady (wife), 56, 125, 152, 157, 158, 159, 282, 290, 309, 313, 354, 365

Churchill, John Spencer, 44, 99

Churchill, Mary, 309

Churchill, Randolph, 362

Churchill, Lord Randolph, 15–16, 17, 18

Churchill, Winston, early life, 15–22; service in Cuba, 18; in India, 19; in Sudan, 20; war correspondent in S. Africa, 30–2; visits U.S. (1901), 35; stands for Oldham, 23–9, 32–35; returned to Parliament, 35; maiden speech, 38–41; relations with Conservative Party, 41–7; sits as Liberal, 47; Member for Manchester, N.W., 48, defeated, 54; Under-Secretary for Colonies, 48; President Board of Trade, 53; stands for Dundee, 54; marriage, 56; Cabinet Minister, 58–9; sends police to S. Wales strike, 61–2; siege of Sidney Street, 62–3; attitude to Lords, 65; views on prisons, 67–8; on military unpreparedness, 67–70, 71–2; First Lord of Admiralty, 73–4; on Home Rule, 77, 78; mobilizes Fleet, 81; goes to Antwerp, 89–91; Dardanelles campaign, 93–8; Chancellor of Duchy of Lancaster, 97, resigns, 99; joins Army, 106–108; urges creation of Air Ministry, 110; Ministry of Munitions, 117; offends Lloyd George, 124; views on Suffragettes, 130; Member for Dundee, 131; Secretary for War, 133; aid to White Russians, 135–7; questionnaire on Army, 140; Colonial Secretary, 145; on Irish Question, 146–9; operation for appendicitis, 151; defeated at Dundee, 154; contests Leicester, W., 155–7; contests Abbey Division of Westminster, 157–9; contests Epping, 160–1; Chancellor of Exchequer, 161; first Budget, 163–5; buys Chartwell, 168; on Indian Question, 173–4; on Disarmament, 178–9; warns on German rearmament, 180, 186; favours Russian alliance, 197; First Lord of Admiralty again, 198; Chairman of Military Co-ordinating Committee, 208; Prime Minister, 214; forms first Cabinet, 216; offers Anglo-French Union, 226; visits U.S., 256, 270, 280, 282, 317, 339, 345, 352; visits Canada, 257, 282, 297, 298, 340, 352; visits Russia, 274, 296; visits Cairo and El Alamein, 274; goes to Normandy, 293; visits Paris, 297, 316; visits Italy, 297; visits Saudi Arabia, 304; visits Syria, 304; visits Egypt, 304; visits Ethiopia, 304; visits Greece, 304, 316; visits Belgium, 316; visits Switzerland, 317; on British Empire, 291; Party defeated (1945), 312–13; refuses Garter, 313, 316–17; urges United States of Europe, 317; celebrates fifty years in House, 335; Prime Minister again,

Churchill, Winston, – *cont.*
337; accepts Garter, 347; celebrates 80th birthday, 353–357; retires from Premiership, 358–9; Member for Woodford, 360; in retirement, 361; honorary citizen of U.S., 362; death, 365; funeral, 366
as parliamentarian, 240–1, 243; parliamentary manner, 38–9; parliamentary indiscretions, 51, 53, 124, 344–5; as statesman, 241–2; daily routine, 201, 236–7, 309
as author, 19, 30, 31, 33, 168, 326
as painter, 99
Citrine, Lord, 323
Clemenceau, G., 123
Clynes, J. R., 137, 171
Coal nationalization, 284–5
Collins, Michael, 146, 148, 149
Cologne, 279, 290, 307
Colvin, Ian, 141
Courageous, H.M.S., 201
Commons, House of, destroyed, 245, 246; temporary meeting-place, 285; rebuilding, 285–8; rebuilt, 334–5
Constantinople, 136
Cooke, Helen, 365
Cooper, Duff, 210–11, 212, 231
Copenhagen, 205
Coronel, Battle of, 86
Cox, Seymour, 285
Craddock, Sir Christopher, 86
Cranbourne, Lord, 189
Crete, 240, 247
Crewe, Lord, 81
Cripps, Sir Stafford, 250, 266, 267, 268, 269, 271, 312, 318, 319, 333
Crisp, C. B., 32, 35
Cromer, Lord, 52

Cummings, A. J., 349
Curzon, Lord, 97, 150, 151
Czechoslovakia, 192–6

D
Daily Graphic, 18
Daily Herald, 141
Daily Mail, 23, 38, 46, 165–6, 328
Daily Mirror, 311, 331, 337, 346, 348, 349, 350, 351, 353
Daily News, 158, 159–60, 164
Daily Sketch, 351
Daily Telegraph, 19
Daily Worker, 250, 328
Dakar, 232
Daladier, E., 191, 192, 193, 194
Dalton, Hugh, 321
Dardanelles, 93–8, 102–4, 114, 136, 149
Darlan, Adm., 225, 275
De Broqueville, M., 89
De Gaulle, Gen., 227, 231, 277, 295, 304
De Valera, E., 146
Demobilization (1919), 133–5
Deniken, Gen., 135, 137
Denmark, 205, 282
Derby, Lord, 156
Dieppe, 297
Dilke, Sir Charles, 48
Dniepropetrovsk, 253
Doenitz, Adm., 307
Dollfuss, Dr., 179
Douglas-Home, Sir Alec, 363
Duke of York, H.M.S., 256
Dundee Advertiser, 153, 154
Dundee Courier, 154
Dunkirk, 88, 222, 223, 228
Dyer, Gen., 141–2

E
Eden, Anthony, 169, 176, 177, 179, 181, 182, 187, 188, 189, 190, 200, 217, 218, 240, 244, 258,

266, 270, 289, 304, 313, 336, 337, 344, 348, 352, 358, 360, 362

Eden, Lady, 358

Edinburgh, Duke of, 358

Edward VII, King, 36, 37–8, 61

Edward VIII, King, 182, 183, 184. *See also* Windsor, Duke of

Egypt, 238, 240, 304, 316, 340, 348, 362

Eisenhower, Gen. D., 275, 277, 282, 290, 293, 295, 307, 329, 345, 346, 350, 352

El Alamein, Battle of, 275

Elgin, Earl of, 50

Elizabeth, Queen, the Queen Mother, 342

Elizabeth II, Queen, 341, 342, 347, 356, 358, 365–6

Elliot, Col., 260

Emmott, A., 23, 24, 27, 28, 33, 34, 35

Enterprise, H.M.S., 297

Epping, 171

Estonia, 238

Ethiopia, 304

Everest, Mrs., 16

Evseyvich, G., 160

F

Falaise, 293

Falkland Islands, Battle of, 87

Feisal, King, 145

Finland, 204, 205

Fisher, Adm., 59, 71, 75, 76, 92, 93, 94, 95, 96, 97, 99, 104, 105

Flying bomb, 294–5

Foch, Marshal, 123

Foster, John, 331

Frankfurt, 290

Fraser, Lovat, 165

French, Sir John, 84, 88, 90, 94, 95, 106, 107

Fulham, 183

Fulton, 317

G

Gaitskell, Hugh, 324, 333

Galitzine, Sophia, 365

Gallagher, W., 152, 299, 303, 323

Gallipoli, 96

Gamelin, Gen., 191

Gandhi, Mahatma, 173, 268, 269, 318

Geddes, Vice-Adm., 117

Geddes, Sir Auckland, 133

General Strike, 165–7

George V, King, 182

George VI, King, 199, 212, 213, 214, 233, 234, 268, 292, 294, 313, 337, 341, 342

George, King of the Hellenes, 299

George, D. Lloyd, 39, 41, 49, 57, 95, 96, 97, 101, 112, 113, 114, 115, 116, 117, 118, 119, 120, 123, 124, 126, 128, 129, 130, 132, 133, 135, 136, 137–8, 139, 146, 149, 150, 151, 157, 172 192, 210, 218, 244, 306

Germany, 191, 197, 334

Giraud, Gen., 277

Glanville, Edgar, 295

Glass, J., 130

Gloucester, Duke of, 272

Gneisenau, 263

Godesberg, 194

Goebbels, Dr., 187

Goeben, 85, 86

Gondar, 253

Gordon, Sir John, 264

Gough, Gen., 116, 129

Greece, 238, 247, 283, 299, 302–3, 304

Greenwood, A., 213, 216, 318

Greenwood, Sir Hamar, 146

Grey, Sir Edward, 52, 57, 59, 69, 81

Grieg, Bill, 331

Griffith, Arthur, 146

Grimond, Jo, 366
Grove Park, 134
Guest, Ivor, 44

H

Haakon, King, 234
Haig, Field-Marshal Sir Douglas,
    107, 120, 122-3, 128, 144
Haile Selassie, Emperor, 182, 304
Haldane, Lord, 57, 71, 81, 92
Halifax, Lord, 191, 196, 213, 214,
    216, 226, 355
Hall, Adm. Sir Reginald, 87
Halsbury, Lord, 66
Hamilton, Gen. Sir Ian, 95
Hankey, Lord, 208
Hardy, Keir, 50
Harington, Sir Charles, 150
Harriman, Averill, 274
Harris, Sir Percy, 219
Hartlepool, 84
Havre, 297
Hayward, Maj., 145
Heligoland, 84
Hess, R., 245, 246
Hills, Maj., 122
Hirohito, Emperor, 253
Hiroshima, 313
Hitler, A., 176, 177, 179, 180, 181,
    186, 187, 190, 191, 192, 193,
    194, 196, 197, 199, 202, 205,
    207, 208, 211, 224, 230, 233,
    249, 307
Hoare, Sir Samuel, 181
Hogge, Mr., 144
Holland, 213, 220
Hong Kong, 254, 256
Hopkins, Harry, 251
Hore-Belisha, L., 244, 247, 248,
    259
Hozier, Clementine, *see* Churchill,
    Lady
Hull, Cordell, 253
Hungary, 247, 295, 314

I

Ibn Saud, 304
India, 291, 316, 318, 321, 322, 325
Indian Home Rule, 268-9
Ineunu, President, 289
Ingersoll, Ralph, 318
Instone, Capt., 157
Iraq, 145, 247
Irish Treaty, 147
Ironside, Gen., 137
Ismay, Lord, 230, 234, 236, 364
Italy, 240, 241-3, 282, 284, 300,
    307

J

Jackson, Sir Henry, 104
Japan, 177, 238, 253, 254, 255, 313
Java, 268
Jellicoe, Sir John, 76, 114-15
Jerome, Jennie, 15, 16
Jerome, Jerome K., 159
Jerome, Leonard, 16
Jodl, Gen., 307
Johore, 260
Joynson-Hicks, Sir William, 48, 66
Juliana, Princess, 217

K

Kearney, U.S.S., 253
Kemal, Attaturk, 149, 151
Kempton Park, 134
Kennedy, President, 362
Kenya, 344
Keyes, Sir Roger, 208-9, 211, 212,
    255, 262, 272
Keynes, J. M., 163, 166
Kharkov, 253, 279, 282
Kiev, 250
Kilmuir, Lord, 354, 359
Kitchener, Lord, 20, 84, 88, 89, 90,
    93, 94, 95, 103, 111
Knox, Sir A., 255
Koltchak, Gen., 135, 136-7
Korea, 333, 338, 340, 342, 343

Krasnodar, 279
Kremenchug, 253, 282
Kursk, 279
Kurusu, Mr., 253

L

Labour Exchanges, 58
Lansbury, G., 178
Lansdowne, Lord, 93, 97
Laski, Nathan, 47
Latvia, 238
Laval, P., 181
Law, A. Bonar, 93, 97, 113, 114, 116, 118, 125, 128, 129, 132, 150, 151, 154, 159
Lawrence, Pethick, 156, 157
Lawrence, T. E., 145
Leahy, Adm., 270, 313, 314
Lease-Lend Agreement, 240
Lee, Jennie, 354
Lees-Smith, H. B., 219
Leningrad, 250, 253, 255, 279
Leopold, King of the Belgians, 220, 221
Liège, 220
Life, 329
Lindemann, Prof., 236, 291, 358
Lithuania, 238
Lloyd, Lord, 178, 231, 350
Lloyd, J. S., 130
Local Defence Volunteers, 229
Locarno, Treaty of, 182
London air-raids, 235–6, 243
Long, Walter, 97
Louis, Prince, of Battenberg, 85, 92
Lowther, J. W., 78, 125
Luxembourg, 213
Lyttleton, Oliver, 266

M

MacDonald, M., 243
MacDonald, Ramsay, 50, 154, 156, 160, 165, 170, 171, 172, 174, 175, 176, 177, 181, 329

McKenna, R., 59, 72
Maclean, Sir Donald, 144
MacLean, Mr., 212
Macmillan, H., 362, 363
McNeil, Ronald, 78
McNeill, R., 164
Macwell, Maj.-Gen., 274
Madagascar, 268
Maginot Line, 221
Malaya, 254, 260, 338, 344
Malenkov, Mr., 346, 350
Malta, 268, 282
Manchester Guardian, 25, 300
Manchuria, 176–7
Margesson, Capt., 213
Markham, Arthur, 111
Marks, Sir Croydon, 122
Marrakesh, 290
Marshall, Gen. G., 329
Marshall Aid, 332
Mary, Queen, 233, 342
Masaryk, Jan, 194
Massingham, Hugh, 344
Masterman, Lucy, 70, 136
Maurice, Sir Frederick, 129
Mawdsley, J., 23, 24, 26, 27, 28
Maxton, J., 198, 218, 219, 287
Mersah Matruh, 271
Metaxas, Gen., 299
Metropole Hotel, London, 125
Michison, G., 345
Mikolajczck, Mr., 270, 298
Milne, Sir Berkeley, 86
Milner, Lord, 51, 123, 133, 145
Molotov, V., 269, 313
Montagu, E., 117
Montgomery, Gen. Sir Bernard (later Field Marshal Viscount), 230, 275, 278, 293, 329, 353, 358, 364
Moran, Lord, 365
Morgenthau, Henry, 280
Morning Post, 21, 22, 29, 31, 158, 166

Morocco, 275
Morrison, H., 209, 211, 217, 312, 325, 326, 330, 331, 342
Morrison, W. S., 354
Morton, Desmond, 236
Moscow, 250, 253, 255, 289
Mosley, Sir Oswald, 173
Mottistone, Lord, 90
Mountbatten, Lord, 321, 322
Mulberry harbours, 290
Munich Agreement, 194, 196
Mussolini, B., 168, 179, 180, 181, 187, 188, 190, 194, 197, 205, 225, 229, 282, 283, 284, 307

N

Nagasaki, 313
Namsos, 205
Narvik, 205, 208, 211
National Liberal Club, 164–5, 281–282
Netherlands East Indies, 268
New York Herald-Tribune, 268, 349, 352
New Zealand, 329
Newcastle Daily Leader, 34
News Chronicle, 349, 352
News of the World, 351
Nicholson, Brig., 222
Nicholson, O. W., 159
Nicolson, Harold, 151, 212
Nijmegen, 298
Normandy, 292
North Atlantic Treaty Organization, 329
Northcliffe, 106, 113, 117
Norway, 205, 206, 207
Norwegian campaign, 205–6
Novgorod, 253
Novorossisk, 282
Nuremberg, 290
Nyon Conference, 188

O

O'Brien, Sir Tom, 345

Observer, 349
O'Dwyer, Sir Michael, 141, 142
Odessa, 136, 250, 253
Oldham, 23–9, 31, 32–4
Oldham Standard, 24, 34
Operation 'Overlord', 292
Operation 'Sea Lion', 234
Oran, 231
Orel, 253, 282
Organization for European Economic Co-operation, 332
Owen, Frank, 93

P

Palestine, 320, 321, 329
Pankhurst, Mrs., 130
Papandreou, Mr., 299
Paris, 226, 295, 297
Patch, Gen., 293
Paul, Prince, of Yugoslavia, 247
Peace Ballot, 181
Pearl Harbour, 253
Peenemunde, 294
Persia, 247
Pétain, Marshal, 123, 225, 226, 227, 244
Peter, Prince, of Yugoslavia, 247
Peto, Brig., 350
Phillips, Adm. Sir Tom, 211, 255, 262
The Pioneer (Allahabad), 19
Poincaré, R., 123, 150
Poland, 197, 202, 296, 298, 302, 314, 315
Poltava, 282
Potsdam Conference, 313, 314
Pound, Adm. Sir Dudley, 199, 201, 211
Prague, 314
Prince of Wales, H.M.S., 251, 254, 255, 261
Prinz Eugen, 263

Q

Quebec Conferences, 282, 292, 298

Quisling, 205

R

Rangoon, 268
Reith, Lord, 266
Repulse, H.M.S., 254, 255, 261
Reynaud, P., 225, 226
Rhineland, 182
Rhodes, Cecil, 45
Rhondda, 333
Ribbentrop, J. von, 203
Richards, R., 260
Riddell, Lord, 96, 97, 98
Robeck, Adm. de, 94
Robertson, Sir William, 113
Rockets, 296-7
Rome, 282, 292, 297
Rommel, Field Marshal E., 273
Roosevelt, President F. D., 238,
    240, 248, 250, 251, 252, 253,
    256, 270, 274, 277, 280, 289,
    297, 298, 304, 306, 318, 329,
    340
Ross, Mr., 345
Rostov, 253, 279
Rotterdam, 220
Royal Oak, H.M.S., 202, 203
Rumania, 295, 314
Runciman, Walter, 23, 25, 26, 27,
    28, 33, 35, 192
Russia, 197, 202-3, 204, 249, 298,
    313, 314, 317, 327, 328, 333,
    346, 353
    British forces in, 136
Russian Revolution, 135
Russo-German Pact, 197

S

St. Laurent, Mr., 352
Saklatvala, S., 155
Salerno, 282
Salisbury, Lord, 356
Samuel, Sir Herbert, 167, 174
Sankey, Lord, 174

Scapa Flow, 201, 202
Scarborough, 84
Scharnhorst, 263
Scobie, Gen., 302
Scott, C. P., 119
Scrymgeour, E., 54, 130, 131, 152,
    154
Second Front, 269, 270, 292-3
Seely, Maj.-Gen., 78, 158
Selborne, Lord, *see* Wolmer, Lord
Sevres, Treaty of, 149
Sforza, Count, 300
Shackleton, David, 47
Shawcross, Sir Hartley, 319
Shinwell, E., 244, 260, 300, 323,
    328, 336, 344-5
Shukri, President, 304
Sicily, 282
Sidi Resegh, Battle of, 253
Silesia, 302
Simon, Sir John, 174, 181
Sims, Adm., 115
Sinclair, Sir Archibald, 217
Singapore, 254, 260, 263
Sino-Japanese War, 187-8
Skrine, H. D., 21
Smith, F. E., *see* Birkenhead, Lord
Smithers, Sir Waldron, 316
Smolensk, 253, 282
Smuts, Gen., 292
Snowden, P., 49-50, 125, 165, 169-
    170, 171, 173, 174
Somerville, Adm., 232
Spain, 196
Spectator, 164, 366
Stalin, J., 250, 251, 275, 277, 289,
    295, 296, 298, 304, 317, 329,
    346, 353
Stalingrad, 281
Stanley, Arthur, 44
Steevens, G. W., 23, 38
Stephen, Mr., 219
Stettinius, Mr., 270
Stevenson, Frances, 81

Steward, Capt. J., 236
Stewart, FitzRoy, 21
Strachey, J., 330
Strasbourg, 331
Suez, 362
Suffragettes, 27, 53–4, 67–8, 130
Sunday Pictorial, 346, 350
Sutherland, Graham, 354
Sweden, 206
Sydenham, Lord, 168
Syria, 247

T

Taganrog, 282
Tedder, Air Marshal Sir Arthur, 274
Teheran, 289, 290
Templer, Gen. Sir Gerald, 344
Thomas, J. H., 167, 173, 174
Thompson, Inspector, 236
Thomson, Mr., 153, 154
Thorne, Will, 298
Times, 259, 302, 303, 304, 352
Times of India, 28–9
Tirpitz, 251
Tobruk, 244, 271, 273, 274
Trades Disputes Bill, 168
Tripolitania, 281
Trondheim, 206, 209, 211
Truman, President, 313, 317, 339, 340
Tunisia, 275, 281
Turkey, 277, 289, 291

U

United Nations, 279
United States, 225, 226, 240, 248, 250–1, 252, 253, 315, 329, 340

V

Vandenberg, Senator, 340
Victoria, Queen, 35–6
VE Day, 307–9
VJ Day, 314
Vienna, 307

Von Spee, Vice-Adm., 86, 87
Voroshilovgrad, 279

W

Walker-Smith, D., 319
Wall Street Slump, 172
Walter, Francis B., 362
Warbey, W., 352
Wardlaw-Milne, Sir John, 259, 271, 272
Warsaw, 280, 295, 297
Warwick, Countess of, 161
Watt, Brig. Harvie, 236
Watten, 294
Wavell, Field Marshal, 240, 247, 256, 274, 280, 321
Webb, Mrs. Beatrice, 57, 58
Webb, Sidney, 57, 58
Wedgwood, Col. J., 139, 208
West Essex Gazette, 160
Western Desert, 240, 242, 271
Westminster, Duke of, 60
Weygand, Gen., 225, 226
Whitby, 84
White, Sir George, 31
Wilde, Jimmy, 158–9
Wiley, Senator, 341
Wilhelmina, Queen, 217, 234
Wilkie, A., 130, 131
Wilson, Sir Arthur, 71, 72, 104
Wilson, Field Marshal Sir Henry, 72, 147
Wilson, Harold, 333, 366
Wilson, Maitland, 240
Windsor, Duke of, 280. *See also* Edward VIII
Windsor, Duchess of, 280
Winterton, Earl, 178, 243, 245, 247, 261, 272, 305
Wolmer, Lord, 97, 178
Wood, Sir Evelyn, 20
Woodford, 336
Wrangel, Gen., 135
Wyatt, Woodrow, 143

Y

Yalta, 304
Younger, Sir George, 129
Ypres, 90
Yudenitch, Gen., 137
Yugoslavia, 247, 283, 295

Z

Zagreb, 314
Zaslavsky, Mr., 331
Zinoviev Letter, 160
Zurich, 317, 328
Zuzenko, A., 155